Spirit of the New England Tribes

SO-AEK-145

Spirit of the New England Tribes

INDIAN HISTORY AND FOLKLORE,

1620–1984

William S. Simmons

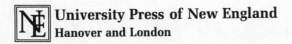 University Press of New England
Hanover and London

LIBRARY
COLBY-SAWYER COLLEGE
NEW LONDON, NH 03257

E
78
.N5
S54
1986
c.1

#12973700

To Cheryl and Riva

University Press of New England
Brandeis University
Brown University
Clark University
University of Connecticut
Dartmouth College
University of New Hampshire
University of Rhode Island
Tufts University
University of Vermont

© 1986 by University Press of New England

All rights reserved. Except for brief quotation in critical articles or reviews, this book, or parts thereof, must not be reproduced in any form without permission in writing from the publisher. For further information contact University Press of New England, Hanover, NH 03755.

Printed in the United States of America

This publication has been supported by the National Endowment for the Humanities, a federal agency which supports the study of such fields as history, philosophy, literature, and languages.

Library of Congress Cataloging-in-Publication Data
Simmons, William Scranton, 1938–
  Spirit of the New England tribes.
  Bibliography: p.
  Includes index.
  1. Indians of North America—New England—Folklore.
  2. Indians of North America—New England—Legends.
  3. Legends—New England. 4. Indians of North America—
New England—History. 5. New England—History, Local.
I. Title.
E78.N5S54 1986   398.2'08997074   85–40936
ISBN 0–87451–370–7
ISBN 0–87451–372–3 (pbk.)

5   4

LIBRARY
COLBY-SAWYER COLLEGE
NEW LONDON, NH 03251

Contents

Preface

I present in this volume examples of southern New England Indian folklore from the earliest European contact to the present day. Two conversations shaped this folklore—one between the living and the dead and the other between the living and the changing world into which they were born. Each generation inherited a body of legends, symbols, and meanings from their predecessors and revised this heritage in recognition of their own experiences. Over the last four centuries the southern New England tribes merged more and more with the larger Euro-American society, and the tribes' oral traditions show strong influences from American folklore in general. Despite this movement away from their past, ancestral voices continue to speak to the living through oral narratives, and the living in turn attribute new and borrowed customs to ancestral sources. In a world where the New England tribes have little in common with their early predecessors and much in common with non-Indian neighbors, folklore is an important link with and source for their Indian identity. I hope to identify the symbols through which they expressed this identity over time and observe how the succession of historic events affected these symbols. I draw mainly upon three kinds of data. The first is the folklore texts themselves and what can be said about their authenticity, content, and changes. Second is the local and large-scale historical circumstances that acted upon the Indian communities. Third is the Yankee, English, Afro-American, and other folklore traditions from which the southern New England Indians borrowed in rebuilding their own narratives. My overall aim is to represent the symbolism, worldview, we might say spirit, of the New England tribes in the context of their material and historic existence. The folklore texts are divided into chapters on witches, ghosts, giants, treasures, and so on, and each text is presented in chronological order from the seventeenth century to the present. Not a history per se, this book is a commentary upon the folklore narratives in terms of which the southern New England Indians registered their past.

In quoted passages obvious slips of the pen have been corrected without comment. Superscript letters have been lowered to the line of the text, and the thorn has been expanded. Editor's omissions are noted by three ellipsis points if the omission entails only part of a sentence, and four ellipsis points if it comes between sentences or if it entails more than a sentence but less than a paragraph. A row of ellipsis points is used if the omission includes a paragraph or more. Words added to clarify texts are placed within brackets. The dates given above the individual texts reflect the approximate recording date, or the earliest publication date.

The design elements facing the title page and on chapter openings are taken from historic period southern New England Indian painted baskets. The design element on the Preface opening is taken from the end of Roger Williams's *A Key into the Language of America*.

I drew the folklore texts together from published and manuscript sources and from interviews with contemporary New England Indians. I first visited Gay Head, for four days, in March 1981; in July 1981 I spent several days in Mashpee on Cape Cod. I was more successful at Gay Head than at Mashpee even though several friends and colleagues (principally the Reverend Harold Mars, James Deetz, and Anne Yentsch) had given me good contacts in the latter community. This was perhaps due to the fact that the Mashpee Wampanoag Tribal Council, Incorporated, had recently lost a major court case in which they attempted to gain federal recognition as an Indian tribe, which would have enabled them to file suit to reclaim thousands of acres of land they had held jointly as a proprietorship until the late nineteenth century. Nonetheless, a number of Mashpee residents, including the tribal historian Amelia Bingham and a young woman who identified herself as Nosapocket, were very hospitable. Carol Bennett of the *Vineyard Gazette* and Gale Huntington of the Dukes County Historical Society provided contacts for me with several Gay Head people, including Wenonah Silva, Leonard Vanderhoop, and Eloise Page, who were generous with their knowledge of Gay Head legends. Donald Widdiss of the Wampanoag Tribal Council of Gay Head, Incorporated, was drafting a petition for federal recognition for Gay Head and saw that my research on oral traditions would strengthen their case. Widdiss introduced me to his mother, Gladys Widdiss, and uncle, Donald Melanson, who spoke to me at some length about Gay Head landmarks, folklore, and history. Again, I visited Mashpee and Gay Head for several days each in

April 1983 but obtained no new interviews at Mashpee. At Gay Head, Silva, Page, Vanderhoop, and Melanson furnished new materials, and Silva introduced me to her aunt, Ada Manning, whom I also interviewed. In April and again in June 1983 I taped a number of ghost stories and other legends with old Narragansett friends, the Reverend Harold Mars and his wife, Laura Mars of Charlestown, Rhode Island. On several occasions in spring and summer 1983 and summer 1984 I visited Gladys Tantaquidgeon and Courtland E. Fowler of the Mohegan Tribal Office in Uncasville, Connecticut. Both were very interested in the folklore research and talked at some length about Mohegan history and traditions. Tantaquidgeon had done extensive folklore research in Mashpee and Gay Head about fifty-five years earlier; she still had her extensive unpublished field notes as well as the outline for an unfinished manuscript on New England Indian culture heroes, which she generously offered for use in this study. Like an archaelogist who leaves part of the site in the ground, I copied the legends and folktales from Tantaquidgeon's notes but did not transcribe her information on plant lore and medicine. She also conducted me through the collections of Mohegan and Niantic material culture in the unique Tantaquidgeon Indian Museum that she and her brother, Harold Tantaquidgeon, have run for many years. Fowler, who looks like his eighteenth-century ancestor, Samson Occom, gave me the typed text of a ghost story involving the anthropologist Frank Speck and also showed me his personal collection of bowls, baskets, carvings, papers, and other heirlooms that he had inherited from his Mohegan forebears. In spring 1984 I interviewed Eric Thomas, a Narragansett who is currently an undergraduate at the University of California, Berkeley, who had worked for several years to prepare the Narragansett petition for federal recognition. In 1984 I interviewed another old friend, Ella Seketau, of the Narragansett Tribe, Incorporated, in the Narragansett Longhouse in Charlestown, who told me several legends I had not heard before. I am extremely grateful to all of these New England Indian people for their openness, kindness, patience, and generosity, and for enabling me to connect the historical record with living tradition. I also should like to acknowledge Earl Mills and Selena and Kenneth Coombs of Mashpee, June MacDonald and Tony Pollard of Plimoth Plantation, Jane Waters of North Dartmouth, Helen Attaquin and Clinton and Daisy Haynes of Middleboro, John Brown of Narragansett, and Dorothy Scoville of Gay Head for some important discussions.

Many colleagues in anthropology, folklore, and history contributed to this effort. Alan Dundes of the Berkeley anthropology department introduced me to the basics of contemporary folklore scholarship and offered many ideas and suggestions over the last several years. Folklore was an unknown territory to me when I began this research, and I am fortunate to have had the most important living folklorist in my own department. Stanley Brandes and the late William Bascom, also of the Berkeley anthropology department, freely listened and offered their expertise on several occasions, as did Michael Bell, the state folklorist for Rhode Island. Several Berkeley graduate students, particularly Lee Davis, Marcelle Williams, Phyllis Passariello, Peter Nabokov, and Constance Crosby, helped with ideas and references that improved the final outcome. For ethnographic and anthropological questions I turned most often to Ives Goddard and Kathleen Bragdon of the Smithsonian Institution, Gordon Day of the Canadian Ethnology Service, Anne Yentsch, then of Plimoth Plantation, Dena Dincauze of the University of Massachusetts at Amherst, Elizabeth Little of the Nantucket Historical Association, and Ethel Boissevain, now retired from Herbert H. Lehman College. For linguistic questions I consulted Ives Goddard, George Aubin of Assumption College, William Cowan of Carleton University, and David Pentland of Winnipeg. William Sturtevant and Wilcomb Washburn of the Smithsonian Institution, Neal Salisbury of Smith College, Karen Kupperman of the University of Connecticut, and James Axtell of the College of William and Mary have had an important influence on my ethnohistorical research over the years. Special thanks are due to Kathleen Bragdon and Neal Salisbury for reading and commenting upon the completed manuscript. I particularly wish to thank Gladys Tantaquidgeon for the many unique texts that she contributed to this study.[1]

I visited many libraries in the course of this project, including the John D. Rockefeller and John Carter Brown libraries at Brown University. Duane Davies of the Rockefeller Library was particularly helpful during my sabbatical there in 1982–83. Glenn W. LaFantasie of the Rhode Island Historical Society and Thomas Norton of the Dukes County Historical Society assisted on several occasions, as did Kenneth Cramer of Dartmouth College Library, Dorothy King of the East Hampton Free Library, and Dorothy Koenig of the Berkeley Anthropology Library.

My wife, Cheryl Leif Simmons, read and commented insightfully upon many chapters, despite her own heavy schedule. My nephew, Robert M. Simmons, Jr., of Middleboro, traveled to New Bedford to photocopy the Mary C. Vanderhoop texts from old issues of the *New Bedford Evening Standard*, and my daughter, Riva C. Simmons, assisted me during the Narragansett fieldwork interviews. Barbara Quigley, who is uncommonly careful and accurate, typed the entire manuscript; Lee Davis prepared the summary motif index. Grace Buzaljko, our departmental editor, carefully examined the entire manuscript, and Judith Ogden drew the map.

Finally, I should like to credit my sources of financial support. The University of California contributed significantly with a sabbatical in fall and winter 1982–83, a Humanities Research Fellowship in spring 1983, and several awards through the Committee on Research. The American Philosophical Society granted a Phillips Fund award that provided for some travel and other field research expenses while in New England in 1982–83.

I am grateful to all of these individuals and institutions for their abundant assistance; surely this is a better effort because of these many influences. Any inaccuracies, misinterpretations, or other limitations of this work are my own responsibility.

W.S.S.

Berkeley, California
August 1985

Spirit of the New England Tribes

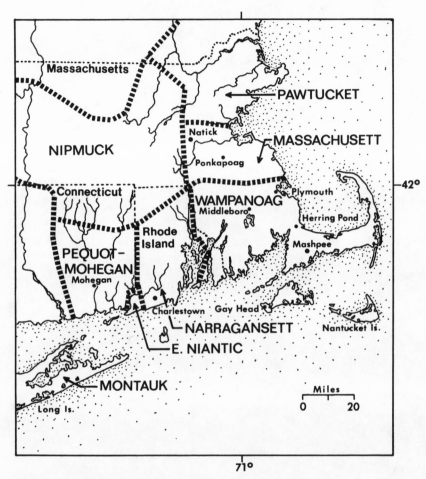

The southern New England region showing tribal distributions in about 1630 and the locations of communities mentioned in the text. Based upon Salwen 1978:161.

1 Introduction

I

When Europeans colonized the coastal areas of southern New England they encountered a number of small principalities with names such as Massachusett, Pokanoket, Narragansett, Niantic, Pequot, and Mohegan. These groups played an active part in the early political and military dramas of North Atlantic colonization and imprinted themselves on the imaginations and memories of the early generations of English settlers. These dramas reached an abrupt and early ending, for by 1676, less than sixty years after the first settlement at Plymouth and long before most North American Indians had laid eyes on Europeans, English colonists had overrun all tribes within the areas of what is now Massachusetts, Connecticut, and Rhode Island. Those Indians who survived became an almost invisible minority around the edges of the American farming villages, seaports, mill towns, and commercial centers that sprang up in the Indians' original territories. To most contemporary New Englanders, these Indians are known vaguely through legends such as that of the first Thanksgiving and by curious place names, such as Aquidneck, Ponkapoag, Naugatuck, and Nantucket, which survived from prehistoric time.[1] The theme of the extinction of New England Indians has appealed to writers since the colonial period, and Squanto, King Philip, Uncas, and many others since have been portrayed as the last of their people.[2] New England town historians often reserve a nos-

3

talgic paragraph for the last Indian to have lived in that vicinity and characteristically mention how he or she earned a humble living by making and peddling brooms, splint baskets, and home remedies among whites. Despite their traumatic defeats in the seventeenth century and the pronouncements of their death, found in history as well as fiction, some Indian communities survived the stressful colonial years and today define themselves as Indian. After three centuries of submersion in American society, they resemble neighboring non-Indian Americans more than they do their seventeenth-century ancestors. In fact they resemble their ancestors hardly at all. If one looks at their economic and political activities, their language, churches, homes, and appearances, one sees in most cases little that can be attributed to the indigenous sources of New England Indian culture. The major exception is folklore, for a continuous tradition of beliefs and legends has lived in their imaginations, and much of it has been recorded over the years. This is not to say that the oral traditions of twentieth-century persons of Indian descent are identical with those of their prehistoric ancestors, for most of their aboriginal folklore has died out, changed, or been infused with borrowings from the majority culture. Nevertheless, their oral narratives show stronger connections with autochthonous traditions than is evident in any other aspect of their society and culture.

II

The raw materials of this study consist of some 240 texts culled from early colonial writings, newspapers, magazines, diaries, local histories, anthropology and folklore publications, a variety of manuscript sources, and from field research with living people. In most cases, whites recorded the texts, particularly in the earlier years. Whites may have heard the narratives directly from Indians or from other whites who heard them from Indians, but when they retold the narratives or wrote them down they often introduced unconscious bias and conscious embellishments that interfered with the Indian voice. A few white collectors, such as Frank Speck, who worked with the Massachusett, Wampanoag, and Mohegan in the early part of the twentieth century, and Mabel Knight, who gathered some important Wampanoag texts in the 1920s, presented Indian narrative materials in a way that respected the words of Indian speakers. Too many others, including nineteenth-century folklorist James Athearn Jones and twentieth-century folklorist Elizabeth Reynard, buried the Indian contribution beneath their own literary improvisations. Jones, Reynard, and others also combined information from different individuals or mixed oral and written sources, which further weakened their anthropological value.[3] I have incorporated a few such texts in this study, with cautionary introductions, either because I wanted to salvage the cultural information they contain or because later Indians read these texts and incorporated them into their traditions.

Fortunately, at least ten persons of New England Indian ancestry have recorded their own folklore. The most prominent of the Indian authors is an eighty-five-year-old Mohegan, Gladys Tantaquidgeon, who lives in a brown-shingled cottage atop Mohegan Hill in Uncasville, Connecticut, where she still bakes cornmeal muffins and drinks her afternoon tea. In her youth Tantaquidgeon studied anthropology with Speck at the University of Pennsylvania and conducted field research during several summers in Gay Head and Mashpee, Massachusetts, in the late 1920s and early 1930s; in addition she has done extensive work on Mohegan medical lore, beliefs, and legends. She published much of this material but generously gave me access to her Mashpee and Gay Head field notes, including many important and heretofore unpublished texts about culture heroes, buried treasure, witches, ghosts, and other legendary subjects that no one except a well-connected and traditional Indian would have been able to obtain. Nothing quite like these traditions has been recorded in this area before or since.[4] The Narragansett, under the auspices of Princess Red Wing, began a journal in the 1930s, *The Narragansett Dawn*, that featured folklore contributions by Red Wing and other Narragansetts who, in keeping with the the Pan-Indian spirit that appeared about this time, also identified themselves by Indian names.[5]

Although the Christian Indians of Massachusetts had been literate in their own language from the seventeenth to the late eighteenth centuries, they limited their writing mainly to public records and did not record folklore. Only one Algonquian speaker from the whole southern New England region, Fidelia Fielding of Mohegan, wrote of religious experiences and folklore in her native language. Speck also collected from Fielding the only legend to have been narrated and recorded in a southern New England tongue. All others who reported Indian narratives did so in English. One prominent contributor to Gay Head folklore, Mary Cleggett Vanderhoop, was of partial Indian ancestry, but from Pennsylvania and not New England. Vanderhoop moved to Gay Head on Martha's Vineyard after marrying a man from that community and became an authority on their traditions around the turn of the twentieth century (Vander-

hoop 1904). Her daughter, Nanetta Madison, also compiled a manuscript collection of Gay Head legends which I had the good fortune
to be able to include in this research. In addition, I wrote down or
tape-recorded a sizable collection of texts during field visits to Gay
Head, Mashpee, Charlestown, Mohegan, and other nearby towns in
southern New England in 1981, 1983, and 1984.

III

No author, English or Indian, provided an Indian folk-classifica-
tion of oral narrative genres. Thus I have drawn upon categories,
such as *memorate, legend, myth,* and *folktale,* from comparative
folklore scholarship to refer to the Indian texts. The memorate is a
concrete account of a personal encounter with the supernatural.
Reverend Harold Mars of the Narragansett country told me one such
memorate that he experienced in his youth: "The hour was rather
late . . . as I came up what we call Belmont Avenue in Wakefield,
when I was suddenly reminded that that headless horse was just
ahead, and true enough I saw the headless horse, a white horse with
no head" (H. Mars 1983). The memorate can be communicated in
the first person or it can be retold by others who did not share the
experience. Memorates told over and over again by second, third,
and subsequent parties may lose their individual details and approximate the more impersonal and collective genre of legend. Folklorists have interpreted memorate experiences in ways that parallel
functional and structural explanations in anthropology. Lauri
Honko, for example, argued that Finnish spirit beliefs support social
norms and that persons who violate such norms through negligence,
drunkenness, quarreling, and so on are the ones most likely to encounter a supernatural figure that warns or punishes them for their
behavior (Honko 1964:17–18). Folklorists also attribute such experiences to situations of great stress, anxiety, and change (Honko
1965:172; Lindow 1978:45–59; Ward 1977:220). Despite the sponta-
neous and authentic qualities of the experiences narrated in memorates, the genre is governed by custom, and the visions follow well-
worn paths. New England Indians experience supernatural visits
from their own storehouse of cultural creations and not from Finnish barn spirits.[6]

Legends are set in real places in the recent or more distant past
and pertain to culture heroes, ghosts, witches, and fairies as well as
to real people. Some legends and memorates, known as negative legends and memorates, end by explaining seemingly extraordinary experiences in commonsense terms. Harold Mars, for example, ended

the memorate of the headless horse by disclosing that the horse had been grazing behind a stone wall that concealed its head. Scholars have attributed a number of functions to legend. The Grimm brothers and Bronislaw Malinowski commented on the ways in which legend animates the landscape and strengthens the bond between living people, their environment, and their past (Malinowski [1922] 1961:298; Ward 1981:3). Folklorists see the legend as an improvisational art that is loosely structured if structured at all. Like the memorate, and in contrast to myths and folktales, legend content is particularly sensitive to social and historical changes, and legends are constantly proliferating to the point that they are difficult to classify. With few exceptions, all the New England Indian folklore materials are memorates and legends.[7]

Myths generally are thought to be truthful accounts of what happened in the earliest possible time; they account for basic creation, are sacred, and provide the authority for existing social institutions, religious beliefs, and ritual (Bascom 1965:4). Anthropologists and folklorists have studied myth far more than any other narrative genre, and a large literature exists on the social and psychological functions of myth, its symbolism, and structure. One dominant interpretation is that myth reinforces the solidarity and identity of the group. Claude Lévi-Strauss, the preeminent figure in myth research, is less concerned with the functions that can be attributed to myth than with its meaning, which he locates in universal organizing principles of mythical thought and the relationships of these principles to the working of the human mind (Lévi-Strauss 1962). We know far less about New England Indian myths than we do about their legends and memorates, for although early Europeans recorded bits of indigenous mythology, Christianity swept this genre away, or rather, replaced it with Christianity's own biblical equivalents. Myth forms a tiny part of the corpus of this study.

The folktale, in contrast to memorate, legend, and myth, is said not to have really happened. Folktales are, in William Bascom's words, "prose narratives which are regarded as fiction" (Bascom 1965:4). They happened out of time or "once upon a time," are told to amuse or to convey moral lessons, and possess well-defined narrative structures (Dundes 1964; Propp [1928] 1979). Although folktales are known throughout North America and even among Indian groups adjacent to southern New England, very few examples of this genre were recorded in the Wampanoag, Mohegan, Massachusett, and Narragansett areas, where presumably the folktales died out early in the historic period.

I have grouped the texts into chapters that reflect dominant or key subjects, such as the arrival of Europeans, Christianity, ghosts, treasures, witches, the giant Maushop, Little People, and dreams. These categories are not the only ones possible, and they are not mutually exclusive; most treasure narratives, for example, also involve ghosts, witches, or the devil. Nevertheless, these key subjects are the major symbolic representations that recur throughout the collection, and most memorates and legends are based upon one or more of them. Within each chapter I have arranged the texts and the accompanying interpretations in chronological order to show the complete course of each key subject as it passed through history by word of mouth.[8]

A smaller and more specific unit of analysis is needed to supplement the genre and key subject distinctions, for although an entire legend can diffuse from one historic and cultural milieu to another, smaller elements also diffuse across cultural boundaries, independent of the larger narrative in which they originally occurred. The Wampanoag of Martha's Vineyard told many legends of how the giant Maushop built a causeway of stones from Gay Head to Cuttyhunk. At one point in the history of this legend, the giant carries his boulders in an apron. This small modification, which probably originated in New England Yankee or British folklore, thereafter became a permanent element in Wampanoag giant stories. Other examples of the cross-cultural transmission of specific narrative elements are abundant in the texts and require a smaller unit of analysis, the motif, that will enable us to recognize these specific innovations and trace their historical origins. Stith Thompson, in *Motif-Index of Folk-Literature*, defined motifs loosely as "those details out of which full-fledged narratives are composed," including anything "worthy of note because of something out of the ordinary, something of sufficiently striking character to become part of a tradition, oral or literary" (Thompson 1955, 1:10, 19). Thompson's motif index is a sensitive tool for identifying specific changes within the texts over time and for determining the possible historical sources for these changes.[9]

IV

The present collection is unusual. It represents one of the oldest continually recorded bodies of Indian folklore known in North America and is the longest-term historical study of oral narratives that I am aware of in the anthropological, historical, or folklore literature. I am interested in the relation between this stream of folklore and the historical events that affected these Indian communities: which symbols persist, which ones change, where innovations come from, and what can be said about the pattern and timing of change. Traditions about fabulous birds, giants, floating islands, ghosts, and things heard and seen in the air provide a window into the content, meaning, and functions of Indian symbolic life and a chronicle of how that symbolic life expressed, and in turn was changed by, historical events. We have recovered the voice of a people who lived through the whole of American history and now will listen to the private and indirect way in which they told their story.[10]

Abundant resources are available for reconstructing the historical context of the narratives. Many historians, ethnohistorians, and anthropologists have written about New England, and there are many historical societies, public archives, rare book libraries, church libraries, museum collections, and private collections where new discoveries reward the careful eye. With these resources I have been able to outline the social histories of the Indian communities where the folklore originated and to connect these local histories with the larger historical currents that affected the region and nation as a whole. I will add another dimension to the context of this Indian folklore—the folklore of non-Indian groups, mainly English and Afro-American, that lived near the Indian settlements. This context is important because new legends and motifs that enter the Indian narratives often originate from these nearby traditions. In addition, many of the Indians were whalers, so theoretically there was no limit to the folklore sources available to them since whaling brought men from faraway ports to settle in New England Indian villages. Hawaiians, Surinamers, West Africans, West Indians, Germans, Scots, and others turn up in the genealogies. The reader may recall from Herman Melville's *Moby Dick* that the three harpooners, Queequeg, Daggoo, and Tashtego, were respectively from Oceania, West Africa, and an Indian village named Gay Head on "the most westerly promontory of Martha's Vineyard, where there still exists the last remnant of a village of red men" (Melville [1851] 1956:107). With over 360 years of written sources in its treasury, southern New England is particularly favored for this combination of anthropological, historical, and folklore analysis.

2 From the Past to the Present

The Indian people seen by the first Europeans to reach New England had ancient prehistoric roots in North America. The Paleo-Indian hunters who pioneered the New World reached New England around 12,500 years ago, after the last continental glacier began its northward retreat.[1] As the glacier and its associated cold weather fauna such as mammoths and mastodons disappeared, the early Indian inhabitants of northeastern North America entered a long archaeological period known as the archaic, which lasted from about 10,000 years ago until about 700 B.C. The archaic hunters and gatherers made intensive use of forest game and local food resources such as fish, shellfish, seeds, nuts, roots, and berries. By the end of the archaic, knowledge of ceramic manufacture and horticulture had diffused to New England, thus initiating the early horticultural or woodland period, which extended from 700 B.C. to A.D. 1000 (Snow 1980:262). Subsistence during the early horticultural period was characterized by a combined hunting and gathering economy with corn, bean, squash, and tobacco cultivation. Because of their enhanced economy, good soils, adequate summer growing season, plentiful food resources, and a warming trend that favored the northward spread of farming, the southern New England populations entered a new period, the late prehistoric (A.D. 1000 to A.D. 1600), which was characterized by increasing populations and denser settlements. Corn, bean, and squash horticulture spread as far north as the Saco River in Maine, but Algonquian tribes that lived in the forests north of this boundary continued the earlier archaic hunting and gathering patterns.

Hundreds of generations of attention to the materials and conditions of the eastern forests and waterways had gone into producing the Indian cultures seen by Europeans at the threshold of the historic or contact period. Stone predominated throughout the prehistoric record as the primary material for projectile points, axes, knives, and other cutting implements, and each archaeological culture is identified by a specific assemblage of points and other tool types that differentiate it from others. Prehistoric New England Indians did not know the use of iron and bronze, although they occasionally pounded raw native copper into beads and cutting tools; they relied mainly upon bone, wood, and shell, in addition to stone, for their productive raw materials. Although very few examples of early historic perishable manufactures survive in contemporary museums, European observers often commented upon the intricate crafting of their baskets, mats, dwellings, beadwork, and clothing. From a technological perspective, the late prehistoric and early historic New England Indians resembled the earlier Neolithic people of Europe, who flaked and polished stone implements, hunted and gathered wild foods, cultivated garden crops with hoes, and manufactured pottery vessels. Unlike their Neolithic counterparts who invented the loom and raised domestic cattle, sheep, and goats, prehistoric New England natives had no knowledge of looms and raised no domestic animals other than the dog.

All southern New England Indians spoke languages related to the Eastern Algonquian family, which extended along the Atlantic drainage from the maritime provinces to North Carolina. Speakers of one Eastern Algonquian dialect could generally converse in the one spoken by their neighbors, but communication became difficult the farther one traveled away from home. Contemporary linguists have identified three Eastern Algonquian languages in the area covered in this study: Massachusett (including the dialects spoken from the Saco River to Massachusetts Bay, Cape Cod, Martha's Vineyard, Nantucket, and southeastern Rhode Island); Narragansett (primarily on the west side of Narragansett Bay and on Conanicut Island); and Mohegan-Pequot (including a range of dialects in southeastern Connecticut from the Pawcatuck to the Connecticut rivers) (Goddard 1978:72). We do not know the early populations of these language areas precisely, but recent estimates have ranged from about 50,000 to as high as 144,000 for the combined Massachusett, Narragansett, and Mohegan-Pequot domains (Cook 1976:29–59; Salisbury 1982:27–30; Snow 1980:33–35). European diseases such as smallpox and bubonic plague ravaged these groups so pervasively in the late sixteenth and early seventeenth centuries that by the time Europeans established permanent colonies in the 1620s and 1630s, some groups had been reduced by as much as 80 percent of their former strength and others had been obliterated. Indian populations fared worse after settlement because of repeated exposure to new diseases, internecine and intercultural warfare, and the disintegration of their social and religious underpinnings.

Language and dialect boundaries reflected social and cultural differences, but in themselves the linguistic groupings had no unifying political structure. The important unit of political organization, referred to here as the sachemdom, from the word *sachem*, meaning chief or leader, consisted of a small territorial domain that in the late prehistoric period was probably independent from other such entities but could be subdivided into smaller subsachemdoms.[2] On Martha's Vineyard, for example, in the early historic period, four sachems presided over distinct territories, each of which included smaller subdivisions ruled by minor sachems. The Nantucket Indians were grouped into two sachemdoms, one on the east and the other on the west of the island. The Narragansett, often thought to include all Indian groups on the western side of Narragansett Bay, actually comprised only one sachemdom among many along the Rhode Island coast.

The sachems ruled by hereditary authority, and the title passed generally in the male line from father to son or from elder brother to younger brother—or to a daughter or sister in the absence of male heirs. Although they were the exceptions, several notable female sachems presided in the seventeenth century, such as Awashonks of the Sakonnet (a small sachemdom in what is now Little Compton and Tiverton, Rhode Island) and Quiapen, also known as Magnus, of the Narragansett. Matthew Mayhew wrote of the Martha's Vineyard sachems, for example, that "The *Crown* (if I may so term it) always descended to the *Eldest Son* (though Subject to usurpation) not to the *Female*, unless in defect of a *Male* of the Blood; the Blood Royal, being in such Veneration among this People, that if a Prince had issue by divers Wives, such Succeeded as Heir who was Royally descended, by the Mother" (Mayhew 1694:7–8). The sachems administered justice, received guests, sponsored rituals, conducted diplomacy, allocated land, and collected tribute, all with the assistance of counselors and ordinary subjects. They ruled by persuasion and consensus rather than by command, and subjects could transfer allegiance to another sachem if displeased with their own. Daniel Gookin wrote in the seventeenth century that "Their sachems have not their men in such subjection, but that very frequently their men will leave them upon distaste or harsh dealing, and go and live under other sachems that can protect them; so that their princes endeavour to carry it obligingly and lovingly unto their people, lest they should desert them, and thereby their strength, power, and tribute would be diminished" (Gookin [1792] 1970:20). Sachems collected tribute from those to whom they granted hereditary and temporary use rights to land and enjoyed other benefits such as the right to whales and goods from wrecks that washed ashore in their territory, the skin of any deer killed in their ponds and rivers, the forequarters of any deer killed in their woods, and the first fruits from the annual harvest. Sachems lived in larger homes and enjoyed more wealth than most, and (along with their more prominent subjects), sometimes married more than one wife. Roger Williams noted two causes generally alleged by the Indians for their several wives. The first was "desire of Riches, because the Women bring in all the increase of the Field, & c. the Husband onely fisheth, hunteth, & c.," and "Secondly, their long sequestring themselves from their wives after conception, untill the child be weaned, which with some is long after a yeare old" (Williams [1643] 1936:147).

Trade, religious gatherings such as harvest and funeral rituals, military assistance, and marriage helped bind neighboring sachemdoms together. Ruling families commonly intermarried, thereby strengthening peaceful relations between independent groups. In the early historic period, as a consequence of the differential impacts of disease, profits of the fur trade, and military alliances with Europeans, several well-located sachems imposed jurisdiction and tribute relations over weaker groups to form larger, more hierarchical, extended sachemdoms. Sassacus, a prominent Pequot sachem from the lower Thames River valley, ruled as many as twenty-six distinct principalities in the territory between the Pawcatuck and Connecticut rivers in the 1630s, and Massasoit, paramount sachem of the Pokanoket (centered near Barrington, Warren, and Bristol, Rhode Island), had authority over several sachemdoms in southeastern Massachusetts, Martha's Vineyard, and Nantucket, which became known collectively as the Wampanoag. The Narragansett sachems extended their sovereignty over at least one Massachusett sachemdom (that of Chickataubut at Weymouth, part of Massasoit's domain), certain Nipmuck bands to the north and west of the Narragansett country, the eastern Niantic (around Westerly, Rhode Island), and a number of small sachemdoms (the Coweset, Shawomet, Pawtuxet, Mashapaug, and Manisseans near their homeland on Narragansett Bay). An early Narragansett legend attributes their sovereignty to the sachem Tashtasick, whose lineage was said to be more noble than all others: "The antient Indians reported that in those Countries of *Narraganset, Niantic, Coweesit, & parts adjacent* there was *one great Sachem* which *had all* the parts *under him* and ruling over all; his Name was TASHTASICK. He had only a *Son* and a *Daughter*; and he, esteeming none of Degree for them to marry with, *married them together*" (Stiles 1916:28). The Narragansett domain did not include the Mohegan-Pequots, their political and economic rivals to the west, with whom they fought for control of frontier lands in western Rhode Island, nor could they subjugate Uncas, the resourceful Mohegan sachem who cast off Pequot rule. English leaders easily used rivalries between sachems to their advantage in securing a foothold in southern New England. Cotton Mather described Indian rivalry as "*a division in the kingdom of satan* against itself, as was very serviceable to that of our Lord" (Mather [1702] 1820, 2:480.

At the domestic level, men attended to construction, politics, trade, hunting, and war while women cultivated, shellfished, cooked, cared for children, and manufactured mats, baskets, and clothing. Occasionally several families lived together in a single circular house, and co-wives of leading men were known to live in separate dwellings. Residence patterns varied with the season through a cycle of dense inland winter villages, to spring fishing camps, to dispersed summer homesteads by cornfields near the sea, to isolated inland hunting camps in autumn and early winter. The men built the traditional wigwam by setting a circle of poles in the ground and then binding them inward to form a hemispherical frame reinforced by withes wrapped and tied horizontally around the structure. Women then covered the frame with bark or mats, leaving a smoke hole at the top over an interior hearth. The family slept on mats on the floor or on raised platforms alongside the fire. When they moved, the women simply rolled up the roofing materials and left the frame intact for the next occupation. Roger Williams recalled, "I once in travell lodged at a house, at which in my returne I hoped to have lodged againe there the next night, but the house was gone in that interim, and I was glad to lodge under a tree" (Williams [1643] 1936:47).

Mothers carried their newborn infants "greased and sooted, wrapped in a beaver skin, bound to his good behavior with his feet up to his bum upon a board two foot long and one foot broad, his face exposed to all nipping weather" (Wood [1634] 1977:114). Some English considered relationships between Indian parents and children to be overly affectionate and permissive by their standards. In Roger Williams's opinion, for example, "This extreme *affection*, together with want of *learning*, makes ther children sawcie, bold, and undutifull" (Williams [1643] 1936: 29). Yet Edward Winslow observed, "The younger sort reverence the elder, and do all mean offices, whilst they are together, although they be strangers" (Winslow [1624] 1910:348).

THE MASSACHUSETT

A group of sachemdoms known as the Massachusett once lived along the shores and estuaries of Massachusetts Bay.[3] To the north they were bounded by the Pawtucket or Pennacook, who lived mainly in the lower drainage of the Merrimack River, and to the south by the Pokanoket or Wampanoag. Both the Pawtucket and Pokanoket spoke dialects of the broader Massachusett language. The Nipmuck lived to the west in central Massachusetts and northern Connecticut. Regular contact between the Massachusett sachemdoms and Europeans intensified during the earliest years of the seventeenth century, particularly after Samuel de Champlain's first visit in the summer of 1605. European seamen surely brought the epidemic of 1617–19 that nearly obliterated the Massachusett on the threshold of permanent English colonization. Thomas Morton, who lived among them, commented on the impact of that epidemic:

the hand of God fell heavily upon them, with such a mortall stroake, that they died in heapes, as they lay in their houses. . . . For in a place where many inhabited, there hath been but one left a live, to tell what became of the rest, the livinge being (as it seemes) not able to bury the dead. . . . And the bones and skulls upon the severall places of their habitations, made such a spectacle after my comming into those partes, that as I travailed in that Forrest, nere the Massachussets, it seemed to mee a new found Golgatha. (Morton [1632] 1947:18–19)

Puritan colonists poured into Massachusetts Bay in the 1630s, and it quickly grew into New England's largest colony. By 1674 Daniel Gookin wrote that the Massachusett "could, in former times, arm for war, about three thousand men" but that "There are not of this people left at this day above three hundred men, besides women and children" (Gookin [1792] 1970:10). Mainly through the efforts begun in the 1640s by the Reverend John Eliot of Roxbury, the Massachusetts Bay Colony Puritans initiated a program for converting the

Massachusett to Christianity and resettling them in English plantations known as praying towns. There Eliot and others instructed the
Indians in English trades and farming and taught reading and writing in the Indian language, for which Eliot provided the alphabet
and orthography. By the outbreak of King Philip's War in 1675, the
Massachusett and some Nipmuck had formed fourteen praying
towns, including Natick, the first and best-known Christian Indian
community in New England, and Ponkapoag, in Canton. The English dealt the entire praying town experiment a lethal blow in King
Philip's War, for although they relied extensively on Christian Indians in the conflict, many of the English distrusted them and con-
fined large numbers to Deer Island in Boston Harbor.[4] After the war,
during which many Christian Indians had vanished, died, or been
killed, the four surviving praying towns suffered declining populations and morale, and a new generation of settlers pressured them
for their remaining land. Beginning in 1719 the Natick Indians lost
most of their common lands, and by 1749 they lived scattered
throughout their township amidst English homesteads. Non-Indians
bought the last Natick property in 1828, and the Ponkapoag guardian
sold that group's remaining tracts around 1840. Rebecca Davis, who
was seventy-one years old in 1861 when her name appeared on a list
of Ponkapoag Indians, in her last years visited Canton regularly from
Boston "just before Thanksgiving; and her old friends furnished her
with pork, eggs, turkeys, and other comforts" (Huntoon 1893:39). As
did many Indian survivors in this region, Davis enjoyed a reputation
as an herbalist and "gained some money by the sale of a salve, which
she prepared from herbs according to the prescription of some ancient medicine man" (ibid.). Although some individuals in southeastern Massachusetts still can trace their ancestry to the early praying towns, these communities had evaporated by the end of the
nineteenth century and very little folklore is known to have been
recorded from this source.

THE WAMPANOAG, MASHPEE, AND GAY HEAD

The Pokanoket sachemdom, centered at Sowams, now Warren,
Rhode Island, also embraced surrounding areas of southeastern Massachusetts. By the early historic period Massasoit's authority extended to the sachemdoms of Cape Cod, the Elizabeth Islands, Martha's Vineyard (also known as Nope), and Nantucket. The great
mortality of 1617–19 especially affected the Wampanoag area, including particularly the Patuxet sachemdom in Plymouth, which
was exterminated. Robert Cushman, a contemporary of the Pilgrims

who visited Plymouth, left a bleak account of the Indians who "were very much wasted of late" and that "together with their own civil dissensions and bloody wars . . . I think the twentieth person is scarce left alive; and those that are left, have their courage much abated, and their countenance is dejected, and they seem as a people affrighted" (Cushman [1622] 1910:231–32). Pilgrim settlement moved first into the ghostly meadows and woodlands once inhabited by the Patuxet and then overflowed into areas still utilized by functioning Indian populations. By 1627 Plymouth Colony men had established the Aptuxet trading post in what is now Buzzards Bay; in 1632 they created a trading station at Massasoit's home village of Sowams on Narragansett Bay; and by 1642 the first English had settled on Martha's Vineyard. Massasoit, and later his son Metacomet or King Philip, accommodated to the English need for more land and reluctantly submitted to English law, but both also tried to maintain authority within their Indian constituencies and drew the line at religious conversion. According to Puritan legend, "It was particularly remarked in *Philip* the ring-leader of the most calamitous war that ever they made upon us; our [John] *Eliot* made a tender of the *everlasting salvation* to that king; but the monster entertained it with contempt and anger, and after the *Indian* mode of joining *signs* with *words*, he took a *button* upon the *coat* of the reverend man, adding, *That he cared for his gospel, just as much as he cared for that button*" (Mather [1702] 1820, 1:514). Despite the independent course steered by their paramount sachems, some lesser Wampanoag sachems accepted English authority and converted to Christianity. Of the several missionaries who worked in the Wampanoag region, the most successful and best known were Thomas Mayhew, Jr. (ca. 1621–57), who worked among the Indians of Martha's Vineyard, and Richard Bourne (ca. 1610–82), who converted a cluster of small sachemdoms known as the "South Sea" Indians in and near what is now Mashpee on Cape Cod. By 1675, when English settlement had overrun most available land in Plymouth Colony, war erupted that ultimately pitted Massachusetts Bay, Plymouth, Connecticut, New Haven, and their Mohegan, Sakonnet, and Christian Indian allies against Philip's remaining Wampanoag, some Nipmuck and Pocumtuck from western Massachusetts, and the Narragansett. By the end of fighting in fall 1676, the English had killed Philip and most of his closest followers, but many converts and some pro-English groups survived in a number of enclaves throughout southeastern Massachusetts and on the islands. From the late seventeenth century to the early twentieth century, many of these enclaves either coalesced with others or simply died out, leaving two principal concentrations of Wampanoag at Gay Head on Martha's Vineyard and at Mashpee.

Mashpee

The early history of Mashpee is closely bound up with the activities of Richard Bourne, a Massachusett-speaking English farmer from nearby Sandwich who, with John Cotton, Samuel Treat, and Thomas Tupper,* brought Christianity to the Wampanoag of Cape Cod.[5] Bourne followed Eliot's example of gathering the convert population together into an English plantation, governed by Indian proprietors, where they could acquire English customs, attend church, learn to read and write in their native language, and eventually earn recognition as a township of Christian Indian freemen. Toward this end, in 1665, Bourne persuaded the two principal sachems of the Mashpee area to give up some twenty-five square miles to "the South Sea Indians and their children forever: and not to be sold or given away from them by anyone without all their consents thereunto" (Hutchins 1979:48). By this remarkable deed the newly converted Indians of the south Cape acquired permanent collective title to Mashpee plantation, and like their Christian Indian contemporaries in Massachusetts Bay Colony and on Martha's Vineyard, they enjoyed protection as English subjects. In 1670 a group of Congregational clergymen ordained Bourne as the first minister of the Mashpee Indian congregation, and by 1674 he had baptized ninety at Mashpee and converted about four hundred more throughout the Cape. During King Philip's War in 1675–76, many English in Plymouth Colony felt uneasy about the numerous Christian Indian villages in their midst and may have required some to resettle in Mashpee. Nevertheless, the peaceful Christian Indians of Mashpee, Cape Cod, and the islands emerged from the war in substantially better shape than did the survivors of Eliot's praying towns.

Thereafter, however, they experienced the same difficulties that afflicted all other Indian enclaves in southern New England—racism, exploitation, indebtedness, drunkenness, harsh legal penalties, and declining populations. One way to repay debts and fines and to avoid indentureship for themselves and their children was to sell common land. Bourne died around 1682, and Simon Popmonet (?—ca. 1720), his Indian successor to the Mashpee pulpit, lacked Bourne's authority in the English community and his ability to protect his parishioners and their property. In 1685 the Mashpee proprietors wisely sought to stem the demands on their land by obtaining an agreement from the Plymouth General Court that made approval by the court and the consent of all Mashpee Indians necessary for any subsequent land transactions. Joseph Bourne (1701–67), a great-grandson of Richard, succeeded Popmonet as minister in 1726, and the Indian Solomon Briant (ca. 1695–1775) followed him in 1742. Both Bourne and Briant preached in Massachusett. By the early years of the eighteenth century, Mashpee men were working in the whaling industry as well as in farming and fishing; the women learned to spin, weave and make tailored clothing, and many proprietors could read and write in Massachusett. As was the case throughout New England and Long Island during much of the historic period, they also earned some income by making and selling Indian brooms and baskets to the English. Many continued to live in wigwams, although some constructed fireplaces to replace the open hearth, and one man who built an English-style frame house heated it with a chimneyless open fire. Although the Indian proprietors owned all Mashpee land, individual families could enjoy use rights for home building and farming and could pass these rights on to their descendants. In the absence of heirs, a user's estate returned to the proprietors. Residents could use the common pasture and woodlands, streams, and marshes as sources for firewood, timber, shellfish, fish, deer, and salt hay. Each year in spring a moderator presided over the proprietors' meeting and a clerk kept records. No liquor could be sold on the plantation, and there were no taxes.

This taste of democratic self-government ended in 1746 when the Massachusetts General Court appointed three English guardians to administer the plantation and lease surplus land to English farmers. The Mashpee people resisted this intrusion, since in their estimation they had no surplus land to lease. In 1760 a Mashpee Indian teacher, Reuben Cognehew, went directly to King George III of England to voice Mashpee grievances, after which the king instructed his governor in Boston to "give the Indians a better government," with the result that Mashpee became a district, free of guardian rule, in 1763 (Freeman 1869:687). The proprietors again had the power to control local affairs and elect their own officers, including three Indian and two English overseers, an English moderator and treasurer, two wardens, and one or more constables (Mazer 1980:41).

District status brought new freedoms and many changes to Mashpee, including the authority to enforce laws and admit new proprietors. The Indians could not, nor did they wish to, sell district land to whites without court approval, and they could not vote for representatives to the Massachusetts General Court. As a consesquence of the opening up of proprietor status in 1763, many newcomers came to Mashpee, including Indians from other New England tribes, some Europeans, and many Afro-Americans. Francis G. Hutchins, a contemporary historian, associated this increase in newcomers with a rapid weakening of Indian cultural traditions, seen most clearly in the decline of the Massachusett language and in an architectural shift from wigwams to shingle houses (Hutchins 1979:77–88). The Revolutionary War also took a heavy toll of Mashpee enlisted men, for an early petition states, "After the war our fathers had sixty widows left on the plantation whose husbands had died or been slain" (Todd 1907:164). Some of these Mashpee women presumably found it necessary to seek mates from outside the local Indian community.

Again, Mashpee's experiment with self-government came to an unwelcome end. The Massachusetts General Court repealed district rule in 1788 and restored the unpopular regime of appointed guardians. The guardians imposed and policed their own regulations and could evict non-Indians or any others who lacked clear proprietary credentials, thus reversing the inflow of Afro-Americans and other strangers into Mashpee, which had increased since the creation of district status in 1763. The Reverend Gideon Hawley (1726–1807), a Congregational minister who had shared the Mashpee pulpit with the Indian Solomon Briant since 1757, influenced the court's decision to impose guardians. Originally appointed to preach in English for those who could not understand Massachusett, he succeeded Briant at the latter's death in 1775 and preached in English until his own death in 1807. According to Hawley, who previously had served as a missionary among Indians in western Massachusetts and northern New York, the influx of non-Indians had weakened the Christian and Indian character of the Mashpee people, who needed guardians for their own good:

At Marshpee are between eighty and ninety Indian houses, if we reckon those who are in affinity with them. This blood is mixed; but the Indian blood prevails in a very considerable degree; and all this people value themselves on being christians, and some of them are an honour to their profession, although too many are not so. These are more civilized than any Indians in the commonwealth, but utterly unable to govern or protect themselves, being surrounded by white people, many of whom would defraud and oppress them without good men to defend them. (Hawley 1795:66)

Hawley concluded, "The present regulation of Marshpee has been the salvation of the Indian interest; and every year proves its utility to them" (ibid.). Having already served as an elected overseer during the district period, Hawley was appointed by the court as a guardian in the new administration.

Edward A. Kendall, who visited Mashpee shortly before Hawley's death in 1807, recorded his impressions of the community at that time and commented on their fear of the supernatural:

But, when the inhabitants of this plantation are called Indians, the denomination must be qualified; for a very large proportion are Europeans and negroes, or at least largely mixed with one or both. It is said that many Hessians [actually four], from the army of General Burgoyne, married into this community; and there are also Englishmen, and descendants of Englishmen, to be found here. . . . From these and various other causes, of the whole four hundred souls [actually between 357 and 380], there is at this day only a very small number, perhaps not twenty, that are pure Indians. . . .

Of the Indians who reside near the missionary house, the greater part have wooden houses, after the manner of the country; one family, however, still possesses a *wigwam*, though with some mixture of European architecture. The smoke passes through the middle of the roof; but the fire-place is of brick: the inside of the wigwam is perfectly neat. The furniture in the houses, here, is generally of the same description with that of the poorer whites.

. . .

The Indians on this plantation, as in other parts of New England, are in some particulars under the peculiar protection of the law. They cannot be sued for any debt exceeding the amount of twenty-four shillings currency, unless contracted with the consent of their guardians: and their lands are in no case answerable. To many of their white neighbours, these provisons are believed to be very offensive; since, but for them, they might, at the cost of a little New England rum, long since have deprived the objects of them every acre in the Plantation of Marshpee.

These people are very superstitious, and very fearful of going about in the dark, in which they are constantly apprehensive of being presented with terrifying visions. (Kendall 1809:178–80, 182–83)

Many Mashpee people expressed their unhappiness with Hawley and the guardian system by leaving his Congregational meeting for Indian Baptist preachers. When Hawley died in 1807, the overseers worsened the situation by appointing another English minister, the Reverend Phineas Fish, who lost almost all Indian support by the end of his thirty-three years in the Mashpee pulpit. After 1830 the legendary Indian Baptist preacher "Blind Joe" Amos captivated the majority of Mashpee churchgoers. Some state officials who attended his service described him:

One feature of the service left a fresh and pleasant impression. It was the appearance of Mr. Amos, the native preacher. He was one of the choir; and, when he struck the first note upon his accordeon, the associations of so novel an instrument, we confess, somewhat disturbed our notions of propriety; but, as he warmed to the service, and stood tall and manly . . . with his

face turned to heaven, and his sightless sockets swimming with tears, he
seemed the very personification of the loftiest spirit of rapt devotion. (Bird,
Griswold, and Weekes 1849:34)

In 1833, after years of political frustration, the Mashpee tried unsuccessfully to evict Reverend Fish, reclaim their meetinghouse, and
prevent outsiders from exploiting their wood and hay. The following
year they finally persuaded the General Court to restore district status, so once again the Mashpee proprietors could elect their own
officials, including the three selectmen. District status precluded citizenship, but most Mashpee people did not desire citizenship at this
time because it would have meant an end to state protection against
being sued for debt and loss of land. In 1840 the court gave the proprietors control over their own religious affairs, whereupon they
swiftly reclaimed the meetinghouse and dismissed Reverend Fish.

In 1842 a radical change in landholding patterns occurred. The
proprietors voted with court approval to divide up ten thousand of
the twelve thousand acres of common land into private allotments
that could be bought and sold among the proprietors. In 1869 the
court removed all restrictions on the sale of land to outsiders and
enfranchised the Indians, and in 1870 Mashpee was incorporated as
a town. Most Mashpee natives preferred the security of district government to the right to vote and feared their community would dis-
integrate after the loss of safeguards they had enjoyed since the
"South Sea" sachems signed the original deed in 1665. It soon followed that whites began acquiring much valuable ocean front property, and by 1920 whites owned more land in Mashpee than did the
Indians (Mazer 1980:64). Meanwhile the Indians turned increasingly away from the traditional livelihoods of farming and fishing to
day labor jobs as guides for fishermen and hunters, domestic workers, farm hands, and cranberry pickers. Since most whites who
bought property in Mashpee maintained permanent residences elsewhere, Indians continued to dominate town politics.

By the 1920s a spirit of cultural revivalism spread among most
North American Indian people, and the Mashpee Indians began to
take more interest in their past and in the traditions, folklore, dress,
and customs of other North American Indians. In the early 1920s,
for example, they restored the Indian meetinghouse which had been
abandoned a number of years, and in 1928 they joined with the Gay
Head and Herring Pond Wampanoag to form the Wampanoag Nation,
thus reestablishing a system of Indian leadership apart from town
politics. That same year they also organized the Mashpee summer
powwow, a public festival that is still an important occasion for dis-
playing their Indian identity and hosting Indians from other north-

eastern communities. Mashpee folklore from the 1930s shows many effects of this revival in the form of conscious borrowings from early published sources and from publications about more distant Algonquian people such as the Delaware and Ojibwa. As Indian consciousness and tribal organization flowered, however, real estate and eventually political control passed steadily and irreversibly into white hands. By the early 1960s whites outnumbered Indians in Mashpee, and by 1969 whites had won a two-to-one majority on the Board of Selectmen. Having lost economic and political control in the community where for over three hundred years they had been the majority, the Indians formed the Mashpee Wampanoag Tribal Council, Incorporated, in 1974, to be their governing body. Two years later the Mashpee tribe filed suit against a large developer (the New Seabury Corporation), the town of Mashpee, and over 140 large landowners to reclaim their entire territory, which, they asserted, had been taken from them illegally. One purpose in filing suit was to "regain control of the land in order to preserve the ecology and to curtail the overdevelopment of the land" (American Friends Service Committee 1978:4). Another was "to reclaim what it considered its sovereign rights as a tribe to rule its own affairs within its own territory" (Mazer 1980:180). After a monumental three-year struggle, the suit failed, leaving a divided community and a more politically astute Indian minority which is still perplexed over the reality of becoming marginal in their ancestral home. In the words of one Mashpee activist, Amelia G. Bingham, "It is our desire to recoup a small portion of the precious Indian land, before the rest of the world moves in, and the land of the Wampanoag is no more" (Bingham 1970:47).

Gay Head

Gay Head was one of four distinct sachemdoms on Martha's Vineyard in 1642 when the English under Thomas Mayhew first settled on the opposite end of the island in what is now Edgartown.[6] Mayhew's son, Thomas Mayhew, Jr., learned the local Indian dialect and followed the missionary calling until he disappeared at sea in 1657. For years after his death the Indian converts on Martha's Vineyard honored his memory (and perhaps his ghost) by dropping stones on the site where he last spoke to them before leaving for his voyage. This memorial, a heap of stones known as the Place on the Wayside, which can be seen today in Edgartown on the West Tisbury Road, embodies the synthesis of Christian and Indian influences that has long coexisted on this island. The senior Thomas Mayhew as well as Thomas Jr.'s sons, Matthew and John, continued the family missionary work and eventually converted the entire Indian population of the island to Congregational Christianity. The people of Gay Head, being the most isolated as well as the most independent of the island's Indians, were also the last to convert, following their sachem Mittark, who converted in the mid-1660s. Mittark served as the first Christian minister at Gay Head, where he preached in Massachuset until his death in 1683. By the time of the senior Mayhew's death in 1681, the Indians of the Vineyard had regrouped into Christian communities separate from and subordinate to the English but under the local authority of Indian sachems, magistrates, and ministers. Matthew Mayhew described this Christian Indian society:

> I shall as to their *Government* only add; that in their several *Plantations* or *Town-ships*, they Elect *three* or more to joyn with the *Sachims* (or Lords of the place) who hold *Courts*, for issuing such Controversies as happen among them, the *Sachim* presiding in such Courts, or in case he decline that Office, another is Elected in his place: if either party dislike the judgment given, he Appeals to a *Superiour Court*, which consists of some of the most esteemed of each place, being some of their *Magistrates*, where some *Principal Sachims* is Elected to preside for one year: and from this Court an Appeal lyes to the *English Court*. In giving Judgment, they observe such rules and orders made and recorded among themselves, and the *English Law*, the knowledge whereof they much aspire unto. They have likewise some among them, whom the less able to declare, or defend their own Cases, improve as *Attornies*; some of which are to admiration *Critical* in their pleadings. (Mayhew 1694:38)

Children in these plantations learned to read and write in Massachusett.

Due to its location on a peninsula on the remote western end of the island and its lack of attractive resources, such as timber, extensive farmland, or a good harbor, Gay Head always enjoyed more isolation and autonomy than did most other Indian settlements in southern New England. By the late seventeenth or early eighteenth centuries the greater number of Gay Head Christians left the Congregational church begun by the Mayhew family to form a Baptist meeting, thus erecting an additional boundary between themselves and the English population. Indian autonomy was fragile, however; Joseph Mittark, who succeeded his father as sachem, sold Gay Head to Matthew Mayhew, who in turn represented Thomas Dongan, royal governor of New York, who at that time claimed jurisdiction over the island. Dongan then created the lordship and manor of Martha's Vineyard and named Mayhew as its lord. A number of Gay Headers challenged the legality of Joseph Mittark's sale, but in 1703 a committee appointed by the province of Massachusetts Bay considered and dismissed their complaints (Massachusetts annexed Martha's

Vineyard in 1691). The Indians requested a review two years later that ended with the same results. The London-based missionary society, the Company for the Propagation of the Gospel in New England, then bought Gay Head from Dongan to encourage the Indians to cultivate what had been their land and to protect the Christian Indians from land-hungry English neighbors. Unfortunately, the company leased some of the best Indian acreage to whites until 1727, when the Gay Headers agreed to relinquish an eight-hundred-acre parcel in exchange for the company's commitment to protect the rest of the peninsula for exclusive Indian use. The population of the Gay Head community in the 1740s ranged between 113 and 165 souls, a dramatic reduction from the late prehistoric population which may have numbered as many as 10,000 for the entire island. Estimates of Gay Head (as well as Mashpee) population in the historic period have always been approximate because of the many who were away for extended lengths of time working in whaling and other industries.

In 1746 the Massachusetts legislature voted to appoint three guardians for Gay Head, and for over a century thereafter the Indians lived under the intermittent authority of overseers whose financial and land management practices they found to be a perpetual source of annoyance. They petitioned frequently, for example, against the overseers' leasing policies, the removal of their households from leased land, the necessity of renting land for their own purposes, the lack of sufficient grazing for their cattle, the inadequate supplies of firewood, and the nonpayment of leasing revenues that were due them. By 1764 the racial composition of the community had begun to change; mating with Afro-American and English had been reported among all Indian populations of the island, and of the 276 persons identified as Indian at Gay Head, only about one-quarter could claim unmixed descent.

The Company for the Propagation of the Gospel, being an English organization, apparently forfeited its title to land on Martha's Vineyard in the course of the American Revolution, and the commonwealth of Massachusetts subsequently administered all Indian lands within its borders. For almost a century thereafter, the state considered the Gay Head Indians to be its involuntary wards, who could not buy or sell land except to each other and could not make any legal contracts, sue or be sued by the courts, or vote in state or national elections.

From the seventeenth to the nineteenth centuries, the Gay Head people enjoyed a distinctive communal existence based upon collective rights to land and frequent sharing of food, tools, labor, and other resources between neighbors and kin. The Baptist church also played a unifying role in the community as the older Congregational church declined (Tripp 1893:250–53). Many observers noted that any native-born Gay Header could homestead unused common land as needed, and at death it could be inherited by his children if they maintained an interest in it; otherwise it would return to the common pool. Kathleen Bragdon, in her dissertation on Massachusett texts, suggests that the Indian emphasis on communal land use, active participation of the populace in government, reallocation of land according to need, and joint use of economic resources represent the adaptation of indigenous patterns to new historical conditions:

The native emphasis on the communal use of land, the flexible inheritance rules, and the joint use of resources set them apart, particularly in the eighteenth and nineteenth centuries, from the non-Indian communities. The reinterpretation of the traditional custom of corporate land holding along the lines of the early English agricultural system introduced to the natives in the seventeenth century, is another instance of the manner in which change in native society and culture served to reinforce their distinctiveness in the late seventeenth and eighteenth centuries. (Bragdon 1981:118)

In addition to the tracts that individual Indians enclosed for their own use, the tribe as a whole cultivated common fields and kept common pasture. They also earned income for the support of the poor, elderly, widows, and orphans by leasing unused land to the English and earned occasional income by selling local clay and cranberries. The following passages depict Gay Head life as seen through the eyes of three early- to mid-nineteenth-century visitors:

The great body of the Indians is at Gay Head. They have here a tract of excellent land, containing three thousand acres, reserved to them. It is destitute of trees; but there are many swamps, some of which afford peat, and others springs of good water. The land is broken into hills; and there are no roads. The Indians have twenty-six framed houses and seven wigwams. The framed houses are nothing better than mean huts. . . . The number of families is thirty-four; and of souls, a hundred and forty-two: beside whom about a hundred Indians are absent from Gay Head; some of whom are children put out to service in English families; and others whale-men. . . . Every native, whether he lives off or on the island, is considered as a proprietor; and every child born to him is entitled to a right, which is equivalent to the pasture of three sheep. . . . Of the Indians nine men are pure, and still more of the women; the rest are intermixed, chiefly with negroes. (Freeman 1815a: 93–94)

The Indians, like those of Marshpee, are a mixed race, and two hundred and forty in number, in which the women and children make more than the due proportion. On the soil, there were not at this time more than fifteen or sixteen men and boys, the rest being at sea, in the fisheries. This is a favourite employ, to which they give themselves, and to which they are anxiously solicited. Ship-owners come to their cottages, making them offers, and persuading them to accept them; and so rarely is Gay Head visited for any other purpose, that this was supposed, at the light-house, to be my errand. This business of inviting the Indians is a sort of crimping, in which liquor, goods and fair words are plied, till the Indian gets into debt, and gives his consent.... The Indians find their fishing-voyages as little for their ultimate benefit ... and their obstinate addiction to spiritous liquors makes their case still worse: hence, an Indian, that goes to sea, is ruined, and his family is ruined with him. (Kendall 1809:193—95)

The pursuits of this tribe are agricultural, with the usual exception of seafaring men; and of those even, the families usually own and occupy land, to which they look for partial support, and upon which the head of the family almost invariably settles for life, after following the sea for a few years....

Generally, they live in framed houses, perhaps a majority having barns.... Their territory is separated from that of the whites, by a rail fence, and the separate lots are fenced, usually safely. Almost the only articles cultivated, are Indian corn, with occasionally other grain, and potatoes....

The legal condition of this tribe is singularly anomalous.... None of the lands are held, as far as we could learn, by any title, depending for its validity upon statute law. The primitive title, possession, to which has been added, inclosure, is the only title recognized or required. The rule has been, that any native could, at any time, appropriate to his own use such portion of the unimproved common land, as he wished, and, as soon as he enclosed it, with a fence, of however frail structure, it belonged to him and his heirs forever. That rule still exists. A young man arrives at maturity, and wishes for a home for a prospective family, or a shelter when he returns from sea; he encloses half an acre, five acres, or ten acres, as the case may be, and he has acquired a fee in the estate; and the most singular and most creditable fact, in connection with this, is, that, while one proprietor has but half an acre, and another has over a hundred acres, there is no heart-burning, no feeling that the latter has more than his share. (Bird, Griswold, and Weekes 1849:18—21)

In 1774 the General Court of Massachusetts appointed a Gay Head man as one of the three overseers, and by 1855 the tribe was electing its own Indian overseers, who became selectmen when Gay Head became a district in 1862. In 1870 the Massachusetts Senate and House of Representatives approved legislation to incorporate the district of Gay Head into the town of Gay Head, the Indians became citizens, and most communal land was allotted to individuals, who could now buy and sell as they wished. At this time the Gay Head population was 227, of whom 188 were native born and 39 originated elsewhere, mostly from other Indian communities on Martha's Vineyard, Mashpee, and other New England towns. Some could trace their ancestry to Surinam, Africa, the Cape Verde Islands, the Sandwich Islands, and Santo Domingo. Most worked as farmers and seamen, and a few made their living as teachers or laborers.

Although vestiges of communalism persisted for almost a century after incorporation, in shared pastures, a town cranberry bog, and cooperative fishing enterprises, the allotment of land to private owners weakened the older communal system and introduced fuel for factionalism along a range of kinship, political, and economic lines. As happened also at Mashpee, a clear transition took place in land ownership from Indian to non-Indian hands, but because many non-Indian landowners were summer residents only, the Wampanoag retained control of the town's political offices. As whaling, fishing, farming, and stock raising declined in the late nineteenth and early twentieth centuries, construction, service, and tourist-related jobs took their place to some extent. By the early twentieth century some Gay Headers displayed a scholarly interest in their history and folklore, and in the 1920s and 1930s they participated in new Indian organizations such as the Wampanoag Nation and the Algonquin Council of Indian Tribes. They also hosted annual powwows, known locally as pageants, where they performed Gay Head legends for Indians and summer tourists to see. Not until 1951 did electricity reach Gay Head, and not until 1955 the first dial telephone. Although the federal government has never recognized the Gay Head (or even the Mashpee) Indians as a tribe, the Wampanoag Tribal Council of Gay Head, Incorporated, is currently petitioning for such recognition and is seeking to reclaim some of its hereditary land.

THE NARRAGANSETT

The Narragansett, who lived throughout most of Rhode Island on the western shores and hinterland of Narragansett Bay, first encountered Europeans in the spring of 1524, when Giovanni da Verazzano visited them for fifteen days: "we saw about twenty small boats full of people, who came about our ship, uttering many cries of astonishment, but they would not approach nearer than within fifty paces; stopping, they looked at the structure of our ship, our persons and dress, afterwards they all raised a loud shout together, signifying that they were pleased. . . . This is the finest looking tribe, and the handsomest . . . that we have found in our voyage" (Verazzano 1841:46). Roger Williams and other English began settling in their midst in 1636, and by 1675 the Narragansett, along with Metacomet's Wampanoag, found themselves committed to a life or death struggle with the Puritan colonies. On December 19, 1675, English soldiers stormed the fortified Narragansett sanctuary in the Great Swamp in South Kingstown and killed large numbers of men, women, and children: "after much Blood and many Wounds dealt on both Sides, the English seeing their Advantage, began to fire the Wigwams, where was supposed to be many of the Enemies Women and Children destroyed, by the firing of at least five or six hundred of those smoaky Cells" (Hubbard [1865] 1969, 1:148). In the following months English war parties pursued the Narragansett survivors and captured or killed many hundreds, including the sachems Canonchet and Quiapen or Magnus. Major John Talcott of Connecticut described the extermination of a large band of Narragansett who had retreated into a swamp in what is now North Smithfield, Rhode Island. Talcott's Connecticut troops and Mohegan allies "assaulted them who p[re]sently in swamped them selves in a great spruse swamp, we girt the s[ai]d swamp and with english & Indian sould[ier]s, drest it, and with 3: hours slew and tooke prisoners 171: of which 45: prisoners being women and children that the [Mohegan] indians saved alive, and the others slayne . . . among which slaughter that ould peice of venume sunck [queen] squa Magnus was slayne" (Talcott [1677] 1934:11). By the war's end the Narragansett had been reduced from as many as five thousand to perhaps two hundred, many of whom fled the area or lived among the English as servants and slaves.[7] Some Narragansett survivors merged with the eastern Niantic, a small and closely related sachemdom in the area of Charlestown and Westerly, and the combined population became known as Narragansett. This small enclave of perhaps five to six hundred people lived a fairly autonomous existence for a few years after the war under Niantic sachems of the Ninigret family. The sachem Ninigret I had assured the English in 1675 that he would not fight against them, thereby escaping the conflict that all but extinguished the Wampanoag and Narragansett. In 1709 Ninigret II (?–1723) quitclaimed to Rhode Island Colony all title to Indian land except a sixty-four square-mile tract in Charlestown that the English agreed to protect as a reservation. From then until the sale of this reservation to the state in 1880, the Rhode Island legislature exercised legal control over the reservation and its Indian inhabitants. Although the sachems enjoyed the rights of freemen and lived the lives of country gentlemen, most other inhabitants of the reservation did not become citizens until the reservation was sold and tribal relations were terminated in 1880.

Because Roger Williams had never attempted to convert the Narragansett and Niantic in any systematic way, and because the seventeenth-century sachems resisted Christianity to protect their own authority, the Narragansett converted to English religion considerably later than the weaker groups around Massachusetts Bay, Plymouth, Martha's Vineyard, and Nantucket. Although some members of the Ninigret family supported the Church of England in the early eighteenth century, the main body of the Narragansett did not convert until 1743, when the itinerant evangelists of the Great Awakening ignited the towns and backwoods of southern New England with their appeals to the unconverted. Shortly after their conversion, around 1750, the Narragansett separated from their parent Congregational church to form a Freewill Baptist church under the Narragansett minister Samuel Niles. This church body, under a succession of Indian ministers, has persisted from the eighteenth century until the present and remains today an important focus of Narragansett community life.

Despite its earlier commitment to protect reservation lands for Indian use, the Rhode Island legislature recognized the sachems as executives of the tribal estate and allowed them to sell reservation property to repay their personal debts. By the mid-eighteenth century many Narragansetts began to perceive that they eventually would lose everything, including land, livelihood, and protection from servitude, if the land sales continued. They petitioned the General Court on many occasions but were unable to prevent the sachems from conveying the most valuable farms and oceanfront acreage to the English. The land controversy became particularly intense during the life of sachem Thomas Ninigret (1736–69), who accumulated vast debts and sold much of the best land. The common people of the reservation under Reverend Niles's leadership retained a lawyer and enlisted several English ministers in their cause, but ultimately the sachem sold whatever lands he pleased. After 1775 many Narragansett moved with other poor and dispossessed Connecticut and Long Island Indians to Brothertown, New York, on the Oneida reservation, where they attempted to establish a self-supporting Christian Indian township. Those who continued to live on the old Charlestown reservation governed themselves by an elected council after Thomas Ninigret's nephew, George Sachem, died around the end of the American Revolution. In the 1830s and 1840s the Brothertown Narragansett moved farther west to Brotherton, Wisconsin, where they established a permanent home. In 1880 Rhode Island purchased the remaining 922 acres of reservation land, leaving a small tract including the church, burial ground, and powwow ground in Indian hands. Eighty-one tribal members became citizens and their children began to attend public schools (rather than the reservation school established in the mid-eighteenth century). Many Narragansett made their living at this time by raising sheep, selling wood, farming, fishing, and stone masonry. Pan-Indian consciousness probably surfaced here around 1907, when William (Buffalo Bill) Cody visited Uncas's gravesite in nearby Norwich, and by the 1920s the Narragansett with the Wampanoag joined the Algonquin Council of Indian Tribes. In 1934 the Narragansett retribalized under Rhode Island law as a private, nonprofit corporation; in 1983 they became a federally recognized Indian tribe with a core population in and around Charlestown of about four hundred persons. They still elect a tribal council, attend the church, use the burial ground, and participate in the August Meeting or Powwow which probably has been going on since prehistoric times. The Narragansett presence in Charlestown has always been strong, and in recent years, as a consequence of their active political programs, their yearly pilgrimage to the Great Swamp Fight site, and other ceremonial occasions, their presence is even stronger.

THE MOHEGAN

The Mohegan, whose homeland centered around Norwich and New London, Connecticut, along the west side of the Thames River, began historically as an offshoot of the Pequot.[8] Uncas (?–1683), the first Mohegan sachem, supported the English assault against the palisaded Pequot village at Mystic in 1637. Therafter, Uncas and his Mohegan remained firm allies of the United Puritan Colonies and contributed significantly to the English victory over the Narragansett in King Philip's War. In later years, Mohegan men also enlisted in the Seven Years' War and in the Revolution. The history of Mohegan land ownership is complex and confusing mainly because Uncas, in 1640, gave most of his lands to the governor and magistrates of Connecticut, and again in 1659 deeded all Mohegan lands to his patron, John Mason, possibly intending that the English would hold these lands in permanent trust for Mohegan use. Whatever Uncas's intentions may have been, Connecticut maintained that the Mohegan had extinguished claims to all or most of their domain. In 1671 Mason drew up a deed that conferred a large tract to the tribe, known as the Sequestered Lands, that would be inalienable by grant or sale. For a hundred years after Mason's death in 1672, much confusion existed regarding succession to tribal leadership and the extent of Indian landholdings, the result of which was a one-way flow of Indian land to English hands. On one side, John Mason and his descendants, with what appears to have been a majority of the Mohegan people, fought a long and ultimately unsuccessful legal struggle to place the tribe under royal rather than colonial authority in order to provide the tribe with greater autonomy in selecting its leaders and in conserving its land. On the other side, the Connecticut assembly and English overseers (overseers were first appointed in 1719) supported a particular lineage of hereditary sachems who sold, leased, and rented tribal land to whites for individual profit, much as the Ninigret family was doing with the Narragansett reservation about this same time. By about 1730 the Mohegan had split into two principal factions that resided at Ben's Town (named for the sachem Ben Uncas II) and John's Town (named for his rival, John Uncas) respectively. Samson Occom, an eighteenth-century Mohegan minister, schoolteacher, and popular leader, described his early life in the Mohegan community about this time:

I was Born a Heathen [in 1723] and Brought up in Heathenism, till I was between 16 & 17 years of age, at a Place Called *Mohegan*, in New London, Connecticut, in New England. My Parents Liv'd a wandering Life, as did all the Indians at Mohegan; they Chiefly Depended upon Hunting, Fishing, & Fowling for their Living and had no Connections with the English, excepting to Traffic with them, in their Small Trifles; and they Strictly maintained and followed their Heathenish Ways, Customs, & Religion, though there was some Preaching among them. (Blodgett 1935:27)

By the early 1740s, when most Mohegans converted to Christianity, they numbered about four hundred people and owned about five thousand acres, the best of which were leased and rented by white tenants. As whites settled and fenced Mohegan wilderness tracts, the Indians found it increasingly difficult to practice their traditional mixed economy of gardening, hunting, and gathering. Many turned to alcohol, perhaps to escape the necessity of becoming more like whites in order to survive the political, economic, and demographic pressures that were choking their traditional way of life. Those Indians who identified with the new order looked to Euro-American religion and education as keys to their survival in colonial society. Samson Occom, the most prominent New England Indian clergyman in his day, stressed the importance of education in his personal account of Christian conversion:

Once a Fortnight in the Summer Season, a Minister from New London used to Come up, and the Indians to attend; not that they regarded the Christian Religion, but they had Blankets given to them every Fall of the Year and for these things, they would attend: and there was a Sort of a School kept, when I was quite young, but I believe there never was one that ever Learnt to read any thing. And when I was about 10 Years of age there was a man who went about among the Indian Wigwams, and wherever he Could find the Indian Children, would make them read; but the Children Used to take

Care to keep out of his Way:—and he used to Catch me Some times and make me Say over my Letters; and I believe I Learnt Some of them. But this was Soon over too; and all this Time there was not one amongst us, that made a Profession of Christianity—Neither did we Cultivate our Land, nor keep any Sort of Creatures, except Dogs, which we used in Hunting; and we Dwelt in Wigwams. These are a Sort of Tents, Covered with Matts, made of Flags. And to this Time we were unacquainted with the English Tongue in general, though there were a few, who understood a little of it.

When I was 16 years of age, we heard a Strange Rumor among the English, that there were Extraordinary Ministers Preaching from Place to Place and a Strange Concern among the White People: this was in the Spring of the Year. But we Saw nothing of these things, till Some Time in the Summer, when Some Ministers began to visit us and Preach the Word of God; and Common People also Came frequently, and exhorted as to the things of God, which it pleased the Lord, as I humbly hope, to Bless and accompany with Divine Influences to the Conviction and Saving Conversion of a Number of us; amongst whom, I was one that was Impresst with the things we had heard.

These Preachers did not only Come to us, but we frequently went to their meetings and Churches. After I was awakened & converted, I went to all the meetings I could come at; & Continued under Trouble of Mind about 6 Months; at which time I began to Learn the English Letters: got me a Primer, and used to go to my English Neighbours frequently for Assistance in Reading, but went to no School.

And when I was 17 Years of age, I had, as I trust, a Discovery of the way of Salvation through Jesus Christ, and was enabled to put my trust in him alone for Life & Salvation. From this Time the Distress and Burden of my mind was removed, and I found Serenity and Pleasure of Soul, in Serving God. By this time I Just began to read in the New Testament without Spelling, and I had a Stronger Desire Still to Learn to read the Word of God, and at the Same Time, had an uncommon Pity and Compassion to my Poor Brethren According to the Flesh. I used to wish, I was Capable of Instructing my poor Kindred, I used to think if I Could once Learn to Read I would Instruct the poor Children in Reading,—and used frequently to talk with our Indians Concerning Religion. Thus I Continued, till I was in my 19th year: by this Time I Coud Read a bit in the Bible. (Blodgett 1935:29–30)

Occom soon emerged as a spokesman for the majority faction that opposed the sachem, and when Ben Uncas III died in 1769, Occom urged that rule by sachem be abolished. Although the Mohegan sachemship in fact ended with Ben Uncas's death, the colony continued to control tribal affairs through appointed white overseers, the old divisions persisted, and the majority still lacked control over the disposition of rents and leases. Occom and Joseph Johnson, his son-in-law, then envisaged an alternative for those Mohegans and other southern New England Indians who wished to follow the English model in religion, government, and subsistence but who found it difficult to realize their intentions among land-hungry white settlers and merchants. They obtained land from the Oneida in western

LIBRARY
COLBY-SAWYER COLLEGE
NEW LONDON, NH 03257

New York where they planned to establish a self-governing Christian Indian community in this more isolated environment. In 1775 the first Mohegans emigrated to Brothertown, New York, to be followed by several other migrations from Mohegan and six other southern New England Indian communities after the Revolution. The state redistributed the remaining Connecticut lands in 1783 among those who stayed behind, and did so again in 1790. In the years following the distribution of 1790, some landholding families died out and their holdings returned either to the state or to the tribe. A tribal overseer leased the vacant common lands, using the revenues to provide spring and fall rations of beef, flour, and one dollar for each tribal member. The agent later discontinued rations and used the funds for repairing buildings, medical services, and burying the dead (Hebard, Kingsbury, and Haven 1861:8). By the early nineteenth century the tribe began electing its own (Indian) overseers, and the state permitted individual families to sell the land they occupied to outsiders in order to repay debts. In 1861 the state made a new distribution of common lands among the hundred or so Mohegans who lived on or about their tribal property, which by then consisted of about twenty-three hundred acres. The commissioners who made the division reserved one farm to be rented for common income and opposed selling any more lands, for "in many instances brought to the knowledge of the Commissioners, where individual rights of land have been sold, the entire avails have been squandered or lost in a short time, and the seller pauperized" (p.6). They further advocated that overseers manage all rental agreements on behalf of Mohegan landowners, thus suggesting that the Mohegan had often come out on the short end of such transactions in the past. According to Speck, the late-nineteenth-century Mohegan population was a composite of Pequot, Tunxis, Nipmuck, and Niantic, as well as Mohegan and English (Speck 1928b:207).

Buffalo Bill Cody visited Uncas's grave site in 1907, creating a stir among local Mohegans who admired Cody's western Indian entourage. In 1920 they formed the Mohegan Indian Association to represent the tribe politically and socially and to preserve its traditions. (Unlike the Wampanoag of Mashpee and Gay Head, the Mohegan had lived among whites and had never controlled local politics.) For many years, until 1938, tribal members gathered in September in front of the Mohegan Congregational Church (built for whites and Indians in 1831) to celebrate the Mohegan Wigwam Festival, which, like the Narragansett August Meeting, probably originated in an older harvest ritual. This little community is still very much alive,

LIBRARY
COLBY-SAWYER COLLEGE
NEW LONDON, NH 03257

and in 1972 approximately 150 persons of Mohegan descent lived in New London County (Taylor 1972:228). One who drives over Mohegan Hill on the Norwich–New London Turnpike can visit such interesting historic sites as Uncas's Fort Shantok, the Mohegan chapel, and the Tantaquidgeon Indian Museum, a remarkable small repository of Mohegan and other American Indian material culture that is owned and managed by Gladys and Harold Tantaquidgeon, descendants of Uncas, Samson Occom, and other early Mohegan leaders.

The four communities that contributed most of the folklore in this study (Mashpee, Gay Head, Narragansett, and Mohegan) traveled different courses through the historic period, but they shared some experiences along the way. By the late seventeenth century all had been transformed from autonomous tribes to subjugated minorities within colonial society. They exercised a measure of self-government based upon English and even traditional institutions such as the hereditary sachemship and a tribal council. English replaced the native languages, which died out except for a few words that continue to be remembered. Narragansett ceased to be a spoken language in the early nineteenth century, the last Massachusett speakers died around the end of the nineteenth century, and the last Mohegan speaker passed away in 1908. The inhabitants of all four communities enlisted in colonial armies, converted to Christianity, and adapted to roles as whalers, fishermen, stone masons, sheep farmers, basket makers, servants, herbalists, and day laborers in the American economy. Each enclave retained land tracts where, until the mid to late nineteenth century, they enjoyed a degree of protection from debt and servitude and particularly from losing their territorial base. During this long sequestered period they neither paid taxes nor voted in colony, state, and federal elections. Despite legal safeguards, all four groups found it difficult to keep their land, and each generation confronted new challenges to their shrinking resources. The Indian enclaves were mainly endogamous, although marriages were common between Indians and other ethnic groups such as Afro- and Anglo-Americans.

Although the federal government did not recognize these New England enclaves as tribes, their nineteenth-century history paralleled that of many federally recognized tribes throughout the nation that were affected by the General Allotment Act of 1887. This act provided that reservations were to be broken up, tribal governments dissolved, lands divided in severalty, and Indians given citizenship, all in the belief that such measures would help Indians enter the mainstream of American life. By the late nineteenth century all southern New England Indian communities had given up their corporate tribal arrangements, and individuals had acquired citizenship and the right to buy and sell land. For the New England tribes, as for many larger tribes elsewhere in the United States, termination of their corporate holdings and communal institutions hastened a period of economic and political decline for many. As they felt the impact of the national trend toward allotment in the nineteenth century, they also participated in the national revival of Indian identity and tribalism in the twentieth century. The New England groups welcomed the rekindling of Indian consciousness that culminated in the Indian Reorganization Act of 1934. The Mashpee, Gay Head, Narragansett, and Mohegan all expressed interest in indigenous traditions and in a wider Indian identity and experimented with new forms of tribal and intertribal leadership. This cultural and political revival continues vigorously into the modern period, and each group is considering or has attempted to attain federal recognition. The Narragansett succeeded in this effort, the Mashpee did not, the Gay Head petition is pending, and some Mohegan are considering it. Tribal leaders today are still searching for ways to hold back the non-Indian population, culture, and political and economic interests that move like an undertow over the remains of their heritage.

3 Worldview

Recognizing continuities and innovation in Indian folklore as it evolved over the last three hundred years requires that we first understand indigenous religion, myth, and worldview during the earliest years of contact with Europeans, when Indian cultures had changed the least. This portrayal of Indian symbolic life during the seventeenth and early eighteenth centuries is the starting point for identifying the Indian cultural wellsprings of the later historic-period legends. Seventeenth- and eighteenth-century Englishmen who lived and traveled in the region provided most of the source material for this reconstruction. The biases of their day clouded these authors' perceptions, but many showed a lively curiosity about Indians, and all shared many beliefs and interests with their Indian contemporaries. For example, New England Puritans as well as Indians attributed larger, if different, symbolic meanings to natural calamities such as storms, earthquakes, and epidemics, and both groups believed in witchcraft and in divine intervention in personal and national affairs.[1]

Bias is apparent in the English descriptions of Indian religion. Typically the English glossed over native concepts, such as *powwows* (or shamans) and guardian spirits, as if they were identical with English witches and devils, about which the English had preformed and emotional opinions. The Puritan and non-Puritan English alike assumed that Indian *powwows* were witches and that Indian culture suffered from a kind of diabolical enchantment. The authors of *New England's First Fruits*, an early Puritan treatise on Indian conversion, assured their readers that "we are wont to keep them at such a distance, (knowing they serve the Devill and are led by him) as not to imbolden them too much, or trust them too farre; though we do them what good we can" (1643:16). This view has much in common with that of the Pilgrims' free-spirited critic, Thomas Morton, who in recent years has been praised for his empathic accounts of Indian culture. According to Morton, the younger Indians deferred to the elder, "the Elder [are] ruled by the Powahs, and the Powahs are ruled by the Devill" (Morton [1632] 1947:40). Such perceptions gave the colonists a moral basis for depersonalizing and subduing the Indian people who lived across the thoroughfares of English migration and also provided the narrative plot for Puritan historians who interpreted Indian-white relations. Cotton Mather, for example, saw Indian warfare as inevitable because "These *parts* were then covered with nations of barbarous *indians* and infidels, in whom the *prince of the power of the air* did *work as a spirit;* nor could it be expected that the nations of wretches, whose whole *religion* was the most explicit sort of *devil-worship,* should not be acted by the devil to engage in some early and bloody action, for the extinction of a plantation so contrary to his interests, as that of *New England* was" (Mather [1702] 1820, 2:479–80). Christian Indians even testified to the truth of such perceptions when they confessed their sins and disowned Indian ways in conversion ritual. Nevertheless, these early accounts are the only written sources we have. They contain many cultural insights that can be recovered by comparing accounts for patterns and by being attentive to areas of bias and self-interest on the part of individual authors. Seventeenth-century and later accounts of Indians around the periphery of southern New England, and accounts of the area written at a later date, also enhance our perspective on the early sources.

The Indian Pantheon

New England was alive with deities, known in the Algonquian dialects as *manitos*. These included gods of women, children, animals, the sun, moon, fire, water, sea, snow, earth, directions, seasons, winds, houses, the sky, corn, and even colors. According to Narragansett mythology, the southwest deity, Cautantowwit, created man and woman from a stone and, disliking his first creation, made a second couple of wood who became the ancestors of all humankind. The Narragansett communicated with Cautantowwit through sacrifice, prayers, and praise, but he lived in an afterworld inhabited by the souls of the dead; the living saw him neither in dreams nor visions. Edward Winslow observed that among the Pokanoket or Wampanoag,

At first, they say, there was no sachim or king, but Kiehtan [Cautantowwit], who dwelleth above in the heavens, whither all good men go when they die, to see their friends, and have their fill of all things. This his habitation lieth far westward in the heavens, they say; thither the bad men go also, and knock at his door, but he bids them *quatchet*, that is to say, walk abroad, for there is no place for such; so that they wander in restless want and penury. Never man saw this Kiehtan; only old men tell them of him, and bid them tell their children, yea to charge them to teach their posterities the same, and lay the like charge upon them. This power they acknowledge to be good; and when they would obtain any great matter, meet together and cry unto him; and so likewise for plenty, victory, etc., sing, dance, feast, give thanks, and hang up garlands and other things in memory of the same. (Winslow [1624] 1910:342)

Winslow learned also that tribal groups differed in the degree to which they emphasized Cautantowwit in ritual and that the Narragansett exceeded all others in their "blind devotion."

The principal deity who appeared to humans in visions and dreams was Hobbamock (Abbomacho), known also as Cheepi (Chepi, Chepian), whose name was related to the words for death, the deceased, and the cold northeast wind. Into his "deformed likeness they conceived themselves to be translated when they died; for the same word they have for *Devil*, they use also for a *Dead Man*" (Eliot and Mayhew [1653] 1834:202). Hobbamock was associated with the color black, and the Indians saw him often at night "in the most hideous woods and swamps" in the shapes of Englishmen, Indians, animals, inanimate objects, and mythical creatures (Johnson [1654] 1910:263). Although he often startled and terrified those who believed they saw him, many desired such visions, for he appeared not to all, wrote Winslow, but to "the chiefest and most judicious amongst them; though all of them strive to attain to that hellish height of honour" (Winslow [1624] 1910:343).

The *pniese* was a person who attained a particular vision of Hobbamock in a difficult ordeal. This status is attested in the Massachusett and Wampanoag areas, but not among the Narragansett or Pequot-Mohegan. The strongest and most able male children were selected as candidates for this ordeal, which involved loss of sleep, fasting, and drinking mixtures that may have been hallucinogenic. These included "the juice of sentry and other bitter herbs, till they cast, which they must disgorge into the platter, and drink again and again, till . . . it will seem to be all blood" (pp. 345–46). Josselyn described a similar ritual in which the neophytes drank white hellebore, which he likened to opium: "The English in New England take white Hellebore, which operates as fairly with them, as with the Indians, who steeping of it in water sometime, give it to young lads gathered together a purpose to drink, if it come up they force them to drink again their vomit, (which they save in a Birchen-dish) till it stayes with them, & he that gets the victory of it is made Captain of the other lads for that year" (Josselyn [1675] 1833:251). The initiates drank until "by reason of faintness, they can scarce stand on their legs, and then must go forth into the cold. . . . they beat their shins with sticks, and cause them to run through bushes, stumps, and brambles, to make them hardy and acceptable to the devil, that in time he may appear unto them" (Winslow [1624] 1910:346). The spirit Hobbamock "maketh covenant with them to preserve them from death by wounds with arrows, knives, hatchets, etc." (p. 345). By virtue of having experienced this vision, the pniese acquired a voice as the sachem's counselor, collected tribute from the sachem's dependents, and participated in decisions about war. He also was an exemplary male warrior "known by . . . courage and boldness, by reason whereof one of them will chase almost an hundred men" (ibid.). Two of the first Indians to walk into the Pilgrim settlement at Plymouth were named Hobbamock and Squanto. Hobbamock, Winslow's close friend and a graceful and courageous man, was a Pokanoket pniese, and Squanto was probably named for a god or for his ability to communicate with gods. Before they died, both men hoped to add the Christian God to their personal arrays, and the English counted them, although tentatively, among their first converts.

All persons, whether sachems or commoners, had access to many other spirits through dreams and visions, which they carefully heeded. A Martha's Vineyard Indian told Roger Williams that the sun god had sent a beam into his chest, which the Indian took to be an omen of his death. The warning may have been reversible, for he "call'd his Friends and neighbours and prepared some little refreshing for them, but himselfe was kept waking and Fasting in great Humiliations and Invocations for 10. dayes and nights" (Williams [1643] 1936:20). Daniel Gookin wrote of relationships between individuals and particular deities that also may have originated in dreams: "Some for their God, adore the sun; others the moon; some the earth; others the fire" (Gookin [1792] 1970:20). English thieves once waylaid, stabbed, and stole the possessions of a Nipmuck Indian who lived among the Narragansett. As he lay dying he called "much upon *Muckquachuckquànd* [the children's god], which . . . appeared to the dying young man, many yeares before, and bid him when ever he was in distresse call upon him" (Williams [1643] 1936:125). Such visions appeared while awake or in trance and occurred privately to one individual and even collectively to more than one person at a time.

In brief, the New England Indians recognized large numbers of gods or *manitos*. The Narragansett gave Roger Williams the names of at least thirty-seven, and a prospective convert on Martha's Vineyard "reckoned up about 37. principal gods he had" (Whitfield [1651] 1834a:111). Although no native classification of these gods is available, we may distinguish at least four types of supernatural figures. The first includes only the great southwest god, Cautantowwit, who created and ruled humankind and who sent them their first seeds to grow. He did not appear in visions, often sent misfortune when angry with his human subjects, and controlled the afterworld in the southwest. The second category includes all forms of the spirit known as Hobbamock or Cheepi, which originated as souls of the dead. These spirits appeared in many forms in dreams and visions and imparted extraordinary supernatural gifts to those such as the *pniese* and *powwow* whom they chose to honor. The great majority of gods, such as those for the heavenly bodies, directions, animal species, the elements, and social categories, make up the third group. These gods appeared in visions and dreams and protected those to whom they appeared. Fourth, some evidence attests to widespread belief in a giant humanlike culture hero named Wétucks or Maushop, who figured prominently in New England Indian myths and legends. Sources regarding the giant will be presented in chapter 9.

Shamanism

The *powwow*, like the *pniese*, differed from others because one or several images of Hobbamock had appeared to him in a vision or dream. John Eliot asked two Massachusett Indians how one became a *powwow*, and they replied "that if any of the *Indians* fall into any strange dreame wherein *Chepian* appeares unto them as a serpent, then the next day they tell the other *Indians* of it," whereupon the others "dance and rejoyce for what they tell them about this Serpent, and so they become their *Pawwaws*" ([Wilson] [1647] 1834:20). A Wampanoag *powwow* on Martha's Vineyard who abandoned his calling to become a Christian confessed to Thomas Mayhew, Jr., that he first "came to be a *Pawwaw* by Diabolical Dreams, wherein he saw the Devill in the likenesse of four living Creatures," and then gave Mayhew the most detailed known account of a southern New England shaman's vision. One of the creatures

was like a man which he saw in the Ayre, and this told him that he did know all things upon the Island, and what was to be done; and this he said had its residence over his whole body. Another was like a Crow, and did look out sharply to discover mischiefs coming towards him, and had its residence in his head. The third was like to a Pidgeon, and had its place in his breast, and was very cunning about any businesse. The fourth was like a Serpent, very subtile to doe mischiefe, and also to doe great cures, and these he said were meer Devills, and such as he had trusted to for safety, and did labour to raise up for the accomplishment of any thing in his diabolicall craft. (Whitfield [1652] 1834b:186)

Tequanonim, another prominent *powwow* from Martha's Vineyard, also disclosed the identity of his many guardian spirits:

he as they said, and in their ignorance conceived, never did hurt to any, but alwayes good. . . . And as himself said he had been possessed from the crowne of the head to the soal of the foot with *Pawwawnomas*, not onely in the shape of living Creatures, as Fowls, Fishes, and creeping things, but Brasse, Iron, and Stone. (P. 187)

John Eliot talked with a Massachusett *powwow* who confided (to his apparent regret) that a little hummingbird looked after him and helped him distinguish right from wrong:

There was, Mr. Eliot told us, a famous Powah, who, coming to Punkapog while he was at that Indian village, gave out among the people there that a little hummingbird did come and peck at him when he did aught that was wrong, and sing sweetly to him when he did a good thing or spake the right words; which coming to Mr. Eliot's ear, he made him confess, in the presence of the congregation, that he did only mean, by the figure of the bird, the sense he had of right and wrong in his own mind. This fellow was, moreover, exceeding cunning, and did often ask questions to be answered touching the creation of the Devil and the fall of man. (Huntoon 1893:15)

Similarly, Winslow was informed that "Hobbamock appears in sundry forms unto them, as in the shape of a man, a deer, a fawn, an eagle, etc., but most ordinarily a snake" (Winslow [1624] 1910:343). The word *powwow* was related to *taúpowaw*, which Williams glossed as meaning "*A wise speaker*" (Trumbull 1903:160; Williams, [1643] 1936:57).

By virtue of their control over spirits, the *powwows* advised their sachems, but how they differed from the *pniese* in this regard is unclear. The inspired role of shaman and the hereditary role of sachem did not overlap generally in one individual, and the few persons who combined these roles were thought to be extremely powerful.

Tispaquin, the "Black Sachem" of Assowampset (now Middleboro, Massachusetts), who supported Metacomet in King Philip's War, was said by the Wampanoag to be "such a great *Pauwau*, that no bullet could enter him" (Church [1716] 1827:144). Most prominent southern New England sachems (Massasoit, Metacomet, Canonicus, Miantonomi, Canonchet, Ninigret, Uncas, Corbitant) were not known to be shamans. Although it was said to be a "very impious matter for any man to derogate from the words of these Powahs," the sachems could discipline or even execute them for inappropriate behavior (Morton [1632] 1947:26).

Hobbamock (or Cheepi) appeared ordinarily and was most conversant with three categories of religious practitioner. The first category, Winslow confessed, he neither knew "by name nor office directly; of these they have few, but esteem highly of them, and think that no weapon can kill them; another they call by the name of *powah*; and the third *pniese*" (Winslow [1624] 1910:343). The first of these may have been the role-combined *powwow*-sachems such as Tispaquin, or Passaconaway, a renowned *powwow* and sachem of the Pawtucket who lived north of Massachusetts Bay at the mouth of the Merrimack River. Within the *powwow* category we may discern a number of functional distinctions regarding the services the *powwows* performed. The Narragansett had "an exact forme of . . . Priest, and Prophet" whom they evidently referred to as *powwows*: "Their Priests, performe and manage their Worship: Their wise men and old men of which number the Priests are also . . . whom they call *Taupowaüog* they make solemne speeches and Orations, or Lectures to them, concerning Religion, Peace, or Warre and all things" (Williams [1643] 1936:128). Although Indian terms existed for religious practitioners described by the English as conjurers, diviners, overseers of worship, priests, prophets, and witches, the above passages by Winslow and Williams suggest that these terms designated the different kinds of powers that the shamans possessed and the distinct functions that they consequently performed (Trumbull 1903:236, 309, 345; Williams [1643] 1936:128). Occasionally several shamans participated in tribal and curing rituals, but no evidence points to the existence of shamanistic societies comparable to the Midewin of the Central Algonquian area.

Most English writers (Eliot, Mayhew, Morton, Williams, Winslow, Wood) noticed parallels between Indian cosmology and their own expectations regarding heaven and hell. Eliot understood that the Massachusett observed "some principles of a life after this life, and that good or evill, according to their demeanour in this life," and

Williams noted for the Narragansett that "Murtherers thieves and Lyers, their Soules (say they) wander restlesse abroad" (Williams [1643] 1936:130; Winslow [1649] 1834:82). These authors may have projected a relationship between the moral works of the living and the rewards of the dead, which originated in their own worldview and misrepresented Indian thought. John Josselyn, who was neither a Puritan nor a missionary, provided another view of Indian notions of death: "they dye patiently both men and women, not knowing of a Hell to scare them, nor a Conscience to terrifie them" (Josselyn [1675] 1833:299). The creator, Cautantowwit, was not wholly good: "they somewhat doubt whether he be simply good, and therefore in sickness never call upon him"; nor was Hobbamock or Cheepi wholly bad (Winslow [1624] 1910:343). The English may have interpreted the fear and awe with which Indians regarded Hobbamock as evidence that such spirits were evil, although it is possible that Christian ideas had shaped Indian accounts of their own beliefs even at this early date. In either event, Williams's observations on Narragansett soul beliefs provide the basis for another interpretation of Indian cosmology that would account for the two afterworlds mentioned by English writers but would also distinguish these afterworlds from the Christian concepts of heaven and hell. One word for soul, *cowwéwonck*, was

Derived from *Cowwene* to sleep, because say they, it workes and operates when the body sleepes. *Michachunck* the soule, in a higher notion which is of affinity, with a word signifying a looking glasse, or cleere resemblance, so that it hath its name from a cleere sight or discerning, which indeed seemes very well to suit with the nature of it. (Williams [1643] 1936:130)

Belief in multiple souls, associated with dreams and reflections, is widespread among North American Indians. Williams did not specify that these were names for two distinct souls, although his account suggests that this was the case, and he did not explain whether these two entities followed the same or a different course at death. The Indians associated both the creator and the shamans' god Hobbamock with disembodied souls, except that those who returned to the creator enjoyed an afterlife resembling that on earth, whereas those affiliated with shamans appeared and disappeared in many forms like images in a dream. Williams's dream soul could have remained on earth as the shamans' helper, while the soul "in a higher notion" returned to the creator in the southwest. One departing soul lit up the sky at night:

They have a remarkable observation of a flame that appears before the death of an *Indian* or *English* upon their *Wigwams* in the dead of the night: The first time that I did see it, I was call'd out by some of them about twelve of the clock, it being a very dark night, I perceived it plainly mounting into the Air over our Church. . . . look on what side of a house it appears, from that Coast respectively you shall hear of a Coarse within two or three days. (Josselyn [1675] 1833:300)

Frank Speck collected a Penobscot legend regarding a woman who dreamed accurately of events that occurred some miles away. While she slept, a ball of fire was seen to leave her mouth, during which time others feared she had died. When the flame returned through her mouth, she awakened and recounted the dream (Speck 1919: 288). Twentieth-century Mohegans and Wampanoags referred to what they translated as the ghost, spirit, or devil, seen as light in foxfire, as dji•bai or tci•pai, which is clearly derived from the earlier Cheepi (Speck 1928b:263). Williams's dream soul, cowwéwonck, would seem to be the entity known after death as Cheepi, the shaman's helper, and also to have shown at times as a light in the evening sky.

Seasonal and Life-Cycle Rites

The southern New England Indians referred to their dominant ritual form as a commoco or nickommo, which Williams and Winslow translated as a feast or dance. The Indians held these rituals regularly at fixed times in the yearly calendar (early spring, late summer when the corn ripened, and midwinter), at turning points in the individual life cycle (naming, puberty, marriage, and death), and in times of general crisis (sickness, drought, famine, and war).

The sachems hosted the seasonal rituals, and powwows coordinated worship: "These doe begin and order their service, and Invocation of their Gods, and all the people follow, and joyne interchangeably in a laborious bodily service, unto sweatings, especially of the Priest, who spends himselfe in strange Antick Gestures, and Actions even unto fainting" (Williams [1643] 1936:127). Accounts of the seasonal rituals are meager. In spring when they gathered at their best fishing sites "they have meetinges from severall places, where they exercise themselves in gaminge, and playing of juglinge trickes, and all manner of Revelles, which they are delighted in" (Morton [1632] 1947:20). In May 1637 Williams saw the Narragansett sachems "this fortnight busy (that is keeping of a kind of Christmas)" (Williams 1874:20). Following harvest, the Narragansett built a house one-to-two-hundred-feet long near the sachem's court, where thousands of men and women gathered: "he that goes in danceth in the sight of all the rest; and is prepared with money, coats, small breeches, knifes, or what hee is able to reach to, and gives these things away to the poore, who yet must particularly beg and say . . . *I beseech you"* (Williams [1643] 1936:180). In August 1637 Williams commented upon "a strange kind of solemnity" which lasted ten or twelve days, during which time "the Sachems eat nothing but at night, and all the natives round about the country were feasted" (1874:56). This could have been the harvest ritual, which continued "night after night" (Gookin [1792] 1970:19). Among the Housatonic Indians of western Massachusetts, the person who provided the food eaten in ritual ate none of it "to signify it is a gift" (Hopkins [1753] 1911:25). This custom probably explains why the Narragansett sachems refrained from eating during the day at harvest ritual, for having allocated land to those who cultivated it, the harvest was in a sense their gift. During the winter *nickommo*, the Narragansett "run mad once a yeare in their kind of Christmas feasting" (Williams [1643] 1936:127).

The Narragansett hosted an elaborate ritual in which the participants offered "almost all the riches they have to their gods, as kettles, skins, hatchets, beads, knives, etc.," all of which the shamans threw "into a great fire that they make in the midst of the house, and there consumed to ashes" (Winslow [1624] 1910:344–45). This ritual resembled the Northwest Coast potlatch, for the more wealth a person contributed to the event, the greater the admiration he or she enjoyed. The Wampanoag associated this ritual with tribal well-being: "This the other Indians about us approve of as good, and wish [their] sachims would appoint the like; and because the plague hath not reigned at Nanohigganset as at other places about them, they attribute to this custom there used" (p. 345). Winslow indicated that this property destruction ritual honored the creator and that the Narragansett held it "at certain known times" which he did not specify. The Wampanoag of Martha's Vineyard also performed a version of this ritual in times of widespread sickness.

Individuals often changed their names during the course of their lives to symbolize changes in personal status, and they also celebrated such changes with ritual feasts. "All their names," wrote Winslow, "are significant and variable; for when they come to the state of men and women, they alter them according to their deeds or dispositions" (Winslow [1624] 1910:349). According to Samson Occom, the nearby Montauk on Long Island did not name children at birth but did so somewhat later at a public feast:

They use to make great dances or frolicks. They made great preparations for these dances, of wampum, beads, jewels, dishes, and cloathing, and liquors, &c. Sometimes two or three families join in naming their children, so make great preparation to make a great dance. When they have got all things ready, they will call their neighbours together, very often send to other towns of Indians, and when they have all got together, they will begin their dance, and to distribute their gifts, and every person that receives the gifts or liquors, gets up and pronounces the name that a child is to be called by, with a loud voice three times. But sometimes a young man or woman will be ashamed to pronounce the name, and they will get some other person to do it. Very often one family will make small preparations, and call few old people to name a child; and it was very common with them to name their children two or three times over by different names, and at different times, and old people very often gave new names to themselves. (Occom 1809:108)

Hardly anything is known about the *rites de passage* for young women, which probably reflects the male interests and personal networks of the majority of authors. Winslow's comment that "Boys and girls may not wear their hair like men and women, but are distinguished thereby," indicates the importance of stylistic differences between child and adult status for both men and women (Winslow [1624] 1910:348). The same author also informs us that the men smoked much tobacco, but it was inappropriate for younger boys to do so, and that boys aspiring to recognition as adults first had to show great courage or succeed at some other notable act. Isaack de Rasieres, a Dutch visitor to early Plymouth, described a rite in which young Wampanoag men demonstrated their readiness for manhood. The rite resembles, and may in fact be identical with, the ordeal for selecting the exemplary male warrior known as the *pniese*:

When there is a youth who begins to approach manhood, he is taken by his father, uncle, or nearest friend, and is conducted blindfolded into a wilderness, in order that he may not know the way, and is left there by night or otherwise, with a bow and arrows, and a hatchet and a knife. He must support himself there a whole winter with what the scanty earth furnishes at this season, and by hunting. Towards the spring they come again, and fetch him out of it . . . until May. He must then go out again every morning with the person who is ordered to take him . . . to seek wild herbs and roots, which they know to be the most poisonous and bitter . . . which he must drink. . . . And if he cannot retain it, he must repeat the dose until he can support it. (Rasieres [ca. 1628] 1963:78–79)

Marriage provided another occasion for entertainment and feasting. Parents could betroth their infant children, but adult males also might select mates with the consent of the parents, friends, and sachem of the bride. The man gave gifts to the father, mother, or guardian of his bride-to-be, and she displayed her change in marital status by cutting her hair and wearing a covering on her head until it grew out again.

Individuals probably took new names at marriage, for they often changed their names to symbolize real or hoped-for changes in their personal lives. One Narragansett woman, because of various hardships and the loss of many close relatives, appointed a day and place where she made speeches concerning her troubles, expressed her desire for future prosperity, and "now and then danc'd a considerable time, gave many Gifts, and had a new Name given to herself" (Kittredge [1690–91] 1913:154). During King Philip's War, when the embattled sachems may have longed for an improvement in their personal fortunes, they frequently held dances at which they changed their names.

Although they feared death and the spirits of the dead, individuals accepted their own death without emotion, even if they died from torture or execution. Mourners painted their faces black and comforted the relatives of the deceased with visits and kind words. The living abandoned and fled from the home where someone had died and even dropped the deceased's name from their speech for a period of months and sometimes years. Persons with the same name as the deceased would change their names to avoid offending the close kin and mourners by causing the name to be spoken. The kin protected the name as they protected a living relative by avenging themselves against anyone who deliberately ignored the taboo. Occom's account of Montauk death, burial, and mourning behavior in the eighteenth century closely resembles the southern New England pattern described by earlier authors:

> They use to wash their dead clean, and adorn them with all manner of ornaments, and paint the face of them with divers colours, and make a great lamentation over their dead. When they carry the corpse to the grave, the whole company, especially of the women, make a doleful and a very mournful and loud lamentation, all the way as they go to the grave, and at the grave; and they use to bury great many things with their dead, especially the things that belonged to the dead, and what they did not bury they would give away, and they would never live in a wigwam, in which any person died, but will immediately pull it down, and they generally mourned for their dead about a year, and the time they are in mourning the women kept their faces blackt with coal . . . neither would they wear fine cloathes, nor sing, nor dance, neither will the mourners mention the name by which their dead was called, nor suffer any one in the whole place to mention it till some of the relations is called by the same name; and when they put off their mourning habit, they generally made a great nightly dance. (Occom 1809:109–10)

Despite the *powwow*'s intimate familiarity with spirits of the dead, no writer indicated that the shaman directed burial or mourning ritual. That function belonged to "*Mockuttásuit*, One of the chiefest esteeme, who winds up and buries the dead, commonly some wise, grave, and well descended man hath that office" (Williams [1643] 1936:203).

The creator, Cautantowwit, resembled the sachems more than he did the *powwows*, for he ruled human society, had provided the first corn and beans for his subjects to grow in the mythical past, and continued to patronize rich harvests in the historical present. The sachems, upholders of the hereditary and hierarchical order, honored him in seasonal ritual by following his example as ruler and benefactor. Cautantowwit's preeminence in Narragansett ritual may have reflected the political ascendancy of their sachems in the early contact period. *Powwows*, on the other hand, achieved prominence by having received visions of Hobbamock. They mediated as priests at most public rituals and put their guardian spirits to work for the sachems and others in divination rituals, weather and hunting magic, curing, sorcery, and a variety of other ritual situations.

Divination

As diviners, the shamans determined the causes and outcome of events in the past, future, and at a distance by conjuring visions which they read as good or bad omens, by direct encounters with external spirits and by the insight provided by their own guardian spirits. In addition to providing answers to questions about illness, war, and politics, they also identified thieves and murderers.

A divination rite may have preceded the first visit by the Wampanoag to the Pilgrim camp at Plymouth. For several weeks after the Pilgrims came ashore, the English and Indians watched each other warily. William Bradford reported, "the Indians came skulking about . . . and would sometimes show themselves aloof off, but when any approached near them, they would run away" (Bradford 1966:79). Then an Indian named Samoset came boldly and unexpectedly among the Pilgrims and prepared the way in broken English for the visit of their sachem, Massasoit. According to English hearsay, before Massasoit decided to make contact, an assembly of shamans from all over the area met together, possibly to divine the best course of action for the sachem to follow: "before they came to the English to make friendship, they got all the Powachs of the country, for three days together in a horrid and devilish manner, to curse and execrate them with their conjurations, which assembly and service they held in a dark and dismal swamp" (p. 84). Nathaniel Morton of Plymouth later interpreted this ritual, as did the Pilgrims, as a sign of "how Satan laboured to hinder the gospel from coming into New England" (Morton [1669] 1826:63n).

Shamans typically divined the cause of illness to learn whether or not it was curable, and a variety of guardian spirits, including crows, hawks, and rattlesnakes, helped them in searching for answers. Edward Ward, a late-seventeenth-century visitor to Boston, witnessed a ritual (of unspecified tribal provenience) in which the shaman divined in trance:

> Upon the breaking out of a War, or such extraordinary Occasions, as the old *Romans* consulted their *Oracles*, so do the *Indians* their *Pawaws*, which are a kind of *Wizards*: And at a General *Pawawing*, the Country a Hundred Miles round assemble themselves in a Body; and when they are thus met, they kindle a large Fire, round which the *Pawaw* walks, and beats himself upon his Breast, muttering out a strange sort of intricate Jargon, until he has Elivated himself into so great an Agony, that he falls down by the Fire in a Trance; during which time, the *Sagamores* [sachems] ask him what they have a mind to know: After which, he is convey'd thro' the Fire, in the same posture that he lies, by a Power invisible, in the sight of the Spectators; then awakes, and Answers the several Questions ask'd by their *Kings* or *Sachems*. (Ward 1905:67)

Thomas Cooper of Gay Head recounted a partly fanciful but essentially credible description of trance and soul journey that he attributed to a Wampanoag ancestor whom he identified as grandmother, who was born before the English came to Martha's Vineyard. The account probably pertains to the period before 1642, when the English settled on the island:

> BEFORE the English came among the Indians, there were two disorders of which they most generally died, viz. the consumption and the yellow fever. The latter they could always *lay* in the following manner. . . . After the rich had thus given away all their moveable property to the poor, they looked out the handsomest and most sprightly young man in the assembly, and put him into an entire new wigwam. . . . They then formed into two files at a small distance from each other. One standing in the space at each end, put fire to the bottom of the wigwam on all parts, and fell to singing and dancing. Presently the youth would leap out of the flames, and fall down to appearance dead. Him they committed to the care of five virgins, prepared for that purpose, to restore to life again. The term required for this would be uncertain, from six to forty-eight hours; during which time the dance must be kept up. When he was restored, he would tell, that he had been carried in a large thing high up in the air, where he came to a great company of white people, with whom he had interceded hard to have the distemper layed; and generally after much persuasion, would obtain a promise . . . which never failed of laying the distemper. (Basset 1806:140).

Some common themes recur in the rituals described by Ward and Cooper. A male (said by Ward to be a shaman) enters a trance, the trance state being associated with insensitivity to fire; the person in the trance communicates with otherwise inaccessible spirit powers and then regains consciousness to report on the experience. Since Cooper associated the trance state with death, this ritual may have caused the temporary absence of the dream soul, which left the body forever at death.

If the Indians had written their history of King Philip's War, they might have emphasized the importance of shamanistic divination in the formulation of strategy. For example, on the morning of May 8, 1676, a war party of more than three hundred Indians appeared in the rain-soaked meadows around the town of Bridgewater, Massachusetts. While they were burning several buildings, a thunder and lightning storm broke overhead, and they withdrew without killing any of the twenty-six male defenders. According to a legend told in the area long after King Philip's War, the warriors "had a Pawaw when the Devil appeared in the Shape of a Bear walkg on his 2 hind feet." If the appearance had been a deer, the Indians said, "they would have destroyed the whole Town & all the English." Because the vision was that of a bear, they "all followed him & drew off" (Stiles 1916:232). Tispaquin, the warrior sachem who was also a great shaman, led this party and presumably divined the inauspiciousness of the day despite his advantage in numbers.

Divination by trance mediumship may have been involved in a curious wartime ritual described in the *Narrative of the Captivity of Mrs. Mary Rowlandson* (Rowlandson [1682] 1913). Philip's men captured Mary Rowlandson, wife of the minister of Lancaster, Massachusetts, early in 1676, when they fell upon that frontier settlement. For nearly three months she traveled with her captors until she was ransomed and returned to her husband. In April of 1676 her captors and numerous other bands attacked and devastated an English force in the battle for Sudbury. Before that battle Rowlandson witnessed a ritual which she described in detail but which she did not understand:

Before they went to that fight, they got a company together to *Powaw*; the manner was as followeth. There was one that kneeled upon a Deerskin, with the company round him in a ring who kneeled, and striking upon the ground with their hands, and with sticks, and muttering or humming with their mouths; besides him who kneeled in the ring, there also stood one with a Gun in his hand: Then he on the Deerskin made a speech, and all manifested assent to it: and so they did many times together. Then they bade him with the Gun go out of the ring, which he did, but when he was out, they called him in again; but he seemed to make a stand, then they called the more earnestly, till he returned again: Then they all sang. Then they gave him two Guns, in either hand one: And so he on the Deerskin began again; and at the end of every sentence in his speaking, they all assented, humming or muttering with their mouthes, and striking upon the ground with their hands. Then they bade him with the two Guns go out of the ring again; which he did, a little way. Then they called him in again, but he made a stand; so they called him with greater earnestness; but he stood reeling and wavering as if he knew not whither he should stand or fall, or which way to go. Then they called him with exceeding great vehemency, all of them, one and another: after a little while he turned in, staggering as he went, with his Armes stretched out, in either hand a Gun. As soon as he came in, they all sang and rejoyced exceedingly a while. And then he upon the Deer-skin, made another speech unto which they all assented in a rejoicing manner: and so they ended their business, and forthwith went to Sudbury-fight. (Rowlandson [1682] 1913:152–53)

The warrior with the muskets behaved as if he had been entranced by the other participants, who then brought him back to conscious-ness. They apparently learned something encouraging from this event, for "they went without any scruple, but that they should pros-per. . . . they acted as if the Devil had told them that they should gain the victory" (p. 153). Rowlandson also noticed that when these warriors returned from their triumph they were depressed as if they had learned of their forthcoming doom. Cotton Mather attributed this transformation in Indian morale to shamanistic divination:

But NOW was the time for deliverance! There was an *evil spirit* of *dissention* strangely sent among the *indians*, which disposed them to separate from one another: the *daemons*, who visibly exhibited themselves among them at their *powawing* or conjuring, signified still unto them, that they could now *do no more for them*. . . . an unaccountable terror . . . so dispirited them, that they were like men under a *fascination*. (Mather [1702] 1820, 2:495)

Mather and other English writers of course disapproved of shaman-istic divination because of its presumed source in devil worship, but they also clearly believed in the ability of some notable *powwows* to peer into and control the spirit world. During the few years before conversion, when English settlers coexisted with pagan Indians on Martha's Vineyard, they knew one shaman with "Familiarity with *Infernal Spirits*" who "could precisely inform such who desire his Assistance, from whence *Goods Stolen* from them were taken, and whither carried; with many things of the like nature: nor was he ever known to indeavour the concealing, his knowledge, to be im-mediately from a *god Subservient to him, that the English wor-shipped*" (Mayhew 1694:12). An Englishman "worthy of Credit," who had "formerly been an eye witness of his ability," in fact con-sulted the powwow regarding a problem of his own (ibid.).

Sorcery

Seventeenth-century shamans deliberately attempted to bewitch personal enemies and political rivals on their own behalf as well as on behalf of patrons. Magical intrusion and dream soul capture best describe their two major techniques. For magical intrusion, the *powwow* prepared a physical object, such as a leather arrowhead, a hair, or a bone, which his spirit ally was believed to project into the victim's body. The guardian spirit was reported to have become "the real body of a Serpent, which comes directly towards the man in the house or in the field, looming or having a shadow about him like a man, and do shoot a bone (as they say) into the Indian's Body, which sometimes killeth him" (Eliot and Mayhew [1653] 1834:204). One woman who "lay in great Extremity and wholly impotent" could not be cured by local shamans, and her relatives sent to Martha's Vineyard for more famous healers, one of whom caught the troublesome spirit in a deerskin, whereupon she recovered right away. The shaman determined that this spirit was that of "an *Englishman* drowned in the Adjacent Sound" which had been sent by a *powwow* who lived near the woman's home. The *powwow* who caught the spirit warned her that "*unless she removed to* Martha's Vineyard, *she would again be Sick, for being an English Spirit he could not long confine it*" (Mayhew 1694:15). As English power grew, the shamans' confidence in their powers waned, so in this case the unruly English spirit gave the shaman an apt explanation for an almost incurable illness.

The shaman responsible for the most explicit case of sorcery between close relatives claimed to have made a mistake:

Another well known *powaw* designing to kill an Indian, who accidentally lodg'd in the house with him and his brother, went forth to inchant an hair. While he was abroad, his brother alter'd his place about the fire, where they slept, and the strange *Indian* came into his place. The conjurer coming in with his devilish implement, gave it a direction to the back of his enemy, which by his mistake, proved his brother, and the devil therewith immediately kill'd him. (Mather [1702] 1820, 2:387–88)

Powwows acknowledged, and others observed, that such magical objects and intrusive spirits entered the victim's body "without any outward breach of the *Skin*" (Mayhew 1694:13).

Dream soul capture worked "by their Seizing something of the *Spirit* (as the Devil made *them* think) of such they intended to Torment or kill, while it wandered, in their Sleep: this they kept being in the Form of a Fly, closely imprisoned; and according as they dealt with this, so it Fared with the *Body* it belonged to" (p. 14). The Pequot warriors, confident in their shamans before their disastrous clash with the Puritan army, "blasphemed the Lord" in the language of soul capture sorcery, "saying Englishmans God was all one Flye" (Johnson [1654] 1910:164).

New England shamans quickly lost confidence in their ability to injure the English by magical means, and the English themselves seldom feared bewitchment from Indian shamans and did not generally explain their own misfortunes in these terms. One shaman threatened a Connecticut settler named Stanton and probably went back to Long Island with a few doubts about his professional future:

sometime after the English lived at Stonington, there came an Indian (of that place) to Mr. Stanton (who had the Indian tongue) and told Mr. Stanton, there was an Indian (of that place) that had a quarril with him, and had sent for a greate powaw from Long Island, who had undertaken to revenge the quarril; and thereupon shewed a greate feare; whereupon Mr. Stanton sent for the powaw, and desired him to desist, telling him that Indian was his pertecaler friende, but the powaw refused without so greate a rewarde might be given, that the Indian could not be able to give, and the Indian powaw grew still more high and positive in his language, until he told Mr. Stanton he could immediately tare his house in pieces, and himself flye out at the top of the chimney; and grew at length to be so daring that he raised the old gentlemans Temper, so that he started out of his greate chayre and layed hold of the powaw, and by main strength took him, and with a halter tyed his hands, and raised him up to a hook in the Joyse, and whipped him untill he promised to desist and go home, which he did and the poore fearefull Indian had no harm from the powaw; there were many Indians without the house, who came as neare as they dare, and saw the disipline, and expected the house to be tore in pieces (as they said), who, when they saw the matter so concluded went away much Surprised. (Indian Powow 1848:44)

English dogs were another matter, for it was "particularly affirmed, that the *Indians* in their wars with us, finding a sore inconvenience by our *dogs*, which would make a sad yelling if in the night they scented the approaches of them, they sacrificed a *dog* to the *devil*; after which no *English* dog would bark at an *Indian* for divers months ensuing" (Mather [1702] 1820, 1:506). One group of non-Puritan settlers suspected that Indian sorcery had affected them. In 1625 Captain Wollaston initiated a small plantation on the south shore of Massachusetts Bay near the site of an earlier abandoned settlement at Wessagusset. After two years this colony failed and the inhabitants moved to Virginia. Increase Mather heard that Wollaston conceded "that the *Indian* Powas had brought that Place under some Fascination, and that *Englishmen* would never thrive upon *Enchanted Ground*" (Mather [1677] 1864:104). God preserved Plymouth from a similar fate, Mather surmised, because he saw that the Pilgrims designed something "better than the World in their planting here" (p. 107). Despite these exceptions, the English considered Indian shamans to be "weake witches," but they did not doubt the effectiveness of Indian sorcerers on other Indians (Morton [1632] 1947:25).

Indians feared sorcery from the English, however, and suspected that some of their contact period diseases originated from this cause. In 1637 the Narragansett sachem Canonicus accused Roger Williams and the English of "sending the plague amongst them, and threatening to kill him especially." Williams replied authoritatively that "the plague and other sicknesses were alone in the hand of the one God, who made him and us, who being displeased with the English for lying, stealing, idleness and uncleanness, (the natives' epidemical sins,) smote many thousands of us ourselves with general and late mortalities" (Williams 1874:17).

In his study of the psychological characteristics of northeastern Indians, Irving Hallowell emphasized a "multifaceted pattern of emotional restraint or inhibition" characterized by the inhibition of anger in interpersonal relations (Hallowell 1967:132). Although Hallowell used no seventeenth-century New English sources, they would have sustained the pattern he described, for numerous writers attested to the Indians' sensitivity to ridicule, long vindictive memories, and displays of violence when intoxicated, all of which can be interpreted as consequences of inhibition in day-to-day interpersonal affairs. Sorcery, being a covert form of interpersonal aggression, flourished in this environment of cultural restraint, where fear of anger was a major preoccupation. Not surprisingly, individuals inflicted sorcery on or expected it from those with whom they had experienced conflict in domestic and political relations.

Curing

Seventeenth-century shamans offered two explanations for misfortunes—those caused by the creator's anger, which they could not prevent, and those caused by the sorcery of another shaman, over which they had some control. The behavior that triggered the creator's anger is unclear, but some evidence suggests that the shamans attributed great collective misfortunes, such as the contact period plagues, to this cause. The Plymouth-area Wampanoag, for example, speculated that their losses in the epidemic of 1617–19 could have been avoided by performing the property destruction ritual in which the Narragansett honored the creator. Furthermore, shamans "seldom come amongst them" during such general illnesses (Josselyn [1675] 1833:299). The creator may have announced his anger by earthquakes and comets which preceded mass misfortunes. The Narragansett also attributed some individual afflictions to their high god. As Roger Williams recalled:

I have heard a poore *Indian* lamenting the losse of a child at break of day, call up his Wife and children, and all about him to Lamentation, and with abundance of teares cry out! O God thou hast taken away my child! thou art angry with me: O turne thine anger from me, and spare the rest of my children.

If they receive any good in hunting, fishing, Harvest &c. they acknowledge God in it.

Yea, if it be but an ordinary accident, a fall, &c. they will say God was angry and did it, *musquàntum manit* God is angry. (Williams [1643] 1936: 123–24)

If a shaman was called to effect a cure, he first divined to learn if the problem was curable:

Another power they worship, whom they call *Hobbamock* . . . is the devil. Him they call upon to cure their wounds and diseases. When they are curable, he persuades them he sends the same for some conceived anger against them; but upon their calling upon him, can and doth help them; but when they are mortal and not curable in nature, then he persuades them Kiehtan is angry, and sends them, whom none can cure. (Winslow [1624] 1910:343)

The Massachusett called shamans who could not cure them *squantams powwows;* since *musquàntum manit* meant "God is angry," this name probably referred to the *powwows'* inability to cure, which they would have explained by saying that God was angry (Johnson [1654] 1910:263; Williams [1643] 1936:124).

One or several shamans, the patient, and an audience participated in the cure, which sometimes lasted for hours. Winslow and Hobbamock found the ailing Massasoit in the midst of one such gathering when they hiked from Plymouth to his home at Sowams, now Warren, Rhode Island, on the east shore of Narragansett Bay:

When we came thither, we found the house so full of men, as we could scarce get in, though they used their best diligence to make way for us. There were they in the midst of their charms for him, making such a hellish noise, as it distempered us that were well, and therefore unlike to ease him that was sick. About him were six or eight women, who chafed his arms, legs, and thighs, to keep heat in him. When they had made an end of their charming, one told him that his friends, the English, were come to see him. (Winslow [1624] 1910:307–8)

The *powwow* and audience commenced with a musical invocation; throughout the ritual he sang and the onlookers responded, sometimes joining with him "like a Quire" (Williams [1643] 1936: 198). His utterances are described as "horrible outcries" and "hollow bleatings" (Eliot and Mayhew [1653] 1834:204), some of which resembled animal cries. His physical movements involved "odd," "fierce," and "laborious" gestures over the patient which caused the *powwow* to sweat until he foamed (Gookin [1792] 1970:20). The most extraordinary feature of the cure, noted also in divination ritual, was the shaman's self-beating of his chest and thighs:

the parties that are sick or lame being brought before them, the powwow sitting down, the rest of the Indians giving attentive audience to his imprecations and invocations, and after the violent expression of many a hideous bellowing and groaning, he makes a stop, and then all the auditors with one voice utter a short canto. Which done, the powwow still proceeds in his invocations, sometimes roaring like a bear, other times groaning like a dying horse, foaming at the mouth like a chased boar, smiting his naked breast and thighs with such violence as if he were mad. Thus will he continue sometimes half a day, spending his lungs, sweating out his fat, and tormenting his body in this diabolical worship. (Wood [1634] 1977:101)

Williams added that the *powwow* threatens and "conjures out the sicknesse" (Williams [1643] 1936:127). Such actions could lead to fainting and "extasie" (Lechford [1642] 1867:118). Perhaps the self-beating helped the shaman reach a trance state during which he spoke with his guardian and enemy spirits in their own language, which would explain the animal cries and other peculiar noises heard by English observers.

The shaman removed intrusive magical objects from the patient's body with the cooperation of his guardian spirit and by laying on hands, sucking, and spitting or blowing the objects away. If a wound proved curable "he toucheth it not, but *askooke*, that is, the snake, or *wobsacuck*, that is, the eagle, sitteth on his shoulder, and licks the same. This none see but the powah, who tells them he doth it himself" (Winslow [1624] 1910:343–44). On occasion the *powwow* accused of causing an illness could be forced to cure it himself. A Martha's Vineyard native found relief in this way:

his Friends advise him to the *Powaw's*, concluding him to be Bewitched; they being met, and dancing round a great Fire, the Sick lying by; some of the Neighbours entered the House, being perswaded that a great *Powaw*, now called to cure, had bewitched the Sick: they threaten him that as he had *Bewitched*, unless he would *Cure* the Sick man, they would burn him in that fire; after many Excuses, too long here to relate, they took him up, resolving at least to a little *Singe* him; who no sooner felt the heat of the fire near him, but the *Sick* immediately recovered. (Mayhew 1694:14)

A successful *powwow* proudly showed his spirit to the audience: "The *Pawwaws* counted their Imps their Preservers, had them treasured up in their bodies, which they brought forth to hurt their enemies, and heal their friends; who when they had done some notable Cure, would shew the Imp in the palm of his Hand to the Indians who with much amazement looking on it, Deified them" (Eliot and Mayhew [1653] 1834:202). The shaman's admirers then cried "*Much*

winnit Abbamocho, that is, very good Devill" (Johnson [1654] 1910:
263). The Pequot women survivors shouted this same praise to the
English soldiers who devastated their palisaded village at Mystic in
1637.

A number of English acknowledged that Indian shamans could
cure as well as injure non-Christian Indians, even though the English criticized the shamans for collusion with the devil and for taking large fees for their services. The *powwows'* methods succeeded
with psychological as well as physical disorders and included practical skills such as bone setting, wound dressing, massage, and
knowledge of the curative properties of roots and herbs. In curing
rituals and on most other ritual occasions, the Indians gave away or
destroyed large amounts of individual property, perhaps to improve
their health. They believed that such property redistributions affected their collective well-being and even tried (unsuccessfully) to
interest the English in contributing to these occasions. William Harris of Providence once watched a dance hosted by the paramount
Narragansett sachem, Canonchet, which he described as "a kind of
religious ceremony wherein they customarily give away all the
money they have and bid those to whom they give it to go and pray
for them. So accordingly out they go and make a kind of shout that
signifies as much, and their women dance around in a ring" (Leach
1963:59). Williams added that once a person "receives this Gift,
upon the receiving of it goes out, and hollowes thrice for the health
and prosperity of the Party that gave it" (Williams [1643] 1936:129).
The fur trade, and to a lesser extent land sales, had increased the
status of individual Indians and had perpetuated wealth differences
in seventeenth-century Indian society. During those same years the
physical health of these populations had deteriorated badly. By giving away and destroying large amounts of material goods at curing
rituals and on other ritual occasions, the Indians could have been
trying to restore good health and fortune by liquidating the material
symbols of social inequality and rapid change.

Weather, Hunting, and War

Few details survive of shamanistic weather and hunting rituals.
"If the yeere proove drie," wrote Williams, "they have great and solemne meetings from all parts at one high place, to supplicate their
gods; and to beg raine, and they will continue in this worship ten
days, a fortnight; yea, three weekes, untill raine come" (Williams,
[1643] 1936:67). Uncas once summoned his most notable shamans
to end a drought at Mohegan, and when they failed he asked a Con-

gregational minister, the Reverend James Fitch of Norwich, to pray
in their behalf:

> then Uncas with many Indians came to my House, Uncas lamented there
> was such Want of Rain; I asked, whether if God should send us Rain, he
> would not attribute it to their Pawawes? He answered, No, for they had done
> their Uttermost, and all in Vain: I replyed, if you will declare it before all
> these Indians, you shall see what God will do for us. . . . Then Uncas made
> a great Speech to the Indians (which were many) confessing, that if God
> should then send Rain, it could not be ascribed to their Pawawing, but must
> be acknowledged to be an Answer of our Prayers. This Day the Clouds
> spread more and more: and the next Day there was such a Plenty of Rain,
> that our River rose more than two Foot in Height. (Hubbard [1865] 1969,
> 1:289–90)

Uncas used English prayers as he used political alliance with the
Puritan colonies, as instruments for his own survival. In addition to
making rain, some persons "can cause the wind to blow in what part
they list—can raise storms and tempests, which they usually do
when they intend the death or destruction of other people" (Winslow [1624] 1910:351). Perhaps the greatest such feat of weather making for which the powwows took credit was a hurricane that battered
the Boston area in August 1675. The Indians, who for three months
had been at war with the English, "reported that they had caused it
by their Pawwaw. . . . They farther say, that as many Englishmen
shall die, as the Trees have by this Wind been blown down in the
Woods" (Saltonstall [1675] 1867:158).

Hunting rituals existed, but descriptions of them are nonexistent.
In 1677 a group of warriors raided Deerfield, Massachusetts, and
captured an Englishman named Quentin Stockwell, who watched
shamanistic hunting ritual and mentioned it in his captivity narrative:

> all the Indians went a hunting, but could get nothing: divers days they pow-
> ow'd, but got nothing; then they desired the English to pray, and confessed
> they could do nothing; they would have us pray, and see what the English-
> man's God could do. I prayed, so did Serjeant Plimpton, in another place.
> The Indians reverently attended, morning and night; next day they got
> bears; then they would needs have us desire a blessing, return thanks at
> meals: after a while they grew weary of it, and the Sachim did forbid us.
> (Mather [1684] 1890:33–34)

In this case and in the one involving Uncas and Reverend Fitch, the
Indians showed themselves to be pragmatic in their attitude toward
the benefits of English prayer, while adhering to traditional beliefs.

Rituals performed in time of war are not well known. Captain Benjamin Church of Little Compton, Rhode Island, witnessed one such

nickommo among the Sakonnet when they joined with the English
as military allies. In the summer of 1676, with the Narragansett
crushed and Philip in hiding, Awashonks, queen sachem of the Sakonnet, committed her warriors to the English cause in a remarkable
dance which the observant Church described to his son Thomas,
who included the account in his father's memoirs:

> It being now about sunsetting, or near the dusk of the evening, the Netops
> [friends] came running from all quarters loaden with the tops of dry pines,
> and the like combustible matter, making a huge pile thereof, near Mr.
> Church's shelter, on the open side thereof. But by this time supper was
> brought in, in three dishes; viz., a curious young bass in one dish; eels and
> flat fish in a second; and shell fish in a third. But neither bread nor salt to be
> seen at table. But by that time supper was over, the mighty pile of pine knots
> and tops, & c., was fired; and all the Indians, great and small, gathered in a
> ring round it, Awashonks, with the oldest of her people, men and women
> mixed, kneeling down, made the first ring next the fire; and all the lusty
> stout men standing up, made the next, and then all the rabble in a confused
> crew, surrounded, on the outside.
>
> Then the chief Captain stepped in between the rings and the fire, with a
> spear in one hand, and a hatchet in the other; danced round the fire, and
> began to fight with it; making mention of all the several nations and com-
> panies of Indians in the country, that were enemies to the English. And at
> naming of every particular tribe of Indians, he would draw out and fight a
> new firebrand; and at finishing his fight with each particular firebrand,
> would bow to him, and thank him; and when he had named all the several
> nations and tribes, and fought them all, he stuck down his spear and
> hatchet, and came out, and another stept in, and acted over the same dance,
> with more fury, if possible, than the first; and when about half a dozen of
> their chiefs had thus acted their parts, the Captain of the guard step up to
> Mr. Church, and told him, [that] they were making soldiers for him, and
> what they had been doing was all one [as] swearing of them. And having in
> that manner engaged all the stout lusty men, Awashonks and her chiefs
> came to Mr. Church, and told him, that now they were all engaged to fight
> for the English, and [that] he might call forth all, or any of them, at any time,
> as he saw occasion, to fight the enemy. And [then] presented him with a
> very fine firelock. (Church [1716] 1827:91–92)

Shamanistic Feats

Certain shamans believed themselves to be omnipotent and capable of remarkable physical feats, sometimes called juggling by
their English contemporaries. Thomas Morton once praised the "admirable perfection" of Indian senses and added that "the Salvages
have the sence of seeing so farre beyond any of our Nation, that one
would allmost beleeve they had intelligence of the Devill" (Morton
[1632] 1947:33). Others described Indians as "having quick wits,
understanding apprehensions, strong memories, with nimble inven-

tions, and a quick hand" and "by nature admirably ingenious" (Leach 1963:65; Wood [1634] 1977:96). The shamans possessed even finer perceptual and motor skills than other Indians, and the English often admired their performances. Passaconaway, a *powwow-sachem* of the Pawtucket on the Merrimack River near the northern periphery of Puritan settlement, was a celebrity among New England shamans. Accounts of his magical feats reached Massachusetts Bay: "if we may believe the Indians who report of one Passaconaway that he can make the water burn, the rocks move, the trees dance, metamorphise himself into a flaming man. . . . in winter, when there is no green leaves to be got, he will burn an old one to ashes, and putting those into the water produce a new green leaf . . . and make of a dead snake's skin a living snake" (Wood [1634] 1977:100–101).

that Sachem or Sagamore is a Powah of greate estimation amongst all kinde of Salvages, there hee is at their Revels (which is the time when a great company of Salvages meete, from severall parts of the Country, in amity with their neighbours) hath advaunced his honor in his feats or jugling tricks . . . to the admiration of the spectators whome hee endevoured to persuade, that he would goe under water to the further side of a river to broade for any man to undertake with a breath, which thing hee performed by swimming over & deluding the company with casting a mist before their eies that see him enter in and come out, but no part of the way hee has bin seene, likewise by our English in the heat of all summer to make Ice appeare in a bowle of faire water, first having the water set before him hee hath begunne his incantation according to their usuall accustome and before the same has bin ended a thick Clowde has darkened the aire and on a sodane a thunder clap hath bin heard that has amazed the natives, in an instant he hath shewed a firme peece of Ice to flote in the middest of the bowle in the presence of the vulgar people, which doubtles was done by the agility of Satan his consort. (Morton [1632] 1947:25–26)

Passaconaway's feats resemble those observed among Wampanoag shamans in the vicinity of Falmouth, Massachusetts, by Joseph Hatch, the earliest English settler of that Cape Cod town. Lost in the woods one evening, Hatch wandered into a "numerous collection of the natives, of both sexes and all ages," who invited him to spend the night:

He threw himself on a bear skin & closed his eyes, but never slept. The Indians doubtless supposing their guest as calm & unruffled as he affected to be, soon joined in a most hideous Powwa . . . around a bonfire. He lay shivering with fear. When this was through, they engaged in various exercises & amusements in small parties; & performed many wonderful feats of slight of hand. One of them he said, actually pulled out of his mouth a large bird called a Penguin, put it in water & made it swim, & then swallowed it again; others would turn water into solid ice, on the whole, it was clear they were assisted by the evil one himself. (Hatch [1816] 1948:7)

Roger Williams heard of a Pequot shaman who threatened to sink English ships by swimming under water, and forwarded this information in a letter to John Winthrop: "The Pequots hear of your preparations, & c., and comfort themselves in this, that a witch amongst them will sink the pinnaces, by diving under water and making holes, & c., as also they shall now enrich themselves with store of guns, but I hope their dreams (through the mercy of the Lord) shall vanish, and the devil and his lying sorcerers shall be confounded" (Williams 1874:6). Other shamans claimed the ability to resist arrow, hatchet, and musket wounds. The English soldiers who overcame the Pequot stronghold at Mystic in 1637 apparently knew of this belief, for "There were some of these Indians, as is reported, whose bodyes were not to be pierced by their sharp rapiers or swords of [for] a long time, which made some of the Souldiers think the Devil was in them, for there were some Powwowes among them, which work strange things with the help of Satan" (Johnson [1654] 1910:168). Tispaquin, the leader of the war party that saw the bear vision at Bridgewater in King Philip's War, believed himself to be invulnerable to English muskets and had been shot twice to no effect. He surrendered near the end of the war, expecting to serve in Benjamin Church's Indian forces; but instead he "was sent to *Plimouth*, but upon Trial (which was the Condition on which his being promised a Captain's Place under Capt. *Church* did depend) he was found penetrable by the English Guns, for he fell down at the first Shot" (Hubbard [1865] 1969, 1:275).

Powwows had been casting their spells more or less uninterruptedly from prehistoric times until the English began settling after 1620. Even the best accounts by observers such as Williams, Winslow, Morton, Wood, Gookin, and Mayhew depict cultures that had already absorbed many European elements and had experienced a considerable amount of misfortune and stress. In many cases the simple presence of Europeans seemed to threaten Indian belief in the efficacy of native symbols. Daniel Denton, for example, commented on how Europeans could inhibit the shaman's power to generate visions and spells: "if any *English* at such times do come amongst them, it puts a period to their proceeding, and they will desire their absence, telling them their God will not come whilst they are there" (Denton 1670:8–9). The Wampanoag once assured Winslow that he could see Hobbamock after a successful cure, but he replied "of the contrary, which so proved; yea, themselves have confessed they never saw him when any of us were present" (Winslow [1624] 1910:344). Clearly the colonial English with their admirable technology, resistance to diseases, and powerful gods posed a frightening challenge to Indian confidence in their own understanding of how the world worked and how to control its workings. But to abandon ancestral traditions to follow the new English ways also could be very disorienting, as was apparent in the cases of peculiar frights that startled the Indian inhabitants of Boston and Martha's Vineyard shortly after the English colonized these localities. The Indians explained these strange events as the result of their having parted from traditional ways:

About this time [1637] the Indians, which were in our families, were much frighted with Hobbamock (as they call the devil) appearing to them in divers shapes, and persuading them to forsake the English, and not to come at the assemblies, nor to learn to read. (Winthrop 1825:254)

There was this Year 1643 a very strange Disease among the *Indians*, they ran up and down as if delirious, till they could run no longer; they would make their Faces as black as a Coal, and snatch up any Weapon, as tho they would do Mischief with it, and speak great swelling Words, but yet they did no Harm.
Many of these *Indians* were by the *English* seen in this Condition. Now this, and all other Calamities which the *Indians* were under, they generally then attributed to the Departure of some of them from their own heathenish Ways and Customs. (Mayhew 1727:3)

Even Passaconaway, the most prominent New England shaman, concluded that his powers could do nothing to stop the advancing English. In 1660 he spoke to a great gathering of Indians on the Merrimack River to say farewell to his children and subjects and to warn them to run away from war with the English should it come. A "Person of Quality" heard the old shaman's oration and wrote down an English version:

I am now going the Way of all Flesh, or ready to die, and not likely to see you ever met together any more: I will now leave this Word of Counsel with you, that you take heed how you quarrell with the English for though you may do them much mischief, yet assuredly you will all be destroyed, and rooted off the Earth if you do. . . . I was as much an Enemy to the English at their first coming into these Parts, as any one whatsoever, and did try all Ways and Means possible to have destroyed them, at least to have prevented them sitting down here, but I could in no way effect it; (it is to be noted that this Passaconaway was the most noted Pawaw and Sorcerer of all the Country) therefore I advise you never to contend with the English, nor make War with them. (Hubbard [1865] 1969, 1:48–49)

Accordingly, when the final struggle began in 1675, Passaconaway's eldest son and successor *"withdrew himself into some remote Place"* (p. 49).

By 1676 the combined impacts of invasion, conversion, and military defeat had completed the transformation of the native New England people from autonomous tribal entities to low-status subjects at the bottom of a large-scale colonial society dominated by European Christians and capitalists, who themselves acknowledged their subjection to the English Parliament and king. As their internal world broke down, those Indians who survived found themselves dependent on English magistrates and on the limited economic opportunities available to them within the new order. This political and economic transformation deeply affected the symbolic universe glimpsed in this reconstruction, and by the mid-eighteenth century Christianity had replaced most core beliefs and almost all myth and ritual. Despite such massive erosion and change, some Indian concepts persisted with new English names and forms, and a few indigenous symbols survived intact in the historic period. The story of the transformation and survival of the Indian character of these cultures is revealed in the content of their oral traditions, to which we now turn.

4   The First Europeans

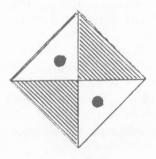

The New England Algonquians said of anything new or remarkable, "*Manittóo*," meaning, "it is a god."[1] Roger Williams commented on how they attributed this quality to the awesome sights and events of English colonization:

> Besides there is a generall Custome amongst them, at the apprehension of any Excellency in Men, Women, Birds Beasts, Fish, & c. to cry out *Manittóo*, that is, it is a God, as thus if they see one man excell others in Wisdome, Valour, strength, Activity & c. they cry out *Manittóo* A God: and therefore when they talk amongst themselves of the *English* ships, and great buildings, of the plowing of their Fields, and especially of Bookes and Letters, they will end thus: *Manittôwock* They are Gods. (Williams [1643] 1936:126)

I

One of the remarkable aspects of first historical contact between European and Indian cultures is the way in which symbolic preconceptions provided the language for perception of these events. Old World explorers began visiting the New England coast in the sixteenth century, and the Indians of Massachusetts Bay preserved in legend the actual moment when they first encountered a European ship. According to William Wood, an Englishman who lived in the Bay Colony from 1629 to 1633, the Indians understood the ship to be a floating island. This was certainly an aboriginal idea, for floating islands and island canoes are familiar motifs in the Algonquian folklore of northern New England and eastern Canada (Beck

1966:78; Rand 1894:232–37; Thompson [1929] 1966:275; D 632.1. *Island canoe).*

1634   OF THEIR WONDERING AT THE FIRST VIEW OF ANY STRANGE INVENTION

These Indians being strangers to arts and sciences, and being unacquainted with the inventions that are common to a civilized people, are ravished with admiration at the first view of any such sight. They took the first ship they saw for a walking island, the mast to be a tree, the sail white clouds, and the discharging of ordnance for lightning and thunder, which did much trouble them, but this thunder being over and this moving-island steadied with an anchor, they manned out their canoes to go and pick strawberries there. But being saluted by the way with a broadside, they cried out, "What much hoggery, so big walk, and so big speak, and by and by kill"; which caused them to turn back, not daring to approach till they were sent for.   (Wood [*1634*] *1977:95–96*)

II

Dreams were an important source of knowledge to the New England Indians and to American Indians generally. A seventeenth-century Nauset man from Yarmouth on Cape Cod dreamed of Europeans and the Bible during the great plague of 1617–19. In this dream an Englishman dressed in black and holding a Bible (or perhaps a black man dressed in black) stood above the assembled English and Indians and attributed the plague to God's anger with the Indians for their sins.[2] The god in this dream, like the Indian creator Cautantowwit or Kiehtan, caused incurable illness when angry: "when they [i.e., their sicknesses] are mortal and not curable in nature, then he [i.e., the shaman] persuades them Kiehtan is angry, and sends them, whom none can cure" (Winslow [1624] 1910:343). The black-robed figure who appeared to the Nauset man reassured him that he and his family would survive.

1648

Fourthly, a fourth and last observation wee took, was the story of an Indian in those parts, telling us of his dreame many yeers since, which he told us of openly before many witnesses when we sate at meat: the dreame is this, hee said "That about two yeers before the English came over into those parts there was a great mortality among the Indians, and one night he could not sleep above half the night, after which hee fell into a dream, in which he did think

he saw a great many men come to those parts in cloths, just as
the English now are apparelled, and among them there arose up a
man all in black, with a thing in his hand which hee now sees was
all one English mans book; this black man he said stood upon a
higher place then all the rest, and on the one side of him were the
English, *on the other a great number of* Indians: *this man told all*
the Indians that God was moosquantum *or angry with them, and*
that he would kill them for their sinnes, whereupon he said himself
stood up, and desired to know of the black man what God would
do with him and his Squaw and Papooses, but the black man would
not answer him a first time, nor yet a second time, untill he desired
the third time, and then he smil'd upon him, and told him that he
and his Papooses should be safe, and that God would give unto
them Mitcheu, *(i.e.) victualls and other good things, and so hee*
awakened."   (Shepard [1648] *1834:44)*

III

Indian converts traced aspects of Christian belief and practice to
aboriginal sources, thus representing change as continuity with their
own past. As they embarked on radical and irreversible changes,
they attributed Indian roots to some of these new experiences. One
Puritan minister heard that many Indians had an apprehension
"That their forefathers did know God, but that after this, they fell
into a great sleep, and when they did awaken they quite forgot him"
(Shepard [1648] 1834:44). An aged Indian of Cape Cod told Thomas
Shepard and others that his people also had known but forgotten the
teachings of the Christian God.

1648

That these very things which Mr. Eliot had taught them as the
Commandements of God, and concerning God, and the making of
the world by one God, that they had heard some old men who were
now dead, to say the same things, since whose death there hath
been no remembrance or knowledge of them among the Indians
untill now they heare of them againe.   *(P. 43)*

IV

Indian legend preserves a number of premonitions and omens of
the arrival of Europeans, including this prophecy recorded by
George Fox who, being a Quaker, would have been particularly attuned to prophecies. According to this (Narragansett?) tradition, Indians should behave lovingly toward whites or else be destroyed.

The warning functioned in a way similar to the next premonition, attested by Cotton Mather (in "The Unknown God"), as an inducement to Indians to embrace English religion and ultimately English rule.

1672

And an Indian said, before the English came, that a white people should come in a great thing of the sea, and their people should be loving to them and receive them; but if they did hurt or wrong the white people, they would be destroyed. And this hath been seen and fulfilled, that when they did wrong the English they never prospered and have been destroyed. So that Indian was a prophet and prophesied truly. (Fox 1952:624)

V

In this anecdote, recorded late in the seventeenth century by Cotton Mather, an Indian woman of Martha's Vineyard claimed to have had knowledge of the Christian God before Christians came to live on her island. This woman, who had lost her first five children within ten days of birth, dedicated her sixth child to this God and the child lived. When the English under Thomas Mayhew came to the island she surmised that the God of whom the English spoke was the same as the one to whom she had dedicated her child. She and her family thereupon converted, and the child became a prominent Indian minister. Since dedicating one's children to a deity was probably an indigenous pattern, this is another example of an old belief validating departure from tradition.

1696   THE UNKNOWN GOD

Pammehanuit an Indian of prime quality, on Martha's Vineyard, and his wife having buried their five first children successively, every one of them within ten days of their birth, notwithstanding all their use of powaws and of medicines, to preserve them, they had a sixth child (a son) born about the year 1638, which was a few years before the English first setled on that Vineyard. The mother was greatly perplexed with fear that she should lose this child, like the former: And utterly despairing of any help from such means as had been formerly tried with so little success, as soon as she was able, (which among the Indians is quickly and within less than ten days) with a sorrowful heart, she took up her child, and went out into the field, that she might there weep out her sorrows. While she was here musing on the insufficiency of all

humane help, she felt it powerfully suggested unto her mind, that
there is one Almighty God who is to be pray'd unto: That this God
hath created all the things that we see: And that the God who had
given being to her self, and all other people, and given her child
unto her, was easily able to continue the life of her child.

Hereupon this poor blind Pagan resolv'd, that she would seek
unto this god for that mercy, and she did accordingly. The issue was,
that her child liv'd; and her faith (such as it was) in him, who thus
answer'd her prayer, was wonderfully strengthen'd: The considera-
tion whereof caus'd her to dedicate this child unto the service of
that God, who had preserv'd his life; and educate him as far as
might be, to become the servant of God.

Not long after this, the English came to settle on Martha's Vine-
yard; and the Indians, who had been present at some of the English
devotions, reported, that they assembled frequently together; and
that the man who spoke among 'em, often look'd upwards. This
woman, from this report, presently concluded, that their assemblies
were for prayers; and that their prayers were unto that very God,
whom she had addressed for the life of her child. She was con-
firm'd in this, when the gospel was not long after preached by Mr.
Mayhew to the Indians there; which gospel she readily, and cheer-
fully, and heartily embrac'd. And in the confession that she made
publickly at her admission into the church, she gave a relation
of the preparation for the knowledge of Christ, wherewith God in
this wonderful way had favour'd her. But that which adds to this
wonder, is, that this very child has prov'd an eminent preacher of
Christ unto the other Indians. He is living at this time [1696] *a very*
religious christian, and a laborious minister, and one, who not
only is pastor to an Indian church on Martha's Vineyard, consisting
of some scores of regenerate souls, but also has taken pains to
carry the gospel unto other Indians on the main land with a notable
effect thereof. His name is Japhet.   (Mather [1702] 1820, 2: 383–84)

VI

Other impressions of Europeans survived in Indian oral tradition.
John Winthrop (1681–1747), son of Wait Winthrop, heard in 1702
what was apparently an Indian account of a ship that sailed under
water and through the air. Indians throughout this region believed
that shamans could swim beneath the water and fly through the air,
and it is not surprising that they would attribute such powers to
something as strange as a European ship. This legend may have been
influenced by (or even may have contributed to) English folklore, for

in 1648 the settlers of New Haven reported seeing the apparition of a ship in the air and under water (Mather [1702] 1820, 1:84; Winthrop 1826:328).

1702

The Dutch Ship that came into the harbour of New London before New England was inhabited. A ship to sail under water, also through the air.   (Emerson 1935:166)

VII

Another marvelous impression of the early Europeans lived on in the area of Dighton, Massachusetts, until the early nineteenth century. As in texts I and VI, the Dighton legend conveyed a symbolic representation of a historical event, for the Indians described as a giant bird what was probably a European ship. A bird that took hostages (B 31.1. *Roc*. A giant bird that carries off men in its claws) was an important figure in northeastern Algonquian folklore, and its predations are attested in the Wampanoag area. For example, the Nantucket Indians spoke of a great eagle that carried away children: "there was a tradition or fable among them, that an eagle having seized and carried off in his talons a papoose, the parents followed him in their canoe till they came to Nantucket, where they found the bones of their child dropped by the eagle" (Freeman 1815b: 34–35). Edward Kendall, who recorded the Dighton legend, did not specify whether he heard it from an Indian or English informant.[3]

1807

As to traditions, there is, though but in a few mouths, an Indian tradition, which purports, that some ages past, a number of white men arrived in the [Taunton] river, in a bird; that the white men took Indians into the bird, as hostages; that they took fresh water for their consumption at a neighbouring spring; that the Indians fell upon and slaughtered the white men at the spring; that, during the affray, thunder and lightning issued from the bird; that the hostages escaped from the bird; and that a spring, now called White Spring, and from which there runs a brook, called White Man's Brook, has its name from this event.   (Kendall 1809:230)

VIII

Thomas Commuck (ca. 1803–56), a Narragansett from the New England Indian community in Brotherton, Wisconsin, recorded one of the most intriguing Indian legends regarding that magical time when

Europeans arrived in the New World. The Narragansett and many other eastern tribes reported hearing a tune in the air some years before Europeans appeared, and Commuck preserved this tune in his published collection *Indian Melodies* (1845) under the title "Old Indian Hymn."[4] This nineteenth-century Narragansett legend resembles earlier texts that attribute an Indian source to elements of Christian belief and practice.

1845

The Narragansett Indians have a tradition, that the following tune was heard in the air by them, and other tribes bordering on the Atlantic coast, many years before the arrival of the whites in America; and that on their first visiting a church in Plymouth Colony, after the settlement of that place by the whites, the same tune was sung while performing divine service, and the Indians knew it as well as the whites. The tune therefore is preserved among them to this day, and is sung to the words here set. (Commuck 1845:63)

IX

John Winthrop (see text VI above) heard in 1702 of a white whale that lived in a pond on Kataimuk or Naushon Island, the largest of the Elizabeth Islands: "The Indians say before the English came to America, there was a white whale kept in the great pond at the West end of Kataimuk Island" (Emerson 1935:165). This whale story surfaced again in 1925, when Rachel F. Ryan of Gay Head told it to Mabel Knight. In Ryan's account the white whale first appeared as an omen of the coming of Europeans. Maushop and Squant, who are mentioned in the legend, are Wampanoag culture heroes of whom we will hear more later.

1925   THE FORETELLING OF THE COMING OF THE
        WHITE MAN

Before the coming of the white man, a great and wise chief lived at Indian Hill, between Eastskysser Hill and the beach hummock where Moshop and Ol' Squant live. On his death-bed he said that a strange white people would come to crowd out the red men, and that for a sign, after his death a great white whale would rise out of the witch pond below. That night he died and followed the fading glow of sunset to the Happy Hunting Grounds; and that night the great white whale rose from the witch pond. The old chief was buried on Indian Hill, and at its foot the Witch Pond may still be seen. (Knight 1925:137)

X

A second telling of this legend, collected by Gladys Tantaquidgeon from Pearl Ryan of Gay Head in 1928, identifies the sachem as Mittark and includes a warning that Indians should guard their lands from whites lest their race disappear. This warning was timely in the 1920s when whites were acquiring Wampanoag land. Interestingly, the twentieth-century Penobscot also thought it was bad luck to see a white animal (Speck 1935:24). A similar association is likely here; the white whale, in addition to symbolizing Europeans, was the largest bad omen imaginable.

1928 COMING OF THE WHITE MAN

Mitark, the last hereditary chief, called people together on Indian Hill at sunset and told them that he was going to die and while he was talking a white whale arose from the water off Witch Pond and Mitark said thats a sign that another new people the color of the whale [?] but don't let them have all the land because if you do the Indians will disappear. Then he died and shortly after the white people appeared. (Tantaquidgeon 1928)

The Indians of southern New England understood and remembered the unprecedented events of colonial contact by means of indigenous symbolic images. *Manitos*, floating islands, flying and underwater ships, giant birds, thunder and lightning, sounds of music in the air, a strange white whale, dreams, premonitions, and warnings all give us a feeling for how the Indians apprehended this portentous moment in their history. Dreams, prophecies, and sounds in the air reassured them that their ancestors had anticipated these events and may even have traveled this way before.

5 Christianity

Conflict between Indian and European raged over the material issues of land and power but also radiated into the supernatural realm, where the two cultures struggled for years, even after the frontier wars had ended. Four themes dominate Indian legends about Christianity. The first is conflict between the English and Indian religions, which had cultural roots in both the English and Indian traditions. English clergymen such as Eliot, Mayhew, and Williams considered themselves at war with their old adversary, the devil, in the New World wilderness. For their part, the Indians may have accounted for the missionaries' campaigns in terms of an aboriginal pattern of dueling between shamans, or between culture heroes, to see who had the greater power. Such struggles are a widespread theme in North American Indian folklore and are documented among Algonquian-speaking groups immediately north of this area (Fisher 1946:250; Lowie 1908; Speck 1919:264, 282–83). The second theme is the ultimate triumph of Christianity. The third is the importance to both sides of remarkable providences (seen in storms, illness, military defeat, accidents, and so on) that afflicted sinners and rewarded the faithful. The fourth theme, already discussed in chapter 4, is the Indians' notion that they already possessed some Christian beliefs and rituals before Europeans came to America.

English dominance in warfare cleared the path for advances at the religious level, but Indians accepted or rejected Christianity for a variety of motives that reflected their different historical experiences and political adjustments to a risky colonial world. The first groups to convert were the members of small and weak sachemdoms near Massachusetts Bay Colony who lived closest to the most powerful English settlements. Following these, a series of small sachemdoms around Plymouth Colony, Martha's Vineyard, and Nantucket converted as English colonists settled in their midst. More autonomous sachems such as Philip of Pokanoket, Canonicus, Miantonomi, and Canonchet of the Narragansett, Uncas of the Mohegan, and Ninigret of the Niantic resisted Christianity because it undermined their authority over their subjects. Even after their defeat in King Philip's War, a Narragansett sachem resisted conversion because, he said, Christianity had not made better people of the English and the English themselves disagreed over which denomination was best. The Narragansett, Niantic, and Mohegan remained pagan until the 1740s, when they converted during the New Light stir of the Great Awakening. This revival also reached other Indian congregations in Massachusetts which already had begun or then began to favor Baptist views.

I

One of the first apparent Christian triumphs happened at Plymouth in 1623 when the Pilgrims prayed for almost a day for rain to end a drought that had withered their newly planted fields. Massasoit's ambassador, Hobbamock, watched their services and wondered why they prayed for rain on a sunny, cloudless day. To his amazement, "the Clouds began to rise, and . . . the Raine fell in a most sweet, constant, soaking showre" (*New England's First Fruits* 1643:5). Hobbamock confided to one of the Pilgrims that he "was smitten with terror that he had abused them and their God by his former hard thoughts of them; and resolved from that day not to rest till he did know this great good *God*" (ibid.).[1]

1623

Now I see Englishman's God is a good God, for he hath heard you, and sent you rain, and that without storms and tempests, and thunder, which usually we have with our rain, which breaks down our corn, but yours stands whole and good still; surely your God is a good God.   (Morton [1669] 1826:100)

Eleven years later, in 1634, William Wood observed that the Indians about Massachusetts Bay admired the English God "because they could never yet have power by their conjurations to damnify the English either in body or goods," and also because "they say he is a good God that sends them so many good things, so much good corn, so many cattle, temperate rains, fair seasons, which they likewise are the better for since the arrival of the English, the times and seasons being much altered in seven or eight years, freer from lightning and thunder, long droughts, sudden and tempestuous dashes of rain, and lamentable cold winters" (Wood [1634] 1977:102). Not only did Christians seem to control prosperity, disease, and weather, they also prevailed in war. At the outset of the hostilities that led to their ruin, the confident Pequot announced, "we have one amongst us that if he could kill but one of you more, he would be equall with God, and as the English man's God is, so would hee be" (Underhill [1638] 1902:16). As Captain John Mason's tiny army made its way overland toward the Pequot sanctuary at Mystic in May 1637, his Narragansett allies trembled at the mention of the Pequot sachem Sassacus's name, "saying, he was all one a God, nobody could kill him" (Mather [1702] 1820, 2:481). After the precipitous English victory over the Pequot, some three hundred Niantic warriors suspected of hiding Pequot refugees refused a challenge from forty of Mason's men, saying "they would not Fight with English Men, for they were Spirits" (Mason 1736:20). Wequash, a Pequot or Niantic who lived with the Narragansett and helped the English as a guide in the Pequot War, regretted the impression he had first had of the English and their God before he saw them fight: "before that time he had low apprehensions of our God, having conceived him to be (as he said) but a Musketto [mosquito] God, or a God like unto a flye; and as meane thoughts of the English that served this God, that they were silly weake men; yet from that time he was convinced and perswaded that our God was a most dreadfull God" (New England's First Fruits 1643:11). Wequash had "no rest or quiet because hee was ignorant of the English mans God: he went up and down bemoaning his condition, and filling every place where he came with sighes and groanes" (pp. 11–12). Despite his conversion, Wequash confided to Roger Williams two days before his death that he still feared for his unworthiness in the English God's eyes: "Me so big naughty Heart, me heart all one stone!" (Williams [1643] 1936:A7 recto).

II

Several English families colonized Martha's Vineyard in 1642, a few years after the frightening destruction of the Pequot. Thomas Mayhew tried to be fair in land transactions with local sachems and respected their civil authority over other Indians, while his son

Thomas, Jr., challenged Indian religious leadership and began win-
ning converts. During the 1650s English power grew while Indian
authority waned, and by 1675, when war broke out on the mainland,
the Wampanoag of Martha's Vineyard had already subjected themselves to the English God and king. Although the Mayhews gained
political control by peaceful means, they fought a number of religious duels with Indian shamans, who eventually surrendered to the
Christian God. On one occasion a notable shaman threatened a gathering of converts after religious services. Hiacoomes (the first Indian
convert on Martha's Vineyard) in turn challenged the shaman to as-
semble all his colleagues on the island, and together they should try
to harm Hiacoomes if they could. The shaman is said to have backed
down. Thomas Mayhew, Jr., described the confrontation as he heard
it from Hiacoomes.

1650

*Another thing is a remarkable combate between two Indians and
a Pawwaw, who, on the Lord's day after meeting, came in very
angry, saying, I know the meeting [Christian] Indians are lyars; you
say you care not for the Pawwawes; then calling two or three of
them by name, and railing at them, told them that they were deceived, for the Pawwawes could kill all the meeting Indians if they
did set about it; with that one of the young men replyed with much
courage, saying, it is true, I do not fear the Pawwawes, neither do I
desire any favour at their hands, pray kill me if you can. And
Hiacoomes told him also that he would be in the midst of all the
Pawwawes of the Iland that they could procure, and they should
do their utmost they could against him, and when they did their
worst by their witchcrafts to kill him, he would without feare set
himself against them, by remembring Jehovah; he told him also
that he did put all the Pawwawes under his heel, pointing unto it;
which answers did presently silence the Pawwawes devillish spirit,
and he had nothing to say, but that none but Hiacoomes was able
so to do.*   (Whitfield [1651] 1834a:116)

III

Christians believed they were superior to shamans and invulnerable to their sorcery, which proved to be the case. When the shamans
found that they could not intimidate converts (who could count on
English support) and that the pagan population was losing confidence in their ability to cure the sick, many shamans began to
question the vitality of their own spirit powers. One eminent *pow-*

wow-sachem on Martha's Vineyard, perhaps the same who had challenged the Christian Indians and Hiacoomes after church, converted when his guardian spirit (a snake) failed to injure Hiacoomes.

CIRCA 1650

I can inform of a Converted Sachim; who in his Publick Protestation, said as followeth. Viz. That he having often imployed his god, which appeared to him in form of a Snake, to Kill, Wound, and Lame such whom he intended mischief to, he imployed the said Snake to Kill, and that failing to Wound or Lame Hiacooms the first Convert on Martha's Vineyard; all which proved innefectual, and having seriously considered, the said Hiacoombs Assertion, that none of the Powaw's could hurt him, since his God, whom he now Served was the Great God, to whom theirs was subservient; he resolved to worship the true God, from which time during Seven years, the said Snake gave him great disturbance, but that he never after his Praying to God in Christ, ever imployed that said Snake in any thing, which about that time ceased to appear to him.

(Mayhew 1694:43–44)

IV

The following account, told to Thomas Mayhew, Jr., by a converted shaman, reveals the painful struggle fought within the psyche of an individual convert. This shaman feared to surrender his indigenous spirits and felt them struggling to remain, until he finally resolved his conflicts in favor of Christianity and thereafter found peace. Other shamans felt their bodies tremble uncontrollably at the time they gave up their guardian spirits.

1652

A Pawwaw told me, who was of no small note among the Heathen formerly, and also with the best now he hath forsaken his Pawwawing, That after he had been brought by the Word of God to hate the Devil, and to renounce his Imps (which he did publickly) that yet his Imps remained still in him for some months tormenting of his flesh, and troubling of his mind, that he could never be at rest, either sleeping or waking: At length one time when I went down to keep the farthest Lecture about seven miles off, he asked me some Questions, whereof this was one, viz. That if a Pawwaw had his Imps gone from him, what he should have instead of them to preserve him? Whereunto it was Answered, That if he did beleeve in Christ Jesus, he should have the Spirit of Christ dwelling in him,

*which is a good and a strong Spirit, and will keep him so safe,
that all the Devils in Hell, and Pawwaws on Earth, should not be
able to do him any hurt; and that if he did set himself against his
Imps, by the strength of God they should all flee away like Muskee-
toes: He told me, That he did much desire the Lord, it might be so
with him. He further said, That ever since that very time God hath
in mercy delivered him from them, he is not troubled with any
pain (as formerly) in his Bed, nor dreadful visions of the night, but
through the blessing of God, he doth lie down in ease, sleeps
quietly, wakes in Peace, and walks in safety, for which he is very
glad, and praises God.*　　　　(Eliot and Mayhew [1653] 1834:205–6)

V

While the English God warned the unconverted by means of
storms, disease, and other disasters, Indian gods countered with occasional admonitions to those who departed from customary ways.
One such sign manifested itself in East Haddam, Connecticut, where
for years the English reported "awful" underground tremblings and
sounds, known as the Moodus noises. The Reverend Stephen Hosmore of East Haddam heard of an Indian legend (probably Wangunk
from the western periphery of Mohegan country) that attributed the
noises to an angry Indian god.

1729

*I have been informed that in this place (before the English settle-
ment) there were great numbers of Indian inhabitants, and that
it was a place of extraordinary Indian pawaws, or in short, that it
was a place where the Indians drove a prodigious trade of worship-
ing the devil. Also I was informed that (many years past) an old
Indian was asked what was the reason of the noises in this place,
to which he replied, that the Indian's god was very angry because
English man's God was come here.*　　　　(Hosmore 1895:281)

VI

When the Wampanoag around the area of Yarmouth, Massachusetts, deeded their land to the English in the 1650s, the town permitted the Wampanoag to retain certain tracts until they no longer
needed them. The Indian population declined when many men died
fighting for the English in the French and Indian Wars and, in 1763,
when many more died of smallpox (Swift 1884:168–71). One who
survived, Elisha Nauhaught, was "an exemplary deacon in the little
cluster of wigwams, which were standing as late as 1779, at Indian-

town in Yarmouth" (Alden 1814:238). A Cape Cod tradition tells of an occasion when a group of blacksnakes attacked Deacon Nauhaught and of the unusual way in which he drove them away. Legends convey symbolic meanings as well as actual events but vary in the extent to which they emphasize one or the other. The Nauhaught legend is heavily symbolic as opposed to historic, but we can guess at its meaning through familiarity with Indian shamanistic beliefs, particularly those regarding snakes. One interpretation could be that Nauhaught described a personal moral crisis in such symbolic terms, for both European Christians and Indian converts associated snakes with paganism, backsliding, witchcraft, and other evils. Another interpretation is that Nauhaught was protecting himself from sorcery, which earlier generations attributed to magical snakes.[2] In either case, his story resembles those of earlier Wampanoag shamans of Martha's Vineyard, who talked of spirits as if they were actual creatures that could be seen and touched. One shaman, for example, claimed to have "put it under my feet, and hope to trample it down in the dust with the Devill and *Pawwawnomas* (or Imps) I throw it into the fire, and burn it" (Whitfield [1652] 1834b:186).

1794

In the southeast corner of Yarmouth, nigh the mouth of Bass river, at a place known by the name of Indiantown, was, about twenty years ago, a little cluster of wigwams inhabited by some of the remains of the Pawkunnawkutts. In this village Joseph Nauhaught was a respectable deacon. Several anecdotes, which evince his Christian sentiments, are still related of him. He was an honest, temperate, and pious Indian. While on his death bed the reverend parson visited him, and was highly gratified by his rational Christian conversation. When he was asked if he were willing to die, his reply was, "Oh yes, I have always had a pretty good notion about that." He was perfectly resigned to his situation and approaching dissolution. He used to pray in his family, and occasionally with the sick and at funerals, with primitive fervour in his vernacular tongue.

The following adventure attributed to him is singular, and the result curious.

It seems he was, on a certain time, attacked by a number of large black snakes. Being at a considerable distance from any people, he was to be sure in a very critical and alarming situation. He had not even a knife for his defence; and what to do, he knew not. To outrun them he found utterly impossible, and to keep them off

*without any weapon was equally so. He therefore, stood firm on his
feet as they wound themselves about him. In a little time one of
them had made his way up to the Indian's neck, and was trying to
put his head into his mouth:* Nauhaught *immediately opened it for
him: The black serpent put in his head—and he bit it off in a moment!—As soon as the blood, issuing from the beheaded, was discovered by the rest of the party, they left their intended prey with
great precipitation.*   (Beth. *1794:150–51*)

VII

The Nantucket Indians converted to Christianity by 1675. Their
population declined rapidly from about 3,000 at the time of English
settlement in 1659 to 136 following a smallpox epidemic in 1763–
64. By 1854, Abram Quary, the last Nantucketer of Indian descent,
had died. An early nineteenth-century legend tells of an ogre,
known only as the Evil Spirit, who resisted Indian efforts to settle
on the island. The English author of this text, identified only as
Homtas, learned the legend from his great-grandfather, who was said
to have heard it from an Indian named "*Eaaooptooicoo, Great Medicine of the Western Tribe*" (Homtas 1829:2).[3] The author knew of
Maushop legends, for he mentioned "a great and powerful Chief"
who created the island with pipe ashes. The legend mainly concerns
a conflict between good and evil deities that reflect Christian influence. The Good Spirit prepared Nantucket for human habitation and
invited a sachem from Chappaquiddick Island to move his people
there, then banished the Evil Spirit beneath the earth for resisting
human settlement. The many-headed Evil Spirit with serpent legs is
unique in southern New England Indian folklore and appears to be
a composite of Indian, English, and classical folklore images. Like
Maushop he was great in size and shared the ability to shape the
landscape. In common with shamans he controlled dangerous
snakes that he sent to injure his enemies, and like the Indian god of
East Haddam he expressed anger by causing earthquakes. Many-
headed giants are not known elsewhere in southern New England
but occur in English and Irish legends (F 531.1.2.2 *Many-headed
giant*; G 361.1. *Many-headed ogre*). The giant's snakelike legs could
have been introduced from classical mythology by the three generations of Nantucketers who transmitted the legend from its Indian
source to the nineteenth-century author (F 526.1. *Typhon. Human
down to thighs; coils of vipers below*; F 526.6. *Cecrops. Body compounded of man and serpent*). Two points of historical accuracy
may be noted. As the author suggests, Pootar Pond probably ac-

quired its name from the Massachusett word for whale or for a whale
spouting (Trumbull 1903:132, 343; Williams [1643] 1936:113).
Second, the legend specifies that the wise chief who first settled
Nantucket came from Chappaquiddick, and in fact a seventeenth-
century Chappaquiddick sachem had proprietary rights to the western sachemdom of Nantucket, where the Indian narrator lived (Little
1982b:288; Mayhew 1727:3).

1829

*This Island was formed by the ashes from the pipe of a great and
powerful Chief, many moons before any one lived upon it. The
Great Spirit looked down upon it and beheld it was fertile and
green—he planted the trees and they grew—he made the Deer and
many other animals, and they multiplied exceedingly, and the
land was very fruitful. The Great Spirit then said it is good, behold,
I will give this ground to my Red Children! The father of all our
brethren then lived at Chappequiddic—he was a wise Chief. While
before the great Council Fire of his Tribe, the Great Spirit spoke to
him, in his ear, and said, arise, take thy Squaws, thy Pappooses,
thy skins and canoes, and go out upon the great Lake.—He was a
wise Chief, and arose to prepare to do as he was told. All the Chiefs
of his Tribe, and those of the Tribes around, went with him to the
shore, bidding him farewell, and believing him thus singularly
called from them as a reward for his virtues, and that he was destined by the Great Spirit to inhabit the blessed Hunting Ground
and Prairies of the just. He left them weeping behind; but he wept
not—he sung his Death song willingly—and the mournful echoes
of those noble tones as they floated upon the wide waters, mellowed
by distance and struck their attentive ear, were all that they ever
heard from the great the good and the wise Chief of their brave
devoted Tribes. Soon a darkness enveloped the scene, shut the
view of the land from his sight, and left him to paddle his bark
unaided by any but divine assistance—his voyage continued many
days and then he was cast upon the shore of this Island where his
posterity now remain.*

*He had been here but a short time, when the Evil Spirit rebelled
against the Good Spirit, and fought for the possession of the blessed
Prairies. The battle was long and severe; but the Good Spirit prevailed and they fled—the awful voice and fiery arrows of the Good
Spirit struck the rebellious Chief and he fell prostrate—(he was a
Giant, with many heads and arms, and monstrous serpents instead
of legs)—his fall was upon this Island—the force so great as nearly*

to divide it in halves; making thereby the valley called Matticut-Cham, which extends through the whole Island. Many Indians were killed by the fall, at which the Good Spirit was angry, and sentenced him to an everlasting imprisonment beneath us, chained thereto by the whole weight of the Island resting upon him, since which his motion has several times been felt shaking the Island like an Earthquake.—The monster was angry—so much so that he gnawed off his Legs and sent them [as] Serpents into all parts of the great waters to ravage and perplex the Children of the Great Spirit. One of them found its way from under the Earth into one of the two Ponds situated a little westward from Shoukemmo. He was discovered, and the braves of our tribes embarked in their Canoes in pursuit of the Pootar, as they called him, (which in our language means a Whale or other monster of the water.) When closely pressed he dissappeared and arose in the next Pond; thus baffling their skill for a long time—But our men were braves and our Chiefs wise men:—both Ponds were speedily filled with canoes—the monster was killed—and the place ever after was called Pootar Pond, and is so even to this day! (Homtas 1829)

VIII

Fidelia Fielding (1827–1908) was an extremely traditional Mohegan woman who spoke and wrote in her native language. Her diary (translated and published as "A Mohegan-Pequot Diary"; Speck 1928b) is one of a very few pieces of New England Indian autobiographical writing. Fielding was the last Mohegan speaker and knew many supernatural legends of Little People and other figures which disappeared or barely left a trace in the folklore of other southern New England tribes. Fortunately, she told many of her stories to her grandniece, Gladys Tantaquidgeon, and to Speck. Her diary shows not only her integration of Mohegan and Christian thought but the considerable extent to which traditional concepts had persisted until her time. In the following passage, selected from her entry for May 30, 1904, Fielding referred to God by the Mohegan *Mandu* and to spirit by *dji•bai,* a form of Cheepi or Hobbamock. The conflict between good and evil is represented in miniature in the contest between the fish and the snake, which Fielding helped the fish to win.

1904

Birds. I love to see the birds, because [they are] pretty. They do not say anything evil. They eat these things Mandu gives, then

they sing, because they do not want for anything. All things Mandu
gives [them], that is so. All things! Yesterday I saw in the river a
snake; he had a fish in his mouth. I hit him, then he gave up the
fish. The fish is handsome. The snake is horrid, he bites you, too.
The fish is handsome. I am afraid of the snake, snake is a spirit
[dji•bai].

Mandu *is good because he knows all things. Man does not know*
altogether but a little. . . . Mandu is great, very good, must you
and I be good, too. Then when you will die, you will stay in heaven,
so says Mandu. . . . Thither does not come anything not good, be-
cause Mandu can not take money.   (Speck 1928b:247)

IX

Fielding told Speck a Mohegan legend that resembles the earlier
one from Martha's Vineyard (text II above) in which a shaman challenged Christian Indians after church. In the Mohegan version, however, the shaman prevailed. Fielding probably heard the story from
her grandmother, Martha Uncas (ca. 1759–1859), who raised her.
Since it is unlikely that Martha Uncas lived during the Great Awakening in the 1740s, when the Mohegan and Montauk converted, she
probably inherited the story from her parents' generation, unless
shamans survived longer in this region than is currently known. The
long shrill whistle that announced the shaman's arrival is unprecedented in local Indian or English lore but resembles a European motif (G 303.6.3.5. *Devil's coming heralded by piercing whistle*). Northern New England shamans were known for their overpowering
voices (Speck 1919:276).

CIRCA 1905

They say that the old time Mohegans used to go down the
Thames River and across Long Island Sound in dug out canoes.
They were fond of visiting the Indians over there. So, one time
Martha Uncas, who at that time knew no English and was unac-
quainted with Christianity, being in need of a little rest and recrea-
tion, was carried over to Long Island on a visit.

When they arrived, they found the Islanders, probably Montauks,
gathered at a meeting in a large shelter. The Mohegans went in
and mingled with them, but did not understand the words of the
speaker. He was a Christian and was preaching. Soon he began to
pray, and Martha instead of bowing her head with the rest, gazed
around in curiosity. All at once, a long shrill whistle sounded above
the trees. Upon looking up she beheld a figure which she recog-

*nized as moigu´ [shaman], standing in the doorway, beckoning the
worshippers with his hand to come out. They all arose without a
word and left the meeting, following after the moigu´.*

(Speck 1909:197)

X

Early twentieth-century Mohegans told of a memorable providence in the life of Samuel Ashbow (1718–95), a Mohegan who converted about the same time as Samson Occom. Ashbow became a
Separate/Baptist minister and teacher among the Mohegan and western Niantic, studied with Eleazar Wheelock, and also worked as a
missionary among the Iroquois. Although he went through phases
when he drank heavily, Ashbow was known mainly as a temperate
man. This legend resembles earlier accounts in which the English or
Indian gods sent weather signs to reward their followers or frighten
them into improving their ways. By Ashbow's time the Christian
God had won the war, and only He issued such providences.[4]

CIRCA 1924   THUNDER FROM THE CLEAR SKY

*Now, there was a time when an Indian man was a preacher here.
He was Samuel Ashbow. He was a good man, but his wife was not
a very good woman, being fond of "ankαpi" (rum). For many years
she was thus, and it made poor Ashbow very unhappy.*

*Then there came a certain time when something was going to
happen; when something was going to happen from the sky. The
Indians were helping a white man build a mill over on Stony Brook,
and Ashbow used to go and help too. One time he took his wife
along with him. Ashbow was a good man, but his wife had a bottle
of "ankαpi" hidden in her dress. She began to drink, and gave
some to the other men. Ashbow only watched her a while, but soon
got angry, and taking the bottle from her, threw it on a rock. It
broke and the rum spilled on the earth. The wife became furious,
and a few moments later, while Ashbow was stooping over a stone,
she picked up a piece of rock and struck him on the forehead. He
fell down with the blood streaming from him. Then there was a
sharp clap of thunder from above, and all looked up, only to see a
clear sky with a patch of cloud overhead only as large as a hand. It
was a sign to Ashbow's wife, and from that time she never drank
rum, neither did the other men who heard the thunder. Ashbow got
well.*

(Speck 1928b:277–78)

XI

In a sense, Richard Bourne drove the devil away from his ancient sanctuaries on Cape Cod when Bourne converted the South Sea or Mashpee Indians. Bourne's rival in this legend embodies qualities of the English devil and the Wampanoag culture hero Maushop. Like Maushop the devil was a giant who carried boulders in his apron and was distracted in his work by a small animal (in some cases a crab, but in this case, a chickadee), which caused him to drop the boulders where they can be seen today. The motif, *The devil drops stones from apron* (A 977.3.1.), had been known in Gay Head lore since 1904 and is probably of British origin. Elizabeth Reynard typically combined literary sources (in this case from *The Barnstable Patriot*) with oral accounts from Indian informants. An elderly but unnamed informant remembered the Bourne jingle because she skipped rope to it as a child (Reynard 1934:318). Reynard's narrative is included despite the mixture of oral and published sources because it draws in part on Mashpee oral testimony. Conflict between the minister and the devil is a familiar New England Yankee theme, but the wrestling matches could indicate Indian influence (Fisher 1946:250; Speck 1919:264, 282–83).

1934   HOW THE DEVIL MET A CHICKADEE BIRD

Richard Bourne was the only man that the Devil could never defeat. He was pious-good, and he prayed so hard that when the Devil came down from the north, to wrestle with Richard Bourne at night, the Devil always got the worst of it. Now the Devil was six times the size of Bourne, and the Devil's muscles were as sinewy as a young pine tree. No one ever could understand why he always failed to win. Of course, Old Man Bourne had the Lord on his side, and that gave him the strength of an Angel-being. Yet, sometimes, he was hard put to it, for the Devil was crafty and quick.

Richard Bourne lived in Bourneland; and the Indians, who loved him, crept close to his room at night, when they saw the pine knots burning there, and heard him moan aloud. They knew that he was wrestling with the Evil One, and sometimes his cries were so piteous that the Indians fell on their knees and prayed for him, in the dark by his window-light.

Every evening the Devil came, stepping high from hill to hill to keep his feet out of the bogwater. He had built himself a den in the wastelands of the Lower Province; and there, by day, he waited for the bones of wrecked ships, and tried to seize upon the souls of the departed. When dusk came, and he could no longer watch the destruction of fair vessels, he always bethought him of Richard Bourne, who was having things all his way, and that meant the Lord's way, down in Bourneland. So every twilight the Devil decided to walk up-Cape, and take a little of the godliness out of Old Man Bourne.

It took the Devil many years to realize that Richard Bourne was always going to defeat him, no matter how hard he tried. When, at last, the Evil One understood that his giant's strength was of no avail, he grew crafty, and one evening, as he came from the tip of the Cape to Bourneland, he gathered the stones along the beaches, every stone that he could find, and put them all in his apron. He felt exultant as his load became heavy, for he thought that he had found a way to destroy Richard Bourne.

Just after sundown he reached the forest that lies to the east of Bourneland. There, on a tree, sat a chickadee bird watching the Devil who appeared against the sky like a great black eagle, hurrying over the hills. The chickadee waited until the laden Devil was close to the tree on which it perched. Then it opened its beak and sang a song:

> 'Howdy, Giant,
> Howdy, Devil,
> You're gonna wressle
> With Richard Bourne.
> You're gonna git
> The worst of it.
> You're gonna git
> The worst of it.'

The Devil was furious with that bird. He lost his temper entirely, and took a rock from his apron and threw it after the chickadee. But the chickadee flew straight up from the tree and was not hurt at all. As it flew it sang again, till the song echoed through the forest:

> 'Howdy, Giant,
> Howdy, Devil,
> You're gonna wressle
> With Richard Bourne.
> You're gonna git
> The worst of it.
> You're gonna git
> The worst of it.'

The Devil could not endure such contempt. He started to run
after the chickadee bird, and stumbled on a root and fell. His
apron-string broke, and the stones rolled out. There they lie, in
Bourneland, to this day. Look high, look low, there are no stones on
the Nauset beaches, or in Truro, or in the Province Dunes. They
were all brought to Bourneland in the Devil's apron and spilled
there when the apron-string broke. As for the Devil, he knew when
he was thoroughly defeated, and, after that, never came back to
wrestle with Richard Bourne. He went to the lonesome tip of the
Cape; sat down there; waited for the bones of wrecked ships, and
tried to seize upon the souls of sailors who washed up on the shore.
(Reynard 1934:38–39)

XII

By the 1930s, when this material was recorded, Richard Bourne
had become a Mashpee culture hero. Reynard did not identify her
sources other than to attribute them to "oral tradition, Mashpee"
(Reynard 1934:320). The contest between Bourne and the Indian
shaman includes Indian and English motifs. By miring Bourne's feet
in quicksand the shaman may have been performing an indigenous
feat, for Penobscot shamans thrust their opponents' feet into the
ground during magical warfare (Prince 1899:182, 185; Speck 1919:
264). Bargaining with the shaman or the devil is reminiscent of a
widespread motif in English and American folklore that had appeared in Gay Head legend as early as 1904 (M 210. Bargain with
devil). The white dove that rescues Bourne from the shaman's magic
comes from European as well as Indian sources. The dove is important in European folk belief as a symbol of purity and a messenger
from heaven and is capable of warding off evil and disease (Ward
1981:355; B 457.1. Helpful dove). In this text the dove also resembles
the crab and chickadee that foiled Maushop and the devil in other
legends from this general area. The explanatory motif for the origin
of cranberries is an Indian touch, consistent with a twentieth-
century Gay Head belief that cranberries came from a divine source
(Neesqutton 1935:188).

1934

He [Richard Bourne] met a Witch Doctor by a river, and solicited
Christian conversion. The angry magician chanted a bog-rhyme
and Richard's feet became rooted in quicksand. With all his
strength he could not stir. "Let us have a contest of wits," said he.
"If I lose I agree to serve you. If I win, you shall release me and

trouble me no more." The Medicine Devil agreed to this, so for fifteen days and fifteen nights they discoursed by the river. The tide swam up; the tide swam down; the sun climbed over Nauset sea, and paused for a while on the top of the sky to hearken to their wisdom. Still Richard Bourne and the Witch Devil argued by the river. The Medicine Man began to feel empty, like an air-full reed. He swayed where he stood; but Richard Bourne was as firm on his feet as when the contest began. Every now and then, while the Witch Doctor spoke, taking his turn at showing what he knew, a white dove flew down from Heaven and laid a round, red berry on the lips of Richard Bourne. Once the dove let go his burden "one sand-dropping" of the hour-glass too soon. The berry rolled to the edge of the bank and caught in the river mud. Then the Witch Doctor saw what the dove was doing and tried to lay his spells on it. But the bird flew past, merry as a song, and came and went, giving sustenance to the White Sachem and none to the Heathen Witch.

By and by the Medicine Devil could stand upon his legs no longer, so he laid him down on the ground. The minute that he stepped off his feet, Richard Bourne could walk again, and went at once to his house to fetch a bowl of wild turkey soup. Before he took one taste off the ladle, he offered the bowl to the fainting witch who put his lips to the rim and drank till all the soup was gone. Now that bowl, made of pure silver, shone inside as bright as a mirror, and in the bottom of it, when the last drop of soup was drained away, the Medicine Devil saw reflected all Damnation and the Judgment of Sinners. He fell on his knees, and the good White Sachem blessed him and taught him how to become a loyal Christian Brave.

Meanwhile the berry that the dove let fall grew and fattened by the river. Finding it there, the Cape men knew there was truth in the story that the cranberry came down from Heaven in the beak of a winging dove.   (Reynard 1934:83–84)

XIII

Besides tormenting shamans on Martha's Vineyard and Deacon Nauhaught in the Cape Cod woods, snakes also invaded a small Wampanoag church at Herring Pond in the eastern part of Plymouth. The antiquarian Betsey D. Keene, who published this legend, did not identify her oral sources, who presumably lived in the Herring Pond Indian community. The belief that the devil attacks churches with storms is well known in English folklore, but to do so with blacksnakes adds a local Indian element to the story.

1934

Later a small meetinghouse was built on the top of a hill overlooking the waters of Herring Pond. But, because black snakes,
numerous in those days, enjoyed the new church-on-the-hill and
persisted in staying inside, twisting and squirming around the
beams and rafters, the Indian worshippers finally abandoned the
building and made plans for another.   (Keene [1937] 1975:213)

XIV

The Mohegan, Massachusett, Wampanoag, and Narragansett produced generations of respected preachers who gave political as well
as moral leadership to their people. According to Narragansett legend, the preacher Peter Noka prayed forcefully enough to save a
sinking ship. Although an anonymous Narragansett author attributed Noka's deliverance to his moral stature, earlier shamans (or
even Increase and Cotton Mather) would have admired his feat.

1936   THE SHIP THAT NEVER MADE PORT

Peter Noka (and may his soul rest in peace) was a big and mighty
man of much muscle, but 'tis told of him, that he found it easier to
pray away his difficulties, than to use his muscle. Peter was a jolly
good preacher, but also a good seaman, as were many Narragansetts who lived along the seacoast.

One stormy night when Peter was rounding Cape Horn on a
schooner bound for 'Frisco, the gale blew so, the ship began to
loose piece by piece. The Captain shouted orders, the men ran to
and fro. Some were even washed overboard, and all were sore
afraid. Peter was asked to take the wheel, but first he knelt and
prayed aloud, "Master, the tempest is raging! Speak to the winds
and the waves, as you did on Galilee! Calm our troubled seamen,
as you did the desciples of old, etc."

The story has oft been repeated how the ship sailed into a lull,
and was calm aboard. They made port safely a few weeks after;
and here, after some disagreement with Peter, the Captain
discharged him; sailed off leaving Peter stranded in San Francisco,
so far from his native Rhode Island. Many of the men who believed
in Peter, begged the captain not to leave him; but the captain was
hard and resented the credit the men gave Peter for saving the ship
by prayers.

So the ship sailed on without him, but it never made port again.
Peter after many years finally reached the Narragansett country
and lived to preach many more good sermons.

("Fireside Stories" 1936:208)

Indian narrators wove elements of English and Indian cultural traditions into their legends about Christianity. The English represented their conversion efforts as God's warfare with Satan, and Indians may have interpreted these same events as magical contests between shamans to see who had the greater power. Both sides attributed significance to signs and providences (particularly pertaining to weather, warfare, and health) as indicators of victory or defeat, and they agreed upon the meanings of many particular signs. Christian and especially missionary themes have not been important in Indian legend since the 1930s, when the last texts were recorded. In the following half century, as the southern New England tribes asserted their political and cultural identity, the tribes also embraced the Indian sources of their complex heritage. Thus, for example, the indigenous culture hero Maushop enjoyed a revival in folklore, and missionaries such as Richard Bourne, who were associated with the demise of Indian culture, receded into the background. Around this time also, the New England Indians began to refer to God in such Indian terms as the Great Spirit and *manitou*.[5] Today, even the most devout Indian Christians speak of bygone traditions with mournfulness, not as threatening or evil things to be destroyed. In fact, the modern role of "medicine man," a vestige of ancient shamanism, is a respected leadership role in contemporary tribal organizations.

6 Shamans and Witches

Recollections of early shamans survived in legends for many years after Christian conversion, and some aspects of shamanistic practice, such as herbalism, curing, and sorcery, persisted into the present century. By the early twentieth century, when most witchcraft texts were recorded, English, African, and American motifs had freely mixed with native tradition. Witchcraft narratives increased during the years of rapid change and powerlessness in the early twentieth century and subsided with the Indian cultural and political revival in the 1930s.[1]

I

The Reverend Samuel Lee of Bristol, Rhode Island, collected some of the earliest postconquest shamanistic lore. He noted that the shaman's familiar spirits included crows, rattlesnakes, and hawks and that shamans could injure their enemies with herbal preparations (Kittredge [1690–91] 1913:151–52).[2] Not many years later John Winthrop heard a legend of a Cape Cod shaman who sent a rattlesnake to bite an enemy on Naushon Island. This legend also provides an explanatory motif for the origin of rattlesnakes on the island.

1702

The Indians relate a story that a Powow which lived at Moniment Bay before the English came over to the Nothun America meting

*with some affront from the Indians that inhabited Naushauna
Island out of Revenge got the Devell to throw over a Rattle snake
which increased much and soon after a squaw was bit by one.*

(Emerson 1935:166)

II

The Mohegan minister Samson Occom described Montauk shamanism while he lived among the Montauk as a schoolteacher in
1761. Occom based his account on recent memory rather than current practice, for the Montauk had converted about nineteen years
earlier. Clearly Occom believed in the reality and efficacy of Indian
spirits.[3]

1761

*As for the Powaws, they say they get their art from . . . the devil,
but then partly by dreams or night visions, and partly by the devil's
immediate appearance to them by various shapes; sometimes in
the shape of one creature, sometimes in another, sometimes by
a voice . . . and their poisoning one another, and taking out poison,
they say is no imaginary thing, but real. I have heard some say,
that have been poisoned, it puts them into great pain, and when a
powaw takes out the poison they have found immediate relief. . . .
And I don't see for my part, why it is not as true, as the English or
other nation's witchcraft, but is a great mystery of darkness.*

(Occom 1809:109)

III

We encounter nothing new on the topic of sorcery until the early
twentieth century, when Mary Vanderhoop published this legend of
the last witch to die at Gay Head and when Frank Speck began his
inquiries with Fielding and other elders at Mohegan. The Gay Head
witch, Patience Gashum, had a long afterlife in Gay Head folklore,
for she appears again as Patience Gershom in the Tantaquidgeon
texts collected in 1928 (texts XXI and XXII below). Patience Gashum's startling deathbed experiences most closely resemble those of
earlier Martha's Vineyard converts described by Experience Mayhew. He observed in the early eighteenth century, "Thus it seems it
is wont to be when Persons are drawing nigh to Death, the Devils do
then make an Assault on them. . . . the House is filled with them"
(Mayhew 1727:58). In the cases described by Mayhew, the devils
assaulted godly people who, as a sign of their godliness, fought the
devils off. Although Patience Gashum also struggled violently to

drive them away, Gay Headers doubt that she succeeded. Gashum was not the last Wampanoag herbalist but apparently was the last one believed to use her knowledge for evil ends. The herbal explosion is unprecedented in Indian and English witchcraft lore in this area, but the Gay Head people knew how to interpret it.

1904

Near Nab Terry's grave lies Patience Gashum, an Indian herbwoman, who is said to have been very wicked. A watcher at her death-bed, a woman who had seen many die, said it was the first time she had ever been frightened upon such an occasion. Patience held in her hand some long, slender whips with which she violently cut the air, saying she saw the devil coming for her. "There he is" she would cry loudly and then ply her whip savagely. After her death many of her herbs were gathered up and thrown in the fire. This action was followed by a violent explosion and a loud report. Of course the superstitious natives attributed this result to the woman's wickedness; but, whatever the true cause, it is a fact that with the passing of the soul of this wretched gatherer of herbs the practice of the black art among Gay Head Indians died.

(Vanderhoop 1904:July 30)

IV

Frank G. Speck's distillation of shamanistic beliefs and legends portrays the end product of the tradition described by Occom in 1761 and includes some new information and interesting survivals. The early twentieth-century Mohegan word for shaman, moigū´, has not appeared in any other southern New England source; how it differs from the more widely used *powwow* is not clear. Israel Freeman's magical ability to quiet dogs is an old shamanistic trait in this area, for Cotton Mather reported that Indian shamans in King Philip's War also had this power over dogs (Mather [1702] 1820, 1:506).

CIRCA 1904

By putting together the fragments of knowledge which the Indians possess, it is possible to form at least some idea of Mohegan shamanism and personal magic. The shaman, or witch, as he or she is commonly called, is termed moigū´ (animate plural, moígū-waq). Any person who is believed to have communication with supernatural powers is referred to by this word. Such persons, being inclined to malicious actions, were generally feared and avoided in the later days, owing to their supposed relations with the Devil. How witchcraft is acquired is not known, but a wizard is not long in being found out by his magic. Witches are remembered chiefly for having been able to transport themselves instantaneously from place to place, to achieve various desires by special individual magic, to concoct charms for various purposes to cast spells over persons, animals and things, and correspondingly to remove them at will, and also to effect the cure of disease by the use of herb medicines which they knew. Also any peculiar occurrences and uncanny noises not thoroughly understood, were attributed to them, when not ascribed to a ghost (jībai´). It is commonly asserted at Mohegan that the times of the witches or shamans, is past; that, since the Indians have taken up Christianity, the witches have gone off to the heathen where they still flourish and cause evil. Several witches, however, seem to have developed, within the last two or three generations, and died mysteriously.

About the last one at Mohegan was Israel Freeman. He claimed to have cured many complaints and, on the other hand, was thought to be responsible for much affliction. He had two good-looking wives, but became jealous of them and rendered them hideous as a punishment by turning up their eyelids so that they remained permanently disfigured. This may have been a survival of the custom of mutilation for adultery. A remedy of Freeman's for warts was to rub the warts with bean leaves, and throw them away without looking to see where they went. Dogs always growled and snarled at Freeman, but he could quiet them by pointing at them with a handful of weeds.   (Speck 1909:195–96)

V

Either Fidelia Fielding or James Rogers told Speck a legend about a man who planted antlers on his fiancée's forehead which required a shaman's medicine to remove. Although the motif Magic horns (D 992.1.) appears in no other southern New England source and shows the influence of European beliefs about cuckolds who grow horns, this incident nevertheless appears to be a survival of early Mohegan lore (F 545.2.2. Horns on forehead; H 425.2. Horns grow on cuckold).[4]

1904   WHY LOVERS SHOULD NEVER BECOME JEALOUS

A young Mohegan man and girl were very much in love with each other. The older people would say,—

"Ah, k'numshni! Look at that! They are very happy."

One day the young man shot a deer. He brought it to his loved

one and laid it in her house. *Now he suddenly became jealous.*
Well, the reason is not known. Then he seized the horns of the deer
and rushed up to her. He pressed them upon her forehead.
    Now they grew there, and no one could get them off her head.
They were going to grow right through the top of the wigwam. So
her family became very anxious. Then they sent for the shaman.
He brought a magic oil and rubbed it on the joints of the horns.
Soon these joints began to crack, and then they dropped off.
    The young man went away from that town, but never came back.
The girl's head was all right.   (Speck 1904b:184)

VI

Fielding narrated a witchcraft story in Mohegan which Speck
translated into English. It is the only legend in this collection to have
been recorded in an Algonquian language. The figure of the Indian
woman traveling with her basket filled with brooms is typical of
southern New England in the historic period, when Indians commonly made an income by selling such homemade wares about the
countryside.[5] Although the witch is a white woman, her feat of
transforming the house into stone may have been an indigenous
motif, for it was known in Seneca folklore (D 471.2. *Transforma-*
tion: house to stone). English witches, like the woman in this legend,
also were known to change food into cattle dung (Baughman G
265.8.1.1[b]. *Witch turns flour into manure, then turns the manure*
back to flour).

1904

An old Indian woman goes to sell brooms at New London (Conn.).
It becomes very dark. Where is she going to stay? She sees a house.
She thinks, "Perhaps I can stay there tonight." I go rap! rap! on
the door. A white woman comes and opens the door. I know her.
She says, "Come in"; she smiles. I say, "Can I stay here tonight?"
The white woman says, "Yes! Are you not hungry? I made some
bread and cheese, can you eat some?" "I am not hungry tonight. I
will eat if I live in the morning." The white woman says, "You must
not say that you saw me here." (She did not wish it to be known
that she was a witch.)
    Then I put down my back-basket, and then I lie down. I go to
sleep. Early I arise. There is nothing (to be seen) of the house; it is
all a great stone. Then I find my bread and cheese (to be) a great
cold piece of cattle dung and a white bone. Horrors!
                                        (Speck 1904a:470)

VII

One of Speck's informants, probably Fielding or Rogers, recounted a fight that took place in 1645 when a large party of Narragansetts under their sachem Pessicus attacked Uncas's stronghold at Fort Shantok above the west bank of the Thames River.[6] Some shamans, including the Narragansett in this story, were thought to be invulnerable to arrows or bullets, but a Mohegan shaman knew how to enchant a bullet to penetrate such invisible armor. This legend indicates the survival of seventeenth-century Mohegan belief.

CIRCA 1905

When the Narragansett had landed on Shantic Point and taken up their position of siege, it looked to the Mohegan as though they were to lose; for the enemy outnumbered them. Now, there was one Narragansett who had climbed a certain tree not far off, where, by means of his elevation he could command an advantageous view of the Mohegan behind their palisades. From his perch he directed a destructive fire into them, adding insult and raillery to his attacks. "Are you hungry?" he would ask in taunting tones. In order to remove such an obnoxious element from their view, the best of the Mohegan marksmen engaged in trying to bring him down, but without result. His abusiveness increased as their shots failed to touch him. Then they concluded that he was a moigū´. At length, a Mohegan, who possessed power equal to that of the Narragansett, appeared and ordered the others to desist. Taking a bullet from his pouch he swallowed it. Straightway it came out of his navel. He swallowed it again and it came out of his navel. Again he did it with the same result. Now he loaded his rifle with the charmed ball and taking aim, fired at the man in the tree. The Narragansett dropped out of the branches, dead. (Speck 1909:196)

VIII

The following story about a black man and several witches hints of George Foster's "image of limited good" (Foster 1967:122–30). The legend depicts a world in which money and other goods are scarce and those who obtain them are suspected of doing so at the expense of others. The "image of limited good" is linked to witchcraft because those who benefit from another's loss often are said to do so by supernatural means. That people are poor because someone mysteriously deprives them of their due is a common belief in economically marginal village communities. The contents of this legend reveal little that is identifiably Indian, but some likely borrowings from African and European beliefs are apparent. For example, the gathering of witches who meet to share their spoils is reminiscent of Senegambian witch lore (Simmons 1971:96–101; 1980:455). The Mohegan narrators (probably Fielding or Rogers) associate witch-craft with a schoolhouse, which may have represented change and the repression of Indian language and culture.[7]

CIRCA 1905

In the olden times no one could keep anything. The witches stole nearly everything, even money. Then, when they had taken the things, they had to divide them in shares for each. On one occasion, they entered a schoolhouse. A black man got in there before them and hid himself in the place where the ashes from the grate are put. Then along came the witches. They did not know that the man was in the building. So they started to divide the money, and hand-ing each one his share, they said, "This is yours. This is yours." And so on. Now the black man jumped up from the ashes. "Where is mine!" he shouted. The witches, seeing such a sight as the black man all besmeared with ashes before them, ran away in confusion. So the black man had all the money. (Speck 1909:197)

IX

As in the previous text about a man who stole the witches' money, another trickster-like black man gets the better of witches, who are depicted as white people. The motifs of persons becoming stranded by forgetting the witches' formula and witches passing through key-holes are British and Anglo-American (G 249.7.; Baughman G 242.7[e].). Flying great distances in an instant is both an Indian and European motif.

CIRCA 1905

Two men lived together in a house and had a black man to work for them. They were very strange people. Once the black man over-heard some strange things going on in their room, and being curi-ous to know about them, peeked in through the keyhole. There he saw his mistresses standing near a big tub of water in the center of the room. In the bottom of the tub was an animal's jawbone. Now one of the women got into the tub and repeated the following words "in the keyhole, through the keyhole." Immediately she disappeared. Then the other woman got into the tub and said the same, and she vanished too. Now the man thought they must be witches, so being a curious man, he went in and got into the tub.

He repeated the words he had heard them say, and the next thing he knew, he was over in England. He found himself in a crowded street. People were going in and out of the shops. It was London. Thinking that he had better have something bracing, he bought a bottle of rum. He soon saw his mistresses in the street, but was afraid to meet them. They would be angry with him. Pretty soon he thought that he had better be going home. So he tried to recollect the words he had heard. But he could not recall them, try as he would. He never could think of them again. He must be there now.

(Speck *1909:198*)

X

Speck's informants spoke of an old woman at Mohegan who had a grudge against a man and was suspected of bewitching his cattle. The man shot with a silver bullet a goose that was bothering the cattle; the next day the woman appeared with a wounded arm, thus proving that she had bewitched the cattle while transformed into a goose. Witches who cause illness among cattle are widespread in British and Anglo-American folklore (Baughman G 265.4.2.1.; Dorson 1973:43–44; Kittredge [1929] 1972:163–73). Although transformation into an animal is common in Indian, Afro-American, and Anglo-American belief, the witch in the form of a goose is specifically known in England (G 211.3.3. *Witch in form of goose [gosling]*). Accounts of using silver bullets to kill witches abound in English and American legend. The closest example concerns a Yankee woman, Granny Mott, who lived in Westerly, Rhode Island, around 1740.[8] One of her neighbors, annoyed by a flock of heath hens, tried but failed to shoot them; finally he loaded his musket with a silver bullet, killed their leader, and soon learned that Granny Mott was about to die (Denison 1878:165). Although death by a silver bullet is surely a European element, Speck attested that Penobscot shamans who transformed themselves into animals could be killed by killing their animal familiar (Speck 1919:251–52).

CIRCA 1905

A long time ago a woman had a grudge against a man who owned some fine cattle. Soon after, the man noticed that something was bothering the herd. At night, they would not sleep and so became greatly run down. He sat up one night to watch. He saw a goose come into the yard and bewitch the cattle. Having a gun loaded, he fired, but the goose flew away unharmed. This was repeated several nights, until at last he loaded the piece with a silver bullet and wounded the goose in the wing. The next day the old woman who

*had the grudge against him was found to have a badly wounded
arm. By that they knew that she was a witch who took the form of a
goose.*   (Speck 1909:197–98)

XI

This Mohegan story about a woman who rode her black hired man
as a horse hints of economic or sexual exploitation and possibly of
punishment for some unspecified offense. The witch rider motif (G
241.2. *Witch rides on person*) is widespread in British, Anglo-
American, and Afro-American legend (Jones 1982:92; Kittredge
[1929] 1972:219; Puckett [1926] 1968:151–53; Rickels 1979). One Rebecca Sims, an English woman who lived in Westerly around 1800,
also had a reputation for witch riding: "One man averred that she
had often visited him in the night-watches, and putting her witch-
bridle upon him, had ridden him great distances as a horse, greatly
to his fatigue and suffering" (Denison 1878:166).

CIRCA 1905

*There was another woman around here who had a black man to
work for her. Every morning when he woke up he found that he
was as tired as though he had been working hard all night. He tried
every way to get rest, but in spite of it all, he couldn't. Nobody
knew what to make of it until one night some person saw that
woman riding as though on horseback, at breakneck speed through
the country. When the person looked closer he saw that she was
riding on the back of the black man, and he was bridled and sad-
dled like a saddle horse. That was how they found out that she was
a witch.*   (Speck 1909:198)

XII

A curious Gay Head legend explains that the origin of kinky hair
among Indians is due to witchcraft. The possibility of Afro-American ancestry has been a sensitive issue in this and other New England Indian communities, particularly in the twentieth century
when individuals identified more consciously with their Indian heritage. Gloria Levitas observes that "the Gay Head Indians are often
described by native islanders as 'straight-haired' or 'kinky-haired'
and they themselves often make the distinction in the heat of disputes or arguments" (Levitas 1980:391).[9]

1908   SNARLY HAIRED INDIANS

*It seems that a hundred years or so ago the Indians were all
straight haired, but a certain squaw got into bad company consort-*

ing much with witches and other adepts of the black art. Her curiosity, however, finally led her too far, and there came a time when she saw more than her friends thought good, whereupon the witches clawed her hair over her eyes and snarled it all up, and ever after the race has been snarly haired.   (Hine 1908:196)

XIII

We first hear of Betsy Dodge in 1926, when Edward Burgess published a series of Gay Head legends that he had collected over his lifetime. Burgess does not indicate when he heard this story, but since his and Tantaquidgeon's informants knew Betsy Dodge, it probably originated in the latter half of the nineteenth century. With her backbaskets, she appeared even then as an unusually traditional Indian woman. The notions that a witch travels quickly and that a sympathy exists between a witch and her footprint are consistent with English, Afro-American, and Indian belief.

1926

Gay Head's most lively memory of a backbasket now, is that of another one that was . . . borne by a woman, plodding home right where we stand; old Betsey Dodge, a niece it is said of John Occooch. She lived in his house after him, and though bent and seemingly feeble, moved rapidly about Gay Head, beneath her well-filled backbasket, so fast that everybody said she must be a witch; none but a witch could move so; "Yes," said one, "when I was a little girl with mother once, driving home, we overtook Betsey bent so under her backbasket that we were sorry and said, 'Let us take it for you, we have room in the wagon.' So we did, and hurried on; but pretty quick, there she was, walking right beside us again, so fast she came; I never saw any one move so quick."

"And I," said another, "when I was a boy and I heard that she was a witch, I said, 'How can you prove it?' and they told me, if you can find a witch's footstep where she has walked, and you follow and step in it, she will turn right around and look you in the eye. So I did next time I saw her pass, and no sooner had I put my feet in her footprints than I saw her turn round, though she was far up now on yonder hill; there she turned round, and she looked me in the eye."   (Burgess [1926] 1970:33)

XIV

Indian folk healers served Indian and white clients during the colonial and postcolonial periods. An early historian of Natick ob-

served that the town once teemed with Indian physicians and doc-
tresses, one of whom, Joshua Bran, "was the most celebrated in his
day" (Biglow 1830:12–13). In the 1920s Matthias Amos, Jr., of Mashpee was "well known even among the white people on the Cape as
a remarkable physician, who employed only the traditional Indian
lore of herbs and simples" (Hutchins 1979:136). As recently as 1928,
when Gladys Tantaquidgeon began her field research at Gay Head, a
number of Wampanoag women still practiced herbal cures. Rachel
Ryan was careful to inform Tantaquidgeon that her deceased aunt,
Tamson Weeks, used her knowledge only to heal, which she did by
expelling the spirit Cheepi from the patient's body.

CIRCA 1928

*While the medicinal properties of many of the plants were quite
generally known, there were, it is said, certain of the old women
who were more adept in the art of preparing and administering the
medicines. I am most fortunate in being able to quote one, Mrs.
Rachel Tauknot Ryan, who spent the greater part of her early life
with several such practitioners. Mrs. Ryan's mother and her aunts,
Tamson Weeks and Esther Howossowee, were herb-doctors of great
renown, both on the islands and on the mainland. The teachings of
those women have been handed down to posterity through individuals considered by them worthy of the right to minister to their
kindred.*

*The cures were regarded to be, to a certain extent, secret property.
The women went out at odd times to places where desired roots
and plants grew, when others would not know of their whereabouts.
Mrs. Ryan does the same, but gives as the reason the desire to
protect plants from being gathered wastefully. In connection with
the preparation of roots and herbs to be used for medicinal purposes, there are certain rules which must be observed in order to
preserve the potent properties of the plants and to cause the remedy to effect a cure. The plants must not be gathered during "dog
days," but just prior to that period. It is believed that the sun is
a great healer and strengthener, therefore plants and roots to be
used for medicine should be dried in the sun. When gathering
bark, only the inner bark is taken. No metal should be used in the
preparation of roots and herbs; they must be pounded or crushed
between two stones or beaten in a small wooden mortar made especially for that purpose.*

*Here, as on the mainland, we note the predominance of the single
herb remedies and the absence of magic and ritual. My informant*

said that Tamson Weeks attributed the cause of disease to the presence of a "tcipai" in the system, and when called in to treat a
case, she always assured the victim of complete recovery as soon
as it was removed. However, she is known to have resorted to herbal remedies only in expelling the "tcipai" from her patients.

(Tantaquidgeon 1930b:16–18)

XV

Tantaquidgeon compiled a biographical sketch, from unnamed
oral sources, of William Perry, a prominent herbalist and healer of
the Wampanoag community in Fall River, Massachusetts. The Mashpee, Herring Pond, and Fall River Wampanoag all knew Perry's reputation, and white families also called on him for help. Perry's
method of divining illness through the client's fingernails has not
been mentioned in any source pertaining to Indians in this area, but
comparable beliefs are known elsewhere in the northeastern United
States (Hand, Casetta, and Thiederman 1981:1688–89). Tantaquidgeon noted that Perry owed some of his powers to the diminutive
spirit Granny Squannit and ended the biography with a hint that
Perry was something more than mortal.

1928   DR WILLIAM PERRY

One of the most noted herbalists among the Massachusetts Indians was Dr. William Perry of the Fall River Band. He travelled
among the people performing miraculous cures and he was well
known not only in Massachusetts but also among the Indians of
Rhode Island and Connecticut. Frequently he was called upon to
minister to a number of white families.

Dr. Perry was a psychic and a practitioner of the old school of
Massachusetts Indian belief attributing his success to the power
and guidance of the Great Spirit through the agency of Granny
Squannit. His cures were secret and he never told what herbs he
used. He could go out mid night and dig up King and Queen root
or any plant which he needed to make medicine for a patient. One
time when he was riding down to Mashpee from Sandwich with
Dorias Coombs, when they were passing along a thickly wooded
section Dr. Perry said "Stop a minute." Mr. Coombs stopped and Dr.
Perry got out and went into the woods. In a few minutes he
returned holding up a plant and said "I've been wanting this plant
for a long time."

His method of determining the nature of the malady from which
a person was suffering was to look at his finger nails through a

glass. Sometimes he could sense the trouble without seeing the person. He is described as being a quiet, sensitive type of person with a strong aversion to things of a worldly character. One time he had been treating a patient in one of the Indian homes on the Cape and during the evening several men and boys came in and were indulging in rather boisterous talk. Dr. Perry was in a meditative mood and sat with the palms of his hands over his eyes. He finally told the mother of the patient that he must be off to the "pine tree" where something awaited him. It was late, but he insisted upon going where he could find solitude and obtain the gift which he felt was ready for him at the "pine tree." (Evidently Dr. Perry had placed the customary food sacrifice offering near a pine tree for Granny Squannit and he was going back to get the plant which he desired).

On one occasion a boy had become ill and was losing his mind. Several doctors had been called in on the case but they were unable to cure the boy. Dr. Perry appeared after the boy's mother had expressed a desire to have him see her child. She knew that Dr. Perry was far away and it would be impossible to reach him. He said that he knew of the trouble and right away started back to Herring Pond. The sick boy sat up in bed constantly casting out an imaginary line and catching fish. When Dr. Perry looked at him, he remarked, "You won't catch many more fish, my boy." Dr. Perry went out into the back yard and returned shortly with some roots which he had dug up. He prepared the roots and made a strong tea which he administered to the boy who fell into a deep sleep. After several hours, the boy awakened and called for his mother. He said, "Where have I been." His mental and physical condition were normal and he had no more trouble.

The daughter of a white family was suffering from tuberculosis and several doctors and specialists had been called in to treat her but she was steadily becoming worse. Her father in desperation decided to ask Dr. Perry to look at his daughter and offer treatment. Dr. Perry visited the girl and lamented the fact that she had been allowed to endure so much suffering. He told her parents that he could help her and that before long she would be out riding her fine horse. This seemed improbable but Dr. Perry administered some herb medicine and in a short time the girl was feeling stronger. After a while he ordered her to sit up and then in a few days she was out of doors. She made rapid progress under his care. . . .

Dr. Perry died about 1885 but he will ever live in the memory of

his Indian descendants for the great work of healing which he
did among the people of the period in which he lived.
     It was said that Dr. Perry was a wizard and following his death
the violin which he owned could never be tuned and played again.

(Tantaquidgeon 1928)

XVI–XXIV

Tantaquidgeon wrote that one Gay Head witch "could transform
herself into a bear at will; another took the form of a bird or a white
feather when she wished to pry into the affairs of others; and some
simply annoyed the members of the community by their presence
and harmless pranks." Others, she noted, "were known to have
employed roots in their malevolent practices" (Tantaquidgeon
1930b:26). Texts XVI through XXIV from Tantaquidgeon's interviews
with Rachel Ryan provide detailed insight into Wampanoag witchcraft belief. The accounts probably pertain to the late nineteenth
century, for Patience Gershom, as we have seen, was already a legend
by 1904. The incidents attributed to witchcraft, such as startled
horses, peculiar birds, and a fire that would not light, in earlier days
would have been explained as caused by manitos or spirits. Here
they are seen as evidence of malevolence on the part of Indian community members, particularly elderly women. We observe in these
texts a dynamic known elsewhere in small-scale communities that
are changing and losing autonomy; people blame misfortunes on the
ill will of others who are near at hand. Such beliefs provide sanctions for peculiar or antisocial behavior but mainly serve to displace
frustration onto those more vulnerable than one's self, usually elderly marginal women.
     Most motifs in these legends could be either Anglo-American or
Indian in origin (G 211.2.1. Witch in form of bear; G 211.4. Witch in
form of wild bird; G 249.3. Witch enters and leaves house by chimney; G 265.6.3. Witch causes horse to behave unnaturally). As early
as 1660 an English woman in Massachusetts testified that a neighbor's wife appeared to her in the shape of a bear, which suggests that
English folk-belief was friendly to the survival of such beliefs among
Indians (Freeman 1869:200). Afro-American motifs could also have
influenced these Gay Head stories, for the notion that one can immobilize witches by sticking objects in their footprints, transform
one's self, create image magic with tar babies, and place medicine in
someone's path to injure them occur also in Afro-American folklore
(Baughman G 273.7. Objects driven into tracks of witch immobilize
witch; Puckett [1926] 1968:39–41, 149, 156, 222–23, 228).

The first text describes a common situation in Old and New England where a traveler asks to spend the night and the host feels obliged to comply. As this custom died out with modernization and the disappearance of small interdependent communities, persons who turned away passersby sometimes felt guilty and thereafter suspected the traveler of causing misfortune and even practicing witchcraft. For example, my great-grandfather, Byron Fenner of Cranston, Rhode Island, lost his farmhouse in a fire and believed it had been caused by a traveler whom he had refused to accommodate many years before. The suspected witch in Ryan's story was not turned away, but neither was she given a bed.

Rachel Ryan mentioned Aunt Esther Howwoswee (ca. 1796– 1883), a Gay Head woman known throughout southeastern Massachusetts as an herbalist and midwife. Although Aunt Esther was not suspected of witchcraft, she had the ability to see through a witch's disguise. Betsy Dodge's reputation for witchcraft seems to date to around the 1870s.

XVI
1928   WITCH STORY

Years ago there were many people who had studied the art and were in league with the Devil. There were some who handled poisonous roots too. One of the women who used to play tricks and bewilder people was old Aunt Betsy Dodge. She was of pure Indian blood and she always carried two buckets, one large and one small, when she went about from house to house. "We never knew" said Mrs. Ryan, "what she had in the buckets because the children were never allowed to ask questions nor peep into packages that belonged to other people."

One time there was someone sick at Jonathan Francis'—and they sent for Aunt Emily Johnson. When she was getting ready to go who should appear but Aunt Betsy Dodge with her two pails. She asked Aunt Emily if she could stay all night. Aunt Emily didn't want her, but told her that if she wanted to sit up she could stay. Finally Aunt Emily was ready to go and started off. She had to go across the fields and through a pair of bars. When she had gone a short distance, a great bird came circling overhead until Aunt Emily became so bewildered that she couldn't find the bars. While she was wandering around night came on and the people where she was going to nurse the sick were wondering what had happened to her. My mother happened to go to Mr. Francis' on an errand and they asked if she had seen Aunt Emily. No one had seen her. My mother did what she could for the sick ones and then went over to find out about Aunt Emily. When asked, her husband Uncle Simon said "The Devil's got her I guess." Aunt Emily was out all night and Uncle Simon said, that old Aunt Betsy Dodge left right after you did last night and she got you all bewildered.   (Tantaquidgeon 1928)

XVII

1928 WITCH STORY

One time when Aunt Julie was visiting mother, there came afloating out through the bedroom door, a feather. It came along just as smoothly through the air and went into the fireplace and up the chimney. It was white and slightly curved. We looked at it in astonishment and Aunt Julie said, "What in the world was that feather doing going along like that?" Aunt Esther How[woswee] happened to come in and she said "Why don't you know who that was! That was Betsy Dodge. She came in here to listen."   (Tantaquidgeon 1928)

XVIII

1928 WITCH STORY

One time when I was a girl I was sent to get a terse [cask] in which my people were going to salt fish. The horse that I had was high spirited but I could manage him. When the men folks had gotten the terse loaded on to the two wheels I wanted to get out of the yard before the other horses in the yard got out. So I clapped my hands to frighten the horses back so that I could get out of the gate and close it behind me and at that moment someone laughed right behind me and away went my horse like a flash. I cut across the fields to try to head him off and just as I got to the bars there was old Aunt Betsy. "Ha Ha, horse ran away, eh?" she laughed sneeringly. How she got over there is more than I can tell.

(Tantaquidgeon 1928)

XIX

1928 WITCH STORY

Another time my Father looked out of the window and saw Aunt Betsy coming. He turned and said to Mother, "There comes that old witch Betsy Dodge." Mother said "Let her come, she doesn't bother me." Father said "Well, I don't like her. She doesn't strike me right." Anyway, she came in and sat down right next to the stove where Father was trying to kindle a fire. As long as she sat there the fire wouldn't burn at all.   (Tantaquidgeon 1928)

XX

1928   WITCH STORY

No one had any faith in old Betsy Dodge. She could get around so fast that everyone knew she was in league with the devil. One time my brother William tried a trick on her. He took a brand new darning needle and when she went out of the house we followed her and stuck the needle in her track and she couldn't move until he took the needle out of her track.   (Tantaquidgeon 1928)

XXI

1928   WITCH STORY

Another very wicked woman was Patience Gershom. She was in league with the devil too. One time a mother sent her child on an errand to the home of Patience Gershom—when the child arrived at her house, there was Patience sitting before the fireplace talking to some tar babies that she had suspended on a string. They seemed to be dancing while she talked to them. The child talked to her but she paid no attention. The child became frightened and ran home. The mother then made the child go back to deliver the message and Patience was still before the fire. When the child appeared there a second time Patience became angry and said, "Don't you dare to come in here again or I'll send something after you." The child ran out of the house and just as she got out on the road, out of a clump of bushes came a great black bear with red eyes. The child told her mother that it was Patience Gershom because she had red eyes. No one had ever seen a bear before.

(Tantaquidgeon 1928).

XXII

1928   WITCH STORY

Patience was so adept in the workings of the Black Art that she could not be restrained by anyone nor kept in jail. On one occasion she was apprehended by the authorities in New Bedford and put in jail along with one of her followers Jane Wabbey. The latter objected to being placed in the same cell with Patience Gershom. She was, however, and in the night Patience Gershom was carrying on terribly. Everyone knew that she was in league with the devil. Finally, Jane Wabbey heard her talking to someone. He was a black man in oil skins in the cell and he asked her, Patience Gershom, if she wanted some money. He gave her money and went away. In the morning Jane Wabbey told the keeper that Patience Gershom had *a man in there during the night. The keeper questioned her but she gave him no satisfactory answer. They finally decided that it was useless to try to keep her so she was sent back to Gay Head. Some of the people from Gay Head went over to testify for Jane Wabbey. She wasn't such a bad woman as Patience Gershom.*

(Tantaquidgeon 1928)

XXIII

1928   THE GIRL WHOM THE DEVIL CLAIMED

There was once a girl who went away and studied the Black Art. When she came back the people knew that she was in league with the devil so they wanted to pray for her. So all the good Indians circled around the house to pray for the girl. For three days they stayed there and then they were forced to go because they wanted to get some wood. They decided to take the girl with them so that the devil wouldn't get her. After they got started on their way they heard an ox cart coming squeaking along. The girl said "My time has come. I must leave you." The people said, "Let us stop and pray for you again." But the girl said "It is no use. My time has come and you must leave me lest you be hurt too." So they left and when they returned there was only a few shreds of her dress here and there in the rocks and briars. They never saw her again.

(Tantaquidgeon 1928)

XXIV

1928

Along with the various capers of the witches we might consider the practice of "rooting" or "laying roots" for people. Certain individuals were said to possess knowledge pertaining to certain roots which were deadly to human beings. Some roots were so potent in the hands of the practitioners as to cause a person's death if layed where he was apt to step over the root. Some were more adept in the use of these deadly roots. *(Tantaquidgeon 1928)*

XXV–XXVIII

The following "projects" collected by Tantaquidgeon at Gay Head illustrate a form of black magic or sorcery that differs from herbalism and witchcraft. Anyone could perform a project by reciting certain words and performing the simple ritual, but one who did so risked the consequences of association with dangerous spirits. These Gay Head projects resemble cases of adolescent love magic attributed to Puritan and Yankee girls. Similarities include divination with egg

whites, the custom of throwing a ball of yarn into a dark hole to
catch one's boyfriend, and the appearance of a large semihuman
monster (Boyer and Nissenbaum 1974:1; Denison 1878:163–64).

XXV
1928

*Once there was a minister who had four daughters. One night
when their father had gone out to preach, the girls decided to try a
project. They took off their underclothes, hung them before the
open fire and retired to an adjoining room. Before long, the wind
began to blow a gale and they heard a terrific clawing and pounding at the door and windows. The girls being alone in the house
were terribly afraid. Their father, returning home, heard the disturbances and there he saw a terrible creature—part human and part
animal. He was also very much alarmed and hurried into the
house. He called to his daughters but they did not answer. When
he observed their underclothes hanging before the fire he knew
that they had been trying projects and he became angry. He called
again and the girls came out from their hiding place. Their father
told them what he had seen outside and he reprimanded them for
meddling with the works of evil spirits.*   (Tantaquidgeon *1928*)

XXVI
1928

*Girls would sometimes break an egg in water and put it in the
sun and in time it would take the form of a certain object. If a ship,
the girl's future husband would be a sailor, if land objects, he
would be a landsman. (Tantaquidgeon 1928)*

XXVII
1928

*Take a ball of cord or yarn and throw it down into a cellar or
dark pit holding the end. Start to rewind. While you repeat the
following: Here I wind, here I wind, here I hope my true love find.
Your lover will appear holding the ball in his hand.*

(Tantaquidgeon *1928*)

XXVIII
1928

*Prick your finger and with the blood write your name on a hand-
kerchief or a piece of cloth and hang it out the window for nine*

consecutive Sundays. A girl did this once and on the 9th Sunday
the following appeared written in blood: If tricks and projects are
your notion, Hell, damnation be your potion.   (Tantaquidgeon 1928)

XXIX

The two Screecham sisters, Hannah and Sarah, lived on what is
now called Grand Island off the town of Cotuit near Mashpee. Being
unable to live with each other for long, Sarah moved to the lonely
south Mashpee woods, while Hannah remained on the island to
help pirates conceal their gold. Elizabeth Reynard gathered the details of their legend from Mrs. Frederick Gardner, a Mashpee Wampanoag, and then rewrote them in her own style. Most of the motifs
are consistent with treasure, ghost, and witch lore from southern
New England Indians and Euro-Americans. For example, killing
someone to provide a guardian ghost for treasure is a widespread
motif; so too is the belief that a witch can transform herself into an
animal such as a horse or deer which can be killed only with a silver
bullet. The will-o'-the-wisp leading people astray is known in Mashpee and Narragansett lore as well as among local blacks and whites.
The hunter's method for identifying the witch transformed into
a horse by attaching a silver horseshoe is new but similar to motifs attested in American, British, and other European legends (F
551.1.2.1. Woman with horseshoe on one foot; G 211.1.1.2. Witch as
horse shod with horseshoes; Wintemberg 1907:213). We already
have seen an Indian example of the marksman who kills an animal,
later to learn that a witch has died elsewhere. Mrs. Gardner, who
told this legend, was Wampanoag, but she and her ancestors borrowed many non-Wampanoag motifs in constructing their Mashpee
legends.

1934   THE SCREECHAM SISTERS

Off Cotuit lies Screecham's Island, now called Grand Island. For
years no one could settle there, for the ghost of Hannah Screecham
frightened men away. She and her sister, Sarah, lived alone on the
island; but one day they quarrelled, and Sarah moved to South
Mashpee and built herself a hut in the forest by the place called
the Witches Pond. Both sisters were evil, and while Sarah became
a witch, Hannah befriended the pirates who sailed along that coast.
Captain Kidd, Black Bellamy, Paul Williams, Baxter, all of them
knew her, feared her, yet trusted her with their gold. While a pirate
sloop lay off shore, the Captain flew signals to Hannah. Then a
boat put out from the pirate ship, a boat with the Captain and one

sailor and a treasure of Spanish Pieces-of-Eight (such as are found
on the beaches today), or perhaps bars of bullion, or caskets of
jewels from Spain. Hannah went down to the sea-beach, kissed the
Captain, and nodded to the sailor. The Captain gave her a shawl,
or a locket of hair, or a finger ring. At her direction, the sailor carried the treasure into the interior of the island where a deep pit
had been dug. When the last bar was laid in place, and the last
coin safe in its box, Hannah pushed the sailor into the yawning
pit. Quick-running sands seeped over him, and he was buried
alive. Then she screamed like the gull in storm, a cry that mingled
with the wind in stunted trees, or the waves shrilling on the outer
beach. At that signal, the Captain put back to his ship; and even
the Black Bellamy, cruelest of buccaneers, shivered as he heard her
wail. Yet he knew that his treasure was safe, its whereabouts known
to only two, Hannah Screecham and himself.

She was never able to dig for gold. The moment that earth-buried
metal touched her, the sand-pits on the Island opened and the
ghosts of the men that she had murdered put their blue hands to
her throat. She has been dead this long time, but at evening, when
you hear her calling over the waters from Grand Island, you will
know that she warns the pirates that someone approaches their
gold.

While Hannah lived on Screecham's Island, Sarah, her sister,
built a house in South Mashpee by the Witches Pond. The forest
there was without moon. The shooting looked good and when deer
were scarce the hunters were often tempted to track in her forest,
although they never succeeded in bringing game to ground. Whenever they appeared, Sarah Screecham grew angry, and threatened
evil luck. She appeared, now here, now there in the forest, and
always, just after she went from sight, a young deer leaped through
the brush, or occasionally, after dusk, the hunters saw a great black
mare. Whether they shot with bows and arrows, or with the white
man's thunder, it made no difference—they could not kill the deer
in her forest, nor catch the great black horse.

Once Sarah fell in love with a Mashpee man. He was afraid and
would have none of her. She grew angry and brought him bad luck.
He became tired of her threats and that he might discover the secret of her magic he invited her to spend the night at his house.
She came, and after dusk, turned into a horse. She was still sufficiently friendly to the man so that she let him catch her. He shod
her with three iron shoes, and a silver shoe on her left front hoof,
and tied her to a tree in his yard. The next morning when he looked

*out of the window, the black mare had disappeared. He went to a
neighbour's, told his story, and they started for Sarah Screecham's
house. They found her moaning in pain. She tried to hide her hand
in the folds of her skirt, and when they seized her by the arm they
saw that a silver horseshoe was nailed to her left palm.*

*She was so cruel a witch that the tribe longed for her death.
Game grew very scarce in the land, and hunters went often to Sarah's forest in the hope of breaking the charm. Always the wind
blew their arrows aside, their guns missed fire, or for some other
reason the bullets took no effect. Always Sarah appeared in the
forest and taunted them for lack of skill.*

*One day a man who remembered the story of the horseshoe fash-
ioned a silver bullet and put it into his gun. He went at dusk to
the forest beside the Witches Pond. Old Sarah laughed her witch-
cackle, but he paid no attention. Just after the sun went down,
Sarah disappeared, and a few minutes later a young doe leaped
through the brush. The man raised his gun to his shoulder and
took careful aim. He had only the one silver bullet with which to
shoot but that flew straight to its mark and lodged near the heart of
the deer. The animal jerked into a high leap, keeping stiff in the
mid-body. Then it sped away. Swiftly the hunter followed, he who
was swiftest tracker in Mashpee, for he knew that the deer was
mortally wounded and could not travel far. Yet almost immediately
he lost its trail, while, in the forest, night shadows thickened until,
like black furry cats, they slunk around his knees. Tei Pai Wankas
called from the swamps, making voices like maidens. The Marsh
Owl woke in the Cedar Tree and cried "Gone, gone," in the Mono-
moyick tongue, his favourite night-speech. The Indian Tracker
spoke no word to shadow or swamp or wild Marsh Owl. He
searched steadily for the wounded animal until Geesukquand's
Sun Canaries nested in the tops of pine trees. Then he returned to
Sarah Screecham's house. No smoke issued from the stone chimney; and when he entered the dwelling-room he found a very old
woman lying dead by the hearthside, with a silver bullet in her
breast.*   (Reynard 1934:50–52)

XXX

Reynard collected a second Mashpee witchcraft story from Gardner about a mother who left a magical corncob doll to protect her
children while she searched for food. A witch burned the doll, thus
causing the mother to lay down her corn and run to the house while
the witch then stole the corn. The guardian doll may derive from
indigenous New England Indian belief, for dolls appeared some

years earlier in a Mohegan folktale collected by Speck (see appendix, V).[10]

1934   THE CORN COB DOLL

When Mercy Lowe's husband died, she was left with four little children to feed. She lived in Mashpee where the corn grows tall, but she had not enough food to keep her children from starving. A short distance from her house lived Ordihon, a kind-hearted Indian who was sorry for her, and ready to give extra supplies from his broad fields. There came a day when no corn was left in the little hut where Mercy lived, and her children were crying for food. Mercy gave them a Corn Cob Doll and told them to play with it. Then she strapped her basket over her back, and went down the road to get help from Ordihon.

The Corn Cobb Doll had a wooden head, and a bit of cloth wrapped around it for a shawl. The four children took their treasure with them when they went out of the hut to watch their mother depart. After she had disappeared around a bend in the road, they played for awhile with the Corn Cob Doll, but they were too hungry to forget their hunger, and in almost no time they were crying bitterly.

Up the road came a little noise, tap, tap, tap, the pounding of a pointed stick on the ground. An old woman, tiny and bent, hobbled toward them. "Why are you crying, children?" she asked.

"Because we are hungry," the children replied.

"Where is your mother?"

"She has gone down the road to get from Ordihon some corn."

At that the old woman muttered, and tapped her stick sharply against a stone. The children did not know whether she was angry at them for being hungry, or angry at Ordihon for giving them corn. They said nothing, dried their eyes, and the oldest held tightly to the doll.

The old woman was Abisha Pockmonet. She glanced up and down the road and made a circle in the dust with her stick. "Come into the house, children," she said. "I'll wait with you till your mother comes home." They followed her into the tiny hut where she seated herself by the stone hearth and looked into the fire. The children drew close. She turned to speak to them again, saw the Corn Cob Doll, and gave the cry of the Swamp Owl before a killing at night. The doll fell upon the hearth. The children, frightened, backed away to the corner of the room, beside a window that looked upon the road.

Abisha Pockmonet never took her eyes from that image wrapped in a rag. She did not stoop and pick it up. Instead she gave it a poke with her stick, putting the point of the stick well under the cob so that the little doll flipped into the air and seemed to jump toward the fire. As she poked at it, the old woman called aloud, "Look, my pretties, look out of the window. Your mother is coming down the road." The Indian children were frightened. They needed their mother, and they needed food. They forgot about the Corn Cob Doll, and did as Abisha said. The old witch gave the wooden head another poke with her cane, and once more the doll seemed to jump toward the fire. "Keep watch, my children," Abisha called, "your mother is coming now." Even as she spoke, the doll leaped toward the hearth; and every time that the children turned from the window, Abisha told them to keep watch for their mother, and every time that they looked out of the window, she managed to flip the wooden image nearer to the flames. At last she poked her stick directly under its grinning head and the Corn Cob Doll jumped high. "Hark, children, your mother is calling, your mother is calling you now." The children turned to the window to listen, and with one final cast of her stick, old Abisha Pockmonet sent the doll into the flames.

A blinding flash of light shot from the hearthfire, a wild light that banded itself into the colours of the rainbow. Old Abisha disappeared in it, and the frightened children heard their mother gasping. They ran out of the hut, and saw her, breathless, frightened, running up the road, without any basket of corn. "What is the matter?" she sobbed as she came, "Oh, what is the matter at home?" They told her about the Corn Cob Doll and of old Abisha Pockmonet; and then they asked for food. "We must return for it," she said, "I left it near a tree by the road." She spoke with hope, but in her heart Mercy Lowe knew that when they went back to the trailcrossing, where she had set down her basket, there would not be any corn.

Ordihon had given her a full load. She had started home with a thank-prayer singing in her heart, but she had not gone far when Fear came upon her, as though an hundred Swamp Devils were swarming over her basket, putting their dry fingers down her throat, whimpering, "Hurry! Hurry! Sorrow at home! Sorrow at home!" She ran as fast as the weight on her back would permit. Weak from lack of food, to her it seemed as if the basket grew heavier at every step. All the Fear Devils sat in it and laughed. To get rid of them, she hid the basket by a tree and ran swiftly to the hut.

The weary, hungry family crept back to the crossroads. No basket

*of corn was there, though they searched at the foot of every tree.
Then Mercy knew that a Spell had been put upon her. Abisha
Pockmonet, the cruel witch, had taken Ordihon's corn for herself,
and hated Mercy Lowe.*

*This is the first story of Abisha and Mercy. After the burning of
the Corn Cob Doll there were many sufferings in that little house.
Hunger lived with them, sorrow followed them. All dwellers in
Mashpee saw that Abisha Pockmonet brought evil to Mercy; and at
last Ordihon, who was a good Indian, took the little family into
his house and gave them protection and food. Then Abisha stopped
her torments, for she knew that Ordihon would punish her, and
since she could get no more of his corn, her jealous rage was done.*

(Reynard 1934:48–50)

XXXI

Perhaps because Speck and Tantaquidgeon did not work among
the Narragansett, we have less information on witchcraft and folk
healers in this community. Although Narragansett authors published
herbal, medicinal, and ghost lore in *The Narragansett Dawn*, they
scarcely mentioned witchcraft, which is not surprising in a publication intended to promote tribal rebirth. The one witchcraft text to
appear in this magazine treats the subject lightly. Fastening branches
across the path to prevent pursuit by witches appears in no other
source.

1935

*Among the old Narragansetts, who once lived in that locality
[King's Factory Road in Charlestown] was Fannie Ammons, a
strangely fearless woman who travelled wherever she pleased
alone, day or night. She lived alone on her own place. I have heard
this story of her. One dark night she came to the Post Office at
Bradford (Niantic). A friend asked her if she were not afraid to go
home alone. No she answered, with a twinkly in her eye. I tie the
bushes across the path behind me, so the witches cannot follow
me.*
(Ishonowa 1935:179)

XXXII

Leonard Vanderhoop of Gay Head spoke of earlier Gay Headers
who had the power to "root" other people and who did not get along
with each other because their powers clashed. Many avoided the
homes of such people and particularly avoided eating their food.
Vanderhoop did not know precisely what rooting was but described

it as supernatural; a person with it "had some power over you, somehow the person that could root you . . . could get you to do most anything" (Vanderhoop 1983). One Gay Header believed that his neighbor, Jim, had been rooting him and let him know of his suspicion. This simple anecdote could have been collected in West Africa or in colonial New England, where similar beliefs existed.

1983

He was a little thin about six foot six . . . but grew up just like this and he had this funny voice . . . he got sick and this Jim says to him "How be ya, Gil? How be ya." [Gil said] "You know dang well how I be before you asked me." . . . He believed that Jim . . . could root him. (Vanderhoop 1983)

The witchcraft record begins with seventeenth-century accounts of shamans who used their powers to injure enemies inside as well as outside the tribe. With a few exceptions, memories of these early figures receded in postconquest, postconversion legends, but elements of their techniques (whether real, such as herbalism, or imaginary, such as animal transformations) persisted among folk practitioners such as Israel Freeman, Patience Gashum, Betsy Dodge, William Perry, and many others. As Christianity replaced shamanism at the heart of Indian religion, Christian Indians absorbed elements of English and Afro-American folk religion, including their witchcraft lore. Nevertheless, ancient shamanistic powers such as transformation, magical flight, control of spirits, herbal cures, and herbal witchcraft lived uninterrupted beneath the surface of acculturated forms.

Viewed in long-term perspective, Indian witchcraft stories flourished in the decades following the dissolution of the land-based communities in the late nineteenth century. The American historians Paul Boyer and Stephen Nissenbaum observed that in Tudor and Stuart England and in Salem, Massachusetts, witchcraft outbreaks "tended to occur (given a prevailing belief in witchcraft) when the evolution from a communal to an individualistic ethic reached a critical stage in a given locality" (Boyer and Nissenbaum 1974:212). The Indian witchcraft stories retold here do not represent an outbreak comparable to the Salem witch trials of 1692, but they reveal an active interest in the subject which correlates historically with the decline in communal life that accompanied the Indians' transition to private citizenship and the termination of state management of their domains. Gay Head and Mashpee witchcraft stories differ from those at Mohegan in that the persons accused tended to be from the Indian community, whereas at Mohegan witches often were white. Mary Douglas has suggested that when insiders level witch-craft accusations at one another, they may be expressing and fighting out factional differences within the group. To level accusations out-side the group reaffirms group boundaries and solidarity (Douglas 1970:xxvi–xxvii). Douglas's sociological insight fits the New England setting. The Mohegan most needed symbolic boundaries to separate them from others, whereas the Mashpee and Gay Head people had secure geographical and legal boundaries until these were done away with, whereupon they too experienced a growth in political factionalism. Thus the Mogehan asserted group identity by attributing witchcraft to whites, and the Mashpee and Gay Head people used witchcraft to air internal differences. By attributing kinky hair to witchcraft, Gay Headers also expressed a symbolic comment on Indian and Afro-American mating. Interest in witch-craft declined by the 1930s (about the same time that missionary stories also declined), when all southern New England groups re-built their tribal and ceremonial structures and took a more active interest in shaping their future. Symbolic and imagined enemies gave way at this time to more concrete social and political objectives.

7 Ghosts and the Devil

Although ghosts and the devil are distinct figures in Euro-American folklore, I discuss them together because while the Indian spirit Cheepi represented spirits of the dead, the English and their Indian converts glossed it as the devil. Even after Indians adopted the English concepts of ghost and devil, these phenomena retained indigenous content. In particular, Indian elements survived in beliefs about illness, healing, sorcery, and ghostly lights such as foxfire and the will-o'-the-wisp. Ghost and devil folklore are similar functionally. From the earliest contact period, when Cheepi appeared to Indians in Boston to warn them against departing from ancestral ways, both spirits appeared to the living, urging them to uphold custom and guard socially correct values and behavior. These spirits lost their importance in the twentieth century as the face-to-face communities they reinforced lost their coherence.

I

William Wood (in 1634), John Winthrop (in 1637), Edward Johnson (in 1651), and John Josselyn (in 1673) described Indian sightings of Cheepi/Hobbamock around Massachusetts Bay in which the Indian perception of this spirit had already been affected by the presence of English and Afro-Americans in their midst (Johnson [1654] 1910:263; Josselyn [1675] 1833:300; Winthrop 1825:254; Wood [1634] 1977:95). In Josselyn's account, the spirit appeared as a Mohawk and again as an Englishman.

1673

One black Robin an Indian sitting down in the Corn field belonging
to the house where I resided, ran out of his Wigwam frighted with
the apparition of two infernal spirits in the shape of Mohawkes.
Another time two Indians and an Indess, came running into our
house crying out they should all dye, Cheepie was gone over the
field gliding in the Air with a long rope hanging from one of his
legs: we askt them what he was like, they said all wone Englishman,
clothed with hat and coat, shooes and stockings.

(Josselyn [1675] 1833:300)

II

In 1700 Robert Calef published *More Wonders of the Invisible
World*, which contained extensive eyewitness testimony on witchcraft in seventeenth-century New England. John Cotton (1640–99),
who worked with Wampanoag Indians on Martha's Vineyard and
near Plymouth, probably told Calef this account of a meeting between an Indian preacher and a black devil. The devil in this story
fits Indian and English stereotypes except for the registration book,
which reflects English, not Indian, belief. By urging the Indian to
stop preaching to other Indians, the devil both challenged the Christian God and defended Indian custom. In this as in most such con-
frontations, the devil, and the ancestors he represented, backed
down. Perhaps the Indian preacher's memorate reflects his ambiva-
lence for departing from traditional Indian ways.

CIRCA 1697

Know then that this remarkable Indian being a little before he Died
at work in the Wood making of Tarr, there appeared unto him a
Black-Man, of a Terrible aspect, and more than humane Dimensions, threatning bitterly to kill him if he would not promise to
leave off Preaching as he did to his Countrey-Men, and promise
particularly, that if he Preached any more, he would say nothing of
Jesus Christ unto them. The Indian amaz'd, yet had the courage to
answer, I will in spite of you go on to Preach Christ more than ever
I did, and the God whom I serve will keep me that you shall never
hurt me. Hereupon the Apparition abating somewhat of his fierce-
ness, offered to the Indian a Book of a considerable thickness and a
Pen and Ink, and said, that if he would now set his hand unto that
Book, he would require nothing further of him; but the Man refused
the motion with indignation, and fell down upon his knees into a
Fervent and Pious Prayer unto God for help against the Tempter,
whereupon the Dæmon Vanish't.   (Burr 1946:309)

III

Josselyn heard in the seventeenth century that a light sometimes appeared over the wigwam before an Indian died. Experience Mayhew wrote of this association between bright-shining light and death in his enchanting book *Indian Converts: Or, Some Account of the Lives and Dying Speeches of a Considerable Number of the Christianized Indians of Martha's Vineyard, in New-England* (1727). One Indian woman who attended her dying mother in 1710 saw two shining persons dressed in white at her mother's bedside whom her mother took to be guardians sent by God (Mayhew 1727:150). Another woman from Chilmark reported with satisfaction shortly before she died that a light beamed on her one night from a window in heaven (p.160). Several Indians attested to another remarkable light that shone at the death of a young woman named Abigail Manhut, in about 1685. Mayhew considered these lights to be unusual, which suggests that they were an Indian and not a local English phenomenon. In these cases an indigenous symbol may have survived by serving a new master. All New England Puritans, red or white, hoped for signs of their salvation, and Indian belief in light associated with death provided one such sign.

1727

I cannot forbear here relating a very observable thing that happened at the time of this young Woman's Death, of which there are three or four credible Witnesses yet living: It being a dark Night when she died, the Moon not then shining, and many of the Stars being covered with Clouds, the People who were with her and tended her, were on a sudden put to a great Strait for something to make a Light withal, whereby they might see to do what was needful to be done for her, their Dry-Pine or Light-wood, which they had hitherto used for this purpose, being all spent. But while they were in some surprize on this account, they were on a sudden more surprized by perceiving that there was a Light in the House, which was sufficient for them to see to do any thing by, that the dying Maid could need them to do for her. All present wondered from whence it was that this marvellous Light came to them; and several of them went out to see if they could discover the Cause of it, but could see nothing that could afford such a Light as that wherewith they were favoured; and therefore concluded it was something extraordinary, and such of them as are still living think so. They say it was not a sudden Flash of Light only, but lasted several Hours, even from the time they first needed it, till the young Woman

*was dead, and they had no more Occasion for it . . . as tho it had
been as bright as that of the Sun at Noon-Day.*   (Mayhew 1727:221–22)

IV

Mayhew also told of Elizabeth Pattompan, who died in Tisbury in
1710, who asked her father some days before she died to write down
her last words and thoughts for the benefit of her relatives, but he
neglected to do so until his daughter's ghost appeared and reminded
him of her request. In the later Wampanoag legends regarding the
silver pipe and the stone pestle, we also encounter ghosts that returned to protest unfulfilled agreements (texts IX and XII below).

1727

*Tho the Father of this young Woman was so earnestly desired by
her to commit to Writing the Words above recited, yet having for
some time neglected to do so, he does with great Assurance and
Confidence affirm, that the Spectre of his said Daughter did after
her Death one Day plainly appear to him, being so near to him,
that he plainly saw that she appeared with the same Clothes which
she commonly wore before her Death. He also saw some Warts on
one of her Feet, which were, in appearance, such as his Daughter
had on hers.*   (Mayhew 1727:241)

V

While the Wampanoag and Massachusett had been absorbing English religion, the Narragansett, Niantic, Mohegan, and Pequot continued in shamanistic ways until the early 1740s. A Narragansett
shaman expressed his reasons for calling upon Cheepi rather than
the God of his English neighbors.[1]

CIRCA 1730

*Some 40 or 50 years ago there was a great Drought and the Indi-
ans of Narragansett held a great Powaw for sundry Days. One Babcock or Stanton at length, being well known to the Indians, went
among them and rebuked them as serving and worshipping the
Devil: an old Powaw Indian readily owned and justified it—saying
all the Corn would die without rain and Chepi the Evil Power
witheld that—now said he, If I was to beat you, who would you
pray to? to me, or to your Father Ten miles off? you would pray to
me to leave off and not beat you any more: so we pray to the Devil
to leave off affecting us with Evil.*   (Stiles 1901, 1:386)

VI

By the early nineteenth century, Old World devil and ghost motifs had thoroughly penetrated New England Indian folklore. James A. Jones's Wampanoag nurse, for example, claimed to have seen the devil and described him in terms that both resembled and differed from other known Indian and European spirits. His appearance near a husking frolic, as a well-dressed gentleman with a glowing face, suggests definite British, Euro-American, and Afro-American as well as Indian motifs.[2]

1830

Seated in a little chair at her side, how I used to enjoy her long but never tedious stories of the wonderful things she had seen and heard—of the phantoms which had visited her bedside, or whispered strange things in her ear—of the several conversations she had had, face to face, with the Father of Evil! Once in particular she had seen the latter grim personage when she was returning from a "husking frolic," i.e. an assemblage of persons met for the purpose of stripping the husks from Indian corn. She described him as a rather tall and exceedingly gaunt old gentleman . . . his face the colour of flame, his eyes green as grass, an enormous yellow cocked hat upon his head, and his robe of woven sea-weed. She averred that he had neither a club foot as some have pretended, nor a "sooty black skin" according to the opinion of others. She described the spot where she saw him with such exceeding accuracy, that I never thereafter, for more than ten years, passed the particular "bush in the little valley, three steps from the gate," by daylight, without a shudder, and never at all by night.

(Jones *1830*, 1:xi–xii)

VII

Jones's nurse also spoke to him of ghosts that had become fully habituated to the English mode of living, simultaneously resembling pre-Christian spirits described almost two centuries earlier by Thomas Mayhew, Jr.[3] The dead maintained close relationships with the living in the stable face-to-face Christian Indian villages of the early eighteenth century.

1830

There was nothing, I believe I may say in the world, which was not with her a "spirit." The waves were "spirits"—the meteors were "spirits"—the winds singing their lullabies were "spirits"—the thunders were "spirits." In the long winter evenings, when seated before the wood fire, which at that season of the year is perpetually burning on a New England hearth, the sound was heard of a cricket chirping in the hollow wood; starting with alarm she would exclaim "a spirit!" . . . She had seen the spirit of her mother, too, employed in knitting woollen hose for her father's spirit. There was not one of my ancestors to whom she had been personally known—and she was very aged at the time of my birth—who had not appeared to her after death, each "with a circumstance" whose simplicity and truth to nature almost impressed you with a belief that such a thing had really been.   (Jones 1830, 1:xi–xii)

VIII

In 1879 Albert S. Gatschet of the Bureau of American Ethnology visited the Narragansett in southern Rhode Island shortly before their reservation was terminated. Gatschet collected a short vocabulary and a few bits of folklore, including this brief account of the creation of cod and haddock. Earlier sources on Narragansett lore are too sparse to clarify whether or not this legend reflects an indigenous explanatory motif. Variations of this legend are well attested in European, New England Yankee, and Penobscot folklore (Halpert 1957; Jagendorf 1948:163–65; Speck 1935:24; A 1751. The devil's animals and God's; A 2217.3.2. Marks on certain fish from devil's fingerprints; A 2412.4.3. Markings on cod-fish).

1879

after God had created the codfish, the Devil made an exact counterfeit of it, but instead of calling it cod also, he called it haddock.
                                                    (Gatschet 1973)

IX

Mrs. Zerviah Gould Mitchell (ca. 1805–95) claimed descent from the seventeenth-century Wampanoag sachems Massasoit and Tispaquin, and was one of the last of her lineage to live on a tiny reservation at Betty's Neck on Lake Assawampsett in Lakeville, Massachusetts. She and her daughter, Emma Mitchell Safford, continued the aboriginal tradition of straw basket making long after most southern New England Indians had abandoned that craft in favor of splint basketry (Butler 1947:52; Speck 1928b:263; Tantaquidgeon 1930a). Mitchell told this legend to Hezekiah Butterworth of Boston in 1892 when she was eighty-five years old.[4] Some of the motifs (D 1606. Magic objects automatically keep out of reach; E 419.8. Ghost re-

turns to enforce its burial wishes or to protest disregard of them; and
E 555. *Dead man smokes pipe,* resemble ones attested among Algonquian, Iroquois, and Eskimo people, and early-historic-period Indians of this region customarily buried pipes and other prized goods
with their dead. "The Silver Pipe" appears to be an early Wampanoag legend that acquired few Euro-American embellishments during the two hundred or so years that it descended by word of mouth
through Mitchell's lineage.

1892   THE SILVER PIPE

*King James, of England, on hearing of the goodness and virtues
of Massasoit, once sent him a present of a silver pipe. The chieftain
prized it highly as a gift from his "white brother over the sea." But
one of his warriors did a deed of valor that so won his heart that he
resolved to make him a present of the pipe as his choice treasure.
The warrior, finding himself about to die, charged his squaw to put
the silver pipe into his grave at the burial, but she, out of regard
to the value of the treasure, hid it, and covered the grave without
it. One evening she went to the place where she had hidden the
royal present, resolving to smoke from the pipe alone, and to hide
it again. She put out her hand to take the pipe, but it moved away
from her. Again, but it moved away, and again and again, but a
dead hand was moving it. Then she bitterly repented of her disobe-
dience, and promised to bury the pipe if she were able. At this
resolution, the pipe lay still, and she opened the grave, fulfilled
the warrior's command, and was enabled to smoke in peace of
mind and conscience, we may hope, the rest of her days.*

(Butterworth *1893*)

X

Ghosts that wander from their graves, haunt the scene of former
crimes against them, and even drink liquor, are known in English,
Welsh, and American folklore (Briggs 1971, 1:417; Dorson 1946:25,
61, 156–57; Jones 1944:246). Peter Sky's return to the place in Connecticut where he was murdered is distinctive because he holes up
in a rock near where he was killed, calls out for liquor, and hollers
when given enough to feel a little drunk. One cannot dismiss the
possibility of influence from earlier Indian belief because spirits
were known to remain close to their grave sites. Food and liquor
were included in the grave goods, and the souls of persons who suffered unnatural deaths were known to wander.[5] Jim Harris, a Scaticook from Litchfield County, Connecticut, told this story to Speck.

The Scaticook population, although mainly composed of Hudson River Mahican, also included people of Mohegan and Pequot ancestry (Speck 1909:205).

1903   PETER SKY CHANGED TO A ROCK

This is the story of Peter Sky. They said that he lived north of here. He used to go by a swamp that lay near a road. One dark night he and some one else went to town and got some whisky. Then they came down that road until they reached the swamp. They took their whisky down there and began to drink when they had found a nice place to sit on. Soon they fell to quarreling over their whisky, and in the fight that followed Pete was killed. The other Indian got away and was never heard of again. But the next day some people coming by found Pete's body there and a rock with a hole in it close by. That rock was never noticed much by the Indians thereafter until one dark and foggy night, when some of them went down to the swamp on their way home to drink something they had bought. They heard noises from the rock, and one of them poured some of the goods into the hole. Immediately there was a voice from the rock. It called for more, and they kept on pouring whisky in until the voice was the voice of a drunken man. That rock will "holler" now on foggy nights if you pour whisky into it.   (Speck *1928b:278*)

XI

Even today some Gay Headers speak of Cheepi as the Indian devil, despite the fact that English and Amerian motifs have quietly crowded out most indigenous beliefs about this spirit. For instance, as in this legend, the British, Anglo-American, French-Canadian, and Afro-American devil is known to visit dances, card games, and other such recreational gatherings. In a later version of this same Gay Head legend we learn that the cornfield where Cheepi rampaged was the collective field of the Gay Head community, thus dating this event to before incorporation in 1870.[6] Both the aboriginal Cheepi and the devil raised unusual weather disturbances, as did the nineteenth-century Cheepi of Mary Vanderhoop's legend.

1904

Of Cheepii not much is known. He is the all-powerful one, the evil one, the devil. The shapes he assumes are frightful, mysterious, convincing. The story of his last visit to this neighborhood will ever be listened to on wild and stormy nights by men and women and children, whose wide and wondering eyes, abated breath and trembling nerves tell without words that they are all accustomed to "seein' things at night."

Near where the old Peters House now stands, more than a hundred years ago, stood a noble Indian residence. 'Twas dug in the side of a hill, with a warm southern exposure, walled up with stones, well roofed with wreckage from the sea, and at one end was an immense stone fire-place with its broad hearth. The floor was of beautifully pounded earth, kept in a fine state of firmness and black polish by constant sweepings with the wonderful pock-web brooms.

To this mansion, one pleasant summer night, came all the braves and squaws with their papooses, for a night of dancing and merrymaking. In the midst of the mirth and the music, when all faces were beaming with joy, out of doors there suddenly arose a great uproar, so vast and terrifying that no one knew its cause or could comprehend its meaning. A momentary hush fell upon the singers and the dancers, and then every son and daughter of a race that knew no fear rushed madly into the open air.

Some fifty feet away, directly in front of the Indian dwelling, stood a very large field of yepninwaha (corn). Grown to a wonderful height, frequently had its proud possessor watched it waving peacefully in the sunlight. A moment before, at the first sign of disturbance, some one had suggested that the ponies might have been loosened and turned into the corn by some spiteful hand. But now there came from the field of living green such a rushing and stamping and snorting and charging that the ponies instantly received a verdict of acquittal. It seemed more like the stampede of ten thousand Texas steers. The red man of those days was never a looker-on, but rather a lover of action, so with whoops and yells the braves charged into the field of yepninwaha, now wrapped in the uncertain darkness of the night; but, try as they would, pursue as they might, a single dark and horrible form, which seemed invincible at every point and capable of being everywhere at once, held the field against them and prolonged their terror. Finally, puzzled and mystified beyond description, they gave up the unequal contest, admitted the power of their supernatural foe, and returned to the house to await the coming of dawn. In the bright sun light of the morning they again went out to investigate, but their errand proved a fruitless mission. Save for the numerous tracks and the trampled earth which they had themselves produced, there was nothing to show that there had been any distur-

bance whatever. As the unbroken corn waved in the gentle breeze, the braves and squaws stood and looked at each other in silence and amazement, shook their heads, and solemnly muttered "Cheepii."   (Vanderhoop 1904, July 2)

XII

Vanderhoops's ghost story resembles earlier ones by Experience Mayhew and Zerviah Mitchell in which a ghost returns to reprimand survivors for neglecting commitments to the dead. In this case the spirit of a Gay Head woman startles her husband, who had kept her pestle for another mate.

1904

The old folks tell of one good, industrious squaw who died and was buried, and whose sorrowing but thrifty sonnup witheld from her grave the pestle she had been accustomed to use. As he had never been known to personally use the article, it was clear that he must have wanted it for some bride-to-be. It so happened that his better half was buried down near the creek and from the surrounding hills a good view could be had of her grave. One evening the "bereaved" one was seen to approach the grave and disconsolately cast himself thereon in grief. He made a great display of pretended sorrow, but evidently the dead squaw's spirit could not tolerate his hypocrisy and crocodile tears, for the mourning brave was seen to suddenly rise and begin to annihilate distance like a Marconigram. Some say that the departed one had merely raised herself and demanded what belonged to her—her pestle. Others insist that she visited upon his offending head some terrible curse! We cannot tell. We only know that he is running yet.   (Vanderhoop 1904, July 30)

XIII

In the Mohegan legend of Papoose Rock a Montauk woman kills her infant because her Mohegan husband has left her and she cannot raise the child alone. This story closely resembles the Narragansett account of the Bastard Rocks or Crying Rocks in Charlestown, Rhode Island, where unwed mothers abandoned their illegitimate or deformed children (text LVIII below). Precisely what moral the Mohegan conveyed by this legend is difficult to know, but in the most general sense it advocates rearing children in the nuclear family. The ineradicable bloodstain speaks as a physical reminder of the consequences of neglecting familial values.[7]

CIRCA 1905

A short distance south of Shantic Point is Muddy Cove, the Indian name for which was Baságwanantakság (derivative from
baság, mud). Southwest from this cove is a rocky ledge on the hillside, at the foot of which in one place there is a reddish discolora-
tion of the rock, having the general outline of a human figure
sprawled out. It is called Papoose Rock and the following tale
accounts for the peculiarity, according to Mrs. Fielding.

"There was a Mohegan who went across to Long Island and took
a wife from one of the tribes there. After some time, he tired of her
and came home. Soon after, she had a child. She said to herself,
'My child's father has left me to take care of him. I cannot do it
alone.' So she made ready for a journey and set out for the Mohegan
country across the Sound to look for her husband. She found him
at Mohegan and said to him, 'You must take care of me and the
child.' But he paid no attention to her. Then she went down to
where there was a steep sloping rock not far from the river. Standing on the top of this slope, she took her child in one hand and
grasped its head with the other. Then she twisted the head and it
came off the blood flowing down the rocks. The woman cast the
head down, and the body she threw farther out. Where the head
fell there remained a splotch of blood, and where the body struck,
there was left an imprint stained upon the rock in the shape of
the child. That is the story. The blood is there yet, and it tells of her
deed when she has gone." (Speck 1909:186–87)

XIV

Other ghosts visited the early-twentieth-century Mohegan. Speck
wrote, "Ghosts or wandering spirits, (jībaí) are believed to be round
about. Besides indulging in many mystifying capers, such as appearing suddenly before people at night and making peculiar and
terrifying noises, they are thought to take vengeance on their enemies and help their friends on earth in various ways. It is hard to
separate the Indian from the European elements in such tales"
(Speck 1909:202). Both the Indian Cheepi and European ghosts lin-
gered around swamps. One such place between Uncasville and New
London was well stocked with spectral creatures. An unnamed Mohegan informant told Speck an anecdote that combined Anglo-
American motifs (E 421.2. Ghosts cast no shadow; E 421.3. Luminous ghosts; E 530.1. Ghost-like lights) with an earlier Indian belief
in the association of lights with departed souls (E 742. Soul as light;
Josselyn [1675] 1833:300). Referring to such lights as the will-o'-the-
wisp, Speck noted that the Mohegan "believe it to be caused by spir-

its who are travelling about with lights" and that such lights "are greatly feared, and are thought to be more numerous at certain places and at particular times of the year." He added, "We encounter in this another common Algonkian concept in the association of the disembodied soul with the apparition of a spot of light" (Speck 1928b:262).

Circa 1905

One dark, stormy night a woman was coming down the long hill toward Two Bridges, having been up to New London. Looking across the swamp to the opposite slope she beheld a light approaching in her direction. When they drew near to one another the woman saw that the light was suspended in the center of a person's stomach as though in a frame. There was no shadow cast, and yet the outline of the person could be distinguished as it surrounded the light. The woman was badly frightened and ran all the way home.   (Speck *1909:202*)

XV

Animal ghosts patrolled this same swamp. As Speck observed, separating the Indian from the European in such legends is difficult, for as Indian guardian spirits appeared in animal and human form, Anglo-American ghosts and the devil's helpers also took the form of dogs, horses, pigs, bears, deer, and other creatures (Carr and Westey 1945:116; Hurley 1951:205; Jones 1944:243; B 742.4. *Fire-breathing dogs*; E 423.1.5. *Revenant as swine*; G 211.1.8. *Witch in form of dog*). The ghostly hands that tugged at women's skirts are akin to ghosts known to whites in rural New York which pulled at bedclothes (Jones 1944:246, 249).

CIRCA 1905

Another time [John] Tantaquidgeon was riding home, and when he was passing the same swamp two dogs dashed from the bushes, and from their mouths they breathed fire. They ran along side, blowing flames at the horse's flanks until he had passed the swamp. A white horse's head has been seen lying there too, but when the person approached it, it moved further along just keeping ahead of him. Women who have gone through the bars near the swamp at night have felt hands holding on to their skirts, and even herds of pigs have dashed out to terrify belated travellers at night. Some Indians claim to have felt hands grasping their feet as they went by.   (Speck *1909:202*)

XVI

Spirit or ghostly lights once visited the pasture by Fidelia Fielding's house in the Mohegan woods. She regarded the appearances as unusual but not dangerous. Being the most traditional Mohegan of her generation, she hardly departed from the ways of her ancestors and thus had no fear of their visits.[8]

CIRCA 1905

Mrs. Fielding was aroused one night by a light that shone from the hill above her house, and while she stood watching it from her window, she saw it ascend the hill to a small heap of rocks, where it blazed up high and subsided. Then it moved to another rock and blazed high again, subsiding as before in a few moments. She had reason to be certain that no one was in the pasture, and the next morning she found no evidence of burning about the rocks. The thing was repeated a number of times and she considered herself to have been visited by spirits.   (Speck 1909:202)

XVII

Fielding's explanation for the origin of a facelike wooden growth on a tree is a variation of Thompson's motif, D 215. Transformation: man to tree, which occurs in English, Eskimo, Seneca, Crow, West African, and Narragansett folklore (text XL below). The chestnut knot story also is an unusual version of the widespread European and American belief that ghosts return to the scene of violent death (Briggs 1971, 1:417; Dorson 1946:25, 61, 156–57; Jones 1944:248).

CIRCA 1905

Several years ago a woodcutter in felling a chestnut tree near the river, picked up a roundish knot that dropped from it. He noticed that its outline and marking resembled a human face. Bringing it to Mrs. Fielding he was told it was the head of a woman who had been slain by her husband a hundred years ago. The couple lived in the grove where the man was cutting, and the head of the woman was believed to have transmigrated to the tree, to warn people of the evil of murder.   (Speck 1909:203)

XVIII

In this Gay Head story, told to Mabel Knight by Charles W. Ryan, Sarah Spaniard's nonmalevolent ghost was attuned to English, Yankee, and possibly indigenous Indian belief for it returned on certain misty nights to the place where her grandson is said to have murdered her for her savings.

1925   SARAH SPANIARD AND FOOLISH MARGIE

Sarah Spaniard saved her money so that she might have a decent burial. Her grandson came home from sea; and not long afterwards Sarah Spaniard was found dead. People said her grandson had murdered her for her money.

They took him down to the village to be tried for murder. They took too Foolish Margie, the woman Sarah Spaniard had always taken care of. They took her in an ox-cart. When they came to the court, they told her she must give a truthful answer to all questions, and they put her on the stand.

They asked her, "Did you see this man kill Sarah Spaniard?"

She answered, "The ox that brought us down had but one horn."

They asked, "How came this woman to be killed?"

She said, "Where did you catch those great, big brass buttons, Boston?"

They told her that they did not wish to hear about ox-horns or brass buttons, but wanted to know how Sarah Spaniard came to be killed.

She replied, "Nebuchadnezzar had long claws."

They had to acquit the grandson as they could prove nothing by Foolish Margie. He went away to sea and never came back. It is said to this day that on certain misty nights, the old grandmother is to be seen wandering about the place where the deed was committed.   (Knight 1925:135)

XIX

Speck condensed from Mohegan informants a number of memorates regarding the ghost of an Indian stonecutter and other ghosts that made digging sounds and threw stones. The stonecutter belief is interesting because of a later legend in which Speck himself encountered this industrious spirit (text XLIII below).

CIRCA 1925

A ghost still holds forth on the steep hillside among the rocks. Some of the Indians, in fact most of them, have at one time or another heard the clinking maul and wedge of some one splitting stone there on dark nights.

It is furthermore asserted that persons passing by this place on the roadway after dark are likely to perceive stones being thrown

*at them. Some even have felt themselves struck by the missiles. An
old general Algonkian belief perpetuated. Somewhere, also, in the
vicinity a murdered Indian is said to have been buried. The sound
of digging has been fancied to come from the place, even within
the last few years.*   (Speck 1928b:254)

XX–XXX

The tightly knit and geographically bounded Gay Head community had its share of Indian ghosts, although the island historian
Gale Huntington believes that such supernatural lore began to evap-
orate "a few generations ago" (Huntington 1969:91). In 1926 Edward
S. Burgess published a series of Gay Head legends that he had collected over the years and that dated to about the turn of the twentieth
century. Burgess wrote: "I am dealing here not with written records,
not with things already printed, but with that more shadowy, fast-
vanishing medium, the sensitive impression-plate of the Indian
mind. . . . it is my aim to make a faithful transcript of the way these
past scenes have appeared to the Indian, and have been narrated to
me by him" (Burgess [1926] 1970:2). The Gay Head ghosts known to
Burgess behaved and dressed like other Americans and reflected life
as it was lived in their day. One is hard put to pinpoint the specific
Indian characteristics of most of these apparitions. Gay Head spirits
haunt the neighborhoods where they lived, appear to persons whom
they knew, and particularly favor an area where the South Road
crosses a small, dark, peaty stream known as Black Brook. Living
animals are thought to be especially attuned to the presence of the
supernatural, and as with the Mohegan and Narragansett, animal
ghosts also travel amid humans. The first account describes the
ghostly scare and conversion of Trustram Weeks, a Gay Head schoolmaster in the early nineteenth century and the husband of the herbalist Tamson Weeks. The second legend is the most unusual of Burgess's collection. The Mayhews had founded the Gay Head
Congregational Church, which fell into disuse by about 1810. Weeks
moved this church structure in 1835 to refurbish it as a house for his
family. Once the church had settled on its new site, passersby could
hear "old-world singing" coming from its rafters, "which still vi-
brated to songs of the Mayhews' converts of long ago" (p. 18). Text
XXIV is interesting because the spirit of the deceased blew along the
road as a piece of white paper, reminiscent of Aunt Betsy Dodge who
once floated through the air as a feather. The Burgess texts are vestiges of an earlier time when Gay Headers shared material resources
and a more heightened awareness of the invisible world.

XX

1926

Not always had Uncle Trustram led the exemplary life of his middle and later years, and the story of his sudden change is that of a return late from a dancing party when he heard a horse coming on after him, dragging chains that rattled ominously. "On came the horse and circled right around him, rattling his chains. Trustram was so frightened that he rushed on home, the horse still rattling the chains round the house, as Trustram burst into the house and fell unconscious in the door; there his good Christian wife found him. When she roused him he told her how Chepie had come for him, and he had heard the chains rattle that were to bind him. It so affected him that he turned right about, went to no more drinking-parties, and became a Christian man."

(Burgess [1926] 1970:15)

XXI

1926

No more was the rattling of chains heard, but the house became known as the abode of singing. For upstairs was the big room with many rafters, lighted by a gable window at each end; roofed in with projecting beams which still seemed to give forth the voices of the old church in singing. So it was remarked by X: "It was the Trustram Weeks house which had been the old church, where people as they passed by still heard singing from its old beams, those queer old beams that I used to see upstairs there." Finally, as we have already seen, this reminder of the old meeting house, "the good beams that remained," was moved up the hill to the State Road, to do duty for Mr. Durwood Diamond. But people still refer to the Trustram Weeks house on the Old South Road as "that house where one could hear singing as he passed."

(Burgess [1926] 1970:15–16)

XXII

1926

Let us pause to consider a couple of examples taken from near our path. First, that at the home of one Q, who had survived the perils of the deep, finally to die on land, at home. In life he had been much feared by young children whom he had often scared from his place. Now would he come again? We are told of a neighbor whom we will call N., a resolute man not now himself living.

N's story is this: "I was coming from the Head one night very late. I was almost at Uncle Q's house. The old gentleman had died there the year before. As I came near the house, walking along the hill, there shone a light. I thought it queer, as no one had lived there since. I went up and I looked in at the window, and there was Old Q kneeling to his chest of tools; there was the same old Russian cap on his head and his saw in his hand; fierce and ugly, that's how he looked, that man from Madagascar. I stood up to the window, and called to him, Hello, and then Q looked up, right on to me, and then looked down again; then I called out, You're dead, I know you are! and as I called, the window was dark and I could see nothing more."   (Burgess [1926] 1970:8)

XXIII

1926

Example No. 2, from near by up the hill. "Here, said she, I was out in the field, picking beach-plums; I looked up, and here was my brother coming right toward me, though he'd been dead some years. I faced him, and he vanished."   (Burgess [1926] 1970:8)

XXIV

1926

Example 3. Said one who had lived near, "We'd been up in the pasture, Father and I, milking the cows, and came back along, passing Q's house; and there a roll of white paper showed up and came blowing out. Then as we got opposite to it, it rolled, all itself, right out in the road, and was gone."   (Burgess [1926] 1970:9)

XXV

1926

Example 4. Two sisters were out one day about fifty years ago or more, where the slope east from Gravelly Hill ended in a low bluff, when from below that bluff came a pair of black oxen; "swish, swish, they came, right on, swaying their heads as they came, and were going to pass us by but we ran; we ran home and told Mother. For you know there were no black oxen at all on Gay Head; and we knew that this which we had seen was something that was not right."   (Burgess [1926] 1970:9)

XXVI
1926   THE BOOTS BY THE BROOK

Few brooks, perhaps, have been more diversely linked with the supernatural than this. Besides being not far from the scene of the previous examples, there are other forms of the supernatural that have their abiding-place here. Here "Old people always said that Savvie locked her boots together"; or as later told, that "Savvie slapped them together." But who was Savvie? "Why when we were children, going to school, there was a pair of boots down there, by Black Brook; old leather boots; so old; stood by the road; we asked what it meant, we were told there Savvie locked her boots together; we didn't dare ask more, we never knew who she was." We know it was a custom here in days one hundred years ago, for Indian women to go barefoot, not only at home but through the woods; possessing boots or shoes but treating them as a luxury to be reserved and held in great respect. So my mother, says X, "would go barefoot to church till she had forded the last brook (Laban's Brook), then sit down and make ready to go into church by putting on the boots she had carried tied together and hanging from her neck."

Why Savvie left her boots by the brook so long remains to be discovered; perhaps she was but like many of her neighbors, long in making up her mind to go into church; but the children hurried by,—it was uncanny that the boots should wait for her so long.

(Burgess [1926] 1970:10)

XXVII
1926   THE HEADLESS MAN

Next of Black Brook's tales, is that of the Headless Man who stands by the brook at the next crossing northward. We are safe from him ourselves, there is some distance; and besides, it is broad daylight now. What is more, we are grown-up folks, aren't we? But children couldn't reason it away like this, some seventy years ago, not even by daylight.

"Lots of people have seen him there, that headless man. Old people have always told us that a man was murdered there. And one of the boys was Solomon F., he who went to sea, he got down so far on his way, and there by the brook stood the man without a head. And Solomon, he never came back. And about a year and a half after that, one of our people, his wife lives here yet, he went in there graping with his little boy; there at twilight when picking grapes he saw the headless man and he fell in a fit, and they found

him dead; good honest man he was, but singular part of it was, it was there he was found dead, just there, there where he'd seen the headless man."   (Burgess [1926] 1970:10–11)

XXVIII

1926 THE BRANCHES THAT SCRAPED

"And if it wasn't one thing at Black Brook it was another. My mother was afraid of nothing, daylight nor dark; but there by the brook she heard as she came along, somebody breaking wood; she looked in under the bushes, there was nothing there; moved on again, when the sound began once more, and now she parted the bushes and looked in, and there was nothing there. But yet she was never frightened, not by bug nor beast nor Beelzebub."

There is another localization of this conception on Gay Head, at the "Cracking-twigs Swamp," which some now will not dare to pass after dark, for the sound of someone cracking twigs there; the white man has intensified the tones of this myth in his name for the "Crying-swamp," in another part of the Vineyard; but we go back to Gay Head for the man who has elevated it into a very poem, who tells me of his "Windharp Tree," "where I listen to the music two branches make as the wind rubs them on each other."

(Burgess [1926] 1970:11)

XXIX

1926 THE HARD-BREATHING HORSE

Black Brook is also the seat of the tale of the Hard-breathing Horse. Says the heroine:

"I was a girl in the time of going to school, we children were; it was early yet, and before dark, when we got into this narrow road, and here stood a big black horse right in the brook. We ran frightened, to tell the other children, and when we came back to the brook, from telling them that there was a horse there,—there was no horse there at all any more."

"And my Aunt Tamson Weeks saw it; she wasn't afraid of anything, but on the road by Black Brook she heard a stamping behind her and she felt its breath right in her face as she passed the brook."

"And then my brother saw it; daring young man, had no fear of anything; but as he was going toward Black Brook his horse shied at something; young horse, and jumped and ran; and in a few minutes something large as a horse was following him, and then

soon the animal was running right abreast of him, and breathing so
hard. By this time brother was really frightened, and he shot off
his revolver, for he thought he might just as well let it be known
that he had one; thinking that he might keep it off. And his own
horse never stopped running till he got home."

(Burgess [*1926*] *1970:11–12*)

XXX
1926

Tradition seems to have preserved little else about this spot,
about Abel's spring, but for one superstition; that cattle can see or
feel a presence sometimes which men are blind to; and "when
cattle in that field come near the Mittark Rock, and the thickets
about the burial stones, they become strangely excited, leaping and
bellowing as nowhere else." Shall it remain so, that the cattle alone
recognize that royal line? Furthermore, a light is sometimes seen
there; but the light is in no man's hand. Shall it not light us back to
Abel and to his brother Mittark?   (Burgess [*1926*] *1970:34*)

XXXI

Although the Mohegan distinguished the will-o'-the-wisp from
foxfire, they and all other southern New England Indians associated
such luminous phenomena with ghosts, devils, and departed souls.
Hannah Pells of Mashpee described an occasion to Gladys Tanta-
guidgeon when Pells's husband chased such lights away by shooting
at them.[9]

1928   LIGHTS

Near [   ] bay lights were seen frequently. One time Mr. Pells shot
at the lights and they were not seen for a long time until lately.
Then one night we saw a light come up from the pond and it came
right up by the house and toward the wood. Like one light above
the other. (Tantaquidgeon 1928–29)

XXXII

This next account, collected by Tantaquidgeon from Rachel Ryan
of Gay Head, concerns jack-o'-lanterns, which were probably identical with will-o'-the-wisps. As in Mrs. Pells's memorate, viewers
managed to threaten the light and chase it away. Here and in other
Indian sources, the will-o'-the-wisp lurks near woods, ponds, and
swamps and will lead children and unwary travelers away from civilization. Such beliefs are ubiquitous in the area and are shared by

many other ethnic groups (Hand 1977). Rachel Ryan's story, for example, concerns a runaway slave who certainly was not from the area and probably was not Indian.[10]

1928   JACK-O-LANTERN

The Jack o' lantern was seen occasionally years ago by some of the people. But since the [   ]ks have been around in the swamps we don't see them anymore. One time, years ago, when Uncle Simon Johnson was living, John Randolph, a run away slave was on his way to Uncle Simon's house when he saw a Jack-o-lantern. He followed the light and became more and more bewildered. He was getting deeper and deeper in the swamp and so he called for help. Upon hearing him, Uncle Simon came out and said, "What the devil have you got down there?" John answered, "I can't get out of this swamp." Uncle Simon came out and said "Give him a clip." Then the nearly exhausted man attempted to strike at the light but without any success. Uncle Simon came nearer and struck it with a stick and cut it in two and the fire went in opposite directions. When they got out they looked at the stick and it was black where it had struck the Jack-o-Lantern.   (Tantaquidgeon 1928)

XXXIII

The Mashpee Spirit Fox or Witch Fox, a vestige of the aboriginal Cheepi, was still considered dangerous and a bad omen when Tantaquidgeon worked in the area in the late 1920s.

1928   SPIRIT OR WITCH FOX

The sound or sight of this "spirit fox" is dreaded by the natives who regard it as an omen of death. It is described as "something moving above the ground" something "like a light" and other times its weird cries are heard. The Mashpee call it Tcipai wankas "spirit fox."   (Tantaquidgeon 1928–29)

XXXIV

The following legend, told to Tantaquidgeon by an unnamed Mashpee resident, could have come from anywhere in the northeast, where haunted house stories are not hard to find.

1928   MASHPEE GHOSTS

Woman was annoyed by noises in house and she knew it to be the spirit of man who once lived there. She one day dressed herself in good clothes and invited man (spirit) to go out with her. She went to [another] house and said, "That is my house and this is

your house. Now stay in your house and don't bother me." The
spirit didn't bother her any more.   (Tantaquidgeon 1928–29)

XXXV

The Gay Head legend of a woman who floats in the air is reminiscent of John Josselyn's description of Cheepi in 1673 (text I above).

1928

At a certain spot near the ridge of the cliffs an old woman is
sometimes seen floating thru the air carrying a basket of fish.
                                                (Tantaquidgeon 1928)

XXXVI

Rachel Ryan's Gay Head legend "Mother and Child Frozen to
Death" is a variation of the idea that souls of persons who die a
violent death haunt the scene of their misfortune. The Indian mother
and child were said to have died because white settlers refused to
give them shelter on a cold winter night. Thereafter, corn stopped
growing on this site, and the blight serves to remind Indians of white
injustices.

1928   MOTHER AND CHILD FROZEN TO DEATH

One time, years ago, on a cold winters day an Indian woman
and her baby came to the village of [   ] and as it was nearly night
the woman sought shelter for herself and child with the settlers.
The white folks treated the Indians very badly so they refused to
take her in. Going down to the stream she sat down on a rock,
holding the child in her arms. There was but a thin coating of ice
on the stream and it would be dangerous for her to attempt to cross
it. There she sat and as it was bitter cold weather she soon per-
ished. In the morning the bodies of the mother and her child were
found frozen stiff and without attempting to identify them, the
people buried them right there. Previous to that terrible tragedy,
corn had been cultivated in the fields nearby where the two were
buried but after that corn would not grow there. It was said that it
was because of the unjust treatment received by the Indians from
the whites that caused the blight. A heap of stones marks the site
of the grave.   (Tantaquidgeon 1928)

XXXVII

In 1936 several Narragansetts contributed ghostlore to their tribal
publication, *The Narragansett Dawn.* The first legend, "On the
Tracks," explains the origin of the name of White Dog Swamp, which

is in the heart of Niantic country. Nighttime passengers on the Boston–New York train might remember this ghost when they pass through the Westerly area. Most elements appear to have been borrowed from English and Afro-American superstition.[11]

1936   ON THE TRACKS

Many years ago a tribe of Niantic Indians lived in the location of the town of Bradford, R.I. In the early part of 1800, the New York, New Haven and Hartford put a railroad from Stonington to Providence. There were a number of the tribe who lived there at that time. The railroad crossed a swamp between Westerly and Bradford, which is known as White Dog Swamp. Many years ago an Indian and his dog were going home short cut by the railroad. They were killed by the train. Ever since on dark nights, the dog and the Indian have been seen there. The great white dog will be seen coming down the track cut half in two while the Indian beside him has no head. They go down the middle of the track as far as the brook and then disappear. Many have seen this and the story keeps many away from there on dark nights; but the swamp is still called The White Dog Swamp, to this day.   (Lone Wolf 1936b)

XXXVIII

The anonymous Narragansett author of "A Ghost Story" emphasized the Indian ancestry of Red Fox, who saw the ghost, as if his Indian background were essential to the story. Perhaps Indians saw ghosts more often than their Yankee neighbors did, but this is only speculation. The principal motifs are common in Euro-American and British folklore (E 272. *Road-ghosts;* E 293. *Ghosts frighten people deliberately;* E 422.4.5. *Revenant in male dress*). Gay Head ghosts also disappeared when looked at (texts XXII and XXIII above). The automobile is a twentieth-century symbol of social and geographic mobility away from the small face-to-face community. By stepping on the gas, Red Fox found he could leave one old ghost behind.

1936   A GHOST STORY

Red Fox is a young brave who lives near Westerly with his family, a dear wife and three tiny children of Indian blood from both sides of their family trees. Red Fox is the youngest brother of Lone Wolf and is very typical in nature and disposition. He tells of a spirit or ghost he has really seen. And to hear him tell it, you unconsciously look to see if the old man stands beside you. He says one night he was driving home alone, along a lonesome road (this was before he was married, he never drives alone now) and thinking heavily of what he had left behind, when suddenly a face leaned against the window of his car, as he jogged along. He saw the hand on the sill as if the old man were hanging on. He noticed the figure was dressed in black with a big black hat and a black Winsor tie. His idea was to rush away, so he stepped on the gas, and when he looked again, the man was gone. Once since he is sure he saw the same man, who as he looked up, vanished.

("Fireside Stories" 1936:206)

XXXIX

King Philip figures more prominently in English folklore than in Indian; the following is one of the few Indian narratives regarding the seventeenth-century Wampanoag sachem. According to its Narragansett author, traditions about Philip's burial and ghost had been handed down within the Leonard family of Taunton as well as among Philip's Wampanoag descendants. Although the story concerns an Indian and the ghost appears only to Indians, the motifs are quite common in British and American legend.

Philip was killed at Mount Hope on August 12, 1676, and was then beheaded and quartered. Captain Benjamin Church decided that because Philip had caused so many English to die unburied, not one bone of his body would be put in the earth. Church gave the head and one scarred hand to Alderman, the Indian who shot him, and the head went on display for some twenty five years at Plymouth. Cotton Mather took away one of the jaws. Otherwise, almost nothing is known of the eventual disposition of his remains (Church [1716] 1827:125–26: Hubbard [1865] 1969, 1:272). Nevertheless, Philip's descendants believe that his spirit is still in the area and communicates with them every few years.

1936   UNDER THE LEONARD DOOR-STEP

Stories from the Leonard's and King Philip's families passed down from generation to generation say, that when Philip was killed his faithful warriors, not being able to steal the whole body, for fear of detection, stole the head of their chief and hid it under the door-step of the old Leonard homestead, in Taunton, until they could safely bury it, with all the sacred rituals due the mighty chief, who [died] for home and people. Indian tradition disputes history, and there are those who believe it, that the great sachem's head is buried between Taunton and Mt. Hope, and no one knows

its resting place. Tradition says that every three generations the
ghost of Philip walks abroad, and reveals to a medicine man this
spot.   ("Under the Leonard Door-Step" 1936)

XL

Narragansett beliefs associating spruce trees with the blood and
souls of dead ancestors may reflect an Indian idea, for the motif, D
215. Transformation: man to tree, is represented in several New
World mythologies, including those of the nearby Mohegan and Seneca. A legend, said to be Pequot in origin, claims that the strong
crimson centers of rhododendrons that grow in Mast Swamp in eastern Connecticut are symbolic of Pequot blood shed there in 1637.
Like the Narragansett spruce, these bloody hearted flowers are a "re-
proach to the white people" for their cruelty to Indians (Skinner
1903:129–31).[12] Princess Red Wing, founder and editor of *The Nar-*
ragansett Dawn, heard the Narragansett spruce account from an Indian old-timer, who added a warning to anyone who would try to
cut down too many of these trees.

1936
One day as a party carried your editor over miles of woodland to
find deserted Indianesque spots, an old timer said to her, "You see
those stray spruce trees on that hill side?"
"Yes, they look like sentinels."
"They are," said the old timer, "It is said, that each of those
spruce trees grow where a drop of Narragansett blood was shed.
They will ever grow in South County, no matter how much civiliza-
tion crowds them. It is said of one settler, that he decided to cut
down every spruce on his 500 acres of Indian land because they
haunted him, and he was killed in the attempt. He cut with such
vengeance, when he heard the story, that each spruce was the soul
of a Narragansett killed by a white man, that a stately spruce which
he set out to destroy, fell upon him, and killed him."
They really do look, as they stand here, there, and everywhere
throughout Narragansett country, that they were souls of departed
Red Folk.   (Red Wing 1936)

XLI

Lone Wolf's memorate regarding his meeting with an illuminated
stump is a vestige of pre-Christian belief about spirits of the dead. It
is also an example of the negative memorate and legend that appears
often in recent Narragansett folklore. In the negative memorate or

legend, the narrator plays upon the listener's interest in supernatural marvels by describing what first seemed to be a ghostly phenomenon and then dismissing it with a commonsense explanation. The narrator can eat his nocake and keep it too, first by speaking as a believer and then by exposing the belief. Lone Wolf seems not to have known the Indian name for foxfire; in contrast to Wampanoag belief—that foxfire is a sign of death—it here signifies good luck.[13]

1936   GOOD LUCK

How many of us have seen a ghost? I have! About 20 years ago one evening I went fishing some three miles from my home into the woods. About midnight the fog came in from the sea and hid the moon and stars. I said it is time to go home and after walking about half a mile, I looked up and right beside me was a big pillar of fire. As I watched, it turned to green and then to white and went out. I walked on and there it was again, I thought it moved and changed colors. The wind blew and I was about to head for parts unknown, but I seemed glued to the spot. I said the Great Spirit has sent me a sign, so I stood and watched it. Finally I walked up to where I thought I had seen the ghost and put out my hand. I touched something that was cold, wet and slimy. It felt like something from another world. I backed off and lit a match and there was my ghost. It was an old rotten stump covered with fungus growth; when the damp air settled on it, and the wind blew it, it glowed, changed colors and faded. Look in the woods for them on a damp night. They are a sign of Good Luck *to you.*   (Lone Wolf 1936a)

XLII

The story of John Onion, a young man who met the devil while skating, has been told by the Narragansett for years and is their most popular legend. Although the event took place on Cocumpaug or Schoolhouse Pond in the heart of Narragansett country, nothing in the legend speaks directly from aboriginal tradition. Although English and American devils are not known to have skated, they appear when called upon and compete with mortals (C 12. *Devil invoked: appears unexpectedly;* G 303.9.9.12. *Devil engages in horse race with man*). This legend is probably more than two centuries old, for on September 24, 1732, Reverend James MacSparran of the Episcopal church in Narragansett baptized the children of John Onion, a white man, and Deborah Onion, his wife, an Indian woman. One of their four children also was named John Onion (Updike 1907:509). John Onion's meeting with the devil served as a warning to later Narragansetts not to go too far beyond their peers.

1936   JOHN ONION

*Ever hear the story of John Onion? It has been told for many
years. Old John Onion lived in the Charlestown woods near the old
Narragansett Indian school house located about a mile back of the
Indian church, on what is now called School House Pond. He came
down to the pond to skate one bright cold night, feeling mighty
frisky. He out-skated all the other lads, and vowed he could out-
skate the devil. The other lads left him to his task. It wasn't long
before he realized he wasn't skating alone. The faster and fancier
he skated, this figure followed. He shouted but no reply. Soon he
recalled his vow of the early evening, and John asked no more
questions. Breathlessly he skated to make the shore, but the dusky
figure skated by him and disappeared. John did not stop to remove
his skates but skated right up the banks of the pond right through
the woods, as fast as his legs could carry him, and on right into the
house. He never after tried out-skating the devil.*

("Fireside Stories" 1936:206)

XLIII

One of the most unusual ghost stories in this collection concerns
the anthropologist Frank Speck and his encounter with a Mohegan
Indian ghost. Speck probably told this memorate to a Wampanoag in
the 1940s, who published it several years after Speck's death in
1950. This is a splendid example of supernatural experience reflect-
ing and helping create a feeling of community, for by validating the
Mohegan's phantasmic world Speck strengthened his own standing
among the people with whom he worked. Shared beliefs about the
supernatural help bind the living more closely together, and not to
see or believe such phenomena is to declare one's distance from the
group.[14]

CIRCA 1960   THE OLD MOHEGAN INDIAN STONE CUTTER

*The late and beloved Dr. Frank G. Speck, who spent his life
working as an ethnologist and an organizer among the Indian
Tribes of the east, once related to me one of his strangest and un-
forgettable experiences. He said that as is the manner of many
college trained students, he listened to superstitious stories as related to him by Indian friends, but that he certainly did not believe
in them, that is, until when one time something happened that
was to change his whole viewpoint about Indian ghost stories.*

*Dr. Speck had gone up to do some field work among the Mohegan
Indians who live at Mohegan Hill in the village of Uncasville, Connecticut. He was having supper with a Mohegan couple with whom*

he had spent the day taking notes on folklore and herbal lore. It had been a pleasant day, and they had rambled through the woods in the old Mohegan settlement, and he had worked up quite an appetite. I believe that the name of the couple was Cooper, and as she was preparing a big supper Indian style with corn bread, succotash, Indian Pudding and pork sausage, Dr. Speck said that as he looked out of the window he could see the orange moon beginning to rise through the tree tops. "Oh look" he said, "There is going to be a beautiful full moon tonight." As he said this, he said that the man looked at his wife and said something in a low voice that was not intended for Dr. Speck to hear. He noticed this but said nothing.

When supper was ready, Dr. Speck and the Coopers sat down to a hearty meal and really enjoyed themselves. After the meal they got up and sat down around the kitchen stove and relaxed with the good smell of woodsmoke, and Doc lit up a cigar. He was so relaxed he said that he did not notice the time, and when he looked at his watch he said that it was time for him to go back to Cynthia Fowler's house. The lady then looked at Dr. Speck in a strange way and said that she and her husband thought it best that he remained with them for the night. Doc replied that since Cynthia would be expecting him he thought that he should be on his way. Both husband and wife then looked at each other strangely and seemed to be sort of embarrassed. Dr. Speck then spoke up and asked if there was something wrong. The woman stopped rocking in her chair and looked at Dr. Speck directly and said, "Dr. Speck, the old Indian Stone Cutter will be working tonight!" He looked at the woman relieved and said, "Well that's all right with me. I don't mind if he is working tonight, and I can understand if he has so much work to do during the day that at night he might have to work over to finish up his chores." The woman and her husband looked again at each other, and it was then that Dr. Speck knew by their glances that something was really wrong.

Finally the man spoke up and said, "Dr. Speck, the old Indian Stone Cutter has been dead over 30 years, and when the moon is full he comes out to work and you will have to pass right by the quarry where he works and you will be sure to hear him. We think you had better stay with us tonight!" The Dr. did not wish to hurt their feelings by telling that he did not believe in such things, but he decided to be tactful about the matter. "Now don't you folks worry," he began, "If anything goes wrong I will let you know tomorrow, but I will be all right!" He bade them both good night and started out through the woods whistling. As he came close to the quarry, he felt strange and stopped for a moment. The chink, chink

sound of someone cutting stone was coming from the quarry. Dr.
Speck said to himself, "Oh that is just my imagination playing
tricks upon me." He started to walk again and the closer he came
to the quarry, the louder the sound of stone cutting became. He
thought to himself, I will go see who is out cutting stone at this
hour. Finally as he walked closer to the sound, and as it became
louder he could see no one in sight though the moon was nice and
clear. Suddenly the sound stopped and he felt relieved and knew
that it was only his imagination. He breathed a sigh of relief, but
suddenly the sound commenced again, and this time it was directly
in back of him. He wheeled around and saw no one, and then he
decided to move. He ran through the woods and the sound followed
him and he never stopped until he reached the Cooper home. He
bolted in the door, and there was a note on the table by the lamp. It
said, "We knew that you would be back. Your bed is all turned
down. See you in the morning." He went to bed right away, but said
that he could not forget how those sounds followed him. From that
moment on, whenever the Indian people gave him advice or told
him about some haunted spot to stay away from, Dr. Frank G.
Speck never made light of their superstitions, and if they advised
him not to go to this place or that place, he heeded them.

Hearing the old Mohegan Indian Stone Cutter had made him a
changed man.   ("The Old Mohegan Indian Stone Cutter" ca. 1960)

XLIV–LII

Dorothy R. Scoville, who is not an Indian but who has been living
on Gay Head for many years, has a sensitive ear for local legends and
published many in Indian Legends of Martha's Vineyard (1970).
Scoville obtained some of her material from published sources as
well as from a number of Gay Headers, including Mary Vanderhoop,
Nanetta V. Madison, Rachel Ryan, James Cooper, and Linus Jeffers.
The motifs are more British and Euro-American than they are Indian
in origin, which is not to deny that they are products of Gay Head
collective tradition. Scoville noted, "Almost every one on Aquinnah
[Gay Head] has seen apparitions of a loved one" (Scoville 1970:25).[15]

XLIV

1970

There is a house on Gay Head which long ago stood empty. A
once commonly used path from the shore to the village, passed
through the yard. The house was very old and had been lived in by
a large family, which one by one had "died off" until only distant

relatives were left. So there was no ready explanation as to why
some heard the distinct sound of a baby wailing from an upstairs
room, while others saw a light shining from the kitchen. Yet when
anyone came bravely near to investigate, the house was empty. The
baby's cries were silenced and there was no lamp in the kitchen
window.

Now the house is occupied and the present owners have not, of
late, heard or seen anything unusual. Once the young wife of the
present owner heard steps across the floor but when she went
downstairs to investigate there was no one to be seen and the door
was still bolted.   (Scoville 1970:24)

XLV

1970

In more recent times there was a young student coming home for
the holidays, saddened somewhat because her pet dog had died
while she was away and so would not be there to greet her. She was
hurrying toward the house when suddenly the beloved animal
appeared from around the corner, jumping and wagging as was his
happy custom. She eagerly reached out to pat him when he vanished, never to reappear to her.   (Scoville 1970:24)

XLVI

1970

Another such unexplained incident involved an old dog whose
master died. The dog mourned him and one day not long after,
seemingly heard a familiar step outside. He got stiffly up from his
nap, eagerly wagging, and went to the door as if ready to greet a
well known presence. When the door was opened for him, no one
was there, but the dog showed all the pleasure of a welcome, then
trotted over to the chair which his master customarily had occupied, and lay down there, apparently content.   (Scoville 1970:24)

XLVII

1970

At one of the houses once occupied by a whaleman, a man in
yellow oilskins has been seen down by the stone wall barway. He
usually appears in the half dark, carrying a lighted lantern as if
searching for someone. The road he follows leads up from the
beach, where long ago a ship was lost with all of its crew.

"Looking for his shipmates, most likely," explain the ones who
have seen the ghostly figure.   (Scoville 1970:24–25)

XLVIII
1970

In the old days Aquinnah people often held impromptu dances in their homes. Furniture was cleared out of whatever room was largest and a fiddler would provide the music. Many were talented musically and played or sang by ear, even as they do today.

A lively dance was in progress one night and when an intermission came, the fiddler left his seat for refreshment. Suddenly the music was resumed in a wildly frantic rhythm, but the dancers stood frozen with horror. There in the center of the room sat the Devil, fiddling for all to see. The dancers as well as their own musician, looked then fled. To this day, that fiddle has never been touched by its owner, and the Devil is forever looking for a fiddle to play but no one on Aquinnah will welcome him.   (Scoville 1970:25)

XLIX
1970

A headless man has been seen, standing beside the brook, say the Old People. He was murdered there and he is looking for his killer. Once the headless man was seen by a whaleman on his way to Edgartown to ship out on a whaler. The ship sailed and never was heard from. Again, the headless man appeared before a father and his small son who were picking wild grapes near Black Brook. The father, a strong, seemingly healthy man, fell dead. No one wanted to see the headless man for fear of what his appearance might portend.   (Scoville 1970:22)

L
1970

Then there was the handsome black horse that was seen by several people whose word was never doubted. The animal was always standing by Black Brook as if waiting for a rider but there was no rider and the horse could not be found by those brave enough to hunt for him the length and breadth of Aquinnah. Nor had anyone on Aquinnah ever owned such a horse.   (Scoville 1970:22)

LI
1970

Not so many years ago, a descendant of Moshop's family was walking home one snowy, moonlight night. Nearing Black Brook he heard footsteps coming along behind him. The wind was still and

the sound carried. He stopped and halloed but there was no answer.
Looking back he could see no one and there were no footprints in
the snow.

He said later, "The footsteps followed me all the way to where
the road turns toward the church and fear was riding me like a
nightmare until I reached home."   (Scoville 1970:22)

LII

1970

Two small sisters were out picking berries one day when they
saw a pair of huge black oxen pass by "with a great swishing
sound," and later when the girls rushed home to tell their parents
about it, their parents listened gravely and shook their heads. There
were no black oxen anywhere on Aquinnah.   (Scoville 1970:22)

LIII

Helen Attaquin informs us that Cheepi finally disappeared. Attaquin is a native of Gay Head and one of the few remaining southern
New England Indians with an Algonquian family name. By vanishing in a storm, Cheepi departed in a way that is compatible with
Indian and English beliefs about the devil.

1970

Many, many moons ago, another legendary Indian giant lived at
Gay Head. This was Cheepii, the Evil One, known for his mischief
and trouble-making. He lived in a den in one of the great hills on
the south side of Aquiniuh. One night, after one of his big Pow-
wows, he disappeared in a terrible storm, and was never heard
from again.   (Attaquin 1970:15)

LIV

In 1974 I spoke with Ella Thomas Seketau of the Narragansett tribe
about my visit to the stone marker at Smith's Castle, near Wickford,
Rhode Island, where the English soldiers killed in the Great Swamp
Fight of December 19, 1675, are buried. She too had visited this site,
where she beheld a vision of a silent, frosty-bearded Puritan soldier.

CIRCA 1970

When I visited that place I had a vision of the face of an old man
with white hair and a beard looking frightening and staring at me
with ice in his hair.   (Seketau 1974)

LV

The Narragansett tribal church is a sturdy granite structure that rests on the site of an earlier wooden church in deep woods by an ancient Narragansett cemetery. Even today this section of Charlestown is one of the most secluded corners of southern New England. Ethel Boissevain, an anthropologist who spends her summers in Narragansett country and who has been studying their history and traditions for over thirty years, collected a legend about ghosts heard singing in this church. Perhaps these "haunts" knew those who sang in the rafters of Trustram Weeks's house at Gay Head, and surely they knew the "Old Indian Hymn" that the Narragansett heard in the air before Europeans came to North America (chapter 4, VIII). The motifs in this legend are familiar ones in West European and Euro-American folklore.[16]

1973

The funeral of Abby Hopstans was to take place at noon. Before it, two members of the council stayed by her coffin then in the church. They got talking about matters supernatural. George related a reminiscence of his aunt: One night as they drove in their ox cart from visiting relatives near the church, a night when no church service was to be held, as they approached the church they saw that it was all lighted up and they could hear singing coming from it. When they came really close to the church it was dark and silent. Seymour Nokastans agreed that he had heard a similar story from his grandmother. He said he didn't really believe in haunts but if this happened in a church something must have happened.   (Boissevain 1973:14)

LVI

One Narragansett recounted to Boissevain an occasion when he thought ghosts were whistling at him. As in the earlier negative memorate "Good Luck" (text XLI above), the experience proved to have a natural (if unusual) explanation.

1973

Seymour told Benjamin about a situation that started to be supernatural but had a natural explanation with the joke on him: One night he wanted to go to the Saturday night dance. His family discouraged him, saying that he might get involved in a fight. But he started out anyway, in fact, wearing his uncle's stovepipe hat.

*As he was walking along he heard a whistling behind him, in his
ears. He walked on, the whistling continued, this went on so much
that he changed his steps and went back home. There he was
greeted by his uncle who said "That ain't no haunt—look at the
vent holes in your hat—the wind comes through and makes a
sound that makes you think the haunts are after you."*

(Boissevain 1973:13)

LVII

Michael Bell, Rhode Island state folklorist, heard a John Onion
story from the late Ferris Babcock Dove (1916–83), a former council
member and war chief of the Narragansett tribe. In Dove's account,
and in the later one narrated by Laura Mars (text LXIV below),
sparks flew from the devil's skates as he passed Johnny Onion on the
ice. Dove heard the story from his mother who learned it from her
grandmother, and he added that the Narragansett generally tell stories at night, particularly in the winter. The moral of the John Onion
story, said Dove, was that "anything you speak up against—either
good or evil (the devil or the Great Spirit)—you're not going to beat
either one" (Bell 1981). Although this is an understandable moral
for a people who have coped for centuries with being a powerless
and marginal minority, Dove's own career as a businessman and the
tribe's success in 1983 in attaining federal recognition suggest that it
may no longer ring quite as true as it once did.

1981

*John Onion was about the fastest skater in the area and he knew
it. And he was quite cocky about the whole thing. So this evening
he was around skating, skating around, skating around his friends
and everything else. It was just about dusk and he said to his
friends, well he says if anybody wants to I'll race up to the other
end of the Pond and back again. And, one of the Indians said "You
think you're quite good, don't ya?" He said, "Yes, I know I'm good."
He said, "Why I can even beat the devil skating." So with that he
took off. Some of the other young fellows started out, but he was so
fast he got way ahead of them and in the distance toward the
schoolhouse, he happened to see a figure. And he noticed there
were sparks coming down where his skates hit the ice. So, and he
kept skating towards it. He said "Well, whoever that fellow is, he is
really skating cause he's got sparks coming right out of his skates."
And when he got up close to him he observed that he had little*

horns sticking out of his head and not only that, but this fellow as fast as he was going, he just kept skating around him, backwards and cross-toed in front of him and everything else. And John Onion got nervous then, in fact he got scared. And so he high-tailed it down the pond, back to Quacumpaug area, to go off to go home. And in the meantime, this little fellow—he skated around him dozens of times on the way down, with his skates, with the sparks coming from his skates. And John Onion realized then that he couldn't of beat the devil, because that had to have been the devil—skating like that and with that he took off right over the ice, right home with his skates on—didn't bother to take 'em off. And that is the story of "John Onion" skating against the devil. (Bell 1981)

LVIII

The Reverend Harold Mars, who lived part of his life in Gay Head, where his father was pastor, served the Narragansett for many years as minister of their church. Now retired, he and his wife live in the woods of the old Narragansett reservation. Reverend Mars told me about a Narragansett tradition involving the Crying Rocks, a glacial stone formation in Charlestown where the sounds of ghostly children can be heard. Mars's Crying Rocks seem to be the same as the Bastard Rocks described in 1761 by Ezra Stiles. A Narragansett named John Paul told Stiles that before the English came, Narragansett mothers who gave birth to illegitimate children would do so in the woods and then kill the infant near the rocks, "where they killed so many Infants, & their Bones lay about so thick, that they go by the name of the Bastard Rocks to this Day" (Stiles 1916:145). Speaking more than two centuries later, Mars did not mention illegitimate children but attributed the sounds to deformed and handicapped children abandoned because they could not survive the rigors of aboriginal life. Although the legend has changed, this site and its ghostly associations are connected with early historic and probably prehistoric Narragansett belief (see also a Mohegan version in text XIII above).[17]

1983   THE CRYING ROCKS

The story that I've always heard about the Crying Rocks, they have to do with a large mass of big rocks there somewhat north of the old schoolhouse and right on the edge of the cedar swamp. Now one of the older Indian men who was a member of the family would tell of passing by these rocks certain hours of the night,

*late at night, and perhaps if the wind happened to be in the right
direction and he would hear what sounded like babies crying and
we have heard that story all of our lives and that's how it got its
name, the Crying Rocks. Now the story behind that is that, the
legend is, that the Indian recognizing the fact that they were exposed to life in the raw so to speak, that when a child was born
deformed or crippled in any manner, it was the plan and practice
of the Indian people, with proper ceremony, to put that child to
death because obviously the child would be handicapped. If he
was a man child he would be handicapped as a boy and as a hunter
or as a fighter, and so it is said for that reason why they would put
the child to death, and this thing having gone on for many years,
why there was a build up of little skeletons, and out of this came
the Crying Rock story. It's been kind of a scary thing, most folks
wouldn't go down there two or three o'clock in the morning to hear
about it. . . . . This big mass of rocks is located just about, I would
say, about a little less than a mile from the church going in a westerly direction down through the woods by the spring . . . on the old
reservation right at the edge of the cedar swamp.*   (H. Mars *1983*)

LIX

While the Mohegan spoke of a ghostly horse's head that moved
about their haunted swamp (text XV above), the Narragansett and
Gay Head Wampanoag (and many English New Englanders) spoke of
a headless horse. Reverend Mars thought that he too had seen the
headless horse one night, but changed his mind in daylight. This is
another Narragansett negative memorate that concludes with a natural explanation.[18]

1983   THE HEADLESS HORSE

*I remember another story that Granddad told me of the headless
horse. These are probably not far from our home. And of course
they would elaborate on these things, and of course as children
you had to sit around and listen. And they become indelibly imprint in your mind, of course, with the oohs and the aahs and the
sweat, perspire; why, you always knew that you wouldn't venture
out after dark. But one night as a boy scout, having attended the
boy scout meeting in town, the hour was rather late now getting
home about eleven o'clock, and as I came up what we call Belmont
Avenue in Wakefield, why I was suddenly reminded that that
headless horse was just ahead, and true enough, I saw the headless*

horse, a white horse with no head, and of course I slipped into high gear. And I'll never forget I was so frightened I just fell up against the door at home and broke the door in getting out of the way of the headless horse. But I saw about the next day when I went by there, there was a white horse in a field but he had—they had low stone walls in that area, and evidently the horse was grazing and I couldn't see his head, I just saw his big body. But nevertheless, many of those kinds of stories they would tell us, and I've forgotten many of them, but had to do with dogs barking, chains rattling, and voices crying out at night and groans and things like that—that of course was part of the tradition of our people.

(H. Mars 1983)

LX

Some of the rattling chains and ghostly dogs lurked around a place known as the four corners between Peacedale and Kingston Village.[19]

1983

We had in our area, we had another superstition . . . as children there was a corner, a section of the highway between Peacedale and Kingston, where another road crossed the main road, and it was called the four corners. At this four corners, at a certain time of night, you would hear the rattle of chains and these chains held two big dogs, and just why they told the story I don't know, but one thing is certain, nobody went by that corner much after dark.

(H. Mars 1983)

LXI

Reverend Mars narrated a legend of Indian Run, a small stream in Peacedale, Rhode Island, which encapsulates the feelings held by generations of Narragansetts regarding their suffering as a colonized people. The story resembles many other American ghost legends in that the ghost of a murdered person remains close by the scene of his violent death (E 334.1. Ghost haunts scene of former crime or sin; E 334.2.1. Ghost of murdered person haunts burial spot; E 411.10. Persons who die violent or accidental deaths cannot rest in grave). In common with the Mohegan Papoose Rock and the Pequot legend of bloody heart rhododendrons, and other English and American legends, the murder left an ineradicable bloodstain (E 422.1.11.5. Revenant as blood; E 422.1.11.5.1. Ineradicable *bloodstain after bloody tragedy).* Ghostly cries and screams also are known in British and American folklore (E 402.1.1.3. *Ghost cries and screams).* Interestingly, the Yankee people from this area have a different legend about the origin of the name Indian Run. Theirs also goes back to colonial times when Indians pursued an English settler who had killed one of their number, but the Englishman avoided capture by hiding among nearby rocks ("A Tradition of Indian Run" 1884; Gardiner 1883:115).

1983   INDIAN RUN

Then there was the story of Indian Run that my dad used to tell me. Indian Run is a little brook that runs side of the old Kingston Road opposite what we call the Old Mountain Field in Peacedale, and . . . it runs into Old Mountain Pond, I think, but anyhow the ghost story attached to that is the screams of a murdered man. They call it the Indian Run because an Indian man was murdered there and throwed in that brook. . . . The eerie sounds that come from there are attributed to the fact that this Indian man was killed by, I guess, one of the Hazards.[20] *You see, the Hazards were migrating into this area; many times in their land transactions if it didn't work out, well, you lost your life. But that was one of the stories attached to the Old Indian Run. I've heard it said that at times they would see blood in the stream. What happened was, many times in those days our people would tell these stories, many times to keep you from trespassing on properties because many times they would do bad things to people, they would whip you, or . . . they would take you and send you away for indentured service somewhere. . . . Many of our people were lost, many things were done; of course, we had no way of documenting these things, no proof to it. . . . The old people would discuss it between themselves and they'd often do it rather close mouthed because you'd be punished if you dared to point your finger at anyone.*   (H. Mars *1983*)

LXII

Reverend Mars's geological explanation for the talking ghosts on Sugarloaf Hill in Wakefield, Rhode Island, is yet another negative legend.

1983

They further claim that that hill was made, you see, by the Indian people, and old lady Watson, she used to come do the laundry and she would tell us that in that hill there were the bodies of these

Indian people, and that at night they would talk. Now I happened to be there one night and we heard this sound, but the explanation that we had later was that the heavy trains moving past the Kingston railroad station there seems to be some strata of rock that would come under the land here that would echo and re-echo when that big train went by; now this [is] just another legend that would kind of justify the peculiar sound we heard there and somewhat alleviate the fears, but nobody spent any nights on Sugarloaf Hill. This is always a legend of our people, and it's still true. (H. Mars 1983)

LXIII–LXV

Laura Mars lived most of her years in the Indian area of southern Rhode Island. As a child growing up on the former reservation, she heard many stories from her mother, including the following one about a man who stopped playing cards once he realized he had been playing with the devil. This legend appears in numerous variations throughout the eastern United States and among a range of ethnic groups, including the twentieth-century Wampanoag of Gay Head. Mrs. Mars's second story, which resembles the first, is the John Onion story that we have seen before. In both of Laura Mars's legends the devil's feet do not touch the ground, reminiscent of earlier Indian sightings of Cheepi. As a child, Mrs. Mars also heard of ghostly lights that led children into dangerous swamps and quicksand. Such beliefs surely discouraged children from wandering too far from home.[21]

LXIII

1983

This man . . . used to play cards, was always playing cards, and she said that he was told by the family that he should not do it, but in drinking they got to playing cards this night, and he said he could beat the devil playing cards, so while he was playing these cards this man came and set down on the other side of the table and begun to play cards with him, and no matter how many games he played, he never could seem to win. And so in the end he gave up, and when he did, this man got up from the table and walked out, and when he did, his feet didn't touch the ground, and he found out he'd been playing with the devil. And from then on he wouldn't play cards any more. (L. Mars 1983)

LXIV

1983

And the same thing happened to another man who used to skate, was a beautiful skater, another Indian, and this Indian man said [he] was a beautiful skater and no matter who he skated with, he always won, and he made the same statement: "I can beat the Devil." So he was out skating round the ice, and this man came on the ice and began to skate with him, and they skated round the pond for quite a while and this figure outskated this Indian man, and when he looked, he skated off and left him, and when he did they said was fire coming out the back of his skates and his feet didn't touch the ice at all. That was another one they put out.

(L. Mars *1983*)

LXV

1983

And then another one Mother told us was when the children didn't behave here on the reservation, in fact she used to tell us the same thing to make us children behave, that there was a light that would come out of the woods from down by the spring, and this big light would come out on the edge of the woods, and the bad children would follow this light and it would carry 'em back into the woodlands to where there was . . . what do they call it, sinking sand we used to call it, or the quicksand, and they never were heard of again. And of course when we got that, you can imagine how us children would quiet down and behave ourselves. But she said the same thing could happen to us if we did not behave that happened to those children.

(L. Mars *1983*)

LXVI–LXIX

Ghosts still wander about Gay Head, but mainly now in people's memories. Donald Melanson, chief of the Gay Head Wampanoag, heard of several that resemble earlier sightings from Gay Head, Mohegan, and Narragansett.[22]

LXVI

1983

At the Jeffers homestead, when they came home at night they would see a man with a lantern walking up the hill, except that he would continue right on up into the air.

(Melanson *1983*)

LXVII

1983

The yellow house on this side of town hall, a ghost was often seen there when it rained. It would then disappear, in a raincoat.

(Melanson *1983*)

LXVIII

1983

At four corners a guy would come out and play a violin with no head, at certain times of year.   (Melanson *1983*)

LXIX

1983

During World War I a guy's brother was in the service. The night he was killed there was a dance here. He looked up from playing the concertina and saw his brother dancing. He wouldn't play any more. He heard that his brother was killed.   (Melanson *1983*)

LXX–LXXII

Wenonah Silva, a granddaughter of Mary C. Vanderhoop, lives on the road to Gay Head, where she makes pottery and baskets. She spoke of the Vanderhoop dog, an animal ghost that glowed like the will-o'-the-wisp and led people astray. Silva also told of how her Aunt Hattie's cat was sensitive to spirit presences and reminisced about Black Brook's former mysteries.[23]

LXX

1983   THE VANDERHOOP DOG

There was a family story that was connected with the Vander-hoops, and it was called "The Vanderhoop Dog." And this dog was supposed to have been real, but it was supposed to glow at night and it would come at night and try to lead the person to an evil place or an evil circumstance, and several Vanderhoop people apparently were supposed to have seen this dog, and I grew up in the absolute fear of coming across the Vanderhoop dog, which would have been, to my way of expecting, would have been fiery, and you know, sort of eerie and scary, but several people were supposed to have seen this, you know, and heard a growling sound.   (Silva *1983*)

LXXI

1983

Aunt Hattie said that her cat would be sleeping in the chair and sometimes growl real low and watch something crossing the room. She would say spirits are walking tonight. She believed animals could see spirits that humans couldn't.   (Silva 1983)

LXXII

1983

Black Brook was supposed to be the habitation of . . . people who had died and came back, and they stayed around here and haunted people, they approached them, you could hear the foot- steps on a foggy night in back of you, and it might have been some- one from Black Brook, a spirit from the other world, and they were, you know, attuned to this and, I don't know, I guess I grew up with such feeling for that that my husband called me sinsaid, which in Portuguese means witch.   (Silva 1983)

LXXIII

Ada Manning, another elderly Gay Head woman who lives in a cottage near the lighthouse and cliffs, also commented on the sensi- tivity of animals to spirits.

1983

My stepfather said . . . that at Black Brook, he had a horse and wagon because he delivered mail. He said lots of times when going to Black Brook his horse would stop and he couldn't get him to go for a few minutes, because there was something there.

(Manning 1983)

LXXIV

The author heard the final ghost story from Ella Seketau while visiting the Narragansett longhouse in June 1984. The Narragansett church, where similar lights were seen, is close to the old Peckham house, where several Narragansetts recently saw a strange lantern glow.

1984   OLD PECKHAM HOUSE

This happened recently. My daughter and another kid went near where the old Peckham house stood, past Signal Rock near Church

Road. They went there junking. It was light. They were looking for copper, brass, lead—things to sell. They were in the place and it started to get dark. They had flashlights with them. They drove out and one wanted to go back to look in a shed. They looked back and there was a light in the upstairs window. One said, "Did you leave a flashlight?" He said no. It looked like a lantern light, yellow light. They went back and went through the whole house, and nothing. No sign of a lantern or anything else. And the sun had been set for over an hour and a half. They went again and there it was again, but they said that's something that should be there. (Seketau 1984)

As shamanism and Indian autonomy collapsed in the seventeenth century, the spirits from whom they derived authority also conceded their central place in Indian religion. Cheepi or Hobbamock withdrew to the periphery of curing and other minor rituals, remaining important mainly to folk healers who worked in the shadows of Christianity. After more than three centuries of intermingling with Old World folklore, Indian supernatural folklore is quite similar to that of the larger society. However, some aboriginal motifs persist, and the societal functions of ghost and devil lore have shown considerable continuity throughout the historic period. Ghosts in memorate and legend have authority that the dead lack in reality—the ability to compel the living to follow through on their commitments to the dead. Ghostly lights that lead people astray also shine in society's behalf by reinforcing parental authority over children. The devils and ghosts that frighten people at dances, card games, and frolics are acting in the service of societal norms and domestic responsibility. Legends about tragic places stress kinship values through geological reminders of the sufferings that befell children who did not have proper families to care for them. Other environmental features, such as the bloody water at Indian Run, Narragansett spruce trees, and the blighted cornfield where the mother and child froze to death, quietly pass judgment on whites for their cruelties to Indians. Even if the belief that ghosts return to the scene of their murders does not prevent such crimes, it communicates sadness and sympathy for the victims, who always have the last word. The ghost at Indian Run protected property, and the devil startled John Onion for flaunting his ability. In these and other cases, ghosts and devils work diligently behind the scenes without much credit as upholders of the moral order.

Where relations between the living are intense and continuous through the generations, where the present recapitulates the past to a greater degree, spirits of the departed figure authoritatively in religious consciousness. The role of ghosts and devils declined in the twentieth century as the communities they protected moved closer to the mainstream of American society.[24] As the roads, crossroads, railways, and other thoroughfares filled with strangers, the ghosts that once helped regulate social life in these localities found it harder to be seen and heard. Ghosts still appear in negative legends and memorates, where they are a source of humor, but they no longer play a significant role in informal social sanctions. The ghosts of contemporary folklore are like the victims of rapid change whose jobs have become obsolete.

8 Treasures

The treasure story is a category of folk narrative that is widespread and particularly well represented in historic American, West European, Caribbean, and Latin American oral traditions. The stories are not indigenous to the New England Indians, and none were recorded among them until the twentieth century. All legends presented here, including the Mashpee tradition of the Screecham sisters (chapter 6, XXIX), are clearly adapted from Euro-American prototypes in which the treasure is rarely found. Early historic New England Indians often buried their most valuable possessions with the dead and did not excavate graves to obtain their contents. This attitude exists even today, for contemporary New England Indians would rather see archaeological sites and burial grounds left undisturbed. Thus, not only was the treasure story alien to aboriginal tradition but Indians disapproved of attempts to recover whatever treasures their ancestors might have buried.

The Euro-American treasure legend usually involves pirates who bury their ill-gotten wealth and kill one of their crew, whose ghost guards the chest or kettle filled with gold. Ghosts of dogs, snakes, and other animals occasionally protect the treasure in place of, or in the company of, human ghosts. Treasure hunters usually fail in their quest because one of their group breaks the rule of silence that all are required to observe, whereupon the treasure disappears or sinks deeper into the ground. Sometimes the devil owns the treasure and offers it to someone in exchange for his or her soul or the soul of a close friend or relative. In this and in many other folklore traditions, treasure is considered dangerous. Treasure is thought to be evil, according to John Lindow, because the sudden acquisition of wealth would be socially disruptive to most human communities. Narratives of fortune hunters who refuse the treasure or who fail to find it thus reaffirm support for the status quo (Lindow 1982:275).

I

In 1972 Gladys Tantaquidgeon published a Mohegan treasure story told by her uncle, Burrill H. Fielding (1862–1952), about an incident that probably occurred in the late nineteenth century. Tantaquidgeon repeated this legend to me as recently as June 1984, adding that the large black animal may have been a bear.[1]

CIRCA 1900

For three nights I had the same dream. I was walking in the old Shantup burying ground along the banks of the river. There I saw a stand of three white birches near a flat rock. I decided that was the place to dig. So I asked Henry Dolbeare, a Mohegan Indian, to go with me on a certain night. At last the time came and we took our shovels and went to the burying ground, arriving there about midnight. There were the three white birches and the flat rock, the same as in my dream. It was a bright, moonlight night. We began digging and not a word was said. Just as I felt my shovel hit what seemed to be a board, a large black animal ran between me and my partner. We let out a yell and ran from the place leaving our shovels behind. After a few days, we went and got the shovels, but never tried digging at midnight again. (Tantaquidgeon 1972:92)

II

Judging from the numerous Captain Kidd stories along the Atlantic coast, the pirate spent most of his days burying treasure and killing members of his crew. The following Mohegan legend collected by Speck is typically American in that the site is located in a dream (N 531. *Treasure discovered through dream*) and the treasure is not recovered. The dream element also could have Mohegan roots, for all northeastern Indians, including the Mohegan, attributed significance to dreams (Speck 1928b:274–75). However, the ghostly guardians of the chest, the taboo against speaking, and the practice of driving a stake or nail into the chest to subdue the ghost were widespread in British and Anglo-American folklore traditions.[2]

CIRCA 1905   CAPTAIN KIDD AND THE PIRATES

In the days of Captain Kidd he and other buccaneers used to come up the Thames River [of Connecticut] in their boats and lie to during the periods of pursuit. Up there among the Indians they could pass the time pleasantly, and also find secluded regions wherein to bury their booty. So the Mohegans have some tales of these visits from the pirates which have furnished the motive for many nightly excursions to dreamt-of spots where treasure is thought to exist. Until this day futile attempts are made to lay hands on some of the gold that is said to be buried along the river shores.

One time two Mohegans, having dreamed of a certain spot where Kidd's money was buried, went down to the river with spades. They began their trench, and soon had the good fortune to disclose the top of a great iron box with a ring in it. Their surprise was so great that one of them said, "Here it is!" At that moment a tremendous black dog appeared at the rim of the pit and growled. At the same moment the chest vanished. The men were so terrified that they never tried to find the place again.

Sometimes the animal, instead of being a black dog, is a pig, and it has even been reported as a terrible-looking man with long robes and clotted hair. It is explained by the belief that Kidd, when he buried his loot, always killed some animal or man and threw him into the pit in order that his spirit might guard the spot.

The following are the instructions that must be observed by the treasure seeker, else his search end in disappointment and fright. The golden disclosure is only made in dreams, and those who are so fortunate as to be visited with one at once engage the help of a trusty friend. The treasure must be sought for in the exact place indicated by the dream. The searchers must provide themselves with a stake or nail to drive into the box the moment it is seen. And, above all, not a word must be spoken until the stake is securely fastened, else the whole thing will disappear and the guardian spirit be released upon the scene. If the taboos be properly kept, success is insured; but unfortunately no one has so far succeeded in keeping them and the treasure yet remains untouched.

A story is told about a family who occupied the house where Captain Fitch lately lived. It seems that Captain Kidd and a band of his followers stopped at this house once, and the mistress served them all with a hearty and bounteous dinner. After they had consumed it Captain Kidd arose, and after instructing the hostess to hold out her apron, poured gold pieces into it until the strings broke, as a reward for her goodness.   (Speck 1928b:276–77)

III

This Mashpee account of the devil's offer to give a Frenchman gold for his soul is one of many New England legends in which the devil trades valuables for human souls (Dorson 1946:47–51). The Mashpee legend is distinctive because people are said to refuse the treasure in order to protect themselves from the curse that afflicted those who tried to recover it. One can read several morals into this story: treasure is evil, the price for finding it is high, and Indians are unwilling to pay the price. Mabel F. Knight collected the text from Chief Massipaug of Mashpee.[3]

1925   A POT OF GOLD

A Frenchman came to South Mashpee. One day the Devil appeared before him in the woods, and showed him a kettle of gold. He offered it to him in return for his soul. The Frenchman sold himself to the Devil for the pot of gold. As soon as the Devil had disappeared, the Frenchman was frightened; he could not bear the thought of touching the money. He buried the pot of gold, and fled. The curse, however, had already come upon him, and within thirty days he died.

The kettle of gold remained buried in the woods. One day an Indian came that way holding his pointed moneystick. Suddenly it bent downward, and he knew he had come to the place of buried treasure. He dug it up; but within thirty days that Indian died. So all the inhabitants of Mashpee discovered that the curse was still upon the hidden treasure, and no one wished to dig for it. This happened many years ago, and today only a few still know the site of the hidden treasure.   (Knight *1925:134*).

IV

Knight learned another devil or ghost legend involving an elusive buried treasure, from Charles William Ryan, a Gay Head Wampanoag. Many elements in Ryan's story recur in white American folklore, such as the ghostly figure in sailor clothes, the kettle filled with gold, and the mysterious theft of the treasure by an unknown hand (Hurley 1951:204; Skinner 1896:267, 271). The transparent human figure (F 529.5. *Person with transparent body*) occurs in western European and American folklore but has not been attested previously in the southern New England Indian setting. This Gay Head legend resembles Chief Massipaug's Mashpee story in that the treasure is believed to come from an evil source and a good person ignores such temptations. In both accounts the affluence symbolized by treasure is unattainable and morally undesirable, despite the Indians' humble material resources.

1925 A GHOST STORY

One night at Gay Head, an Indian woman and her children were all alone in the house. The children were sound asleep in bed and the woman sat knitting by the fire-place. As is the custom today with many Indians, her door was standing open. The woman was sure she heard some one come to her door and went to see who it was. There was a sailor standing in the open doorway. The woman asked him what he wanted, and the sailor said he would like to come inside and get warm, because his clothes were wet and he felt chilly. The woman placed a chair by the fire and the sailor sat down in it.

The woman put another log on the fire, and as she sat there knitting and watching the fire, she noticed that she could see the fire right through his feet, for his feet were stuck out, so that they came between the woman and the fire, but that did not prevent her from seeing the blaze, just as if his feet were not there. This made her very much afraid, but she was a brave woman and said nothing, merely kept right on knitting. Finally the sailor turned to her and said,

"Do you want any money?"

She didn't answer at first, so he repeated his question, and then she replied, "Yes."

The sailor told her that if she really wanted some, all that she would have to do, would be to go outdoors to the back of her house and there beside a rock she would find buried a kettleful of money. After he had given the Indian woman directions for finding that kettle, the sailor thanked her for her hospitality and went away.

The woman didn't go out at first, as she was very badly frightened. But after a while she thought she might as well go and see if there were any truth in what the sailor had told her. She took her hoe, went out doors and easily found the place the sailor had described. She began to dig, but every time that she stuck her hoe in the ground, her children who were sound asleep in bed would cry out as if they were in great pain. She rushed into the house every time that they cried, to see what was the matter with them, but she always found them just as she had left them. After this had happened several times, she decided to give up digging for that night, thinking she would try it again in the morning when it was bright daylight.

When morning came, she wondered if she had dreamed all this
and went outdoors to the place where she had dug the night before.
There was her hoe standing where she had left it, but somebody
else had been there and finished digging while she was asleep,
because there was a big, round hole. She looked in the hole and
saw that some one had surely been there ahead of her and dug up
that hidden treasure, so that she was too late after all.

Considering everything, perhaps she was not too late, because it
may have been the Devil in disguise, who tempted her to see
whether she cared more for her children than she did for gold.

(Knight *1925:136*)

V

In Rachel Ryan's "Pirate Story," the ghost tires of his fate and helps
fortune hunters discover the treasure. Such cooperative ghosts are
known in Afro-American folklore, but the ghostly oxen are a distinctive Gay Head touch (Hurley 1951:201, 209–10).[4]

1928   PIRATE STORY

Phoebe and Chickadee have a similar call. It [the phoebe] is
called the money-bird. It says, "There is plenty of money.
Cheer up."

And there is too. All around here, for long ago in the time of the
pirates and press gangs, they came here and buried it in bakin'
cauldrons. They did bury it all around near the ponds, Menemsha
and Squibnocket, and for years, until lately, most of them spent all
their time hunting for treasure chests of silver, household
goods, etc.

Terrible days around the islands. People were awfully scared
when they saw off island and especially when strange craft an-
chored off shore and the men came off 'em for they used to come to
the houses and take all the young and able bodied men. The press
gang you know (preceding the War of 1812).

Ships would come some of them dreadful pirates and others just
in need of men, carry the men away and force them to be sailors.
When they were pirates they would come ashore and bury their
treasures some place, kill a man, bury him with it to keep watch
and sometimes these ghosts would get tired of keeping guard, and
would be willing to tell certain people where it could be found.

The islands were a terrible place for such doings and many a
vessel came to hide treasure. Ikis Hill was one place where the
people around here were digging over to find it. They would some

times dream of it and if the Mohegans think a person has to dream three times of it I don't think thats right because here there were certain ones who had the power to make the ghosts that guard come and talk to them telling them how to find the treasure. My sister was one and my aunt another. There were plenty of them here a few years ago when they used to be up to such doings. And sometimes the guardian would appear to people in broad daylight so it wasn't all in dreams, and they always wore a red shirt and black pants. Now that always goes with the treasure hunt. Its always a man with a red shirt and generally with black pants. My aunt [went] one time with an Old Indian woman on Ikis Hill and as they went toward the foot of the hill near the wall where the spring is she saw a man with red shirt and black pants bare headed, driving a pair of peculiar looking oxen—seem to have yellow stripe around body—different from any they ever had around here. She said to the other woman—"Do you see that man with red shirt and those queer oxen?" At first she couldn't see anything and all of a sudden she saw the same. He was going around there near an old grave so they knew there was treasure buried there.

(Tantaquidgeon 1928)

VI

Here Ryan suggests that whites sometimes find Gay Head treasures, thus stigmatizing whites, while vindicating Indians for being poor. Thomas Jeffers, who was more concerned with burying the murdered pirate than with recovering the treasure, is a model of Indian decency.

1928 PIRATE STORY

Years ago old Thomas Jeffers had a house on south shore over looking Squibnocket. Where the ships used to make harbor sometimes he saw one day a great ship heave to and a great crowd of men with red shirts come ashore and busy themselves for a long while up and down the place. They all had the red shirts so he knew they must have been pirates. Thinking they were coming off to get men like the press gang he sent word all over the Head for the men and boys to run hide for when they came ashore they took anything they wanted. He stayed there because he was too old to be taken and lame besides and kept watch on what they did. After a while they all went off to the ship, hoisted sail, went to sea. When the ship showed only a spot on the horizon, he went down to where they had been to see what it was. Sand was all tramped down and in one place he found a new grave so shallow that the man's knees stuck up above the ground. He took him out and found him a fair looking man with fair hair and blue eyes but he had the red shirt and black pants that all the pirates wore. He said a prayer over him, dug a deeper grave and gave him a decent burial. Put stones at head and foot.

Years after there came a man one night to his son's house. An old and Stalwart fellow who showed signs of having spent his life at sea. He asked for a night's lodging and altho they were suspicious of him on account of the Press group and pirates who were travelling the country they couldn't refuse him so they took him in but kept watch on him to see what he was up to. That evening he went off down the shore for a walk and came back with a square box under his arm and went away with it the next day.

(Tantaquidgeon *1928*)

VII

Again Ryan stressed Indian restraint and social virtues. The old man in this legend knew where the treasure was buried but would not tell. He apparently did not guard the treasure for himself, simply choosing not to disclose his secret. Not revealing one's knowledge is considered to be an old Indian character trait at Gay Head.

1928 PIRATE STORY

One of the old Indians had house near shore on South side. One night four great stout men came to get him to go with them down to the shore. He didn't want to go but he couldn't refuse because they were such rough looking men, so he went with them. They went to a place and marked off a place on the sand with sticks and told him not to cross those lines. Put a pistol in his hands and told him to stand guard and see that nothing happened. He had to do it. They went somewhere inside the bound and went digging, whether they got anything or not nobody ever knew even? Because Indians like him wouldn't tell if he knew when asked—all he said was he didn't know.

(Tantaquidgeon *1928*)

VIII

During her field research at Gay Head, Gladys Tantaquidgeon collected a version of the story first recorded by Mabel Knight in 1925 (text IV above) regarding the transparent sailor. In this text the transparent person is not the devil, but he is dangerous, as indicated by the red shirt and black pants which symbolized pirates in Gay Head lore. This version lacks the moral speculation attached to the end of the earlier version, but the message is still implicit in the story: One who obtains treasure is suspect and perhaps willing to sacrifice the well-being of others for personal gain.

1928   PIRATE STORY

It was terrible here. What evil things the Pirates did. Another time there was a woman who had a young baby who lived near the shore. A man came one day to her house. He had a red shirt and black pants and his hair seemed to be wet, drip on his shoulders. She was scared. More so when she noticed that when she looked at him she could see right thru him. He seemed tired. He began to tell her that right behind her house was buried treasure that she could have it if she wanted with very little trouble. Just to go back of the house and in the thatch she would dig out a box of money.

Although she was terribly scared and didn't want to leave her baby who was asleep alone with him, she went out back and began to dig. She had not gotten started before the baby began to cry and the baby stopped crying. She did this three times when he encouraged her to try again telling her how easy it was, the baby cried louder each time when she gave it up. Third time struck lid and bail of bakin pot but the baby cried so loud she left it and hurried back. When the man went she closed up the doors and wouldn't go out any more.

Next am she went to look in hole and found it dug out and pot gone. Somebody else had seen her digging and had come and taken it away.   (Tantaquidgeon *1928*)

IX

Laura Mars of the Narragansett spoke of a treasure buried on Sugarloaf Hill in Wakefield, Rhode Island. As with many treasure stories told by English and Indians in this region, the treasure is guarded by a mysterious animal and is never found.

1983

On Sugarloaf Hill in Wakefield . . . they claimed years ago, I used to hear my brother-in-law tell this, and his father, and they said there was a treasure that was hidden in that big hill and many, many people that tried to get that treasure and had dug into it, and whenever they got almost to it there's a big snake comes out and it scares 'em, and the treasure goes back in that much further and they never was able to get a hold of that treasure. They claim [it] is still there.   (L. Mars *1983*)

X

Ella Seketau's grandfather told her of an incident that happened in Lebanon, Connecticut, in the nineteenth century. This is a version of the negative memorate because what seemed to be supernatural lights proved to have been caused by an old man who was secretly burying his gold at night. Apparently the treasure fell into white hands.

1984

My grandfather or his father saw a light about a quarter of a mile away by the spring. It appeared often. They looked for the source and thought it was a ghost. They never saw any footprints, and if there were any, they were going in the opposite direction. They could never see anyone, they would wait but never saw anything. Then, years later, some developers were capping the spring and found the gold of this old man who went down there with his light and buried it. The workers divided up the money.   (Seketau 1984)

The treasure stories reflect Indian life and perceptions even if they are not derived from Indian cultural sources. They emphasize that Indians are poor because they are unwilling to bargain with the devil or to compromise their own codes of decency in order to acquire wealth. Most treasure stories appeared in the early twentieth century, when Indians had lost or were losing their land and when the Great Depression caused widespread economic hardship. Although Indians borrowed legends and motifs about hidden treasures from American folklore, they never gave up their conviction that no one should disturb Indian graves. The site of the Narragansett sanctuary in the Great Swamp Fight (1675) is still not known with certainty, for Indians who knew its location would never reveal their secret.

9   Giants: Maushop and Squant

The story of the so-called "Culture Hero," who gave the world its present
shape, who killed monsters that infested the land, and gave man the arts that
make life worth living, is one of the most widely distributed Indian myths.
In what we might call the prehistoric era there was no clear distinction
between man and animals. At last the culture hero appeared, and transformed
some of the beings of those times into animals, others into men. He taught
the latter how to kill animals, how to make fire, and how to clothe themselves.
He is the great benevolent being, the helper of mankind. (Boas 1898:4)

    Gay Head oral tradition states that the first Indians to populate
Martha's Vineyard found a giant named Maushop, who had been
living there with his wife Squant and their children. This giant created many topographical features of the New England landscape,
protected the Indians from a huge cannibal bird, and helped them
in other ways until Europeans arrived to settle, whereupon he withdrew, leaving only indirect evidence of his presence, such as coastal
fogs, which were said to be smoke from his pipe. All Indian groups
that lived in southern New England and on eastern Long Island
probably knew of Maushop, a local manifestation of a broader northeastern culture-hero pattern of giants that included Gluskap of the
Algonquian-speaking tribes of Maine and eastern Canada. Although
Maushop legends died out in most of southern New England by the
end of the seventeenth century, the Christian Wampanoag continued
to speak of him and his wife Squant throughout the eighteenth, nineteenth, and twentieth centuries. Fortunately, many persons, both English and Indian, wrote these stories down, thus providing a contin-

uous series of Maushop legends that extends from the early historic period to the present.[1]

Maushop's name seems to be derived from the Proto-Algonquian word meaning "big man" or "giant," and this in fact is the meaning that twentieth-century Gay Head Wampanoag gave to his name. Squant, or Ol' Squant (pronounced Squannit at Mashpee), is surely derived from the seventeenth-century *Squáuanit*, the "Woman's God" (Williams [1643] 1936:124).[2]

I

Roger Williams in 1643 described a culture hero named Wétucks who was probably the same figure as Maushop, for Ezra Stiles wrote in 1761 that "Weetucks' name was called Maushump by the Long I.[sland] Indians" (Stiles 1916:157).[3] The derivation and meaning of *Wétucks* is less clear than that of *Maushop*. It might be the same word etymologically as the Ojibwa *windigo*, meaning "cannibal monster," or it might be a kinship term; for example, it resembles the Narragansett *wéticks*, meaning "a sister," and *watòncks*, meaning "a cousin" (Williams [1643] 1936:29).

1643

They have many strange Relations of one Wétucks, *a man that wrought great Miracles amongst them, and walking upon the waters, & c. with some kind of broken Resemblance to the Sonne of God.*   *(Williams [1643] 1936:A5 recto)*

II

The Wampanoag of the Elizabeth Islands converted quietly to Christianity during the latter half of the seventeenth century through the efforts of the Mayhew family, who already had introduced Christianity to Martha's Vineyard.[4] Missionaries as well as converts often referred to Indian deities as devils, and Maushop, too, was sometimes known by that name. John Winthrop (1681–1747) visited the Elizabeth Islands in 1702 and heard a Maushop legend there which he entered in his diary. Motifs explaining the local origin and specific characteristics of animal species are widespread in North American Indian folklore, and the explanation given here for the arrival of crabs on Nantucket is surely indigenous to the Wampanoag. The culture hero's labors with large stones are reminiscent of English, Irish, German, and Scandinavian folklore about giants and devils; but because comparable feats are commonplace in the Gluskap legends of northern Algonquian people, this aspect of Maushop's behavior is probably Indian and not borrowed from Europeans.

1702

The Natives of the Elizabeth Island say that the Devell was making a stone Bridge over from the main to Nanamesset Island, and while he was rowling the stones and placing of them under water a crab catched him by the fingers, with which he snatched up his hand and flung it towards Nantucket, and the Crabs breed there ever since. (Emerson 1935:166)

III

By the late eighteenth century the isolated, windswept peninsula of Gay Head supported an Indian population of about two hundred persons. As other Indian communities on Martha's Vineyard declined, many of their inhabitants moved to Gay Head, which emerged as the historic center of island Indian life. Dr. William Baylies of Dighton, a physician and a Massachusetts state senator, visited Gay Head in 1786 to view the fabled cliffs for which the area was named. There he recorded the first of many Maushop legends attributed to the Wampanoag of this vicinity. In his journal, Baylies described the red, blue, yellow, white, black, and green clays that gave the cliffs their peculiar beauty, and he also suggested (incorrectly) that the bowl-shaped depression near the top of the cliffs, known as Devil's Den, was the crater of an ancient volcano. While exploring the shoreline below, Baylies collected fossil whale bones, shark's teeth, and petrified shellfish that had washed out of the headland. Since Baylies did not mention the Massachusett language, which may have been spoken by only a few at this time, he probably heard the legend in English. In this text Maushop appears as a helpful and industrious giant who maintains a friendly relationship with the Indians before disappearing in the early colonial period. He shared his meals of roasted whale meat and great fish with them; they provided him with enough tobacco to fill his pipe, and he in turn made Nantucket with his pipe ashes. Maushop's whaling, his practice of uprooting trees for fire, his prodigious stonework, and his creation of the island from ashes are recurrent motifs in subsequent Maushop legends, where they serve many explanatory functions. Maushop's practice of pulling up trees accounts for the barrenness of this exposed end of the island, and his cooking fires explain the burned and colored soils and fossil remains that surround his former home like an immense archaeological midden. His need for stepping

stones to catch whales accounts for the dangerous series of sub-
merged rocks known as Devil's Bridge that extends westward from
his den toward the mainland. The arrival of Europeans and the subsequent Christian conversion of the Martha's Vineyard Indians
ended relations between Maushop and his people, whereupon he is
said to have accepted the Christian view that he belonged to the
devil and retreated from his rightful home.

1786

*In former times, the Indian God, Moiship, resided in this part of
the island; and made the crater, described above, his principal
seat. To keep up his fires, he pulled up the largest trees by the roots;
on which, to satisfy his hunger, he broiled the whale, and the great
fish of the sea, throwing out the refuse sufficient to cover several
acres. He did not consume all himself; but with a benevolent hand,
often supplied them with food ready cooked. To facilitate the
catching these fish, he threw many large stones, at proper
distances, into the sea, on which he might walk with greater ease
to himself. This is now called the Devil's bridge. On a time, an
offering was made to him of all the tobacco on Martha's Vineyard,
which having smoked, he knocked the snuff out of his pipe, which
formed Nantucket. When the Christian religion took place in the
island, he told them, as light had come among them, and he belonged to the kingdom of darkness, he must take his leave; which,
to their great sorrow, he accordingly did; and has never been heard
of since.*   *(Baylies 1793:153–54)*

IV

An anonymous author described Maushop about the same time
that Baylies did and in very similar terms, except that he or she
spelled the giant's name Manshop and noted that he retired in disgust upon the coming of Europeans to America.[5]

1787   ORIGIN OF THE ISLAND OF NANTUCKET

*On the west end of Martha's Vineyard, are high cliffs of varie-
gated coloured earths, known by the name of Gayhead. On the top
of the hill is a large cavity, which has the appearance of the crater
of an extinguished volcano, and there are evident marks of former
subterraneous fires. The Indians who live about this spot have a
tradition that a certain deity resided there before the Europeans
came into America, that his name was Manshop; that he used to
step out on a ledge of rocks which ran into the sea, and take up a*

*whale, which he broiled for his own eating on the coals of the
aforesaid volcano, and often invited the Indians to dine with him,
or gave them the relicks of his meal. That once to shew their gratitude to Manshop for his very great kindness to them, they made an
offering to him of all the tobacco which grew upon the island in
one season. This was scarcely sufficient to fill his great pipe, but he
received the present very graciously, smoked his pipe, and turned
out the ashes of it into the sea, which formed the island of Nantucket. Upon the coming of the Europeans into America, Manshop
retired in disgust, and has never since been seen.*

("Origin of the Island of Nantucket" 1787:525)

V

Thomas Cooper of Gay Head told one of the richest Maushop legends to Benjamin Basset, an Englishman of nearby Chilmark, who
published it in the Massachusetts Historical Society *Collections*.
Cooper had heard the legend from his "grandmother," who was
either a classificatory grandmother or else very old, for she remembered the arrival of Europeans in 1643. The Cooper/Basset text
shows clear parallels with Gluskap legends of the northern Algonquian area, particularly in the giant's ability to transform living creatures into animals and stones and in his creation of channels and
islands. His feats provided explanations for the characteristics of
killer whales, the shape of a rock formation off Sakonnet Point on
the Rhode Island coast, the origin of the small island known as Noman's Land near Gay Head, and the colored soils and fossil contents
of the Gay Head cliffs. According to Cooper's legend, Maushop also
showed his kindness toward the Indians by sending them dead or
dying whales that drifted ashore. Such drift whales were an important food resource in southeastern New England in the prehistoric
and early historic periods (Little 1982a). Whether Maushop retreated because of Indian or English settlement is unclear in this
text. The legend begins with the Indian explanation for the first arrival of man and dog on Martha's Vineyard.[6]

1792 FABULOUS TRADITION

*The first Indian who came to the Vineyard, was brought thither
with his dog on a cake of ice. When he came to Gay Head, he found
a very large man, whose name was Moshup. He had a wife and
five children, four sons and one daughter; and lived in the Den. He
used to catch whales, and then pluck up trees, and make a fire,
and roast them. The coals of the trees, and the bones of the whales,*

*are now to be seen. After he was tired of staying here, he told his
children to go and play ball on a beach that joined Noman's Land
to Gay Head. He then made a mark with his toe across the beach at
each end, and so deep, that the water followed, and cut away the
beach; so that his children were in fear of drowning. They took
their sister up, and held her out of the water. He told them to act as
if they were going to kill whales; and they were all turned into
killers, (a fish so called). The sister was dressed in large stripes. He
gave them a strict charge always to be kind to her. His wife
mourned the loss of her children so exceedingly, that he threw her
away. She fell upon Seconet, near the rocks, where she lived some
time, exacting contribution of all who passed by water. After a
while she was changed into a stone. The entire shape remained for
many years. But after the English came, some of them broke off
the arms, head, &c. but the most of the body remains to this day.
Moshup went away nobody knows whither. He had no conversation
with the Indians, but was kind to them, by sending whales, &c.
ashore to them to eat. But after they grew thick around him he left
them.* (Basset *1806*)

VI

A "good old Quaker lady" from Cape Cod told this Maushop legend to the Reverend Timothy Alden, who wrote the text presented
here. This Nauset Wampanoag legend from Yarmouth describes the
giant cannibal bird already described in the account of the first Europeans at White Man's Brook (chapter 4, VII). Beliefs about giant
birds and the culture hero's contests with these and other formidable
creatures are widespread in Algonquian folklore from New Jersey to
Labrador. In addition to revealing another way that Maushop helped
the Indians, this legend provides an explanation for Nantucket and
coastal fogs. The poke that Maushop smoked in his pipe, known
variously as white hellebore, Indian poke, and *tabac du diable*, was
used by seventeenth-century New England Indians in ritual and may
have had hallucinogenic properties (Josselyn [1675] 1833:251).[7]

1797

*In former times, a great many moons ago, a bird, extraordinary
for its size, used often to visit the south shore of Cape Cod, and
carry from thence to the southward, a vast number of small children.*

*Maushop, who was an Indian giant, as fame reports, resided in
these parts. Enraged at the havock among the children, he, on a*

certain time, waded into the sea in pursuit of the bird, till he had crossed the sound and reached Nantucket. Before Maushop forded the sound, the island was unknown to the aborigines of America.

Tradition says, that Maushop found the bones of the children in a heap under a large tree. He then wishing to smoke a pipe, ransacked the island for tobacco; but, finding none, filled his pipe with poke, a weed which the Indians sometimes used as its substitute. Ever since the above memorable event, fogs have been frequent at Nantucket and on the Cape. In allusion to this tradition, when the aborigines observed a fog rising, they would say, "There comes old Maushop's smoke."   (Alden 1798:56–57)

VII

James Freeman, author of the following text, was well acquainted with the people, customs, and history of early nineteenth-century Martha's Vineyard. His Maushop narrative agrees in most particulars with those recorded earlier by Baylies and Basset, except he mentions a malignant spirit that took Maushop's place.

1807

At Gay Head is the Devil's Den; which, notwithstanding the terrour of its name, has nothing formidable in its appearance. It is a depression in the hill, in the form of a bowl, except that it is open on the side that is toward the sea, through which it is not difficult to descend to the strand. If it was on the top of a mountain, it might be called a crater. In this cavity, according to an Indian fable, many years before the English came to Martha's Vineyard, a giant, or tutelar deity, named Maushop, resided. Here he broiled the whale on a fire made of the largest trees, which he pulled up by the roots. Though a malignant spirit has now taken possession of his den, yet the first occupier was a benevolent being, and he kindly supplied the Indians with whales and other fish. After separating Noman's Land from Gay Head, metamorphosing his children into fishes, and throwing his wife on Saconet Point, where she still remains a mishapen rock, he went away nobody knew whither.

(Freeman 1815a:43)

VIII

An unidentified English traveler visited Gay Head in the summer of 1817 and heard a Maushop legend that differs from previous texts in several details. In this version Maushop's transformed children were said to play still in the nearby waters, and the manner of

Maushop's disappearance is described more fully. We also find the first written mention of his wife's name, Saconet, later recorded as Squant. While exploring Maushop's den and cliffs, the English author found deposits of long narrow crystals that the Indians referred to as Maushop's needles.

1817

According to the tradition of the Indians, when their ancestors first came from the west to this island, they found it occupied by Maushop, a benevolent but capricious being, of gigantick frame and supernatural power. His daily food was broiled whales, and he threw many of them on the coast for the support of his Indian neighbours. At last, weary of the world, he sent his sons and daughter to play at ball, and while they were engaged in their sport, drew his toe across the beach, on which they were, and separated it from the island. The returning tide rising over it, the brothers crowded round their sister, careless of their own danger; and while sinking themselves, were only anxious to keep her head above the waves. Maushop commended their fraternal affection, bade them always love and protect their sister, and preserved their lives by converting them into whale killers, a sort of grampus, whose descendants still delight to sport about the ancient dwelling of their great progenitor. The giant then hurled his wife Saconet into the air, and plunging himself beneath the waves, disappeared forever. Saconet fell on the promontory of Rhode Island, which now bears her name, and long lived there, exacting tribute from all passengers. At length she was converted into stone, still however retaining her former shape, till the white men, mistaking her probably for an idol, lopped off both her arms; but her multilated form remains to this day on the spot where she fell, and affords lasting and unimpeachable evidence of the truth of the tradition.

("Visit to the Elizabeth Islands" *1817:318–19*)

IX

James Athearn Jones (1791–1854), an American novelist, folklorist, lawyer, and farmer, grew up on Martha's Vineyard and visited there frequently during his adult life (Flanagan 1939; Pease 1881). A white who had been born "within twelve miles of a principal tribe of Indians, within two miles of a small band, and within six miles of two other small bands," he had been deeply influenced by the Martha's Vineyard Indians (Jones 1830, 1:ix). His grandfather, on whose farm he lived as a boy, employed an old Indian nurse who cared for Jones during his first fifteen years, and he also knew many Indian children whose parents worked on the farm. "So thoroughly has my mind become imbued with their superstitions," he wrote, "that at times I find difficulty in reconciling myself to the plain matter-of-fact narratives of the men of my own creed and colour" (p. x). Mima, his childhood nurse, told about giants, fairies, ghosts, and other strange figures, and inspired in him a lifelong curiosity about Indian folklore: "I implicitly believed all old Mima's stories, for [how] could I be made to entertain a suspicion that she who watched every night by my pillow, and gathered me berries, and waded into the water to pluck lilies for me, and procured me a thousand playthings—the devices of savage ingenuity—could tell me false tales" (pp. xii–xiii). In his late thirties Jones published a three-volume collection of Indian folklore based upon his research on and travels among Indian groups in eastern North America. In this collection he included several accounts that he attributed to his childhood nurse, two of which concern Maushop. Unfortunately, Jones composed his texts "with a careful reference to the manners, customs, rites, opinions, etc., of the people whose history they were supposed to tell" (pp. xxvii–xxviii). In other words, he combined oral and published sources and rewrote these according to his own taste. "The Devil of Cape Higgin" is one such text that combines indigenous folklore with elements from unspecified sources.

Three aspects of this legend are new in comparison with previous texts, namely, Maushop's system of exacting tribute, his role as an intermediary in courtship, marriage, and domestic relationships, and his personality transformation from a helpful, good-natured patron to an irritable nuisance. All three innovations have precedents in Wampanoag history and culture. In his emphasis on tribute, for example, Maushop resembles the influential sachems of the colonial period who exercised control over the disposition of whales. Nantucket sachems in the seventeenth century appropriated all whales that drifted ashore, which they then distributed among their subjects in precise customary ways (Little 1982a:19–21). Jones's comment that Maushop received one-tenth of all whales as tribute is close to recorded practice (Bragdon 1981:121–23; Little 1982a:21, 33–34; Winslow [1624] 1910:347). Even Maushop's concern that his subjects withheld tribute is reflected in historic litigation by Nantucket Indians over the correct allocation of rights and shares. This parallel between Maushop's practices and those of early sachems is apparent also in his relationship with the sachem Hiwassee, who was important enough to be Maushop's equal and therefore paid only minor tribute, and whose daughter reportedly married Maushop's son. Like Maushop, the northern Algonquian giant Gluskap also partitioned whales, and this element of Maushop legendry described by Jones may well have been authentic. Maushop's role as an intermediary in courtship, marriage, and family relations also resembles historic sachems and the legendary Gluskap (Leland 1898:51–58; Thompson [1929] 1966:8; Wood [1634] 1977:99). Thus, the changes Jones noted in Maushop's behavior are historically plausible, for in harassing his subjects with new demands, such as a larger share of their whales, Maushop followed the examples of known sachems (Little 1982a: 33–34). Jones also provides new details that are consistent with northeastern ethnography. Maushop's role as helper is expanded to include giving advice for hunting, fishing, planting, harvesting, and foretelling storms, which are services that traditional shamans provided. We learn for the first time that Maushop has a "brother goblin" on the mainland who gives him tobacco and that the deity Hobbamock is Maushop's master. The latter assertion appears in no subsequent Maushop legend and is probably an example of Jones improving his narrative with information from other sources. The sachem's name, Hiwassee or Howosee, is actually an old Gay Head family name (Pease 1871:31). Other details such as the reference to the frog month, the clam shell labret, the crab claw nose ornament, and Maushop's ritual as he prepared to create Nantucket are probably fanciful embellishments. Interestingly, Maushop's interference with grouse and woodcock snares is reminiscent of Penobscot accounts of shamans who sometimes meddled with hunters' traps (Speck 1919:287–88). Jones published a similar version of this legend a few years earlier in which he inexplicably referred to Maushop as Siwanticot (Jones 1826).

1829   THE DEVIL OF CAPE HIGGIN

A long time ago, before the occupation of the Island of Nope by the white people, there dwelt, upon the north side, and near its western end, a spirit or goblin—a very good-natured, peaceable, clever, old fellow, very fond of laughter and a good joke. The Indians called him Moshup, which signifies a very bad Spirit, but, when the white people came, they named him with reference to the little elbow, or promontory of land, where he had his usual residence, the Devil of Cape Higgin. There is another tradition, in which, it is said, that he once lived upon the main land, opposite Nope, and near the brook which was ploughed out by the Great Trout. It was said, that Moshup came to Nope in search of some

children, which had been carried away by a great bird, and finding
the spot pleasant, people clever, and food abundant, concluded to
take up his abode there.

Moshup, the Devil of Cape Higgin, was by no means so bad as
his title implies. Faults he had, it is true, but no one is without
faults. And then, compared with the vices of men, the vices of the
devil sunk into mere trifles. He was a little loose in his morals, and
withal, rather cross to his wife, but he made up for the latter fault
by his unwearied attentions to the wives of his neighbours. He gave
into very few indulgences, drank nothing stronger than water, and
never ate more than a small whale, or five or six porpoises, at one
meal. His greatest indulgence was in smoking the Indian weed,
which he did to excess. He was moderate in his exactions from the
Indians, requiring, as a tribute, only a tenth part of all the whales,
grampusses, and finbacks, which might be taken by the inhabitants
of the Island, together with all the porpoises caught in the Frog-
Month. The evil of scarcity, so it was not occasioned by indolence,
he bore with much composure. But, if a cheat were attempted to be
practised upon him, by sending him the poorest fish, or if any part
of his share was abstracted, if a porpoise or a halibut was hidden,
or the head of a finback sunk, with a buoy attached to it, or the
fin of a whale buried in the sand, he showed most terrific symptoms
of wrath and anger, and never failed to make the Indians pay
dearly for their roguery. But those who dwelt in his vicinity, indeed
all liable to be called upon for tithes, little disposed at any time to
battle with spirits and demons, paid their dues with great prompti-
tude, and so seldom came in collision with their grim and powerful
neighbour. To tell my brother the truth, it was not for their interest
to quarrel with him. He was of much importance to them in many
of their pursuits, and assisted them with a great deal of good advice
and sound and profitable counsel. He frequently directed them to
a fine school of black-fish, or bade them see whales, or man their
canoes for the chase of the finback; he told them when to plant and
gather in their corn, and foretold to them the approach of storms
with an accuracy productive of the greatest advantages to them. He
also assisted the young people in their courtships up to the time of
joining hands, but this it was whispered he did from a disposition
very proper to a naughty being like himself, who could not fail to
find his account in multiplying human miseries, and thereby increasing the chances of their going to the dominions of Hobbamock,
his master. Was any little rogue of a maiden solicited to become
the wife of a youth, and her parents stood out to the time of more

usquebagh, who but Moshup was called in to negociate for a less quantity? If a father said, "It shall not be," and Moshup could be prevailed on to say, "It shall be," the father was sure to find a pretext for changing his mind. If a young woman was beloved by one, and she pouted and pretended indifference, three words from Moshup were sure to make her reasonable. And, when women were much given to scolding, he had, somehow, a singular knack at taming them. Taking every circumstance into view, it will be readily concluded that he was a favourite with the Indians; indeed some of our fathers say, that he was once their grand Sachem; the greater part, however, think he was the first governor of the whites, and this I believe.

But spirits and demons, as well as the children of this world, whether white or red, are subject to changes of opinion and conduct—to many whims and phantasies. Moshup grew harsh and ill-natured as he grew older. The change was first felt in his own family, the peace of which was soon destroyed by continual strife and quarrelling. He would beat his old woman for nothing, and his children for a great deal less. He soon began to harass his subjects with new demands and querulous exactions. He now frequently demanded the half of a whale instead of a tenth, or took, without asking, the whole of a grampus or finback. Instead of contributing his aid to promote marriages, he was very diligent in preventing them; instead of healing love-quarrels, he did his best to make them irreconcileable. He broke many well-ordered matches, and soured much matrimonial bliss, set many friendly families by the ears, and created frequent wars between the different tribes of the Island. The wild ducks he frightened with terrific shouts, so that the Indian archer could no longer come near them; he cut the springes set for grouse and woodcocks—in short, he became a very troublesome and dangerous spirit. There was, however, no use in fretting; he was seated firmly on their necks, and there was no shaking him off. So the Indians bore his freaks with great patience, calmly took up with the offal of the whale, and only adopted the precaution of removing as far from him as possible. His harsh behaviour unpeopled his neighbourhood; and soon the little elbow of land, which the white people call Cape Higgin, had, for its only occupants, the Spirit Moshup and his family.

Upon the southern shore of the same Island of Nope, at a distance of ten or twelve miles from the residence of Moshup, lived, at the same period of time, Hiwassee, the proud and arbitrary Sachem of that portion of the Island which lies most exposed to the fogs of spring. He was a very rich and mighty man, had abundance of grape-vines, and a vast many ponds, well stocked with clams, oysters, perch, crabs, and wild fowl; many swamps filled with terrapins and cranberries; and much land, well adapted to the growing of maize and other good things. He was accounted the most powerful Sachem on the Island. He was, besides, on excellent terms with Moshup, and so escaped all taxes, contributions, and tenths, merely now and then making him a present of a few baskets of grapes, or a few terrapins. This Sachem had a daughter, young, and more beautiful than any maiden that had ever been seen in Nope. She was taller than Indian maidens generally are, her hair was long and glossy as the raven's, and her step very light and graceful. Then she excelled very far the women of her tribe in the exercises which belong to the other sex. None drew the bow with equal strength, or tortured the prisoner with so much ingenuity, or danced the war-dance with equal agility, or piped the war-song with lungs as efficient. I must tell my brother that, according to the tradition of our nation, the Indian females were first taught by her to introduce the crab's claw into the cartilage of the nose, and to insert the shell of a clam into the under-lip, as ornaments. She was, indeed, a beautiful creature, and understood better than any one else the art of attracting all the brave and best of the land; the love and admiration of the other sex followed her whithersoever she went. Her father's wigwam was filled with the suitors who came to solicit her love. There were the chiefs of the tribes which dwelt at Neshamoyes, Chabbaquiddic, Popannessit, Suckatasset, and many other places; warriors, famed and fearless, who asked her of the Grand Sachem in marriage. But no, she was deaf to their entreaties, laughed at all their presents of conch-shells, terrapins, and eagle's feathers, and carefully and scrupulously barred the doors of her father's wigwam against all the suitors, who, according to the Indian forms of courtship, came when the lights were extinguished and the parents were sleeping, to whisper soft tales at the side of her couch. The truth, which must be told my brother, is, that she had long before placed her affections upon a young warrior, stern to his enemies, but to her all gentleness, who dwelt at the western end of the Island, and was reckoned the favourite, some said he was the son, of the Devil of Cape Higgin. They had loved each other long, and with the truest affection, and all their hopes centered in a union.

But my brother knows—if he does not I will tell him—that fathers and mothers will not always permit daughters to have their

own way in marriage. The proud father objected to the lover, because he had slain but three foes, and was not descended from
a line of chiefs, distinguished by their wisdom or valour. What was
to be done? The lovers talked the matter over and over again, and
finally determined to apply to Moshup, for his aid and advice.
They forthwith repaired to the usual residence of the goblin. It was
a most auspicious moment; they found him in a delirium of joy. A
school of whales, in a recent dark night, becoming bewildered, had
foundered upon a neighbouring ledge of rocks, and a great many
fine calves had been deposited at the mouth of his cave as his
share. Withal a brother goblin, residing somewhere upon the main
land, had sent him some excellent old tobacco; and these, with the
occurrence at the happy moment of other enlivening circumstances, had wrought him up to such unusual good temper that he
quite forgot his very recent determination to annoy all lovers, and
promised to befriend the hapless pair. He rose from his seat, put
a few hundred pounds of tobacco in his pouch, took a half-roasted
grampus from the coals to pick by the way, and set off for Sanche-
quintacket, the place of Hiwassee's residence: the young warrior
perched upon his shoulder, and the maiden, reposing on a litter
formed by his arm, lay horizontally on his breast.

Moshup was no devil with wings, but he had two legs, and could
use them to much advantage. So he set off at a pretty smart trot,
and was very soon at the end of his journey. He found the Grand
Sachem busy at a feast, but this did not prevent him from telling
his errand at once. With great calmness and in perfect silence, for
he was not in one of his talkative fits, he heard the maiden's father
give his reasons for refusing his daughter to the lover. They were
those which have been a thousand times urged before—"Poverty—
poverty—low parentage—low parentage; not sufficiently known—
not sufficiently celebrated."

"Is this all you have to say against the young man, you old fool?"
asked Moshup. "What do you want? What must the young man
have?"

"He must have a great deal of land—he must have an island,"
answered Hiwassee.

"Good," said Moshup, drawing a huge quantity of smoke into his
mouth, and blowing it out through his nose: "follow me!"

At the time whereof I speak, the island of Nope extended to and
comprehended the little island of Tuckanuck. The little island was
then a part of the larger island; but once upon a time there came
a great storm, the winds raged and the thunders rolled, and the

storms beat upon the island, and it was disjointed and became two islands. To a high cliff, upon the eastern side of this same Tuckanuck, Moshup conducted Hiwassee, his daughter, her lover, and a great crowd of other Indians, who followed to see what wonderful feat he would perform. Being arrived, he sat down upon the ground, and commenced his charm. First he dug a great hole in the earth, into which he threw many heated stones, the while muttering many words, which no one but himself understood. Then he filled his pipe with tobacco, kindling it with the rays from a flash of lightning. When this was done, he bowed once to the rising sun, twice to the North Star, blew thrice in a conch-shell, muttered more unintelligible words, and commenced smoking at a great rate. In a few minutes it was as dark as the darkest night, and a terrible tempest arose. The thunders rolled awfully, the lightnings flashed, the rains poured down, and abundance of voices were heard in the east, puffing and blowing as of men in great labour. Presently there was a hissing sound, like that of live embers dropped into water— Moshup had emptied his pipe. There now came up a strong wind from the west, which, gradually dispersing the smoke he had created, displayed to their view a low dark something in the east. It was the promised island—the ashes from Moshup's pipe. The couple upon whom Moshup bestowed this island gave it the name of Nantucket, and such it bears at this day.

I have no more to say.   (Jones 1830, 3:321–30)

X

Jones attributed "The Legend of Moshup" to his Indian nurse and noted that his account is "corroborated in a communication made to the Massachusetts Historical Society, and published in their Transactions; but, not having been able to find a copy in England, I must beg the reader to rest satisfied with my assertion that, independently of my nurse's version, a communication made to the before-mentioned society stamps the tradition as genuine" (Jones 1830, 1:xxiv). Jones refers here to the "Fabulous Tradition" told by Thomas Cooper to Benjamin Basset (text V above). Jones's comment is puzzling because segments of "The Legend of Moshop" follow thought for thought, and in some instances word for word, the Cooper/Basset text. Either Jones worked from notes and had forgotten their source or he concealed his use of the published text, which raises questions about the extent to which he elsewhere represented materials published by others as his own memories. This text also includes many innovations, such as the description of Maushop's appearance, which do not appear in earlier published narratives. Like a giant king known to the early twentieth-century Penobscot (probably Gluskap), Jones's Maushop only had two teeth (Stamp 1915:315). His telling of the cannibal bird story adds details to previous versions, including the fact that the story accounts for the discovery of Martha's Vineyard and not Nantucket. Tackanash, the name Jones attributes to the first Indian to reach Martha's Vineyard on the cake of ice, is certainly a form of the Gay Head Indian name Tacknish or Tokinosh (Gookin [1792] 1970:100; Pease 1871:53). Although the giant tortoise occurs elsewhere in Iroquois and other eastern woodland mythologies, it is not mentioned in any other southern New England source and is probably an inaccurate improvement on the author's part. All explanatory motifs, such as the source of bones and ashes in the Gay Head cliffs and the origin of fog, agree with previously published narratives. In sum, Jones had unique exposure to Indian storytellers but diluted the value of his texts by adding information from uncredited sources and by burying Indian discourse beneath his own artistic efforts.[8]

1829   THE LEGEND OF MOSHUP

Once upon a time, in the month of bleak winds, a Pawkunnawkut [Pokanoket] Indian, who lived upon the main land, near the brook which was ploughed out by the great trout, was caught with his dog upon one of the pieces of floating ice, and carried in spite of his endeavours to Nope. Hitherto, it had remained unknown, and, as our people supposed, unapproachable. Several times they had attempted to visit it, but their canoes had always been swept away, or pushed back by some invisible hand, some friendly Manitou of the water, who feared danger to them, or some angry spirit of the island, who, by these signs, forbade their approach to his dominions. For many years, and ever since the memory of our fathers, the Indians, supposing it the residence of Hobbamock, the being who rules over evil men, sends disease and death to the Indians, breeds storms in the air, and utters the fearful sound in the black clouds, had carefully abstained from attempting to visit it. Nor was it altogether a mere uncertain dread of evil, which had operated on their minds to people it with living and moving beings. They could see at times men of monstrous stature moving rapidly over the island, and at all seasons in the calm evening, or when the winds blew from it, could hear sounds of anger or wailing, or of music and merriment, proceeding from its gloomy shades. And some pretended to have seen distinctly the form of a tall man wad-

ing into the water to grasp whales. The forced visit to its shores of
Tackanash, the Pawkunnawkut, made them see it was not the
dream of a sleeper who has eaten too much meat, but like that
which men see with their eyes when they are awake, and would
talk only what the Good Spirit may hear.

When Tackanash and his dog arrived at Nope, he found the man
whose existence had been doubted by many of the Indians, and
believed to have been only seen by deceived eyes, heard by foolish
ears, and talked of by lying tongues, living in a deep cave near
the end of the island, nearest the setting sun. And this was the
account which Tackanash on his return gave the chiefs of the
strange creature. He was taller than the tallest tree upon Nope, and
as large around him as the spread of the tops of a vigorous pine,
that has seen the years of a full grown warrior. His skin was very
black; but his beard, which he had never plucked nor clipped, and
the hair of his head, which had never been shaved, were of the
colour of the feathers of the grey gull. His eyes were very white,
and his teeth, which were only two in number, were green as the
ooze raked up by the winds from the bottom of the sea. He was
always good-natured and cheerful, save when he could not get
plenty of meat, or when he missed his usual supply of the Indian
weed, and the strong drink which made him see whales chasing
deer in the woods, and frogs digging quawhogs. His principal food
was the meat of whales, which he caught by wading after them into
the great sea, and tossing them out, as the Indian boys do black
bugs from a puddle. He would, however, eat porpoises, when no
larger fish were to be had, and even tortoises, and deer, and rabbits,
rather than be hungry. The bones of the whales, and the coals of
the fire in which he roasted them, are to be seen now at the place
where he lived. I have not yet told my brothers the name of this big
man of Nope—it was Moshup.

I hear the stranger ask, "Who was he?" I hear my brothers ask,
"Was he a spirit from the shades of departed men, or did he come
from the hills of the thunder? I answer, he was a Spirit, but whence
he came, when first he landed in our Indian country, I know not. It
was a long time ago, and the Island was then very young, being
just placed on the back of the Great Tortoise which now supports
it. As it was very heavy the tortoise tried to roll it off, but the Great
Spirit would not let him, and whipped him till he lay still. Moshup
told the Pawkunnawkut that he once lived upon the main land.
He said that much people grew up around him, men who lived by
hunting and fishing, while their women planted the corn, and

beans, and pumpkins. They had powwows, he said, who dressed themselves in a strange dress, muttered diabolical words, and frightened the Indians till they gave them half their wampum. Our fathers knew by this, that they were their ancestors, who were always led by the priests—the more fools they! Once upon a time, Moshup said, a great bird whose wings were the flight of an arrow wide, whose body was the length of ten Indian strides, and whose head when he stretched up his neck peered over the tall oak-woods, came to Moshup's neighbourhood. At first, he only carried away deer and mooses; at last, many children were missing. This continued for many moons. Nobody could catch him, nobody could kill him. The Indians feared him, and dared not go near him; he in his turn feared Moshup, and would seek the region of the clouds the moment he saw him coming. When he caught children, he would immediately fly to the island which lay towards the hot winds. Moshup, angry that he could not catch him, and fearing that, if the creature hatched others of equal appetite and ferocity, the race of Indians would become extinct, one day waded into the water after him, and continued in pursuit till he had crossed to the island which sent the hot winds, and which is now called Nope. There, under a great tree, he found the bones of all the children which the great bird had carried away. A little further he found its nest, with seven hatched birds in it, which, together with the mother, he succeeded after a hard battle in killing. Extremely fatigued, he lay down to sleep, and dreamed that he must not quit the island again. When he waked, he wished much to smoke, but, on searching the island for tobacco, and finding none, he filled his pipe with poke, which our people sometimes use in the place of tobacco. Seated upon the high hills of Wabsquoy, he puffed the smoke from his pipe over the surface of the Great Lake, which soon grew dim and misty. This was the beginning of fog, which since, for the long space between the Frog-month and the Hunting-month, has at times obscured Nope and all the shores of the Indian people. This was the story which Moshup told Tackanash and his dog. If it is not true, I am not the liar.

Moshup, at the time when Nope was visited by Tackanash, had a wife of equal size with himself, and four sons, and a daughter, the former tall, strong, and swift, very expert at catching fish, and nimble in pursuit of deer, the latter beautiful, sweet-voiced, and bounding as the fawn. She would sit in the first of the evening, when the dew began to fall, and the shadows of men lengthened, and sing to her father songs of the land of the shades of evil men,

songs which told of the crimes they had committed, and their repentance, and guilt, and compunction, and shame, and death.
Though Moshup appeared to care little for any body, he nevertheless loved his little daughter, as he called her, whose head peered
over the tallest trees, and whose voice was heard upon the main
land. He shewed by many signs how much he loved his daughter.
He strung up the teeth of the shark as a necklace for her, gathered
the finest shells for her anklets, and always gave her the fattest
slice of whale's meat to her portion.

The story of Tackanash, who very soon returned to Waquoit, and
his description of the beauties of Nope, carried many of the Pawkunnawkuts thither to live. It was indeed a pleasant place, pleasant
to the Indian, for it abounded with all the things he covets. Its
ponds were many, and stocked with fine fish and fat wild ducks; its
woods were filled with deer, and the fertile banks of its streams
overrun with wild vines, on which the grape thickly clustered, and
where the walnut and the hazel-nut profusely loaded both bush
and tree. Soon, the Pawkunnawkuts, at peace among themselves,
and blessed by the Good Spirit with every thing they needed,
became very numerous. There was not a pleasant spot on the island, from which did not arise the smoke of a cabin fire; nor a
quiet lake, in which, in the months of flowers and fruits, you would
not see Indian maidens laving their dusky limbs. The wild duck
found no rest in his sunny slumber on the banks of Menemshe, the
pokeshawit could no longer hide in the sedge, on the banks of his
favourite Quampeche, and the deer, that went to quench his thirst
in the Monnemoy, found the unerring arrow of the Indian in his
heart.

But to Moshup the increase of the Indians seemed to give pain—
none knew why, since the only enjoyments he appeared to covet
were still as numerous as before. Whales were still plenty, poke
was still plenty, and sleep and sunshine as easily enjoyed as ever.
Though he never harmed the Indians, he grew discontented and
unhappy, cross and peevish in his family, and sour and unneigh-
bourly to all around him. He would beat his wife, if she did but so
much as eat a falling scrap of the whale; toss his sons out of the
cave, if, in the indulgence of boyish glee, they made the least noise
while he was taking his nap; and box the ears of his little daughter,
if she did but so much as look at an Indian youth.

Once upon a time, he bade his children go and play ball upon
the beach that joins the hill of White Paint to Nomensland, telling
them that he would look on and see the sport. When they had

played awhile, he made a mark with his great toe across the beach at each end, and so deep that the water followed the mark, leaving them surrounded with it, and in great danger of being drowned. When the tide at length began to flow across the beach, covering with water the whole space between the two high lands, the brothers took their little sister, and held her up out of the water, while Moshup, seated on the high cliffs, looked on. He told them to act as if they were going to kill whales, which they did, and were all turned into the fish called killers, a fish which has ever since been an enemy to whales, and is its greatest terror. As the sister was always a gay girl, painting her cheeks of many hues, and loving many-coloured ornaments, he commanded her to become, and she became, the striped killer. He bade her brothers be always very kind to her, and they have obeyed him.

When Moshup's wife learned the transformation of her children, she grieved very much for their loss. Night and day she did nothing but weep and call for them, till, at length, Moshup grew tired of her noise, and, catching her up in his arms in a paroxysm of passion, he threw her as far as he could towards the country of the Narragansetts. She fell upon the point which juts far into the ocean, and over whose rocks the evil Manitou of the deep throws the great waves. The Indians call it Seconet. There, seated upon the rocks, she began to make all who came that way contribute to her support. She grew to be so cross and cruel, exacting so much from Indians, and making so much noise, that the Great Spirit changed her into a huge rock; the entire shape of which remained many years. But, when the Yengees came, some of them broke off her arms, fearing she would use them to their injury, and her head, lest she should plot mischief; but her body stands there now.

Moshup did not stay long on Nope after he had thrown away his wife, but while he did remain he was very good to the Indians, sending them many whales and other good things. He did very little save watch on the edge of the sea the sport of the killers, and in particular that which was striped, feeding it with certain pieces of fish, talking kindly to it, and always calling it by the name his daughter bore. Sometimes he would remain for many suns perched on the high cliff of White Paint, looking eagerly towards the place where he had thrown his old woman. At last, he went away, no one could say with certainty whither. Some of the Indians supposed they could see him at times walking on the high hills beyond the tides; others thought that he had gone back to his master, the Evil Spirit.   (Jones 1830, 2:263–72)

XI

This anonymous "Devil's Bridge" manuscript probably dates from the late nineteenth or early twentieth centuries and differs from previous sources in some details. In building his bridge, Maushop is said to have excavated earth and rocks from the Gay Head cliffs (which explains the origin of the circular depression known as Devil's Den) and to have carried this material in his shoe. This is a familiar motif in British and German lore, where giants create rock formations and other features by emptying rocks and sand from their shoes (Motz 1982:83; Sikes 1881:370). Maushop appears a bit angrier in this account than in previous ones; he throws his family into the sea along with the earth and rocks because a crab has interrupted his bridge-building activities. The formula "Once upon a time" belongs to the European folktale tradition, which suggests that a Euro-American, not an Indian, wrote this particular text.

CIRCA 1900   THE DEVIL'S BRIDGE

Once upon a time a mighty giant named Maushope lived in the vicinity of Gay Head. He was the tutelary deity of all the surrounding country and, being of a friendly disposition—when not enraged—he taught the natives how to take fish and secure the beaver which were very abundant. From the cliff at Gay Head he was accustomed to fish for whales, often frying one entire for breakfast.

Once while on a benevolent mission to save a papoose which has been carried off by an evil genious, he filled his pipe with helebore, and smoked so furiously that the fogs, which envelop that region and roll along to the Banks of Newfoundland, were caused by the smoke of his pipe, and the ashes emptied from it formed Nantucket.

Finally Maushope projected a bridge by which to cross over to Cuttyhunk and the mainland, and laid the foundation with rocks brought from the opposite shore. The first load of earth—which he carried in his shoe—was filled in when an inquiring crab bit his toe as he was working barefooted in the water, and he left the work in a terrible rage, and the remains of it exist as a sunken reef to this day.

But the demonical nature was fully aroused by the insult of the crab, and a direful domestic disaster followed. He tore off a fragment of Nope and hurled it away six miles into the sea, where it now remains as Noman's Land; then he cast his five children into the sea and tossed his wife over to Seaconnet Point, where she is still to be seen in the form of a shattered boulder, and then left for parts unknown.

A circular depression 300 feet in circumference and 100 feet in depth, on a hillside at Gay Head, where Maushope filled his shoe with earth, and the Devil's Bridge, still remain to authenticate this old Indian legend. ("The Devil's Bridge" ca. 1900)

XII

As whites began to buy the old Wampanoag trust lands and as community isolation broke down, new motifs entered the Maushop folklore. Mary A. Cleggett Vanderhoop (ca. 1857–1935) published a major collection of Gay Head legends (texts XII to XX) that captures this change. Vanderhoop's contribution is considerable, for she provided a large sampling of Gay Head legends from a particular moment in time, something no previous author had done. By 1904 Gay Head lore had begun to show some effects of the Indians' joining the mainstream of American citizenry; the earlier Maushop, once both kind and capricious, had divided into two figures, the benevolent Maushop and the evil Cheepi Unck. Cheepi Unck combines Maushop's great size, strength, and proclivity for building bridges with attributes of the spirit Cheepi and the devil. This version of "The Devil's Bridge" involves two factions, one that supports and another that opposes building the causeway to Cuttyhunk. Factionalism had surfaced in Gay Head over the issue of incorporation, which pitted the foreign born and those with experience outside the district against others who were more locally oriented, and these factions grew in later years (Levitas 1980:32–33, 341, 350, 356). This legend displays conflict between those who favored access to the outside world, who were championed by the evil Cheepi Unck, and those who favored isolation, represented by the symbol of tradition, a wise old Indian woman. The legend achieves through symbol what the conservative Gay Headers failed to achieve in reality, for the old woman prevented her adversary from completing his bridge to the outside world. After many years of relatively little innovation, many new motifs appear in "The Devil's Bridge" legend at this time, including G 303.16.19.4. *Devil (Satan) flees when cock is made to crow;* K 1886.3. *Mock sunrise. Contract is to be fulfilled at dawn;* K 1886.3.1. *Mock sunrise: person causes cock to crow;* and M 210. *Bargain with devil.* These new motifs show probable borrowing from Anglo-American, British, and possibly Cape Verdean oral narrative traditions. Contacts with English settlers and later immigrant groups and participation in far-flung seafaring industries furnished the Gay Head Wampanoag with ready sources of new motifs as they adapted their legends to new historical circumstances.[9]

1904

Another legend is to the effect that there were two factions inter-ested in the building of the bridge to Cuttyhunk. Those on one side argued thus: "There are enough of us here now; if the bridge is built we shall be overrun by our neighbors and become too crowded." The other said: "We must and shall have a bridge." And so they went to one called Cheepii Unck and asked him to build the structure. Cheepii Unck, always willing to be obliging, con-sented immediately to do a good substantial piece of work, and agreed to build a bridge of stone—not a weak, unstable wooden affair. The other crowd was very angry, but as Cheepii Unck was to do the work, there was apparently nothing to do but submit. Nothing to be done? Where ever there is opposition to a great de-gree, there also is to be found the cunning of the fox. Now, it so happened that the compact made with Cheepii Unck read after this fashion: "I, Cheepii Unck, between the hours of sunset and before cock-crow in the morning, do agree to build a bridge from Aquin-nah [Gay Head] highlands to Cuttyhunk. If I fail to finish said bridge of stone before cock-crow this compact is null and void." However, the cunning children of discontent were watching matters closely. One dark night word was passed around that Cheepii Unck had begun his work, and true it was. The all-powerful one had commenced his task with an energy not to be gauged by any known standard. All the tremendous strength and force of his gigantic body was thrown into his work. At last the bridge was well under way. Great rock after rock and immense stone after stone was taken up, carried a greater or lesser distance, and dropped into place. If all went well, before cock-crow the bridge should be in place— there to remain in spite of a defiant opposition. Busy Cheepii Unck had neither thought to give nor time to spend in watching the cun-ning ones. But to one old lady-squaw, whose name has been lost in the mists of the past (it may have been Waukshus, but it certainly was not Mrs. Moshup, nee Squant), a singular fact was well known, and that was this: If a bright light is flashed suddenly before a cock's face no matter what the hour, he will crow. This old squaw, one of the cunning ones, lighted her torch and waved it where the cock would catch the glare. With flapping wings and outstretched

neck, the cock crowed long and loud and lustily. Cheepii Unck's
work was thereby ended, the bridge was unfinished, and the oppo-
sition was triumphant.   (Vanderhoop 1904, July 2)

XIII

Vanderhoop wrote that an unnamed enemy conquered Maushop
on the mainland and drove him to Gay Head (Aquinnah), where he
lived comfortably for a while with his wife and family. Maushop's
retreat to the remote Gay Head peninsula follows the historic migration of Vineyard Indians to this settlement as the English spread over
the island.

1904

Of Moshup more is known. After a long and stubborn conflict on
the mainland, he was finally conquered and forced to flee for his
life. Thus it is, at the height of his renown, we find him living on
the extreme western point of Aquinnah, in a wonderfully sheltered,
well-watered spot, now called the Den. This is a deep and roomy
hollow, resembling the old cellar-holes, but on a much grander
scale. More than a century ago it was described as a grassy glen
whose slopes led gently down to the seashore. It is open to the
southern and western breezes, and its portals and door-steps are
washed by the waters of the broad Atlantic. At the entrance of the
Den stand great rocks on either side: high and broad they form
an imposing doorway which is not only stately, but extremely con-
venient for fishing purposes. Here Moshup made his home, and
here he brought his lovely Squant—now, but not then, "Ol' Squant."
Moshup was big and powerful, and Squant was trusting and beau-
tiful. Such was the beginning of Moshup's home life in Aquinnah.

(Vanderhoop 1904, July 2)

XIV

Following Maushop and Squant's arrival on Martha's Vineyard, an
enemy cut Squant's eyes square, thus obliging her to cover her deformed eyes and face with her long black hair. Speck's legend regarding the Mohegan sorcerer Israel Freeman (chapter 6, IV), who had
two wives "but became jealous of them and rendered them hideous
as a punishment by turning up their eyelids so that they remained
permanently disfigured," suggests that eye mutilation may have been
an indigenous southern New England motif (Speck 1909:196). In one
of the earliest accounts of Martha's Vineyard Indians, Thomas Mayhew, Jr., described how a jealous pagan mutilated the eyebrow of the

sachem Towanquatick and how the sachem thereafter treasured the wound as a symbol of his conversion (Whitfield [1651] 1834a:113).

1904

Squant was broad, but finely proportioned, with coal-black hair, which she wore over her face, so as to cover it as with a veil. The reason for this—as given by the few who had beheld her face while the veil was lifted, and as told by our forefathers in tones of awe— was that Squant's eyes were square. They had been cut and thus shaped by an enemy who one day found her asleep on the marsh. Thus her beautiful hair was used to cover her hideous deformity.

(Vanderhoop 1904, July 2)

XV

By 1904 Maushop's family had grown from the four sons and one daughter in earlier accounts to twelve daughters (in the following text) and even to an indefinite number of sons and daughters (in text XVIII below). Motifs regarding Maushop's prodigious whaling, cooking, and stone-building activities echo earlier texts, but his giant cooking pot or witch's caldron is new. Although giant caldrons occur in Old World witch and giant lore (F 881.1.1. *Gigantic cauldron*), the great try-pots of the whaling industry provide a model much closer to home (Melville [1851] 1956:326).

1904

In the course of time children came to gladden the home and the hearts of Moshup and Squant. These children were all daughters, and there were twelve of them. Their home life was simple enough. From his great doorway, looking out upon the ocean, Moshup could see the whales as we do now when they pass. Standing on the large door-stones, he would catch a whale or some other great fish by its tail, and with one swing of his powerful arm land it into the witches' cauldron, beneath which a fire was always kept smouldering. To replenish this fire, he pulled up the largest trees within his reach. From the whales he threw out refuse enough to cover several acres, and from his vast supply frequently furnished the inhabitants with an abundance of ready cooked food. When the whales did not come within a reasonable distance of the shore, Moshup would throw great rocks and stones into the sea, and on these approach the leviathan he had selected. Sometimes Moshup cooked for himself, and at other times the industrious Squant prepared the food for her lord and his daughters. Thus they all grew and waxed strong as the years went by. This is the tale as it is blown to us upon the winds of tradition. Why the home of this great Indian god should be called the Devil's Den, and why the rocks he cast into the sea are known as the Devil's Bridge, we are not told, but assuredly his characteristics were not wholly evil.

(Vanderhoop 1904, July 2)

XVI

In this account, as in many others, Maushop industriously transforms the landscape by creating islands and rearranging boulders. Carrying boulders in an apron is an interesting new motif (A 977.3.1. The devil drops stones from apron; Baughman A 977.1.2[cb]. Giant carrying apron load of stones for building drops them when apron string breaks) that could derive from local tradition but more probably originated in Yankee and British devil, giant, and witchcraft lore. For example, the nineteenth-century white inhabitants of Easton, Massachusetts, told of how the devil filled his apron with stones and dropped them when his apron string broke, thus creating a rock formation that can be seen today (Chaffin 1886:773–74). The crab that caused Maushop to spill his stones was an old friend to Wampanoag legend.[10]

1904

They say that when Moshop was coming here, was on his way to this headland (which was no headland then, but a part of the mainland), the way being low and marshy, the great chief became greatly fatigued. In his weariness he dragged one foot heavily along the marshy ground, and the track thus made was filled by the ocean. At first the little streamlet seemed only a silver thread, but by force of waves and tides and winds it broadened and deepened, and in the course of time became the wide opening which now separates the Elizabeth islands and No Man's Land. Thus it is that these two places form monuments to the geographical change wrought by Moshup's foot.

But Moshup's rock-bound doorstep was his chief delight, and next to his wife and daughters did he worship it. Here he stood in the pleasant air and sunshine—stood and looked dreamily out on the vast expanse of water, the headlands peeping up to keep him company. One day he decided to go to the island now called Cuttyhunk. 'Twas only a few steps for one like Moshup, but as he did not wish to wet his feet he filled his apron with stones and started to build a bridge as he crossed. On he went, dropping a great stone here and there to step upon. Progressing rapidly, soon his "bridge" was nearly completed. Absorbed in his work, and unmindful of

things watery or otherwise, he failed to note the approach of a
large and watchful seacrab. Suddenly his big toe was caught and
held fast in the sea-crab's vicelike grip. The stepping-stones were
immediately forgotten, never to be thought of again by the great
one. Howling and roaring with pain, Moshup threw and kicked the
remainder of the rocks in every direction, in a wild endeavor to kill
the crab or compel it to release its powerful hold. After a furious
assault the tenacious crab relaxed its jaws and poor Moshup
limped back home with his wounded member. The old "bridge" is
still there, a silent witness to another experience of the great Moshup, though it is now little more than a ledge of sunken rocks
upon which more than one noble craft has met her doom.

(Vanderhoop 1904, July 2)

XVII

In this retelling of the creation of Nantucket, Vanderhoop refers to
Maushop's pipe as his *peudelah*. The origin of this word is puzzling
because it appears in no previous text, is not Algonquian, and does
not resemble any word for pipe recorded in Indian vocabularies
from southern New England or Long Island.[11]

1904

*Moshup loved his great stone door-step. Frequently he would
stand thereon and smoke his peudelah (his pipe.) Once an offering
had been made to him of all the tobacco grown on Martha's Vineyard, which was then called Nope by the Indians. With his peudelah filled with the last of this great gift he one day stood in the
sunshine and smoked while he mused of his past [and] his greater
days. All unheeded his big peudelah suddenly tilted sidewise;
and, as the tide was high, the falling ashes therefrom were carried
out and down to the east by the swift-running tide, until at last,
caught by some drift on a shoal, they became fixed, and in time
Nantucket—or "The Devil's Ash-Heap," as it is called by the older
natives—grew little by little, until she reached her present magni-
tude and prosperity.*

O wonderful ash from Moshup's peudelah.   (Vanderhoop 1904, July 2)

XVIII

Maushop's indefinite number of sons and daughters, the matriar-
chal table manners, and the replication of these manners among
killer whales are new elements that appear only in the Vanderhoop
collection.

1904

But let us now return to Moshup and his home-life on the great
headland. The family was in thriving condition, and, as in Noah's
time, Moshup begat an indefinite number of sons and daughters.
What is more, they were all well trained by their doting father. The
children were so numerous that when the daily board was spread
all could not sit at the table at one time, so Father Moshup said the
girls should come first, while the sonnup (sons or braves) were
taught to wait in accord with the old principle—beauty first,
strength afterward.

At length there came a day when Moshup, either in vision or
reality, saw that the outsiders were coming to his fishing-grounds.
On one hand tradition tells us that the newcomers belonged to the
pale face branch of the human family, while another legend says
that a vast cake of ice, covered with Indians and dogs, lodged here.
The latter would appear to be the correct view, because at that
time Gay Head is said to have had a population of about twelve
hundred—four hundred Indians and eight hundred dogs. However,
whether the one story or the other is true, Moshup's homelife was
gone forever. Hastily calling his loved ones, his children around
him, he thus briefly addressed them: "My children, there will no
longer be room for you in this peaceful home of ours; no longer
may you find happiness in beautiful Aquinnah. The stranger
comes, an unbidden guest, to take that which was ours. Departing,
I bid you remember my teachings. Farewell, my sons and daughters, farewell." And then and there the great Moshup, as if by magic,
transformed his children into killers.

Today in old Ocean, roam these children of the chief at will.
Warm-blooded are they, and they nurse their young. In appearance
they resemble the whale, being fully as large. They are spotted
black and white, though occasionally an all-white one is seen. The
sign by which we know they are the true sons and daughters of
the great Moshup is this: They eat whales. In doing this they invariably eat the tongue first, though why they should unanimously
agree to partake of one particular portion before another must ever
remain a mystery. For many years it has been an item of popular
belief that the killers never eat a whale which is found dead, but
always kill their own. But those who have had ample opportunity
to study the peculiar habits of these denizens of the deep now
insist that though the killers are true to their name and will kill
and eat a whale, they have also come to that point where they will
occasionally partake of one which has been found dead. As in the

old days, however, the females are the first and the favored ones at such a feast, while the males await their turn in patience. And thereby do we also know that they are still the true sons and daughters of our good Moshup—still true to the teachings of the father in their new home and sphere. After the tongue is eaten, all surround the whale and ravenously bite out and devour pieces as large as one's arms can easily encompass. So swiftly do these killers partake of their feast that even expert whalemen must move quickly if they would save the bone.   (Vanderhoop 1904, July 2)

XIX

Maushop disappeared when Indians or Europeans crowded into his territory. Vanderhoop also left open the possibility that Maushop and Squant live hidden somewhere in the hills of Martha's Vineyard where strange noises, mists, and giant footprints sometimes point to their presence. Squant's disappearance into the dunes "without one solitary backward glance" recalls a Gay Head custom noted later by Speck. On Cranberry Day, a former annual community picnic, "a child was given a basket of food to carry into the dunes to set down at a lonely spot as a gift to old Granny Squanit, and cautioned to hurry away without ever looking back" (Speck and Dexter 1948: 264). Clearly Ol' Squant lives somewhere nearby where she still might be seen.

1904

Having disposed of his family in a manner which was wholly satisfactory to himself—for there were none who dared to criticise his action—Moshup had no thought save for himself and his squaw, his faithful companion in so much joy. Here traditions become more numerous and grow less positive. One story says that Moshup completely disappeared after a violent and prolonged quarrel which ended only when Ol' Squant wearily turned her footsteps to the highest point of the towering headland, and, posing herself for a moment while her eyes bade fond farewell to the rugged beauties of fair Aquinnah, jumped far out into the Atlantic and forever passed from sight in its bluest depths. Another says she chose the path along the beach around the cliffs and kept steadily on her stony way until she reached the south beach, where for the remainder of her life she concealed herself in one of the many existing sand hummocks.

But perhaps the most fitting ending of all, and the one that ought

to be true, is found in the version which says that Moshup took
the lead along the path around the cliffs, while Ol' Squant, without
one solitary backward glance, followed his footsteps with all the
stoicism of her kind. Thus, close to each other in the end as in the
beginning, together they sought that farther beach where the sands
had glittered in the sunshine and shimmered in the moonlight of
a thousand years. Together they passed the towering cliffs and
Molitiah's Ledge—passed Peaked Rock and Black Rock—passed
all the old landmarks until Zace's Cliffs were reached. Here at last,
lovers still, they sought repose and disappeared together in a hummock, though a hammock would have been far more comfortable.
Even at this day, when the atmosphere is clear, we may look in that
direction and see the smoke which is said to arise from their abode,
from fire or peudelah. Nor is it an uncommon thing at such a time
to hear a native say, with all assurance of a fixed belief: "Ol' Squant
is smoking." There are also those who tell of a weird, strange cry
that is occasionally heard on the south beach, and they always
allude to it as "Ol' Squant's warning of another shipwreck." Frequently at an early hour of the morning longshoremen will see an
immense track in the wet sand where the tide has gone down. "Ol'
Squant has been along," they say. Thus it is she ever wanders about
and occasionally gives evidence of her existence to the poor pygmies who now find homes in her abiding place of old. Her shape
must be simply grand, for it is said to resemble that of an immense
haystack. And yet she is fashionable. At dawn, we are told, she
leaps far out into the sea for her morning plunge, and at dusk she
duplicates the performance in order to obtain her evening dip.
Nevertheless, our poor senses are not acute enough to catch one
glimpse of her as she moves about in stateliness upon our beach.
We have only the airy nothingness of tradition and the smoke
which arises from the distant hummock to tell us of her past great-
ness and her once-upon-a-time reality.   (Vanderhoop 1904, July 2)

XX
    In the earlier Cooper/Basset legend (text V above), Maushop ban-
ished Squant to Sakonnet Rock for mourning the transformation of
her children into whales. Vanderhoop went one step beyond this
version, seeing in Maushop's behavior an explanation for the origin
of Indian women's submissiveness to their men. Vanderhoop seems
not to have been aware of the earlier published text, for she did not
know where Squant's transformed remains could be seen.

1904

Though Moshup had lived long in the country he never mingled with the common people. And yet he was the first schoolmaster. From his home on the cliffs he taught the natives respect for himself. He also taught them to be charitable—for when he had great stores of broiled fish he gave of his abundance to his subjects. He taught his family obedience—not only ordinary obedience—and secured his wife's quiet submission to his superior authority in all things save one. On account of her rebellion against his disposition of their children (so one of the varying traditions has it) he changed her into a stone. Somewhere on our shores there was once a stone in the perfect shape of a woman, bent over as if she were gathering fish. Curiosity seekers continually chipped at this stone until there was little left, and now, no one knows where even that little is, though "the trail" apparently leads to Squibnocket. At any rate the old god made of her such an example that all squaws are now submissive. Thus Moshup taught. (Vanderhoop 1904, August 6)

XXI

In *Nantucket: The Glacier's Gift* (1911) Eva Folger described an Indian giant that created Nantucket and Martha's Vineyard, but she did not disclose her source. Although Folger's giant closely resembles Maushop, the legend differs in a few details from the Gay Head prototypes and may have originated on Nantucket or Cape Cod. The giant's anger and island-building activities recall the Gay Head Maushop, and his specific method of creating islands with earth from his moccasins resembles "The Devil's Bridge" (ca. 1900) manuscript from Martha's Vineyard (text XI above). His use of Cape Cod for a bed, however, is new.

1911

Once upon a time there lived on the Atlantic coast a giant who used Cape Cod for his bed. One night, being restless, he tossed from side to side till his moccasins were filled with sand. This so enraged him that on rising in the morning he flung the offending moccasins from his feet, one alighting to form Martha's Vineyard, while the other became the since famous island of Nantucket.

(Folger 1911:1)

XXII

Daniel Wing, a Cape Cod antiquarian, attributed the following account of the origin of Martha's Vineyard, Nantucket, and fog to "native Indians," perhaps of the lower Cape. Maushop's wading in the sea, dumping sand from his moccasins to form islands, and creating fog with his pipe have all appeared before, although not in exactly this combination.

1915

The native Indians accounted for the islands Nantucket and Marthas Vineyard by a mythical story which ran somewhat in this wise:

A great many moons ago there lived upon the Cape a giant named Maushop. One day he waded out into the South sea to a great distance, for his legs were exceedingly long and his bodily vigor wonderful. After a time his moccasins became full of sand, which made walking painful. Thereupon he emptied one, and the island of Nantucket appeared above the surface of the water, while the sand which he poured from the other formed the island known as Marthas Vineyard. He lighted his pipe and volumes of smoke arose, obscuring the vision for miles around. Ever afterward, when fog appeared over the water, the Indians would exclaim in their native tongue, "Here comes old Maushop's smoke."   (Wing 1915:6)

XXIII

Wing attributed a second Maushop legend to Captain Loring Fuller of South Yarmouth, whose Indian informants are not identified but who may have been Gay Head seamen, for the legend closely reproduces nineteenth-century Gay Head accounts of the origin of Natucket, the bridge to Cuttyhunk, the aggressive crab, and Maushop's transformation of his wife and children.

1915

A very long time ago there lived a great Indian giant named Maushop, who could wade up and down Vineyard sound without finding the water more than knee deep. His home was in a cave called the Devil's Den on Gay Head. He used to sit on a boulder in the sound to smoke, and the ashes from his pipe, taken away by the currents, formed the island of Nantucket. He undertook to build a bridge from Gay Head to Cuttyhunk by filling one of his shoes with sand and wading out to empty it on the intended line; but a crab bit him on his uncovered foot and made him so angry that he broke off a portion of the cliff and threw it southward, thus forming the island called No Man's Land. He flung his five children into the sea and they were transformed into fishes. His wife remon-

strated with him and he tossed her across the channel to Seaconnet.

(Wing *1915:8*)

XXIV

First noted by Alden in 1798, the legend of the giant cannibal bird persisted in the Cape Cod area until the twentieth century, when an anonymous author published this overwritten version from unspecified sources. The unusual spelling of Maushop (Manshope) occurs in the anonymous 1787 text, which is quite different. Some details are new such as the bird's biannual raids to the mainland and its seizure of the culture hero's own child.

1915   HOW THE FOGS CAME TO THE CAPE

For many, many years the lodges of the mighty Mattacheesits had nestled beneath the shelter of the great oaks which spread their arms out toward the blue waters of the Cummaquid, lying beyond the verdant stretches of the Great Marshes, near where the village of Barnstable now stands. And twice every year since time began, once in the Moon of Bright Nights and again in the Moon of Falling Leaves, the Great Devil Bird from over the South Sea had come to levy his awful toll on the tribe, by grappling in his terrible talons the half-grown papooses; sometimes even seizing young braves who were old enough to handle a tomahawk, and bearing them away to his lair in the Region of the South Wind.

One evening as the Great War Sachem Manshope was returning to his wigwam, swollen with pride from victories won over the Nausets far down the old war trail which leads over Scargo Hill and on down the Cape, and which may still be traced by the curious, he was startled by the heart-breaking wail of the death dirge echoing through the trees on the heavy air of sunset. Quickly his pride turned to rage when he found his faithful squaw, with face gashed and breast torn as a sign of sorrow, bemoaning the loss of her first born, a stalwart young brave of sixteen summers, whom the Great Bird had snatched up in his mighty talons and borne off to his lair, when the sun was within a hand's breath of its setting.

Pausing but an instant to raise his tomahawk in an attitude of defiance toward the South and asking the Great Spirit to see and aid him, Manshope started with giant strides across the Cape, splashing through creeks and watercourses, until ere night-fall he had reached the edge of the low swamp which then lay where the channel is now between Bishop and Clerk's Ledge, and the mainland, and could just discern in the failing light of the dusk, the Great Bird and its human prey sinking below the horizon.

No man before had ever crossed the great South Sea, or discovered if land lay beyond, but the Sachem's eyes saw the waters as blood and his soul called out to Heaven to give him strength and cunning to trail this terrible enemy to his lair and slay him there. Unheeding the darkness of night falling over the turbulent waters, he waded boldly forth, and guided by the stars, soon came to the isle since called Capewack by the Indians, which we know as Martha's Vineyard, and striding on to the high cliffs which rise majestically on the western end of the island he found on the very edge of the land, a giant oak, around whose roots for many paces were strewn the white bones of children brought from the Cape tribes in countless former depredations.

Creeping softly under the deep shadow cast by the great tree, and peering through the branches overhead, he could see the dim outline of the Great Devil Bird, with his wicked head hidden beneath his wing, sleeping heavily after his gluttonous feast, without a thought of danger lurking underneath, for never before had man's foot trodden this island where he made his lair.

Manshope looked to his weapons, saw to it that his tomahawk was secure in the sinew which bound it to its handle, and then with all the cunning and craft inherited from a race of hunters, he swung himself, as stealthily as a panther, from limb to limb, until at last he stood on the top of the gnarled and twisted oak, so near the Bird that the night wind ruffling his feathers blew them against Manshope's cheek.

Slowly and noiselessly, the war axe of the Sachem was raised in air, poised for a moment, and then came down with a sickening swish on the bended neck that was curved so unsuspectingly toward him. With a crash the Great Bird fell through the branches of the oak, and all its limbs quivered as it struck the earth, never to rise again.

Manshope waited patiently until he was certain his arch enemy was dead before he descended and slowly and sorrowfully wended his way to the north shore of the Island. His heart was heavy within him for although he had trimphed over this Great Evil One, his own young brave was gone to the Happy Hunting Grounds of his Fathers, and his soul cried out for his lost son. Pondering deeply over the eternal "why," he sat down to rest and refresh himself on the banks of the island overlooking the Sound, before endeavoring to return to the mainland and home.

From his quiver he drew forth a pipe, but his tobacco was so

dampened by his passage through the waters on the previous eve-
ning that it would not burn, so gathering a quantity of pokeweed,
which was commonly used by our Cape Indians when their tobacco
ran short, and filling his pipe anew, Manshope was soon enveloped
in eddying whirls and rings of smoke that arose and spread on the
morning air, swirling across the Sound on the freshening Southerly
breezes, and curling over the moorlands of the Cape, until, so great
were the clouds of smoke the Sachem blew from his nostrils, they
were wafted even to the wigwam in the land of the Mattacheesits
where his faithful squaw waited his return.

Great was the rejoicing in the Indian Village when the people
saw this sign, for well they knew the Great Bird was slain, and that
Manshope still lived, for was the Sachem ever known to linger on
the trail of a living enemy even long enough to smoke?

The Great Devil Bird came no more to ravage the Tribes of the
Cape; and forever after, when in summer the fog bank drifted in
from across the Sound, enveloping the moorlands in its eddying
whirls and curling around the wigwams in the Indian village, just
as the smoke wreaths did from the Sachem's pipe on that morning
when the Great Bird was slain, the Indian mothers would draw
their children in nearer the camp fire and telling them this legend
while the mists crept silently around them would say, "Here comes
Old Manshope's Smoke!"   ("How the Fogs Came to the Cape" 1915:15–16).

XXV

Gale Huntington, the leading resident historian and folklorist of
Martha's Vineyard, learned two Maushop legends from a Gay Head
Indian neighbor named George Cook, with whom he picked berries
as a child. Huntington wrote to me: "In [James A.] Jones's time and
even much later there were Indians living in white households all
over the Island. When I was a boy there was a Gay Head boy, George
Cook, who was living on the farm of a neighbor. As long as he lived
he was one of my best friends" (Huntington 1980:1). Huntington's
accounts, written from memory some fifty years later, consist of brief
explanatory motifs for the origins of Devil's Bridge, Noman's Land,
fossil bones in the Gay Head cliffs, and Nantucket.

CIRCA 1915

Moshop is supposed to have started the Devil's Bridge because
he wanted a causeway so that he could walk dry-shod to Cutty-
hunk. But he soon became bored with the project and abandoned
it. He is also credited with having separated Nomans Land from

the Vineyard by drawing his big toe across the barrier beach that once made a much larger Squibnocket Pond and that connected the two Islands. Of course the sea broke through the track left by Moshop's toe and washed away all the beach without leaving a trace. Moshop is responsible, too, for the fossil bones that are found in the Gay Head cliffs. They are the remains of the whales and other marine creatures that he feasted on. . . .

Moshop's most spectacular feat of all was the creation of Nantucket. . . . One day Moshop was smoking his pipe while fishing in the shoal water east of Chappaquiddick. The pipe went out and he knocked the dottle and ashes into the water in a little heap. That little heap is Nantucket.   (Huntington 1969:90)

XXVI

Agnes Rothery attributed the legend of the devil and the chickadee to Cape Cod "natives" who could have been white or Indian. Again, the giant carries boulders in his apron and drops them when interrupted by a chickadee, which apparently substituted for the crab in this version.

1918

The natives recalled the old legend about the Devil, who came down the Cape one fine day stepping from one hill to another to keep from getting his feet wet. His apron was full of boulders, and as he entered the town of Bourne a chickadee laughed at him. In a rage he seized a boulder from his apron and started to throw it at the bird. But he stumbled and fell, and the boulders landed in Bournedale and are pointed out from one generation of children to the other as the place where the Devil broke his apron strings.

(Rothery 1918:14)

XXVII

Mabel Knight heard a unique telling of "The Devil's Bridge" from Charles William Ryan of Gay Head. Maushop and the devil are here presented as adversaries. After driving Maushop from Cape Cod to Gay Head, the devil then schemed to acquire the giant's soul through a contract with his wife. Squant, however, denies the devil his prize by outwitting him with the mock sunrise. The motifs M 210. *Bargain with devil* and K 210. *Devil cheated of his promised soul* are traceable to Yankee and British folklore sources (Dorson 1946:51–55; Johnson 1897:241–42; Leather 1912:164; Sikes 1881:203–4). Maushop may be compared here with Gay Head men who often were away from home; as in the 1904 Vanderhoop text (text XII above), the devil symbolizes outside interests that caused Indians to retreat and that still knock hard on their doors.

1925   THE DEVIL'S BRIDGE

Long ago two giants lived on Cape Cod, and one was good and one was bad. The bad one made himself so unpleasant that the good one, Moshop, took his wife Squant and his twelve beautiful daughters and fled with them to Martha's Vineyard. Moshop settled at the end of the Island where the Gay Head Indians live today. On the farthest point, in what is now known as the Devil's Den, he made his home. They had always plenty of food, for when they wanted more, Moshop stood by his door and caught whales by their tails. He threw these on the big out-door fireplace where there was always a fire burning. When they needed more wood Moshop took hold of a tree, pulled it up by the roots and threw it on the fire.

Moshop was often away from home. One day his wife was alone by the door, and the Devil came by. He told her that between sun-down and the time the cock crowed for dawn he could build a bridge from the place where the Coast Guard Station stands today to Cuttyhunk. Squant did not believe him. The Devil made a bet with her, and he said that if he succeeded, he was to have Moshop's soul. Squant was sure he could not succeed, and she accepted the terms of the wager.

At sun-down the Devil began to build the bridge. He picked up huge boulders in his apron. He was in such a hurry to take them to the part of the shore where his bridge must be built that a few of the boulders fell out, and you can see them today where the Devil dropped them. They are always known as the Devil's Boulders.

Squant saw that something must be done at once, for the Devil built his bridge with great rapidity. She took a candle, lighted it, and ran out to find her old rooster. She flicked it in front of his eyes, and he, thinking the dawn had come, crowed lustily. When the Devil heard this, he too thought the dawn had come, and he was so angry that he seized what he had built of the bridge and flung it out into the water where it is today, the cause of many shipwrecks.

Moshop and his family were hard-pressed by the people, and to save his daughters he turned them into "killers" (fishes like whales). He then took his wife around the point to Squibnocket, where the smoke of their fire may still be seen sometimes at twi-

light. He himself may be seen at midnight by one who has drunk
heartily and is coming home through the woods. "Whether this is
true or not, I cannot say, for I myself have never met him."

(Knight 1925:134–35)

XXVIII–XXX

About a quarter century after Vanderhoop published her collection of Gay Head lore, Gladys Tantaquidgeon began fieldwork in Gay Head and Mashpee. Hers is the largest collection of Maushop lore on record and the truest thus far to the words of Indian narrators. Her rapport at Gay Head and Mashpee was excellent, and old people in these communities remember her fondly. Tantaquidgeon wrote, "Both young and old believe, to a certain degree, in the mythological beings Moshop and Squant," and they were "careful not to talk too freely about Moshop at one time, lest he should appear to them" (Tantaquidgeon 1930b:20–21, 24).

One obvious change noted by Tantaquidgeon was in the culture heroes' facial features, for Maushop as well as Squant had only one eye in the middle of their foreheads, suggesting possible influence from the Cyclops of Homer's *Odyssey*, who also was a giant living in a den on a hillside above the sea. The one-eye motif (F 531.1.1.1. *Giant with one eye in middle of forehead*) is known in Irish and Welsh folklore as well. The island called Noman's Land off Gay Head also brings up the possible connection to Homer's Cyclops, but according to island tradition the name originated as a shortened form of Tequenoman, a local Indian sachem (Huntington 1969:94). Like Old World giants, Tantaquidgeon's Maushop wrecked ships on Devil's Bridge by lighting false signals, then gathering the goods from the wrecks in great canoes manned by slaves. This negative image of Maushop, with its antiwhite, cargo-cult overtones, is a folklore inversion of Gay Head reality, for in the nineteenth century the Gay Head men volunteered for lifesaving crews to rescue endangered ships (Attaquin 1970:37–39). It is logical, nonetheless, that Maushop was said to provide the Indians with wreck goods, for he long had done the same with drift whales. Like his northern neighbor Gluskap, he was often helpful but sometimes impetuous and irritable.

The Maushop and Squant of Tantaquidgeon's accounts are more traditional and less affable than in the earlier accounts by Vanderhoop (1904) and the later account by Madison (1955). Perhaps these differences reflect the fact that Tantaquidgeon collected legends told by Indian to Indian, whereas the others were also concerned with conveying Indian traditions to a non-Indian audience.[12]

XXVIII

1928

*Moshop was an Indian, they say, the first one to live on the Is-
land. Although he had only one eye, nothing escaped his vision.
He could see ships from afar and would place his signals so as to
wreck them and get the things they carried. Thats how the Indians
here got all they had. For in the beginning they lived out in the
open like animals—they did not even have wigwams. From the
way some people talked you would think they lived like wolves.
He lived out of the sea on whales and such things that came to him
for we never heard that he went clamming or worked for his living
like other people. He was a lazy old fellow. Uncle [Trustum?] Weeks
used to say Moshop was a hero of the Indians. He was not a good
man but a mighty one. The old folks used to think that if you talk
about him too much he would appear to you. Thats why it was bad
luck to talk about him too much. Thats what they used to tell us. I
never heard however that Moshop was expected to come back and
as for old Skwant they use to tell us, Dont you ever make fun of her
or she'll tear you all to pieces.* (Tantaquidgeon 1928)

XXIX

1928

*Moshop was a giant who had a single eye in the middle of his
forehead. He came to the island from somewhere on the mainland.
Finding it uninhabited, he sought shelter in a cave on the high
cliffs not far from the site of the present Gay Head lighthouse. There
he lived with his wife, who also had only one eye. The couple had
several children. Moshop had a large fireplace near his den, and
he pulled up great trees for fuel. This accounts for the absence
of trees in that locality, and also for the supposed volcanic remains
upon which geologists have commented from time to time. Eigh-
teen years ago, "smoke was seen issuing from the cliffs and scientists pronounced it to be of volcanic origin, saying that the island
was in danger of sinking"; but sage Indian inhabitants assured
them that it was "only the smoke from Moshop's fireplace."*
(Tantaquidgeon 1930b:21–22)

XXX

1928

*Moshop was fond of blasted whale meat and would eat a whole
whale at a meal. Standing near the entrance of his den, he could
reach out over the cliffs, pick up a whale that had been washed*

ashore, and swing it over to his fire, which was burning continually. The blood and grease from the whales stained the cliffs. Moshop taught the people how to build their lodges; how to till the soil and to catch the whale and smaller fish that lived in the sea. He placed false signals and caused many shipwrecks. He sent his great canoe out, manned by slaves, to capture the crews of the ill-fated ships and to bring the cargoes ashore. Thus he obtained goods of various sorts for himself and his subjects.   (Tantaquidgeon 1930b:22)

XXXI–XL

Tantaquidgeon's accounts of the creation of Nantucket, Noman's Land, fog, Devil's Bridge, and the transformation of Maushop's children are close to preceding versions. Squant's sorrow for the loss of her children provides an explanation for the mournful sounds of wind and surf along the south shore of the Gay Head peninsula.[13]

XXXI

1928

Once a big bird carried off one of Maushop's children and so he started off toward the islands to find it. On the way he got tired and smoked his pipe and when he dumped the ashes out it formed Nantucket.   (Tantaquidgeon 1928–29)

XXXII

1928   HOW NANTUCKET WAS FORMED—"DEVIL'S ASH HEAP"

Once there were two lovers. They wanted to get married but the girl's father objected and so did the boy's father so Moshop said that he would help them. So he sat down and lighted his pipe (which it was believed made him think better). As he turned his pipe to let the ashes fall out he moved his arm back and forth. Where the ashes fell an island started to form and he told the lovers to go there. That was how Moshop created Nantucket.

(Tantaquidgeon 1928)

XXXIII

1928

A pair of lovers, whose parents objected to their marriage, went to Moshop for aid. He sat down to smoke, and as he emptied the ashes from his great pipe into the sea, there arose a cloud of smoke, and as it cleared away the lovers beheld a beautiful island. There they dwelt on the island now known as Nantucket.

(Tantaquidgeon 1930b:23)

XXXIV

1928   SKWANT MOURNS

Moshop is said at this time to have been very cruel toward his children. He beat them terribly and their mother Skwant mourns to this day (so it is said of the surf as it beats on the shore).

(Tantaquidgeon 1928)

XXXV

1928

Moshop sometimes treated his family cruelly. One day he sent his children out to play on the beach. Cutting a deep channel across the beach with his big toe-nail, the water rushed in and the children were in danger of drowning, so he transformed them into porpoises. This act caused the mother to mourn, and she later jumped off the cliff. When the wind howls and the surf beats along the south shore, the weird sounds produced are reminders of the fate of Moshop's family.   (Tantaquidgeon 1930b:23)

XXXVI

1928

Moshop was a stout man. He picked up a lot of rocks and started to build a bridge but a crab bit him on the heel and caused him to drop the rocks.   (Tantaquidgeon 1928)

XXXVII

1928

Moshop attempted to build a bridge from Gay Head to Cuttyhunk by placing huge boulders in the sea, but before he had accomplished his task, a crab caught him by the heel and he was obliged to stop work. This made the giant so angry that he threw the crab toward the Nantucket shoals; threw several of the boulders far out to sea and broke off a portion of Gay Head which he cast into the sea, thus forming No Man's Land.   (Tantaquidgeon 1930b:22–23)

XXXVIII

1928   MOSHOP'S BRIDGE

The Indians on Martha's Vineyard and Cuttyhunk were not very friendly. Moshop decided that he wanted to build a bridge from Martha's Vineyard to Cuttyhunk so being very strong he started to carry huge rocks in his apron toward the Head and threw them out to sea. There was an old woman on Cuttyhunk who found out what Moshop was doing. She said, "We dont want those people near here. I'll stop his work." It was generally known that Moshop liked to sleep in the daytime and that he would never work after dawn so the old woman took a lantern and went to the chicken house and put it before the cock and he, thinking it was near day break, began to crow. When Moshop heard the cock crowing he thought that it was near dawn so he dropped all the rocks there. He was so angry that he picked up the biggest one that he could find and threw it as far toward Cuttyhunk as he could. This is now called Saddleback Rock. Many ships have been wrecked on Moshop's or Devil's Bridge. *(Tantaquidgeon 1928)*

XXXIX
1928

Moshop dragged his big toe and loosened up a piece of land which floated out to sea and is called No Man's Land.
(Tantaquidgeon 1928)

XL
1928 MOSHOP MAKES NO MAN'S LAND

Mrs. Ryan said that her Uncle Dan Nevers told her that there were people on No Man's Land and he [Moshop?] was angry because he feared that the giant on No Man's Land had more power than he so he dragged his toe along the beach which separates No Man's Land from Gay Head causing the water to rush in between the two places. *(Tantaquidgeon 1928)*

XLI–XLVI

In Tantaquidgeon's account, Squant had acquired a more violent personality and even killed Maushop following a series of family quarrels. She is said to live somewhere in her old domain, where Rachel Ryan reported seeing her. The taboo against speaking Maushop's name lest he appear could be a remnant of the well-documented seventeenth-century taboo against speaking the name of the dead.

XLI
1928

Finally, Moshop was lured along the south shore by Squant, to her abode on the Wasquabsque cliffs. They quarreled continually and at last the great and powerful giant was slain by the wily Squant. These domestic differences were said to be the cause of

climatic disturbances in that region. Even now, when unfamiliar
sounds are heard coming from that direction, the Indians say that
a storm is brewing. The smoke from Moshop's pipe causes the
dense fogs so frequently encountered by craft operating off Cape
Cod and in Vineyard sound. My informants were even careful not
to talk too freely about Moshop at one time, lest he should appear
to them.   (Tantaquidgeon 1930b:23–24)

XLII
1928

Squant, they say, is still alive and frequents the beaches along
the south shore. She has square eyes, and long hair which hangs
down to the ground, covering her body and concealing her deformity. It appears that originally she was considered to be a supernatural being to whom they prayed for spiritual and material aid.
The later conception, as expressed in current tales and by a number
of writers, is that of a witch who carries off children and bewitches
men.   (Tantaquidgeon 1930b:24)

XLIII
1928

Children were told never to go down to the south shore because
Squant would get them if they did. One day when Mrs. Ryan was a
child she with other pupils left the school grounds and went down
along the shore. Before long she saw a big load of hay swaying
back and forth as though it were an ox cart but there weren't any
oxen pulling it. The children were so frightened that they ran back
to school and the people told them that it was Squant who had
frightened them. "So I still believe that Squant is down there."
                                            (Tantaquidgeon 1928)

XLIV
1928

Maushop takes the form of various creatures and may be sensed
about Gay Head at times as a gust of cold wind that rushes past
one and gives one the [   ].   (Tantaquidgeon 1928–29)

XLV
1928

Tea leaves in cup referred to as Moshop and Skwant and read as
follows. Moshop and Skwant dancing together, guess they've made
up so now we'll get some good weather.   (Tantaquidgeon 1928)

XLVI

1928

An Indian lobster man returning from spearing skates for bait at twilight on a bleak June night throws his iron pail among some rusty implements lying in his shed. "That ends my days work." A series of sparks are given out as the implements clash. "Look at them sparks, Old Moshop's got into em."   (Tantaquidgeon 1928)

XLVII

In 1934 Elizabeth Reynard of the Department of English at Barnard College published a substantial collection of Indian and Yankee folklore from Cape Cod that included some Maushop legends. In her chapter "The Death of the Giant" she attributed much of her oral narrative material to two Mashpee chiefs: "The Indian legends in this section were told to the author by Chief Red Shell [Clarence Wixon], historian of the Nauset Wampanoag Tribe, and by Chief Wild Horse [Clinton Haynes], Wampanoag Champion of Mashpee, who have generously contributed them to this book. The stories, repeated orally from generation to generation, are only known to a few living Indians. These retain and treasure the legendary beliefs" (Reynard 1934:23). When I first discovered Reynard's Mashpee texts I was surprised by what seemed to be some remarkable and little-known linguistic and cultural survivals. After locating Red Shell's personal notebooks, talking with Wild Horse's son and daughter, Clinton and Daisy Haynes, who now live in Middleboro, and spending a few hours in the library, I understood that the legends are unlike any others we have seen thus far. The Mashpee had been asserting their Indian heritage for several years before Reynard published, and Chiefs Red Shell and Wild Horse played a major part in promoting a Pan-Indian awareness among their people. Their legends include motifs and vocabulary from the Ojibwa and Delaware and some linguistic materials that were last recorded by seventeenth-century writers such as Roger Williams and Edward Winslow. Red Shell and Wild Horse combined elements from comparative and ethnohistorical sources with published and oral Wampanoag traditions to create a new folklore that expressed their interest in restoring Wampanoag links with the past and with other American Indian groups. One Maushop legend regarding the origin of Scargo Lake and Hill near Yarmouth combines earlier sources with another well-known Cape Cod legend (said to be Indian) about Scargo Lake. Yotannit (the fire god) and Nanipaushat (the moon god) certainly came from Williams ([1643] 1936:125), available in earlier editions.

1934   HOW MAUSHOP MADE SCARGO LAKE

Once the giant went visiting on the north side of the Narrow Land. The Indians there grew fond of him, and asked him to leave them something to remember him by, when he had gone away. Maushop, in his eagerness to please them, dug a deep hole and placed the earth from it in a large mound on the southern side of the hole. He dug fast and he dug deep, until at last the hole was so great that in it a giant could bury more than the largest Wampanoag village. When Maushop had finished this work, he lighted his pipe and puffed forth smoke that formed into dark clouds whence issued the drumbeats of the Thunder-Spirit and the lightning of Yotannit. After he had completed his smoke, Maushop emptied his pipe. Ashes fell upon the high mound, and rain poured from above. Night extended upon the land without the coming of Nanipaushat, the Moon Spirit. For two days and two nights the waters descended from the heavens. On the morning of the third day the clouds rolled themselves together and drifted north. The sun shone upon the people. They came out of their huts and saw a great lake, where Maushop had dug a hole, and beside the lake towered a high hill covered with pine trees. The hill they named Scargo for the pine trees made from the ashes of Maushop's pipe, and the lake has been known ever since by the name of Scargo Lake.   (Reynard 1934:27–28)

XLVIII

The Little People who besieged Maushop's sons may once have existed in Wampanoag folklore, but Red Shell or Wild Horse probably borrowed the name Pukwudgees and the story itself from published sources. Legends of Little People known as Pukwudjininee abound in Central Algonquian folklore (the name appears in no early New England source), but perhaps Red Shell and Wild Horse found their inspiration closer to home. Thomas Weston, in *History of the Town of Middleboro, Massachusetts* (1906), published several legends that he identified as Wampanoag, including one about Pukwudjees, "a race of little people" that lived on an island in Assawampsett Pond (Weston 1906:425). Weston or his uncredited source had inserted local place names into an Ojibwa legend.[14]

1934   THE BATTLE WITH THE PYGMIES

On an island in Poponesset Bay, below South Mashpee, Maushop kept his wife, a giantess born to a common-size brave and squaw at a place called Cummaquid. Since she did not stop growing when she reached the height of a man-being, she soon became so tall that the highest trees only reached to her shoulder. Even so, she was far shorter than her husband, who knocked trees over as if they were so many weeds, and thought nothing of eating a small whale at a meal.

Maushop's wife, named Quaunt, bore him five sons who were also giants and had good hearts. Quaunt was not so good-natured as these men-folk with whom she lived. Sometimes she nagged Maushop, or beat her sons; sometimes she tried to prevent them from doing good to the Indians of the Narrow Land. Often she repented of her periods of evil, and attempted to befriend man-beings, to make amends for her folly.

In the days when Maushop and his five sons and his quarrelsome wife used the Cape for their Wigwam-mat, a Little People lived in the swamps of maple and birch, and around the salt ponds and bays. They built their homes in high grasses or bulrushes, and divided their forces into seven bands, each with its own leader. These pygmies, or Little People were called Pukwudgees. Only a handful of them were in each band, yet so potent was their magic (even a common Pukwudgee had charms greater than those of the tribal medicine-men), so terrible were their miracles, that Maushop and his sons and his wife could not always prevail against them.

The chiefs among the Pukwudgees had more power than the pygmy-warriors, but the chief of the chiefs, the leader over the seven bands, was the greatest magician of them all. In height he was the tallest Pukwudgee, and at that he scarcely reached the knee of an ordinary man. Around his neck hung a string of bright shells. His body was entirely covered with green leaves, and he carried a white oak bow equipped with arrows which were not a finger long. He and his band lived in the marshes near Poponesset Bay, where he could keep an eye on the doings of Maushop, and trouble the Gentle Giant with small botherings.

The Pukwudgees were bad. Now and then they befriended a man-being, but that was only to show what they could do. They trained the Tei-Pai-Wankas (Will-o'-the-Wisps) to shine lights near the trails at night. Travelling Indians followed these lights and were lured into the marshes where Mahtahdou, the Devil, trapped their feet in quicksands and sucked them into the earth. The Puk-wudgees delighted in scaring women and girls. Sometimes the Little People appeared in the form of bears, and when the hunters shot at them, pulled the arrows out of their hides, broke the arrow shafts and ran away; or vanished into air as soon as arrows touched their bodies. They pushed Indians off high cliffs and killed their victims. In the form of wild cats they jumped upon man-beings and

*fought to the death. Jealous of Maushop, and of the love that the
Indians bore toward him, now and again the Pukwudgees
performed good magic; solely to make Maushop aware that their
medicine was more powerful than his.*

*The Gentle Giant was slow to anger, yet there came a day when
he could endure the tricks of the Little People no longer. He took a
large tree in either hand, waded all the way around the peninsula,
stooping down to inspect the shores, bending low to look into the
marshes and along the reeds of the baywater. The Pukwudgees
kept rabbit-still. The giant could not see them, so he enlisted his
sons in the search. The five sons, who were smaller than their
father, lay down among the pine trees near Poponesset Marsh. The
wind blew from the south. The reeds swayed back and forth and
the giants saw this motion and did not realize that Pukwudgees,
hidden among the salt grasses, were creeping nearer, nearer. Suddenly, the tiny warriors threw bad magic in the giants' eyes, and
the sons of old Maushop were cruelly blinded. With huge hands
they struck at the grass and crushed a few Pukwudgees. But all the
rest of the pygmy warriors escaped to a safe distance; and as the
giants could no longer see them, they stood in the open and threw
poisoned darts into the hides of the sons. The young giants became
so weak that they could not rise. In great suffering they waited for
the coming of Maushop who, when he saw his strong sons stricken
by the Little People, worked all the magic that a giant knows; then
summoned the medicine-men; but neither he nor any Indian could
save the five blind giants.*

*They died beside the marshes near Poponesset Bay. Maushop
lifted their young bodies and carried them to Succonesset Waters.
He heaped sand over their corpses, building it into huge mounds
which became small islands. He planted trees and grasses to grow
on the graves of his sons. These islands are called by white men,
the Elizabeth Islands, or the Town of Gosnold.*   (Reynard 1934:29–31)

XLIX

The Little People in this text represent Europeans who, by firing
on Maushop, caused him to disappear or die. Red Shell or Wild
Horse probably created the legend themselves but may have con-
sulted earlier European accounts by Wood, Kendall, or Basset and
possibly Longfellow's *The Song of Hiawatha* ([1855] 1955).

1934   THE DEATH OF MAUSHOP

*After his children had perished, Maushop became very sad. He
had never known defeat before, and he spent all his time thinking*

what next he should do to rid the land of Pukwudgees. He could think of nothing except that he was old and broken-hearted.

One morning, as Geesukquand the Sun-being cast handfuls of mica pebbles over the Eastern Sea, Maushop saw a small white bird riding upon the waves. As it drew nearer, the giant perceived that it was not a bird but a canoe over which hung two white skins on sticks. He waded through the sea and stooped to pick up the magic boat. Before he could touch it, sharp darts, like flung pebbles or the arrows of Pukwudgees, stung against his legs. In fear that the vessel was an evil charm sent against him by the Little People, Maushop strode back to the Narrow Land, picked up his wife, threw her against Succonesset Point, and made his escape to the South. The Magic of the Pukwudgees, or of that white-winged vessel, may have occasioned his death. He has never returned to the Place of Bays; and the Indians, who love him, believe that he would come if he could.   (Reynard 1934:31)

L

Writing in 1934 of the traditions and history of Bourne on upper Cape Cod, local historian Betsey Keene mentioned giants and a devil that may be Indian memories of Maushop. Their stone-building efforts and the broken-apron-string motif echo Devil's Bridge legends of an earlier day.

1934

There is no lack of Indian traditions nor scarcity of imaginative explanations as to the reason for some peculiarities of rocks and boulders, found so plentifully in the woods of Bourne—the Boulder Town of Cape Cod.

· · ·

"The Devil's Dumping Ground" is almost indescribable, being an uneven plot of woodland covering approximately two acres.

· · ·

A rocky region of uneven ledges, situated on the easterly side of the old Sandwich road just before it enters the Pocasset and Forestdale road, is called the place "Where the Devil broke his apron string." Here the rocks, all sizes and shapes, lie heaped in disorderly layers from the bottom to the top of the incline, just as they fell when the "apron string" broke.

"Squaw Hollow," not far from these apron-string rocks, was, traditionally, depressed into its present shape by the Devil's heel when his Satanic Majesty, bent on one of his mischievous errands, stepped thence to Nantucket.   (Keene [1937] 1975:180–81)

LI

The 1904 Vanderhoop texts marked the first public expression of Gay Head interest in Indian traditions, and by 1928 this interest took political form with the establishment of a Gay Head branch of the Wampanoag Council. Like many other northeastern tribes at this time, Gay Headers sought new ways to establish their Indian identity as the racial, linguistic, territorial, and cultural basis of that identity slipped away. In the 1930s they began a series of annual summer powwows or pageants in which they dressed up in Plains Indian regalia and reenacted local legends for their own pleasure and to encourage tourism to their end of the island. These pageants, held in the evening at various locations including town hall and the Gay Head cliffs, began in 1933 and lasted until the late 1970s (Levitas 1980:386–93; Mayhew 1956:147). Leonard Vanderhoop, an esteemed elder who often played the part of Maushop (see Abbey 1982), owns a typewritten script for one pageant, held around 1955, which he permitted me to copy. Nanetta Madison, author of this text, was a daughter of Mary Vanderhoop.

The 1955 text accentuates the positive side of Gay Head legends, for Cheepi, the evil one, is not mentioned, and Maushop is more considerate of his wife, sons, and daughters than in previous narratives. The old culture hero left his impetuous and tricksterlike qualities behind when he mounted the stage. Maushop's pet frog and toad, their transformation at the time of European contact, and his prescient dreams are new.[15]

CIRCA 1955

In days of long past, we of Gay Head would have welcomed you with the Indian word, Toniketcha. Now we welcome you in the language which best serves all of us in the United States of America. Welcome friends one and all. For the old days are gone, and of that time there remains nothing but the bright threads of memory, woven in a pattern we hope is never lost.

This year marks the 353rd anniversary of our Island's discovery and the arrival of the first white people to record their visit to Aquinnah, as Gay Head then was known.

Tonight we would take you back to that simple, primitive time, long before the coming of the white man to this place. To the age of heroic figures in Indian legendry. And so we welcome you to Aquinnah, home of these legendary figures.

In the spirit of those days, [   ], as Chief Running Deer, will interpret our greetings in a dance of welcome handed down from one

generation to another. They have been collected for tonight's pag-
eant by Nanetta Vanderhoop Madison of Gay Head. The narrator is
Jacqueline Manning and the songs are sung by Helen Attaquin.
Others taking leading parts are Leonard Vanderhoop, Moshup;
Joan Vanderhoop, Squant; John Vanderhoop, Tashmoo; Maysel
Vanderhoop, Quampeche; Lyman Madison, Medicine Man; Wm.
Vanderhoop, father of the bride; Cedric Belain, brave; June Noble
(bride); Luther Madison, Chief; Dougie Vanderhoop, a crab. All are
of Gay Head and descendants of the people who first lived on
Aquinnah.

For proper atmosphere let us imagine ourselves seated on the
earthen floor of an old wigwam, swept with the cornhusk broom
and sprinkled with white sand in honor of this gala occasion, a
night of song and story.

How did the Pawkunnawakutts first come to Gay Head? Legend
tells of Moshup, a great fighting chieftain, who lived on the mainland. Tall was he, and straight as the shaft of an arrow, excelling in
all feats of strength and bravery because he was said to be
endowed with supernatural powers. Indeed, his great prowess in
war and sport often was attributed to magic, and a spirit of envy
and malice soon arose. At last, weary of strife and discord on the
mainland, Moshup decided to lead his followers to a new place
where they could spend their days in peace.

For many moons, Moshup wandered ever eastward, until he
came at last to low marshy lands, where weary and worn, he
dragged his great toes, thus creating the chain of Islands known
today as the Elizabeth Islands. Wishing to make a complete separa-
tion from those with whom he had lived in such turmoil, he again
dragged his great toes, permitting the waters of the ocean to rush in
and surround the land we now know as the Island of Martha's
Vineyard. Thus Moshup separated his people from their former
way of life, choosing as a home for them, these colorful headlands,
where they erected their wigwams and settled in this hollow, which
in time came to be known as the Devil's Den.

Moshup's family consisted of his wife, Squant, their 12 stalwart
sons and 12 beautiful daughters.

Even in those long ago days, feeding a family of that size was a
problem, but behold mighty Moshup as he stands at the edge of the
cliff seeking with keen eyes the whale that will provide their food.
In those times whales came close to shore, for they had not learned
to fear pursuit. Later, whaling became an industry adopted from
the Indian's first crude efforts. Many Gay Head men sailed the

World in early whaleships. . . . Now Moshup makes his catch and hauls it in to be prepared by his wife and daughters for the evening meal. Blood from these slaughtered leviathans of the deep stained some of our cliffs a dark red, so legends say, and that color may be seen today. Whale's teeth, shark's teeth and quahog fossils still to be found in the cliffs, testify that the refuse from Moshup's table was discarded close by his wigwam. Mighty trees were needed to kindle the fires on which the whales were cooked. Day by day the nearby forests were stripped, which accounts, no doubt, for the present scarcity of large trees in Gay Head. Wild blueberries, larger and more succulent than in any other part of the Island, grew on tall bushes, as they do today, so that Moshup's people might vary their menu. But on the low lying marshes between the dunes along the shores of Aquinnah, grew the greatest delicacy of all, the wild cranberry. No one knows how they came to grow there, but we of Aquinnah believe it is another sign from the Great Spirit, who never ceases to watch over his children.

According to custom, men of the family ate first at the family table. The women served them and waited then until the braves had departed before eating their fill of what remained. Dishes were made of clay dug from the cliffs and molded into shape with skillful hands. Today we still make things of clay, following the lessons handed down from our elders.

Legend tells us that Moshup's wife, Squant, was very beautiful, so beautiful that one day, as she lay sleeping, an evil spirit seeking to disfigure Squant because of malice, cut her eyelids so she appeared to have square eyes. So distressed was Squant when she realized what had happened, that forever after she wore her hair as a veil over her face so that none might see her disfigurement.

. . .

On summer evenings, Moshup would sit at his enormous doorway, smoking his great peudeldee, as the Indian called his pipe. In good humor at close of day, well content with his lot, Moshup often gave kindly advice to his people who brought their problems to him for his consideration.

According to legend, a certain brave, son of a wealthy chieftain, wished to wed a poor maiden who was without dowry. But the chieftain had refused to consent to such a union. Knowing that Moshup had helped others, the two lovers sought him out and presented their case.

The great one listened kindly, but said nothing, merely sat and puffed away on his faithful peudeldee. The two lovers were disappointed at Moshup's apparent indifference and were turning sadly away, when he leaned forward and dumped his gigantic peudeldee, whereupon there arose a furious burning and sizzling, accompanied by dense clouds of smoke and vapor. When all was clear again, there lay the beautiful Island of Nantucket, which Moshup presented to the maiden as her dowry in answer to her prayer.

. . .

Although Moshup was happy in his new home, he sometimes thought regretfully of the land he had left behind him. One day it occurred to him he could establish a link with the mainland by building a bridge across the water. To think was to act with this great one. He began immediately to toss huge stones into the water in the direction of Cuttyhunk, for he planned to use that island as a stepping stone to the mainland.

Stone after stone splashed into the sea, and Moshup was so mightily pleased with his efforts he did not observe a crab come sidling along. The crab did not recognize Moshup of course, but saw only Moshup's great toe, which he pinched tightly between his big claws. Startled and enraged, Moshup dropped his rock, flung the crab from him and limped home to Squant without finishing his bridge. But the Devil's Bridge, a dangerous ledge of rock in the waters between Gay Head and Cuttyhunk, is today a mute testimony to Moshup's attempt at bridge building.

As the years passed, Moshup was troubled by dreams, and he spoke often to Old Squant of the visions which told him of the coming of a strange people from a far land. They were a pale skinned people, who spoke a strange tongue and sought new places to make their home. They would come one day to Aquinnah and would live there in harmony, for not one of Moshup's children ever would lift his hand against a neighbor. Other tribes would make war on the pale skinned people, but the Pokonokets of Aquinnah were destined forever to follow the trail of peace.

Because Moshup knew his visions were a warning of things to come, he called a family council.

Soon he told them, there would be no room on Aquinnah for him or Old Squant. After telling them of his troubled dreams he said solemnly, "So you may find a refuge from harm, I will change those of you who wish, into killer whales, that you may roam the sea as your fancy directs."

All but a few chose the sea. How do we know? Because that particular kind of whale still eats as the children of Moshup were trained to do, the males before the females.

Moshup also provided for his many pets, since they too were of unusual size and helpless without his care. Gently he tossed his devoted frog toward the sea, and lo, Noman's Land appeared. A huge toad which often sat beside him, demanded to follow Moshup, and regretfully Moshup turned him to stone. Amid the dunes of South Beach, Toad Rock stands today.

Moshup's favorite pet was a large white whale, and knowing he most certainly would be pursued, Moshup dug a deep pool, connected to the sea by an underground passage. Today the pool is known as Witch Pond, because it is said to have strange properties. The water is black and tastes of the sea. Long ago, when some curious scientists investigated, they declared the pool was bottomless.

Even now, on foggy nights, some people claim to hear peculiar sounds from that direction, while others say they have felt a heavy moisture on their cheeks. Could it be Moshup's white whale, come up to spout?

His pets thus disposed of, Moshup gazed sorrowfully for the last time, upon the home which he had created; the place where he had lived so happily and ruled so wisely for so many long years.

Thus, with Old Squant following, he took the trail to the lonely South Beach, past Peaked Rock, past Black Rocks, past Zach's Cliffs, and there, among the dunes, disappeared forever from the sight of man.

Yet there are times when a faint haze arises and you may hear someone remark, "Ol Squant is smoking her pipe." Or when the fog comes creeping up across the dunes to southward, another will say, "Moshup has dumped his peudeldee."

But we with open hearts know that the smoke stands as a sign of the undying love of Big Chief Moshup, the sign and seal of his love for us, his children. And the faint sigh born on the wings of the wind, is Old Squant, singing a lonely song to her lost children.

So we of Gay Head have shared with you our legends, in memory of Moshup, his wife Squant, and their children.

Now the tribal fire burns low, the last legend has been told and we bid you goodnight.

"Tabut", we thank you, "Ta-but", we thank you very much for your presence here.   (Madison 1955)

LII

Helen Attaquin of Gay Head and Middleboro, Massachusetts, identified Maushop with the Central Algonquian mythical trickster figure, Michabo, whose name may be related etymologically to the Wampanoag culture hero.

1970

In common with all primitive races, the aborigines of Gay Head and Martha's Vineyard had their traditions and myths concerning their origin, their environment, and their Creator. Among the Algonquians, the omnipotent being who ruled their lives was called Mich-a-bo, the Great White Hare. On the island of Noepe, or Martha's Vineyard, the Indians told the same wonderful legends of an omniscient being, but in their telling, they changed the Great One's name to Maushope. He, it was, who came to Noepe from the mainland, bringing with him his wife and children to live in the Devil's Den. Later, he would build the Devil's Bridge, and would create Nantucket. In time, tiring of the Vineyard and feeling that he was being crowded, he disposed of his children, and he and his wife vanished from sight behind Zack's Cliffs.   (Attaquin 1970:15)

LIII

In March 1981 I tape-recorded some Maushop legends from persons of Wampanoag ancestry at Gay Head and Mashpee. Wenonah Silva, a contemporary artist and potter and a granddaughter of Mary C. Vanderhoop, had learned the legends from her mother and had participated in the pageants in her youth. Her accounts give a feeling for some of the ways the culture hero lived in the minds and lives of recent Wampanoag generations.

1981

My mother for instance often called me Maushop because I was forgetful. . . . I wasn't so forgetful as I was . . . a butterfly. I was not easy to pin down and I was always questioning and always planning to do something and getting it half done and leaving it. That was one of Maushop's traits, evidently. And she'd say, "I don't know when you're ever going to settle down and really get anything done. You're too flighty, and you're just like Maushop." She'd often make that parallel between me and the mighty giant.

(Silva 1981)

LIV

Silva remembered Maushop as a "well-muscled, very imposing" giant who used his size and strength to improve the landscape for Indian fishermen. His character is more helpful and innocent and less angry than the older hero of Gay Head lore.

1981

I can't remember why he was out there digging or scraping with his big toe, which was supposed to be as big as a steam shovel or anything, you know, that a child could imagine that was big and able to dig at deep depths. And I guess it was in making a channel around the island 'cause there is one right out off Gay Head where the fishermen and only the Indian fishermen knew that particular route. And he deepened the channel just off the island and he was digging out there, digging with his big toe making the channel deeper so that the fishing boats could go through, so that all the galleys could go through—when he got bitten by a crab and came limping. And that was at the time also that he decided that he was going to build a bridge to the mainland and got bitten by a giant crab that came sidling up. And oh, he was quite a baby when it came to getting hurt, and he came limping ashore holding his big toe and nursing that and never went back to finish the bridge.

(Silva *1981*)

LV

Silva also narrated the story of how Maushop's wife Squant had been disfigured and thereafter concealed her eyes with hair.

1981

She was ordinary [in size]. She had been marked by the evil one, Cheepi, to have square cut eyes. He was supposed to have been jealous of her beauty, and one day when she was blackberrying, she had fallen asleep in the blackberry patch and the evil one, Cheepi, had come upon her sleeping there and had disfigured her, and according to legend, subsequent to that she wore her hair over her face to hide that disfigurement.   (Silva *1981*)

LVI

Gladys Widdiss, a Gay Header in her sixties who now lives near Boston but visits the island often, learned of Maushop from her mother and aunt: "Ma and Aunt Nellie . . . used to talk about somebody that was awfully large—they used to say they were an old Maushop." Widdiss was familar with Gluskap legends from Maine because her mother read these to her and because in her younger days there was "a lot of travel between Gay Head and Maine." In her mind, Maushop and Gluskap were equivalent beings. She recounted a legend regarding Devil's Bridge that hearkened back in many details to the Vanderhoop text of 1904, except Maushop substitutes for the troublesome Cheepi and community factionalism no longer plays a part in the story.

1981

I'm not sure whether it was another chief or whether he was speaking to the tribe, and in order to show them his powers as a chief he told 'em he could build a bridge from the Head to Cutty-hunk before morning or before the cock crows. So they told him that he couldn't, 'twas impossible. And he said, nope, that he could. So it ended up that they were going to meet again the next morning, or they were coming back the next morning, and to see if he would have the bridge finished when the cock crowed. So they went off and he started to build the bridge, throwing big rocks into the ocean to build the bridge. Well, the ones that were betting [against] him decided that they would trick him, so they said they would go and they would get a cock and they would trick the cock into crowing, and then Maushop would have to stop because he didn't say it had to be light—he just said [that] when the cock crowed that he would have it finished. So that's what they did. They went and got this rooster and one of 'em got a light. I'm not sure now whether it was a lantern or just a torch. Well, anyway, they got a light and put it in front of where the rooster of course was sleeping or whatever they do at night. Do they really sleep— chickens? Well, anyway, they went and put it in front of him, and of course, when soon as that light came up in front of him he thought it was morning and he started to crow. And when he started to crow, of course, Maushop heard it and so that was the bet. He had to stop, so he stopped. . . . It's not quite halfway across where Devil's Bridge is, and he had to stop the bridge. So they in a way had won their bet, even if they had done it in an underhand way, and that's why the Bridge was never finished.   (Widdiss 1981)

LVII
Widdiss's telling of Maushop's farewell resembles the 1955 pageant text by Nanetta Madison. Her thoughts about the meaning of fog (as a spirit form of Maushop and Squant) and visiting offshore whales (as metamorphosed forms of earlier generations of Indians) are consistent with earlier Gay Head lore. In her understanding, the fogs and whales return to see how those Wampanoag who chose to remain in human form are making out.

1981

*After many years of living here in peace and quiet he had strange
dreams, and in these strange dreams there were strange people,
white people that were going to come to the island, and with their
coming there was going to be strife again, which was his original
reason for leaving the mainland. There was so much strife there
that he decided that he didn't want to be involved with it, so he
brought his people over here, and in his dreams he saw more or
less that cycle repeating itself with the strange people. And he
didn't want to be involved. Of course, even as a chief, a legendary
chief or chief of supernatural powers, he did grow older—probably
not as fast as we do, but he just couldn't see going through all that
strife with the new people, so he asked his people to make a choice
of whether they wanted to stay or whether they wanted to be
changed into whales. And whichever they chose would be all right
with him. And those that wanted to be changed into whales [he]
. . . threw them back over the bank into the water. And those that
didn't stayed with him. I guess, because at the time he didn't go
over the bank. . . . He had taken care of all of them and his pets [of
which] . . . one was a toad that he turned into a rock, which is
today known as Toad Rock, found off of Moshop's Trail down south
and which later became a post office, forerunner of our modern
post office, because messages were left there from down island.
And the pet crab he changed into a whale, but he threw that over
the bank to the south, and he made an entrance from the ocean
into Witch Pond which is down off the main road as you come in
town, and so that this whale could come in under if it got in trouble
or if it needed a rest or needed to get away from anything that was
bothering it. Then he and Squant, and he doesn't mention specifically if any of his people went with him, but I would imagine some
went with him, some stayed here; they didn't want to go away. They
just wanted to stay here and, I guess, see what came. And they
were willing to take, I guess, a chance with what was coming, the
strife that he told them about, because he forewarned them. So he
and Squant left the Head and walked down South Beach and they
walked, and of course as they walked farther and farther away
they finally disappeared about where we call Zack's Cliffs now.
They disappeared from sight there, and we was always been told
when the fog comes in from south it is their spirits coming back to
check on us, the remainder, the descendants of the remainder that
were left here, to see how we were making out. Also, there are
whales that most summers . . . at one particular time or another
you will find in Menemsha Bight one or two—sometimes more*

*whales, and they'll play around out there for about a couple of
days; then they'll disappear again. We think they're coming back
to check on us to see how we are making out.*   (Widdiss 1981)

LVIII

Widdiss told another story about where Maushop and Squant
went when they disappeared, which she had heard at Mashpee. No
previous writer has recorded this version.

1981

*Have you been to Mashpee? Mashpee has another version of
Maushop and his end. Now, we don't know whether it's a continuation of ours or whether it is a separate one, but the end of him,
their legend tells 'em, that he came back to Mashpee and went into
Mashpee Lake, and this is where he and Squant spent the rest of
their life—they disappeared in that lake. And if you look at the
map of Mashpee and of this lake, you will see an Indian sitting, the
outline of an Indian sitting at the corner of this lake. Mashpee
people say that this is Maushop come back to them. So it could
very well be that when he disappeared from our side that he did go
back to Mashpee.*   (Widdiss 1981)

LIX

Although I heard several times at Mashpee that Mashpee folklore
died out with Red Shell's and Wild Horse's generation, one twenty-
nine-year-old resident spoke freely about Maushop and other legends. Her account differs from most others in that it is a memorate;
she spoke of encounters she had experienced rather than legends
she had heard. Whereas previous texts describe Maushop's departure in the early historic period and his liminal presence thereafter,
in her account Maushop returns in the transformed figure of a little
green bird. The timing of the giant's reappearance at Mashpee cor-
responds historically with the group's resurgence as a political and
cultural entity. This timing is meaningful, for as the Mashpee asserted themselves politically, their ancient culture hero broke
through the veil behind which he had remained dormant for so
many years, emerging still powerful but much reduced in size. Nosapocket's association of Maushop with Bigfoot or Sasquatch indicates that, in addition to representing local Wampanoag tradition,
the giant is one of a broader contemporary family of Indian culture
heroes that connects the Mashpee with other American Indian
tribes.

1981

I've had three encounters with this being and it lives in Asher's
Pass, what we call this wooded area. And there I heard, the first
time I heard it it was walking in the river and the stones underneath his feet was crumbling and crushing, popping, and it was
kind of frightening. And I was with a friend who was Pima Indian
from the Southwest. She got frightened. I said, "Well, let's get in the
car. Just keep your finger on the keys but don't start it until we get
a glimpse of this and see what it is." It came closer and closer and
at the very second it seemed that it was going to pop out, it got
up out of the river and went up the pass and you couldn't see it.
We drove off, anyway, not knowing how big a stride it had or anything, but it was not interested in seeing us. But I took it as an
honor and a message, an omen of some sort, that this thing allowed
me to be near it. My second encounter with that [was] a year later.
My family homestead is right along the Mashpee River, and we're
off about a quarter of a mile from it, and this same being, heavy
footed enough to shake the ground as it walked, came up to my
window and I'd estimate that this had to be—it itself had to stand
about as high as that owl I was telling you about. It leaned on my
windowsill and just breathed. And its chest I would say had to
be about five feet wide. Its lungs were bigger than my body, and it
just breathed. I was paralyzed with fear. I just laid there and listened, and it stood there and didn't do anything. Its nasal passages
made a growling sound . . . maybe I was listening, trying to figure
out what it was doing there and find out if it was hostile or what
was the case. But it just came and stood there for maybe a half an
hour or so, and then it left. The following morning I went out to see
the footprints. I figured they had to be at least two feet long, and I
got out there and there was no footprints near the house or in the
direction that I listened to it going—no footprints whatsoever. And
that's when I began to think of it more as a medicine being, a Bigfoot or a Sasquatch, or a Maushop-type being, and I was not very
frightened, but excited that such beings still lived amongst the
Mashpee Wampanoag people [which] was very special knowledge
to me; so I sought out, I looked for it, and of course they couldn't
find it. But my next encounter with it I was camping in Asher's
Pass on the other side of the river, and I was doing an arts and
crafts program with the young Indian children. They went to the
bay to collect shellfish for our meal, and I stayed at the camp making a sweat lodge. And I heard the footprints again, and wanting
to see it this time for sure, I decided to hide in a hole that had a

dead tree laying on top of it. So I got underneath there and waited
and listened, and when I was certain that it was in the open I took
a peek, and there was nothing there that I expected to see. There
was a small bird, and it was only like three inches off the ground
itself, and very small and a green bird. And the color green is the
calm color, one that will bring you that. So I watched it, and the
bird walked the entire perimeter in a perfect circle around the
camp. It took a long time for it to walk it, but it walked with the
footsteps of a Maushop. That bird I have seen, but it made no sense
to me at all, for how this whole thing came about. The people that
I've heard that have seen this being down at Asher's Pass were
frightened and they didn't stop to really look good enough to find
out what it was. It was just a towering human being that had a
lot of hair, and it just decided that a glimpse frightened them. . . .
So I haven't really found any accurate descriptions or something
that people have said. . . . Other people have heard the same footsteps. . . . The green bird has another symbol and . . . the power
of a medicine being such as a Maushop. . . . The green bird is, first
its size and yet its intensity. Its size [is] a subtle reminder to us,
as a small tribe in itself, that our medicine needn't be regarded as
weak because we're small in numbers. But we have the intensity of
medicine beings, so a reassurance, in those years of my life, studying very hard and looking very deep in our culture and our woods
for ways to reassure and strengthen our tribal self-concept and to
help balance the intrusion of newcoming people into our territory—something that was very, very hard for everyone to deal with.
And I looked to the woods and to the Creator for assistance, and
this is one of the ways that many different experiences, vision
quests, and things, looking for this kind of story to tell my own
people, and it worked. The green bird is symbolic of our tribe, and
calm is being our power for this time rather than rage or demon-
strations. . . . A calm state of clear mindedness is what the bird
was symbolic of.   (Nosapocket 1981)

LX

Nosapocket also narrated an unusual legend regarding Maushop's
departure and death. In her account, the creator changed Maushop
into a white whale because he had been pampering the Gay Head
people to the point of making them lazy. A Gay Head whaleman then
killed Maushop, who thus died at the hands of the people who knew
him best. Since no such legend is known at Gay Head, Nosapocket's
version of Maushop's transformation and death suggests some ri-

valry between these two Wampanoag communities. In her account, Maushop and Melville's Moby Dick have merged into one legendary figure.

1981

He used to come to the Cape, and Mashpee was one of the village sites for the Wampanoags. But he used to swim here and fetch wood for the Aquinnah Wampanoags, the Gay Head [people]. And turns out that it was our feeling as well as the Creator's that he was spoiling those people by doing many of their labors [so] that they themselves became more lazy. And from the tales that I hear—one of my favorites—is a reminder to people not to become lazy, because the Creator had counsel with Maushop and reminded him that he was spoiling the people from being what they could be, what their capacities were. [He] pampered them like little children. Therefore the Creator informed Maushop that he was to be changed into another type of medicine being, a white whale. And so he was given time to say goodbye to the Aquinnah people as well as us, the Mashpee people, and we went to see him at the Gay Head cliffs to say farewell. And his companion, a very huge toad, was overtook with sorrow, seeing his friend was going to leave him and never be with him any more. And in his grief and sorrow the Creator saw that it wasn't good, and so changed him into a stone. So to this day, 1981, there is a stone on the Gay Head cliffs that resembles a huge frog, a reminder to us to not be sorrowful about our Creator's decisions, that they are the very best for all living things. To complete the whole story, Maushop was later through the centuries referred to and called Moby Dick. I met a fellow named Amos Smalley when I was younger, and he told me that he was the one that killed the Moby Dick. He was a very old gentleman when I met him. . . . he was an Aquinnah Wampanoag, Gay Head. He was of the very people that Maushop loved so dearly and pampered as if they were his very own children. And it's not surprising to me or any other Wampanoags that it being an Aquinnah Wampanoag that would change his state of being again. And it could have only been a Wampanoag, in my mind, that could have killed a Moby Dick, sought after by so many whalers.   (Nosapocket 1981)

LXI

Ada Manning, an elderly Gay Head widow, talked with the author in 1983 about a range of local topics including Maushop. Her account of Devil's Bridge was brief but traditional.

1983

*Maushop decided he was going to build a link between the island
and the mainland. Maushop got frightened and let go of his apron
and let all his rocks go and formed the Devil's Bridge—a dangerous
place.*   *(Manning 1983)*

LXII

One February evening in 1983, my father and I dined at a Provi-
dence-area restaurant. The waiter, Louis Colby, happened to be a Gay
Head Wampanoag whose family had moved to the mainland to work.
Between orders he volunteered a brief account of the Devil's Bridge
story. Roger Williams first mentioned the Wétucks/Maushop legends
in 1643, and he would probably be interested to know that survivals
of these "many strange Relations" are still told by people of Indian
descent in the very area where he heard them over three centuries
ago. Colby, a young man in his twenties who had participated in the
Gay Head pageants, added that he did not think the story was "really
true."

1983

*The devil built a bridge of stones from Gay Head toward the
mainland but didn't finish it. There are still many rocks there today
that you can see. He also caught whales.*   *(Colby 1983)*

Creation is an important theme in North American Indian folklore,
which includes explanations for the origin of such basic phenomena
as the earth, people, and agriculture, and such specific phenomena
as islands, rocks, weather, customs, and animal traits. Christian conversion obliterated most basic creation mythology in southern New
England as Christian deities replaced the Indian creator and lesser
gods. Protestant doctrine triumphed in all areas of ritual and world
view where the two cosmologies overlapped, but some specific origin beliefs (such as those expressed in the Maushop and Squant legends) survived. Maushop and Squant continued to be given credit
for phenomena such as Devil's Bridge, Sakonnet Rock, colors in the
Gay Head cliffs, Toad Rock, Noman's Land, Nantucket, visiting
whales, fogs, winds, and so on, which were of emotional and expe-
riential importance to generations of Indians. At the same time, such
beliefs did not seriously challenge Christian doctrine. A core of motifs apparent in the Maushop and Squant texts originated in prehistory or in the early historic period, remained fairly intact during the
long, stable reservation period, and still exist to some extent today.[16]
The long duration of the Gay Head Maushop legends allows us to

observe changes in the texts, some of which, such as details of his appearance, are variable but short lived. By 1904, when Mary Vanderhoop published her collection of local traditions, the two sides of Maushop's personality had evolved into separate culture heroes, Maushop and Cheepi, the devil. As the Gay Head Indians became socially and legally more like other Americans their culture heroes also marched more in step with the dominant model of contrasting good and evil gods. This bifurcation continued to appeal to the Wampanoag until as recently as 1925, when Mabel Knight published a legend in which the devil bargained (unsuccessfully) to win Maushop's soul. In subsequent years, following the renewed spirit of Indian tribalism that culminated in the Indian Reorganization Act of 1934, the benevolent side of Maushop's and Squant's personalities continued to be emphasized and the devil's role diminished. No doubt the folklore pageants that began at Gay Head during the cultural and political renaissance in the 1930s influenced how the Wampanoag represented their culture hero to the outside world. As Indian society became more Americanized, and as American society as a whole came to value Indian tribalism, Maushop took center stage as a wise, more gentle, and less irascible figure. Maushop lore in Mashpee followed a different course in the 1930s but responded to the same historical currents. There, scholarly innovators reconstructed legends from a combination of oral tradition, ethnohistoric sources on the Wampanoag, comparative sources on other Indians, and a strong dose of imagination. Although the Maushop legends are responsive to historical change, they draw surprisingly little from historical events for their narrative content. They do not mention such important figures or watersheds in their history as, for example, Thomas Mayhew, Richard Bourne, or King Philip's War. One major historic event, however, had a profoundly formative effect on the content of Maushop legends: the coming of Europeans. In many texts this event marks the end of Maushop's family life, his and Squant's death or disappearance, and the end of his miraculous creations. This transition from prehistory to history is demarcated by a series of transformations of his children, wife, and pets, after which the giant disappears, but not completely, for both Maushop and Squant are known even today to communicate with living Indians who recognize their signs. Despite the increased penetration of non-Indian motifs into the legends after 1900 and the deadening effect that the arrival of Europeans had on the mythical age, the legends still convey a self-contained magical world where the ancestors, landscape, weather, sounds, and sea creatures are alive in distinctly Indian ways.

10   Little People

No seventeenth- or eighteenth-century authority mentioned fairies, dwarves, elves, or Little People among the southern New England tribes, but they appear in several nineteenth- and twentieth-century accounts.[1] Legends about Little People could have diffused to this region from neighboring Algonquian-speaking areas where such beliefs are widely attested (Adams 1905:24; Beck 1966:58, 81; Fisher 1946:229–30; Harrington 1921:49; Leland 1898:140–69; Schoolcraft 1857:662; Speck 1935:12–13, 16; Stamp 1915; Williams 1956:160–62). West European and West African traditions of Little People are well documented, but little of this particular Old World lore is known to have reached the United States (Baughman 1966:xv, xvii; Hand 1981; Puckett [1926] 1968:145–46). Although the Puritans did not transfer English fairy beliefs to New England soil, they sometimes spoke of the devil as a short, dark man. The Indians, too, described their spirit Cheepi or Hobbamock as dark and sometimes as small (Calef [1700] 1946:312; Dorson 1946:48). That all other northeastern Indian people, including the Iroquois, had beliefs about Little People argues for their autochthonous existence, although in some cases European devil and fairy lore shaped Indian legend. Examples of this influence will be seen in the Gay Head legends "The Mother of the Kinky-Haired Indians" and "Iskisa Hill" (texts IV and V below), which account for Indian-black mating.

I

We first hear of Little People in 1903, when Speck published his earliest interviews with Fidelia Fielding on the Muhkeahweesug, who left behind such curiosities as brass kettles, old glass bottles, bones, and petroglyphs that an archaeologist might attribute to the prehistoric and early historic inhabitants of Mohegan country. In this and other respects they resemble, but probably are not derived from, the European fairies that were believed to have made the arrowheads and other implements found near prehistoric barrows and dolmens in Britain and Ireland.[2]

1903

Now for the oral testimony of the Mohegans themselves. To obtain this let us take the old trail, some evening, over to Fidelia Fielding's, the wisest of the Mohegans, and hear what she has to say. I can do no better than to let her tell it herself, leaving the reader's imagination to supply him with the gestures and quaint mannerisms of an old Indian woman accompanying her deposition. In the quiet of the early evening she begins.

"Yes; the little men were here then. They used to tell about them; my grandmother and the rest. It was long before my time, but my grandmother knew of them from her grandmother. Folks saw more things in the woods then, than they do nowadays. Well it's different. Anyhow, "nonnuh" my grandmother's grandmother, saw the "little men" when she was a child. She was coming down the Yantic river in a canoe with her father and mother. There they were, the "muhkeahweesug," the "little men," running on the shore. A pine woods came down to the water there and she could see them through the trees. But her mother told "nonnuh"; "Don't look at those 'little men.' They will point their fingers at you, then you cannot see them." So she turned her head away. There were not many of them.

And the "little men" would come to your house, so they used to say, asking for something to eat. You must always give them what they wanted, for if you didn't they would point at you, then, while you couldn't see them, they would take what they wanted. That is what the old people told the children about the "little men."

(Speck 1903b:12–13)

II

In this and the previous account we learn almost everything that has been recorded about the Mohegan Little People. Despite their shy and retiring nature, they were not unfriendly to humans, and in this case they appealed to an Indian woman for medical help. They may have died out, as Fielding suggests, but her relatives today on Mohegan Hill still remember that they existed.

1903

The night grows colder, and Fidelia keeps on talking while she builds up her fire with huge chunks of hickory. Down below, in the swamp, a fox barks, though it is too dark to see him. She continues.

"They told their children about those things. Then, once, an Indian and his wife lived here. They were Mohegan. They saw a "little man" too. It was in this way. One wild, stormy night, a rap on the door. The wind blew very hard when the squaw opened it. Someone was standing outside. But she didn't know who it was. When she found out what he wanted, she told her husband that he wanted her to go and take care of a sick woman, a long way off. She then told her husband that she was going, and that she would be back before long. So she packed up a few things, and out through the storm the person led her. This small person was a "little man," but she thought it was a boy. They went on and on through the storm. It was a bad night, even the squaw didn't know where she was being taken. But at last she saw a light before them, and soon there was a house. The "little man" said nothing but led her in, and showed her a "little woman" lying ill on a bed of skins. This "little man" and "woman" were "muhkeahweesug"; and the squaw then saw that they were. But she took good care of the "little woman." For a long time she stayed with them, not saying much but doing very well. Bye and bye the "little woman" got better, and pretty soon she was well. After this the squaw was ready to go, for she had been away from home long enough. So they gave her presents, and she packed her bundle. Then the "little man" wound a piece of skin over her eyes so that the squaw couldn't see, and led her back to her husband's wigwam. You see, the "little people" treated her well. But when the squaw got to her house and took the skin from her eyes, she couldn't see where the "little man" had gone. He was gone. This squaw and her husband wanted to find the "little man" but they couldn't. So they gave it up. The "little people" died out. I guess these were the last. They lived way back in the woods. They kept away from the Indians. All this happened a long time ago, before the white people came down here. My grandmother told it to me."   (Speck 1903b:13–14)

III

Chappaquiddick Island lies across the harbor from Edgartown on Martha's Vineyard. Many Indians lived there when the English came in 1643, but by 1861 only about seventy remained, and perhaps one person of Indian ancestry lives there today (Earle 1862:16; Levitas 1980:47). Early twentieth-century English inhabitants of Chappaquiddick knew of a Little Man who permitted himself to be seen and then disappeared, thus resembling the Mohegan Muhkeahweesug who would point their finger at the viewer and then disappear. The Little Man of Chappaquiddick differed from his Mohegan counterparts by pointing away from rather than at the viewer and then vanishing when one looked in the direction he pointed. He also resembled British and Celtic fairies who would appear and disappear before wondering human eyes. But given how little fairy lore the Europeans transported across the Atlantic Ocean, it is more interesting to speculate that the English adopted the Little Man from Wampanoag storytellers. The English of Chappaquiddick told their best stories "in the island farm-house at dead of winter, before the open fire" (Clough 1918:553). The Indians, too, told their legends in winter, and perhaps one evening they planted the seeds of this story in front of an English fire.

1918

The Little Man is something more than a voice. He can be seen; and some time, when you are walking alone across the Chappaquiddick moors, you may encounter him. He is very small and very strange-looking. Those who have seen him are unable to say more of his physical appearance. But you may know him by his manner. He never speaks: he approaches you, looks at you oddly, and then points off across the sea. You will naturally look in the direction in which he points,—people always do,—and when you look back, he will be gone. Vanished, absolutely! No trace of him anywhere. The story is told of a certain Edgartown man, a lover of practical jokes, that he once asked a Chappaquiddick farmer, "Who was that little man that I saw down in your field?"—"I don't know. Why?" was the rather indifferent answer. "Well, I just wondered. He was sort of queer-looking. I thought I knew everybody in town, but I never saw him before."—"What did he say to you?" asked the farmer, showing a little more interest. "Why, that was the queer part of it. He didn't say a word; he just pointed. Of course, I looked to see what he was pointing at, and then"—"Yes, yes, what then?"—"Why, he was gone. I don't know what became of him. He must

*have gone off pretty quick."—"There now!" cried the farmer, excit-
edly. "You've seen it! Now maybe folks won't say there's no such
thing! I've seen it, and my father saw it, and now you've seen it!"*

(Clough 1918:554)

IV

This Gay Head legend regarding the origin of kinky hair among
Indians presents the encounter between an Indian woman and a
little black man as a journey into an underground kingdom. Journeys
into an underground fairyland are attested in western European
sources but not in white and black folklore from the northeastern
United States (Briggs 1971, 1:182–83, 195–96, 222; Hand 1981:143).
In this narrative by Rachel Ryan, and in the previous one (text II) by
Fielding, the Little People needed Indian women to heal them.
Ryan's Little People are spiteful in comparison with Fielding's
Muhkeahweesug, and their subterranean kingdom suggests an affin-
ity with the devil or European fairies and hints that blacks rank be-
neath Indians.[3]

1925   THE MOTHER OF THE KINKY-HAIRED INDIANS

*Before white men came to Martha's Vineyard, the Indians were
picking berries at Duncan's Ridge. When they had finished, they
went up on Eastskysser Hill to feast, but one beautiful squaw was
so busy picking that she stayed behind. When the people went
to look for her, they found only her berry basket. They hung it on a
tree, for they knew she would come for it.*

*Every year when they went to this place for berries, the basket
was more and more decayed. At last, many years after, a strange
woman came toward them as they feasted after the berry picking.
She had kinky hair. She asked if they remembered the squaw who
had been lost, and she said, "Take me to your chief." They took her
to their chief, and she told her story:*

*As she picked berries, a black, black man with thick lips and
kinky hair came toward her. He told her that his chief had a thorn
in his side which caused him great pain. None of his people could
remove it. He had sent to her for help as a Medicine Woman who
could cure sickness by knowledge of herbs.*

*They went down a flight of stairs until they came to a land of
fruits and flowers. The little man led her to his chief, and she removed the thorn. She stayed on among them, always thinking she
would return to her people. One of the black men wished to marry
her, but she went to the chief and asked only that she be allowed to*

return to her people. He gave her presents, and sent her back with the man who had brought her to that place. They went up the stairs, and when they had come to the place where she had left her basket, the black man took away her presents, and ran his hands through her long hair till it was kinky as his own.

When she had finished her story, the chief commanded them to cast her out. He prophesied that another race would come who would resemble this woman; he said that they would mix with the Indians and that this squaw would be the ancestor of many Kinky-haired Indians.   *(Knight 1925:136–37)*

V

Ryan told her legend again to Gladys Tantaquidgeon three years later, and although some details differ, the story is essentially the same. The Indian chief in the first version reacts more sternly by banishing the unfortunate woman, whereas in the second he only repeats his warning that other persons with such hair will follow and that they will not be good for the Indians.

1928   ISKISA HILL

It was during the berry picking season and the Indians went out to pick huckle berries. One of the party was a young woman who was a doctor. When she had filled her basket she hung it on a tree and sat down to rest. The others went up the hill expecting her to follow but she did not. When they came back to the spot where she had left the things she was not there. Only her pack basket remained hanging on a tree. They waited for her but she did [not] come back. Out of superstitious regard they did not touch the basket. They were very sad because this woman was a good doctor and would be greatly missed by her people.

Every year at the berry picking season the people would go to the spot where the basket hung to await the return of its owner but she never appeared. Finally only the bail of the basket remained on the tree. One day when the people had gathered as usual to watch for the absent one, they saw a woman coming up the hill toward them. She addressed them in their native tongue but they did not recognize her because she had kinky hair. Then the chief arose and spoke to her "We do not know you. You are not like us. The Indians have straight hair but your's is ingrown" and called her a stranger. The woman said "I belong to you." Then she related the following experience: While she sat on the rock resting a little black man came to her and asked her if she would go with him and take a

*thorn out of the King's side. He promised not to keep her long so
she followed him down long flights of stairs. Finally they came to a
beautiful land. The people were very peculiar looking and their
hair was ingrown. She took the thorn out of the King's side and the
people gave her many beautiful gifts. After [   ] she wished to return
to her people but they wanted her to stay there. Then the King's
son fell in love with her and told her that if she would marry him
she would be Queen of all the land. He made many promises to her
but she told him that her people would not allow her to marry one
of his race at which he became very angry. She attempted to run
away but her lover attacked her and pulled her hair and dragged
her around in such a manner that her hair became kinky. After
taking the presents away from her, he allowed her to go up the
stairs which she said took many days. After she had told her story
the Chief arose and spoke to the people saying "This foretells the
coming of another people whose hair will be tight and woe unto
you when they will appear."*   (Tantaquidgeon 1928)

VI

The aboriginal women's god, Squáuanit, survived at Gay Head as
the giant Maushop's wife, Ol' Squant, and at Mashpee as Granny
Squannit. Although the Mashpee Wampanoag also associated
Granny Squannit with Maushop, she developed an independent
personality here as a tiny woman similar to the Mohegan Muhkeahweesug. Both the Mashpee and Mohegan considered these Little
People as patrons who would fulfill wishes if properly remembered
with baskets of food and drink left in the woods. Granny Squannit
is the dominant figure in Mashpee folklore; in addition to being a
source of medical knowledge, she reigned as a bogey over children
and threatened adults who spoke ill of her. One elderly Wampanoag
woman told me in 1981 that the Indian practice of drying clothes on
bushes in the sun was known as Granny Squannit's laundry. In the
following account, told by Susan Poquet Jeffers to Tantaquidgeon,
Granny Squannit serves the same function as the Narragansett light
(chapter 7, LXV), which leads naughty children astray.

1929 SKWANIT

*My grandmother, Susan (Attaquin) Poquet, used to tell us when
we were little children that Granny Skwanit would come and carry
us off when we were bad and made a rumpus. She told us this so
much that we used to call her Granny Skwanit. She used to scare
us by letting us hear how awful she looked, a little old woman with*

long hair hanging down and a long narrow face, how she would
come creeping up on her hands and feet and carry us off into the
woods and we'd never get back. She told us that to scare us so we'd
be good and not run off into the woods and get lost. Then they
used to say that children that get lost and were not seen again had
been carried off by Granny Skwannit.   (Tantaquidgeon 1928–29)

VII

The following collection of short texts from Tantaquidgeon's
notes, provided mostly by Eben Queppish, the last Mashpee basket
maker, fill out Granny Squannit's character in the early twentieth
century.[4]

1929   OFFERINGS TO GRANNY SQUANNIT MASHPEE

Little basket with dumplings and cake hung on branch of tree.
Hannah Pells, Mashpee, 1928–29.

In basket and place in woods. Cover with leaves. Ebben Queppish
1928–29.

On plate with napkin covered over. Place on tree stump. Ebben
Queppish.

In bag and throw into woods by boy. Gardner.

Small quantity of liquor left with offering. Ebben Queppish.

Granny Squannit carried off a boy (William Thompson, Mrs.
Webquish's grandfather's brother). Told [him] not to look at [her]
face. Had cat's eyes.

Squannit teaches about herbs. Tell ailment and leave offering
and she will leave herbs.

For spiritual aid leave offering anywhere. Could track her. Had
moccasins. 3 inch foot like rabbit's foot.

Left Pocasset because people didn't treat her right. More partial
to men.

[If you have a] sincere motive, Granny will aid.

Never allowed to talk about Granny Squannit because she knows
everything they said.

Granny Squannit—small, white hair. Like old woman. Howls on
Screecham's Island.

Mrs. [Dorcas Coombs] Gardner's brother about 1880 (George
Coombs) claimed to have seen Granny Squannit down by the lake
in South Mashpee sitting under an oak tree. She was a little old
woman with long hair hanging down all over her face.

Granny's beans bloom when the herring run.

Square [eyes]. One in middle of forehead.

*Grants wishes, gives spiritual aid, knows when she's talked
about.*
Taught Indians value of medicinal herbs. Directs herb gatherers.
Allowed people to gather plums and wild peas from her gardens.
Provides food for lost shipwrecked people.
*Frightened and carried off children. She would take what she
wanted from people.*
*Places beacon fires on beaches causing ship to put in to shore
and become wrecked.*
Partial to boys and men.
Told captives never to look at her face.
Would point finger at person so that they could not see her.
Could become invisible at will.
Disappeared due to neglect and advance of civilization.
Toys found on beach.
Given food following feast.
Don't leave offering exposed, always cover.
*Small cup of bitters (liquor) and 2 or 3 tobacco leafs left with
Granny's food.*   (Tantaquidgeon 1928–29)

VIII

Chief Red Shell, the source for "The Legend of the Mashpee
Maiden," probably obtained most of this legend from James A.
Jones's fanciful "Legend of Coatuit Brook," first published in 1829,
and the rest from an authentic fragment of Mashpee folklore (see
appendix, XI). To these he added the Ojibwa-derived name for Little
People, Pukwudgees. Jones had given the name Awashanks to the
Mashpee maiden, which Red Shell shortened to Ahsoo. Awashonks
was in fact the name of the seventeenth-century woman sachem of
the Sakonnet.[5]

1934   THE LEGEND OF THE MASHPEE MAIDEN

*In the long ago, there lived among the Wampanoag of the Mash-
pee Village, a maiden called Ahsoo. Her legs were like pipestems;
her chin was pointed and sharp as the beak of a loon; her nose was
humped and crooked; and her eyes were as big as a frightened
deer's. Day after day she sat on a log and watched those around
her. No one cared for her; none of the men desired her friendship.
She was an idle, lazy maiden who would not work in a wigwam
nor carry wood for a fire.*
*Although Ahsoo was ugly, no woman could equal her in singing.
Birds paused on the bough to listen to her, and the river, running*

over rapids, almost ceased its flowing to hear the Mashpee Maiden. On a low hill near the river Ahsoo would sit and sing. Beasts of the forest, birds of the air, fish of the lakes came to hear. Maugua the Bear came, and even the great War Eagle; but Ahsoo was not afraid for she knew that they had only come to listen to her songs. The river at the foot of the hill became alive with fishes, journeying up from the South Sea to hear the voice of Ahsoo. Every animal, bird, and fish applauded in its own manner, since they all greatly desired that Ahsoo should continue.

There was a big trout, chief of all trout, almost as big as a man. Because of his size he could not swim up the river to hear Ahsoo sing. Every night he burrowed his nose further and further into the bank. At length he planed a long path inland and the seawater, following him closely, made Cotuit Brook. This chief of the trout loved Ahsoo and he could not see how ugly she was, for she always sang in the summer evenings after the sun went down. So he told her that she was pretty; and of course the Mashpee Maiden fell deeply in love with that trout. She told him how she loved him and invited him to visit her wigwam.

At this time, the Pukwudgee chief lived with his followers in the marshes near Poponesset Bay. He observed the Great Trout who was making a new brook for the use of the pygmy people, and one day the little chief overheard the trout lamenting because he could not have Ahsoo for a wife.

"The charming Mashpee Maiden and I love each other dearly," sighed the Monster Fish, "but, alas! neither of us can live without the other, and neither of us can live where the other lives."

The chief of the Pukwudgees was sorry for these lovers, so he changed the Maiden into a trout, and placed her in Santuit Pond. Then he told the Monster Fish to dig his way to the Pond, and have the maiden for his wife. The Trout digged so hard and so fast that, when he reached Santuit Pond, he died of too much exertion; and the Maiden who had become a trout died of a broken heart. Indians found the defeated lovers, and buried them side by side in a large mound, called Trout Grave, near the brook dug by the Chief of Trout. (Reynard 1934:31–33)

IX

Betsey Keene, a local historian, corroborated much of Tantaquidgeon's testimony regarding Granny Squannit, in part with an anecdote from an unnamed middle-aged Mashpee man. Here Granny Squannit oversees the supply of wild beach plums, and those who pick them first present her with a food offering. Keene added, "Among Wampanoag relics, found in the Museum of the American Indians at Broadway and 155th Street, New York, is a round, open-work basket about two and one-half inches tall; it contains a few small meal cakes and this label: 'For an offering to Granny Squanet, a mythical personage who, in return, insures a plentiful supply of beach plums'" (Keene [1937] 1975:201). Speck or Tantaquidgeon may have contributed the basket and the information on the label. Granny Squannit could not have been too particular about how these offerings were delivered.

1934

An Indian story tells that many moons ago there lived in a cave on Sandy Neck, Barnstable, a little old Indian woman known as Granny Squanet. Her black hair, so long that it hung down nearly to her feet, she always wore over her face never allowing any one to see her features. She liked little boys and was often visited by them. One day while Granny was asleep on the sand, a boy visitor, after walking cautiously up, looked curiously at the long black hair drawn as usual over Granny's face, stooped, and pulled it aside. Great was his surprise when he saw that Granny had only one eye which was situated directly in the middle of her forehead.

In the season of beach plums it was customary for the Mashpee people to make a trip with ox teams to Sandy Neck where these especial plums grew bountifully. One night after school a young brave with other Wampanoag descendants started for a two-day beach-plumming trip to Sandy Neck. At bed-time the boy chosen according to custom to carry food to Granny Squanet, so that she might give them plenty of beach plums, was this young brave. With bated breath he grabbed the food and rushed off in the dim light toward the cave where Granny was supposed to be. The young brave, now a man of mid-years, thus finishes the story: "I went just as far as my legs would allow, threw the food as hard as I could, and then sprinted back to camp as scared a boy as you ever saw."

(Keene [1937] 1975:200–201)

X

The final word on Little People appears in a short guidebook by Gladys Tantaquidgeon to the Tantaquidgeon Indian Museum. In the book she mentions the similarity between Mohegan and Wampanoag beliefs and summarizes what Mohegans remember today about the Muhkeahweesug.

1981

A small open weave basket made about 1840 is connected with the mythology of the Mohegan and related Algonkian Indians. It is referred to as an "Offering Basket." According to Fidelia Hoscott Fielding, last speaker of the Mohegan-Pequot language, who died in 1908, it was customary to put corn bread and meat in a small basket and leave it in the woods or along the beach for the "Little People" to ensure good luck when going fishing, hunting, gathering nuts or berries, food or medicinal plants. In 1929, Eben Queppish, Mashpee, of Cape Cod, taught Gladys Tantaquidgeon to make a similar type basket. The Massachusetts Wampanoag shared this belief regarding the offering of food to "Granny."

(*Tantaquidgeon 1981:3–4*)

Beliefs and legends about Little People survived in some areas and disappeared in others without a trace. The Muhkeahweesug resemble Penobscot Little People and are probably descended from aboriginal Mohegan prototypes. The Mashpee Wampanoag Granny Squannit is an amalgamation of the pre-Christian women's god and Little People, and the tiny black people from Gay Head apparently combine European devil or fairy lore with vestiges of Indian belief. No one interviewed at Gay Head in 1983 remembered Little People, and no Narragansett source or informant has ever mentioned the subject. Chief Red Shell borrowed the Pukwudgees from Ojibwa folklore, not from Mashpee traditions of Granny Squannit. Like Maushop at Gay Head, Granny Squannit served as a symbol of Mashpee ancestry, traditional lore, and distinctiveness from other people. Still feared and respected in the 1930s, she was the major folkloric symbol of Mashpee Indian identity.

11   Windows to the Past:
Dreams and Shrines

The past, represented by ancestors, ghosts, culture heroes, land-marks, and memories, spoke to the living through folklore and still exercises some authority in the present. Myths, legends, folktales, and other oral narrative genres typically explain origins, account for precedents, warn against infractions, and provide glimpses of reali-ties of another time. Many folklorists, anthropologists, and histori-ans even have tried to interpret folklore texts as codes to the prehis-toric or unwritten past and have had some qualified success in retrieving historical knowledge from such materials. Oral narratives also have their own history, but this has rarely been documented. In this historical approach to New England Indian folklore we have seen that motifs and even entire categories of legends enter and dis-appear from the record in accordance with changes in the relation-ship between the local community and the larger social environ-ment. Often we may identify a historical logic in the selection of new motifs and legends, and the elimination of the old, as traditions pass through time. The voices of past generations that speak in folklore have an effect on the living. Such voices preserve their authority through an implicit agreement that the living have the final word, that they can reformulate these messages according to their own in-terests and experiences. Here we will consider some additional ways that past generations communicate with their living descendants.

I

The gods, culture heroes, ghosts, and Little People who conveyed ancestral wisdom through memorate and legend also communicated directly through dreams. In one of the earliest dreams recorded in the New England area, the ghost of a sachem's mother complained to her son that a party of Plymouth men had stolen her grave goods. When the sachem awoke, he called together his men and attacked the English, but they anticipated his plan and defended themselves.

1632

The Planters of Plimmouth, at their last being in those parts, having defaced the monument of the ded at Pasonayessit (by taking away the herse Cloath which was two greate Beares skinnes sowed together at full length, and propped up over the grave of Chuatawbacks mother,) the Sachem of those territories, being inraged at the same, stirred up his men in his bee halfe, to take revenge: and having gathered his men together, hee begins to make an oration in this manner. When last the glorious light of all the skey was underneath this globe, and Birds grew silent, I began to settle as my (custome is) to take repose; before mine eies were fast closed, mee thought I saw a vision, (at which my) spirit was much troubled, & trembling at that dolefull sight, a spirit cried aloude (behold my sonne) whom I have cherisht, see the papps that gave thee suck, the hands that lappd thee warme and fed thee oft, canst thou forget to take revenge of those uild people, that hath my monument defaced in despitefull manner, disdaining our ancient antiquities, and honourable Customes: See now the Sachems grave lies like unto the common people, of ignoble race defaced; thy mother doth complaine, implores thy aide against this theevish people, new come hether if this be suffered, I shall not rest in quiet within my everlasting habitation. This said, the spirit vanished, and I all in a sweat, not able scarce to speake, began to gett some strength, and recollect my spirits that were fled, all which I thought to let you understand, to have your Councell, and your aide likewise; this being spoken, straight way arose the grand Captaine, and cried aloud come, let us to Armes, it doth concerne us all, let us bid them Battaile; so to Armes they went, and laid weight for the Plimmouth boate. (Morton [1632] 1947:72–73)

II

By the eighteenth century, long after the New England Indians had converted to Christianity, dreams continued to be an important window to the supernatural. English ministers chided the Narragansett and Mohegan New Light converts for attributing their Christianity to dreams and visions rather than to the Bible. The Congregational minister Joseph Fish, for example, wrote of the Narragansett minister Samuel Niles, in 1765, that he was "in imminent danger of leaving *The Word*, for the Guidance of *Feelings, Impressions, Visions, Appearances* and *Directions* of Angels and of Christ himself in a Visionary Way" (Simmons and Simmons 1982:5). Fish also wrote a brief report of an aged Narragansett who dreamed of God, Jesus, and the ancestors.

1773

Talkd with old Tobe Cowyass. . . . Tobe Said he had, Sometime ago, been home, (meaning, to Heaven). Had Seen the Great God, and that he was a Great Gentleman. Had Seen Jesus Christ, A handsome Man. Seen also a Multitude of Folks in Heaven, Resembling Butterflies of Many Colours, etc. Strange, Gross, Horrible Ideas and notions of the heavenly World!

(Simmons and Simmons 1982:93)

III

Gladys Tantaquidgeon, who summarized Mohegan dream beliefs in the early twentieth century, testified to the continued presence of spirits of the dead, who still gave what guidance they could.

CIRCA 1925

Among the Mohegan there is a belief that dreams are messages from their ancestors who are in the spirit world. These spiritual advisers appear in dreams to guide and instruct the dreamer. Sometimes they bear messages of hope and encouragement and on other occasions warn one of impending danger or death. If a person has the same dream three nights in succession the dream will come true. To prevent its recurrence the dreamer must turn the soles of his shoes upward before retiring at night. Never tell dreams which denote ill luck before breakfast.

Several informants said that they had recurrent dreams and one young woman told the following dream which occurs before or during illness of a relative:

"On Fort Hill, near the ruins of the ancient council seat of Uncas, a blazing fire is seen. A huge pot is suspended over the flame. An Indian, tall and straight, wrapped in a bright-colored blanket and wearing a war bonnet, is stirring the contents of the pot with a

long-handled wooden paddle. If the boiling substance rises to the top and flows over the sides the person who is ill dies. If it does not overflow and ceases to boil the person will recover."

Another informant told a recurrent dream in which a black monster with terrible claws and wide spreading wings appears. This is a sign that death will claim one of the tribe within a short time.

Nearly everyone in this group believes that to dream of black animals or objects is an evil omen. To dream of negroes is a sign of trouble and disappointment in the future.

During the past summer a Mohegan woman had a dream in which the spirit of her mother came and told her to tell the people to continue with their plans for the annual wigwam festival. This message inspired the people and with renewed courage they set to work determined to carry out the old custom that it might please the spirits of the departed ones. The affair was a great success.

At the same time, while walking near our burying ground one day, I had the good fortune to pick up a perfect stone ax. Upon showing it to some of my relatives, several of them remarked that it was the spirit of one of my ancestors which led me to the spot where I found the ax. They believed it to be a sign of good luck and to encourage me in my work.

Messages from my brother who is in the spirit world are received quite frequently, by members of the family, in dreams.

To dream of snow and ice denotes good luck. Clear, running water denotes good luck; muddy water, ill luck.

To dream of vermin warns one of illness in the family.

Dreaming of snakes is a sign that you have enemies. If you kill the snake you can overcome your enemies.

Should anyone dream of a snake it is a sign of having an enemy. If on the next day the dreamer should kill a snake he would be able to thwart the evil design. This belief is shared by the Penobscot and their relatives in northern New England.   (Speck 1928b:274–75)

IV

Eric Thomas, a contemporary Narragansett who was instrumental in preparing the Narragansett petition for federal recognition, attributes his political calling to a dream in which he saw the spirits of the dead and the newborn leaving and returning to earth and in which he learned that the earth would end if the eastern Indians lost their land. Since the Narragansett have now regained part of their old reservation, in a great measure because of his efforts, this end seems less inevitable than it once did. A Gay Head Wampanoag woman dreamed of a tidal wave that engulfed Indian homes. Although she did not specify whether ancestors or other spirits appeared in the dream, she obtained her prescience from an Indian woman of an earlier generation who came in contact with the informant's mother before the informant's birth.

1983

I used to dream, have a recurring dream of a tidal wave which came over the south shore and up to the Vanderhoop house and if it came halfway to the window I would wake up and say somebody's going to be very sick in my family. Or if it came above the window I'd wake up and say somebody's going to die in my family I know they are and within two or three days that would happen. And when I told my mother about it she said you were marked that way whatever that meant. You know that she evidently approached someone who had supernatural powers and she felt they had influenced me before birth and that I had the power of predicting something happening. (Wampanoag woman 1983)

V

The living also kept in touch with the dead in a tangible way through memorials or shrines. Indians throughout the area remembered people and events by digging small holes in the ground or by heaping up stones or brush at particular locations that later came to be known as sacrifice rocks, wishing rocks, or "taverns." One such memorial can be seen today in Edgartown, Massashusetts, where Indian converts honored the memory of Thomas Mayhew, Jr., after he perished at sea.[1] Edward Winslow first described Wampanoag memory holes in 1624

1624

Instead of records and chronicles, they take this course. Where any remarkable act is done, in memory of it, either in the place, or by some pathway near adjoining, they make a round hole in the ground, about a foot deep, and as much over; which when others passing by behold, they inquire the cause and occasion of the same, which being once known, they are careful to acquaint all men, as occasion serveth, therewith; and lest such holes should be filled or grown up by any accident, as men pass by, they will oft renew the same; by which means many things of great antiquity are fresh in memory. So that as a man travelleth, if he can understand his guide, his journey will be the less tedious, by reason of the many historical discourses [which] will be related unto him. (Winslow [1624] 1910:352–53)

VI

More than a century after Winslow's account, Ezra Stiles heard of a related practice among the eighteenth-century Wampanoag near Plymouth. These Indians, who by now were Christian, cast a stone or piece of wood on a certain large rock to obtain prosperity and success in hunting deer.

1762

Mr. Williams told me that on the Road from Sandwich to Plymouth there is a large Stone or Rock in a place free of Stones; and that the Indians immemorially have been used, whenever & as often as they pass this large Stone, to cast a Stone or piece of Wood upon it. That Stones not being plenty, pieces of Wood is most commonly used, & that there will once in a few years be a large Pile on the Stone, which is often consumed by the firing of the Woods for Deer. That the Inds. continue the Custom to this day, tho' they are a little ashamed the English should see them, & accordingly when walking with an Eng. they have made a path round at a quarter Mile's Distance to avoid it. There is also at a little Distance another Stone which they also inject upon, but pass it with less scruple; but are so scrupulous that none was even known to omit casting Stones or Wood on the other. . . . The Indians being asked the reason of their Custom & Practice, say they know nothing about it, only that their Fathers & their Grandfathers & Great Grdfathers did so, and charged all their Children to do so; and that if they did not cast a Stone or piece of Wood on that Stone as often as they passed by it, they would not prosper, & particularly should not be lucky in hunting Deer. But if they duly observed this Custom, they should have success. The English call them the Sacrificing Rocks, tho' the Indians don't imagine it a Sacrifice—at least they kill & offer no Animals there, & nothing but Wood & Stones.

N.B. There is such heap of Stones accumulated from such a Custom of passing Indians, between New Haven & Milford about three Miles out of Milford upon the Road. Another Heap at Stockbridge by the Housatunnuck Indians.   (Stiles 1916:161–62)

VII

By 1802 the population of Mashpee was said to number about 380 people of Indian, African, and European descent who lived in wigwams or small cottages and who farmed, whaled, fished, and made woolens, cheese, brooms, and baskets for a living. An anonymous author observed, "The Indians retain few of the superstitions of their ancestors: perhaps they are not more superstitious than their white neighbors" ("A Description of Mashpee" 1815:7). The author noted that the sacrifice rocks were among the few Indian customs to have survived at Mashpee.

1802

They still however preserve a regard for sacrifice rocks, on which they cast a stick or stone, when they pass by them. They themselves can hardly inform us why they do this, or when it began to be a custom among them. Perhaps it may be an acknowledgment of an invisible agent, a token of the gratitude of the passenger on his journey for the good hand of Providence over him thus far, and may imply a mental prayer for its continuance: or perhaps, as many of the vulgar among the English carry about with them lucky bones, and make use of other charms to secure the smiles of fortune, so these sticks, which are heaped on the sacrifice rocks, may be nothing more than offerings made to good luck, a mysterious agent, which is scarcely considered as a deity, which is spoken of without reverence, and adored without devotion.

("A Description of Mashpee" 1815:7)

VIII

Edward Kendall, in his travels through southeastern Massachusetts in the early nineteenth century, also visited the sacrifice rocks and speculated about Indian motives for the custom.

1807

Two Sacrifice Rocks are on the side of the road leading from Plymouth to Sandwich. One of them may be six feet high, and the other four; and both are of ten or twelve feet in length: and they differ in nothing, as to their figure, from the masses of granite and other rock, which are scattered over the surface of all the adjacent country. All that distinguishes them is the crowns of oak and pine branches which they bear, irregularly heaped, and of which some are fresh, some fading, and some decayed. These branches the Indians place there, from motives which they but obscurely explain, and for doing which their white neighbours therefore generally suppose that they have no reason to give. When questioned, they rarely go further than to say, that they do so because they have been taught that it is right to do it, or because their fathers did so before them: if they add any thing to this, it is, that they expect blessings from the observance of the practice, and evils from the neglect.

But, to whom is this worship offered? To a manito; and by manito, through the religious prejudices of the whites, is usually understood a devil. It was with great pleasure therefore that I heard, from the lips of the aged missionary of Marshpee, in this neighbourhood, the enlarged view which he took of this matter: "One day," said he, "as I was riding past a Sacrifice Rock, I saw two Indian women dragging a young pine-tree, and setting about to lay it on the rock. It was so large and heavy, that the undertaking almost exceeded their strength: however, they persevered. My approach a little disconcerted them; but I only smiled on them as I passed; for I considered the act as an acknowledgment of a providence, and therefore not to be too hastily rebuked."   (Kendall 1809:49–50)

IX

Speck visited Mashpee in 1907 and uncovered new information regarding roadside memorials. According to his aged Mashpee informants, these sites mark locations where people encounter spirits of departed Indians (Cheepi or *tcipai*).

1907

The only mention the present Mashpee authorities make of former religious beliefs is that the spirits of the departed (tcipai) frequently appeared in the paths of the living, and that such ghosts required propitiation before they could be induced to clear the way. The ancient Indians, they say, were always telling of meeting spirits on their journeys. Consequently, a religious practice grew out of this belief, viz, that of erecting great square flat-topped lodges covered with brush at certain points along their accustomed roads or paths. At these the Indians used to stop and deposit some piece of property or food, or else pour out a libation of whisky. They also held religious meetings and carousals in these lodges. Such Mashpee of to-day as are superstitiously inclined still observe the custom of throwing a twig or branch upon the rotting framework, or on the former sites of these spirit-lodges, whenever they pass by.   (Prince 1907:495)

X

By the twentieth century the Mashpee Wampanoag (who were the last to maintain the custom) referred to their memorials as wishing places or taverns. Speck's observation that they made offerings of alcoholic beverages at these sites suggests why the Wampanoag called them taverns. Gladys Tantaquidgeon noted in 1935, "At present there are two or three taverns in the territory of the Mashpee. Several very old ones were destroyed when the new highway was built through the town. Of the three, two are old and are located in South Mashpee; the third has been started in recent times on the grounds where the summer gatherings are held. The informants questioned did not know why the brush heaps had been started nor did they know why they felt compelled to cast a stick on the pile when passing it. One man said, 'It may be somethin' to it. I never can pass a tavern. I just have to go back and cast that stick on.' Another suggested that it might have been started to mark the scene of a murder or other calamity. The most logical explanation is found in the words of Eben Queppish who said that the largest tavern of all, years ago, was built up where a lodge or brush wigwam had fallen down" (Tantaquidgeon 1935:49). By the 1930s the Mashpee people also referred to these massive brush mounds as "lucky stick piles" (Hutchins 1979:139). Gertrude Aiken remembered one South Mashpee tavern from her childhood, perhaps in the 1920s or 1930s.

CIRCA 1930

At one place here in South Mashpee there was a so-called wishing place. Each time a person passed this spot, it was a custom, whether in a wagon or walking, to get a stick, or a small tree if one wanted to be unusual. One would spit on the stick and make a wish and throw it upon the pile. We were so superstitious about this custom we actually believed evil spirits would follow us if it was not carried out. (Bingham 1970:20)

XI

Ella Seketau told a Narragansett legend of how people could look directly into the past through a windowpane in a certain abandoned school. Someone has since broken the window because such things "shouldn't be."

1984   WINDOW OF THE PAST

This was an actual window in the old schoolhouse on Chemunganuk Hill Road. . . . Normally looking at the window pane it had one of old, old glass and one area was sort of ridged; it looked warped. When you looked at it straight on it felt smooth, but when you looked at it, it looked warped. And the scene on one side [i.e., when looked at from one direction] was just as it was supposed to. I looked and you could see a sea with Indian people, and it didn't match with the window next to it. The area that I did see

*was a big rock formation down the hill. . . . The people were stand-
ing by that stone outcropping. They were Indian. Everybody who
looked in it who had the experience saw different things at different
times. My cousin's husband said you shouldn't have things like
that, and he broke it. Two of Aunt Nita's children were born in that
room.*   (Seketau 1984)

In a world where change was accelerating and identity was elusive, the ancestors and other spirits gave what illumination they
could, through dreams, memorials, and even an old schoolhouse
window. The practice of adding to wayside memorials to protect
one's prosperity, ask for luck in hunting, make wishes, mark old
agreements, guard against misfortune, and remember the dead is
purely an Indian custom that began in prehistoric or early historic
time. With this simple ceremony the New England Indians literally
touched their past, symbolized by the generations of stones and
branches their ancestors had placed beneath and by the Indian
ghosts that presided over these locations. The Mashpee Wampanoag
were indicating, in a way, that beneath the layers of their identity
they were Indian at bottom, just as they believed that an ancient
wigwam rested at the bottom of the pile.

12 Conclusion: "There Is a Stream That Issues Forth"

When a custom, an art, or an opinion is fairly started in the world, disturbing influences may long affect it so slightly that it may keep its course from generation to generation, as a stream once settled in its bed will flow on for ages. This is mere permanence of culture; and the special wonder about it is that the change and revolution of human affairs should have left so many of its feeblest rivulets to run so long. (Tylor 1874:70)

Each generation does not make its folklore anew; beliefs, symbols, and motifs are strongly prefigured by existing tradition. In concluding this study of Indian folklore from prehistoric to modern times, I first summarize what survived from aboriginal tradition and offer an explanation for these survivals in terms of community continuity. Then I discuss the transformation of folklore texts and the relationship of this transformation to the events of historical change. Finally I comment on the importance of these narrative materials to the ongoing spirit or identity of the southern New England Indian people.

I

Why should some oral narrative symbols have persisted until the present century when most elements of aboriginal culture, including much folklore, died out? In general, these persistencies are not as mysterious as Tylor's passage on the stream of culture suggests, for as cultural transformation and loss can be understood as consequences of Indian submersion within the larger society, cultural survival can be illuminated by attention to the ways in which Indian communities withstood these same disintegrative pressures. These surviving symbols spring from their deepest Indian identity, but this identity alone is not enough to perpetuate itself; for although it may be slow to change it is not primordial. Rather, it retreats or thrives in interaction with specific historical conditions. Indigenous cultural symbols persisted most strongly where persons of Indian descent maintained boundaries through corporate territory, political participation, and internally cohesive social institutions. Continuities in the integument of Indian society are the vehicle for survivals in oral narrative traditions.

The Gay Head Wampanoag community on Martha's Vineyard, where one finds the largest and most continuously recorded body of folklore, also possesses the most robust and explicit survivals. Situated on a remote peninsula on an offshore island, Gay Head is the most bounded of the four enclaves under discussion. In comparison with Mashpee, Mohegan, and Narragansett, the Gay Headers enjoyed the greatest continuity of effective local autonomy, beginning with the Mayhew administration in the seventeenth century and extending to today's Indian control of town selectmen. Gay Head was also the most tightly integrated community, with communal production patterns and Indian churches and ministry. The numerous culture hero legends of Maushop and Ol' Squant, which thrive only here, are clearly derived from pre-European narrative tradition. Beliefs and legends regarding the mischievous aboriginal spirit Cheepi are also more developed here than elsewhere. Beginning as a spirit of the departed and a shaman's helper, Cheepi persisted as an agent in folk medicine, a component in ghost beliefs, and an Indian equivalent to the European devil. Although Little People long ago disappeared from Gay Head lore, they appeared in diluted form in the first quarter of the twentieth century. The folktale "Why the Cricket Is Black," collected by Tantaquidgeon in 1928 (appendix, XII), is one of the very few Indian folktales to have survived in all of southern New England.

Wampanoag Indians in the vicinity of Mashpee, Massachusetts, also converted in the seventeenth century and survived King Philip's War intact on protected lands. Although they enjoyed a considerable amount of local autonomy as proprietors of their plantation, their community was less isolated than Gay Head and more outsiders seem to have settled in their midst. The reimposition of guardian rule in the late eighteenth century had the dual effect of tightening community boundaries to outsiders but weakening Indian control over political and religious affairs within the reservation. By the early nineteenth century the Indians had regained much of this autonomy; but once the push began to divide communal holdings into private allotments, the Mashpee people began to lose control first of their land and then of local government. By comparison with Gay Head, they were less bounded geographically and socially; political control was more fragile, and they participated less in communal forms of production. Mashpee folklore also reveals a less vivid and less varied pattern of survivals than that at Gay Head. Maushop, although known at Mashpee, is emphasized far less than the diminutive Granny Squannit, who apparently represents a fusion of the aboriginal women's god with Little People—a scaled-down culture hero. Beliefs regarding the spirit Cheepi were less developed at Mashpee than at Gay Head, but the practice of leaving roadside offerings of stone and branches known as taverns persisted at Mashpee until the 1930s. Like the numerous place legends at Gay Head that cloak the various rock formations, cliffs, and other landmarks with ancestral commentary, the Mashpee taverns also were a form of communication between living and past inhabitants who walked the same paths and returned as anonymous ghosts.

The Mohegan entered the historic period under English protection, without having suffered defeat in war. However, denser white settlements surrounded and interpenetrated their community, which never was as well bounded as Gay Head and Mashpee. Hereditary sachems governed the enclave internally throughout most of the colonial period, and they were replaced in turn by a tribal council that exercised increasingly less authority. Factional loyalties characteristically diffused political leadership between competing camps throughout Mohegan history. Although Connecticut nominally protected certain tracts, the Indians leased many of these to whites and apparently did not develop communal production patterns. The church was less of a cohesive factor at Mohegan than at Mashpee, Gay Head, or Narragansett, and when the Mohegan chapel opened in 1832, a white minister served a mixed congregation of Indians and whites. Although the Mohegan were less bounded and less autonomous than the Gay Head and Mashpee proprietors, they displayed some interesting survivals, to be explained in part by their late conversion in the 1740s, some seventy-five years after the Wampanoag. The Little People and Cheepi persisted into the twentieth century and are still remembered by a few families that live today around the tribal center on Mohegan Hill, although no new folklore about these figures has been created for some time. Three folktales regarding the trickster Chahnameed survived until the first years of the twentieth century (see appendix, V–VII), as did some legends of ancient shamans. If Mohegan versions of the culture heroes Maushop and Squant existed, they disappeared with no trace at all, except perhaps for a single footprint in a boulder behind the Mohegan chapel, said to have been made by the devil when he left the area. Thus, despite some important early twentieth-century survivals, nothing at Mohegan compares with the strong Maushop narrative tradition at Gay Head, or even with the Granny Squannit legends and taverns from Mashpee.

The United Puritan Colonies dealt the Narragansett of Rhode Island a severe blow in 1675–76, from which they recovered only by merging with the eastern Niantic. Like the Mohegan, hereditary sachems governed in the colonial period, to be replaced by a tribal council. The reservation community was long divided between the sachem's party, which favored selling land, and the majority party, which thereby was left with less and less of the reservation to subsist upon. Those who opposed the sachem supported the Narragansett church, which continues as the religious center of the tribe to the present. The Narragansett had little control over outsiders moving into the reservation, and there is little evidence for corporate economic activity. Their traumatic destruction in the seventeenth century, combined with political weakness and divisiveness during the reservation period and the greater fluidity of their social boundaries, probably explain why the Narragansett show the fewest Indian cultural survivals. The culture heroes Maushop and Squant do not appear in any source after 1643; no writer ever mentioned Little People or the trickster Chahnameed among them; and Cheepi disappeared around 1740. Only a few localities in Narragansett country such as Crying Rocks and Indian Run have old legendary associations. Perhaps earlier ideas about death and the departed survived covertly in beliefs about will-o'-the-wisp and ghosts; recent folklore about the symbolism of the northern lights resembles earlier prophetic symbolism about figures seen or heard in the air. If Speck had worked as intensively with the Narragansett as he did with the Mohegan around 1900, he might have revealed survivals that otherise escaped notice, but existing sources show comparatively little indigenous symbolism in Narragansett folklore for at least fifty years.[1]

Sources regarding the other Indian communities, such as those at Yarmouth, Herring Pond, Dartmouth, Ponkapoag, Fall River, Lakeville, and Natick, Massachusetts, and the southern Connecticut Pequot, are too few and intermittent to be useful for reconstructing the folklore history of any of these communities. The Yarmouth and Nantucket Indians knew of Maushop, but the old culture hero died out with these Indian populations in the nineteenth century. The scattered Wampanoag enclaves of southeastern Massachusetts knew of Cheepi and Squant in the early twentieth century, and snakes frequently retained negative symbolic associations with shamanism. The strongest narrative tradition and the most explicit Indian cultural survivals are found at Gay Head, where we also find the strongest history of political autonomy, group boundaries, and collective forms of ownership and production.[2] When the Gay Head people participated in the widespread awakening of Pan-Indian consciousness in the 1930s, they had ample local traditions to draw upon and therefore emphasized their own folklore more than did any other southern New England Indian group.

II

Explicit survivals comprise only part of the overall content of the folklore narratives, for Indian storytellers borrowed many elements from American and Old World oral traditions and transmitted these to later generations as their own. One trend is clear: as one approaches the modern period, Indian folklore becomes more and more like that of the larger society. Traditional Indian legends such as those of Maushop and Ol' Squant show increasing penetration by non-Indian motifs, and the late historic ghost, devil, treasure, and witchcraft legends closely resemble those of American whites and blacks. The infusion of new narrative elements was neither random nor a simple result of proximity to other oral traditions but correlated closely with a series of turning points in Indian social history. The New England tribes experienced a particularly overwhelming series of events, such as epidemics, military conquest, and political domination, which challenged their confidence and understanding and undercut the infrastructure of their societies. In the aftermath of these and other watersheds, the survivors buoyed themselves up by means of social and cultural constructions that drew upon the new as well as the old.

The pattern of cultural borrowing and loss was shaped to a degree by indigenous structures that influenced the selection of elements from the total range of those available, but historical events also introduced changes independent of internal criteria of acceptance or significance. The earliest encounters with Europeans are interesting in this regard. The folklore texts indicate that Indians of the contact period apprehended unprecedented events in terms of received categories such as *manitou*, floating islands, giant birds, and miraculous shamanistic flights. Thus, certain traditional concepts withstood and may have been validated to a degree by these early encounters. Other aspects of Indian belief collapsed almost as soon as Europeans stepped ashore. Several early observers remarked, for example, that the Indian shamans could not make their guardian spirits appear in ritual if any Europeans were present. As Europeans dampened Indian confidence in ritual, they also terminated an age of miracles in folklore, for Maushop performed his last transformations and then withdrew when Europeans came to settle. Like the shaman's guardian spirit, he evaporated before the gaze of the unbeliever; in folklore terms, he fled from the eyewitness genre of memorate to the hearsay genre of legend.

The Pequot War of 1636–37 and King Philip's War of 1675–76 assaulted the natives' confidence in their beliefs just as the wars turned the balance of power forever in favor of the English, regardless of which side the Indians may have supported. Indians remembered their ancestors' demise mainly through legends about Indian ghosts that hovered around the places where, as humans, they had met their violent deaths. Although there is precedent for such legends in native belief, they closely resemble and surely were shaped by Yankee ghost lore from this same region. In awe of English technology and beginning to question ancestral certainties, many Indians sought the opportunity to identify with the symbols that seemed to give English society its power. The early Puritans exalted conversion above all other religious experiences, and the New England ministers exercised stiff standards in judging the authenticity of professed conversion by English and Indian alike. Although the missionary accounts are self-serving and their achievements may have been more modest than they believed, many Indian converts took their faith seriously and lived exemplary Christian lives. Conversion required the wholesale abandonment of Indian belief, myth, and ritual and a massive infusion of formal Christian belief as well as perhaps English folk belief, although this latter is less well documented. John Eliot and others published biblical texts in Massachusett to supersede indigenous mythology.

Generally, Indian folklore reveals admiration for Christianity despite its association with the colonial adversaries of their old way of life. These positive feelings are understandable, for many Indians who survived did so because Christianity provided a basis for group identity and a future in white-dominated society. While missionaries swept away Indian gods and myths, their converts projected the struggle into folklore, where contests between pagan and Christian continued for many years. Although rivalry between God and the devil was an English theme, an indigenous element, dueling for power, may have persisted within the very folklore of Christian conversion. Also, because the English devil had come to symbolize the totality of pagan Indian religion, he thereby acquired some native Indian characteristics. Converts even conceived of and communicated with the Creator in a way that hinted at indigenous ideas. For example, Christian Indian graves on Martha's Vineyard and at Natick contained burial goods, suggesting that Indian beliefs about the Christian hereafter differed from those of their Puritan teachers (Allen 1938:24–25; Biglow 1830:15–16). The Indian spirit continued to fight against total assimilation even after all had been converted, for the Indian preachers Peter Noka and Samuel Niles were said to have been better Christians than were the whites. Conversion brought about a major discontinuity and transformation of Indian myth, ritual, symbols, and world view, but some Indian elements lived on even in the folklore that depicted the conversion process. As sweeping as the Christian triumph had been, indigenous motifs participated in its victory as surely as Indian allies contributed to English success in war and Indian preachers helped spread the Gospel.

With the political issues decided, Indian survivors gravitated to a number of small reserved or sequestered territories where they experienced a degree of self-government and protection for about two centuries. This interval, which differed in length and historical particulars for each group, was one of relative stability as each community developed its own subcultural traditions, as can be seen in the Maushop legends recorded at Gay Head over these years. The few examples of ghost and devil lore recorded in the eighteenth and nineteenth centuries, and most that appeared later, are close to English and American prototypes and reflect an emphasis on social control within the small face-to-face communities. The devil chastised those who participated in "frolics" and card games, sometimes materializing to informally rebuke those who had challenged local norms. Ghosts reminded the living to respect ancestral ways and to fulfill their obligations to the dead; they haunted them for past crimes, and if we may project backward from later texts, they guarded property and community boundaries. Witchcraft and treasure legends may have existed in the eighteenth and nineteenth centuries before the termination of corporate tribal life, but written evidence does not appear until later, so I will not speculate on their earlier functions except to note that such beliefs often reflect areas of interpersonal conflict. Thus, for about eight generations, from the late seventeenth to the late nineteenth centuries, the southern New England Indians enjoyed relatively stable and repetitive lives. During this time, European-style ghosts embodied the past in the present, guided the living, and protected custom, and in company with devils they provided informal social sanctions.

By the mid- to late nineteenth century, land reserves came to an end in response to a national attitude that culminated in the General Allotment Act of 1887. The purpose of this act was to break up federally recognized tribal governments and reservations in order to speed up Indian assimilation into mainstream American society. Although the New England tribes had been living under state, not federal, guardianship, they nevertheless felt the first ripples of the trend leading toward national policy. By 1880 the Narragansett, Gay Head, Mashpee, and Mohegan either had sold their lands or had seen them allotted to individual Indians. Many Indians did not desire this change, and schisms developed between those who favored and those who resisted the decision. Joshua Noka, a Narragansett who opposed detribalization, argued, "For a colored man to be a citizen, he will remain about the same as at the present time. . . . Why should the Narragansett tribe be willing, just for the sake of being a citizen, to throw away the rights and privileges that they now have?" (Narragansett Tribe 1880:32, 34).[3]

Allotment and detribalization removed the underpinnings of community structure, which in turn opened the floodgates to innovations in folklore. Yankee, Afro-American, and other Old World giant, devil, and witch motifs had been in the air for years, even centuries, before Indians actually incorporated them into their narratives. Innovation in oral narrative was linked to transformation in the social basis of community, as diffusion followed channels that had been opened by social and political events. In a period of stability, storytellers may have been aware of other folklore but drew less upon it in narrating their own, whereas in a period of discontinuity they were more open to change and selected from their own and exogenous traditions that which expressed and accounted for their experience. Thus, Maushop converged more with the Christian culture hero, and his adversary began making contracts and was foiled by tricks that had long worked against the Old World devil. Memorates and legends of Anglo-American and Afro-American witchcraft attest to a raised level of conflict and vulnerability. Treasure stories appeared in the postallotment period and continued during the years preceding tribal revival in the 1930s, after which they faded away.

These accounts reveal ambivalent attitudes toward wealth at a time when Indian land was passing freely into white hands and later when the Great Depression was exacerbating Indian economic problems. Treasure legends imply that wealth is attainable but at an immoral price, that it is never actually attained, that some Indians know where to find it but refuse to because of a sense of honor, and that it is evil and will threaten community values. These attitudes are understandable among a people who believed that the larger society had gained much of its wealth at their expense. Power relations between the cultures strongly influenced the diffusion of folklore elements: as Indian autonomy and boundaries weakened at conquest, conversion, and allotment, Indian symbols and motifs also retreated, while non-Indian motifs of ghosts, witches, devils, giants, and treasures moved conspicuously into their narratives.

By the 1920s the architects of national Indian policy had recognized and moved to correct the disintegrative effects of allotment and detribalization, first under President Herbert Hoover and then under President Franklin D. Roosevelt. John Collier, commissioner of Indian affairs in the Roosevelt administration, took steps to see "the Indian tribal group survive, both as a real and as a legal entity . . . in the face of a prevalent attitude that saw the solution of the Indian problem in the destruction of the tribe" (Washburn 1975: 254). The Indian Reorganization Act of 1934 was an attempt to undo the damage done by the General Allotment Act and to enable Indian communities to turn again to their own land and institutions as sources of pride and strength. Although this act was aimed primarily at federally recognized western tribes, the southern New England Indians responded enthusiastically to the supportive atmosphere and independently created a range of political and cultural institutions. This resurgence of Indian spirit inspired a rekindled interest in Indian folklore, as can be seen, for example, in Gladys Tantaquidgeon's research on folklore, basketry, and other survivals, Princess Red Wing's journal *The Narragansett Dawn*, the public performance of Indian legends at Gay Head pageants, the revival of the Mohegan Wigwam Festival, and an unprecedented amount of Indian scholarly interest in the early ethnohistoric sources and in other Indian narrative traditions. Many texts from this period are more complex than earlier ones because they contain a mixture of Indian, Afro-American, and Euro-American elements bequeathed by oral tradition, facts and vocabulary deliberately culled from early written sources and from the published folklore of other Algonquian people, and a creative synthesis of some or all of this material by a few innovators such as Mashpee's Chief Red Shell and the Narragansett Princess Red Wing. At Gay Head, where local folklore traditions were the most robust, narrators borrowed the least from such other sources, supporting Eric Hobsbawm's observation, "Where the old ways are alive, traditions need be neither revived nor invented" (Hobsbawm 1983:8).

The modern period of tribal activism began in New England after 1966, when Congress established time limits for the recovery of damages resulting from the unlawful purchase of and violation of Indian lands. Since that time the Penobscot and Passamaquoddy in Maine as well as the Narragansett and Mashpee have filed suits to recover thousands of acres that they claim had been sold illegally in the eighteenth and nineteenth centuries. The Gay Head Wampanoag, western Pequot, and Mohegan also initiated steps to clarify or recover territorial claims. This modern period also is linked to changes in folklore, for politically active and aware people whom I interviewed spoke often in the first-person memorate genre rather than in terms of legends of others' experiences. Some spoke of power visions, medicine beings, significant dreams, and direct encounters with Maushop and other supernatural figures.[4] These accounts are only remotely ancestral and are mainly inspired by the wider symbols of Pan-Indian culture. As the southern New England Indians came back to life politically, their folklore revived experientially, but in the process they branched out markedly from the traditional lore of their ancestors. We can observe an ebb and flow of Indian and non-Indian elements in their oral traditions through time, in tandem with a corresponding rhythm in their political history. As group authority declines, non-Indian genres, symbols, and motifs replace and interpenetrate indigenous narrative traditions. As group authority expands, as in the era of the Indian Reorganization Act in the 1930s and the modern period of assertive tribal governments, we see more evidence for the conscious selection of Indian symbols from ethnohistoric and comparative ethnographic sources and from the broader contemporary symbols of Pan-Indian identity.

III

Early anthropologists wrote of the spirit of a people that, like the soul, could be seen as the seat of their particular vitality, and anthropologists today continue to be interested in ways to represent the essence or inner life of a culture. Edward Spicer, for example, refers to "persistent identity systems" as a set of symbols that constitute "a sort of storage mechanism for human experience, a means for organizing the accumulating experience of a people" (Spicer 1971:796).[5] Writing specifically of folklore as a window to the symbolic content of culture, Alan Dundes argues that it serves "as a kind of autobiographical ethnography, a mirror made by the people themselves, which reflects a group's identity" (Dundes 1983:259). Folklore, as we have seen in the New England texts, is the major vehicle for expressing and perpetuating a persistent Indian identity, and the Indians' claim to being a people is more strongly proclaimed in folklore than in any other aspect of their culture. Identity is not a single thing but includes a variety of dimensions such as attachments to ancestors, to local and national communities, to places, and even to shared opposition to other groups.

Most memorates and legends convey the memories, works, and experiences of past generations into the present, and a number of Narragansett, Mohegan, and Wampanoag expressed satisfaction to me when transmitting narratives received from older and bygone relatives.[6] Former generations speak in folklore through anonymous spirits of the dead, through ghosts of remembered persons, and even through purely legendary figures such as Maushop, Granny Squannit, and the Little People. Maushop represents the heroic prehistoric age when Indians ruled New England uncontested. Granny Squannit embodies, among other things, the folk wisdom of old-time Mashpee Indians, and the Little People were said to have been responsible for the graves and artifacts of Mohegan ancestors (Speck 1903b:11–12). Legends about ghostly presences in spruce trees, rhododendrons, rock formations, cornfields, and streams all speak of historical injustices to earlier generations. The ghosts that lived around taverns or memorials urged the living to respect custom as their predecessors had or else lose their luck. Persons whose last wishes are ignored return to chide relatives for neglecting their obligations. The dead appear everywhere to tell the living who they were and how their descendants should behave toward one another in the present. Even domestic dogs, cats, horses, and cattle, which also participate in human social life, were believed to be attuned to the ancestral presence. To acknowledge the ghosts and other legendary figures known to one's parents and grandparents connects the living and the dead and affirms one's commitment (as Frank Speck understood in his memorate of the Mohegan stonecutter) to the collective, symbolic life of the group. Is this past orientation an obstacle to adaptation and survival in the present? Probably not, for the living revise their folklore, and thus their past, as they move forward in time, and change also can be construed as recurrence. Today's ghosts, for example, are not the same as those reported over three centuries ago by Mayhew, Williams, or Winslow. Seventeenth-century Indians who surrendered ancestral traditions in the course of conversion, comforted themselves with the belief that their pre-Columbian ancestors had once known the Christian religion. As the outside world impinges upon indigenous institutions, storytellers expand their repertoire of motifs and legends to account for and to master new experience and draw on old and new symbols in reconstructing their narratives. Rather than being an iron hand that grips their identity regardless of historical circumstances, the ancestral voice in folklore imparts a group spirit, an awareness on the part of the living that they belong to a particular people who have survived dramatic obstacles and will continue to do so, even though specific areas of indigenous custom are lost and replaced with alien practice and belief.

Folklore establishes a strong identification with specific places. Group names such as Mashpee, Gay Head, Herring Pond, Narragansett, and Mohegan are also place names. Coatuit Brook, Santuit Pond, Mashpee Lake, Cocumpaug Pond, Sugarloaf Hill, Devil's Bridge, Devil's Den, Black Brook, Fort Shantok, Nantucket, and many other localities have or had particular meanings that are stored and communicated in memorate and legend. Maushop shaped the landscape in prehistoric time, and later generations remember and add to the stories of his creative activities. Nantucket, or the "Devil's Ash Heap," for example, is a monument to his magical pipe as well as the home of a giant predatory bird that Maushop killed. Even fogs in this region are said to be smoke from Maushop's pipe. A giant trout that forced its way in from the sea ploughed out the channel of Coatuit Brook. Ancient Narragansetts talk together at night on Sugarloaf Hill. The devil skated with John Onion on Cocumpaug Pond. King Philip's ghost rises in the vicinity of a certain home in Wampanoag country where his skull is said to be buried. Ghosts congregate at particular crossroads and at various watery locations such as Black Brook and White Dog Swamp. These areas where the ancestors hunted, fished, farmed, cut timber, and then died, and where the living are raised, have or had many layers of meanings. Through folklore the living stake a magical, emotional, and ancestral claim to their terrain that cannot be shared easily with outsiders who see it mainly as real estate, vacation property, or a natural resource. This claim lives by its own rules and is not immediately erased when others acquire the land.

The most important factor in the formation and development of a persistent identity system, according to Spicer, is the oppositional process, which he defines as "a continued conflict between these people and the controller of the surrounding state apparatus" (Spicer 1971:797). The New England enclaves have always struggled to retain their resources, are struggling today to reclaim political control over a territorial base, and even must work to be recognized as American Indian. All southern New England Indians share a varied racial background that includes white and/or Afro-American ancestry. Local whites often question the legitimacy of the local Indian identity and consider them to be "colored" or "Negroes." In folklore, Indians distinguish themselves from whites, to whom they attribute higher status, and from blacks, to whom they attribute less esteem than themselves. In one account white spirits were said to live "high up in the air"; in others, blacks lived beneath the earth's surface and were associated with devils, witchcraft, and bad luck (Basset 1806: 140). Whites generally are not seen as enviable but rather are often depicted as dangerous or morally inferior, as in the cases of pirates or persons who make contracts with the devil, who offer one thing and give another, who deface Indian landmarks, and who are sometimes even witches. Blacks also appear as clever tricksters and as victims of white people's witchcraft. Nevertheless, Indians differentiate themselves in folklore from blacks and whites. In a world where whites have held the power, Indians such as King Philip, John Onion, and those who would win money at cards and seek treasure should be wary of too much success, for they will pay a price in the end. As the Narragansett Ferris Dove observed in 1981, "Anything you speak up against—either good or evil (the devil or the Great Spirit)—you're not going to beat either one."

An associational process, which may be defined as the ways in which the group identifies with the symbols of the larger society, is also important to their identity. The New England Indians not only exist as distinct enclaves but function well in the larger networks in which they live and embrace many of the symbols and values of the wider society as their own. They owe their survival to identification with the mainstream as much as they do to an oppositional process that has kept them separate. From the earliest colonial years on Martha's Vineyard, Indians believed that those who converted enjoyed better health. Even Maushop, the aboriginal culture hero of Gay Head, became more of a Euro-American figure in the twentieth century. In their first public display of Indian identity, the Gay Head people in 1933 gathered to honor the memories of those Indians who fought and died for their country in World War I (Levitas 1980:372–

80). Identification with other Americans of Indian descent also has been increasing in the last half century. New England Indians borrow freely from the clothing, ornament, folklore, and ritual styles of the Plains, southwestern, and other northeastern Indian cultures. The *Manitou* or Great Spirit of whom they speak bridges Pan-Indian and mainstream American symbolism, for although it is believed to have particularly Indian qualities, it created and oversees all people, not only Indians.

These several dimensions of identity function together in coherent ways. Legends about Papoose Rock, Indian Run, and Witch Pond not only draw attention to particular places and recall past events but provide guidelines to the living who know their stories.[7] The fossil middens and colored soils of the Gay Head cliffs are a monument in a sense to the qualities of generosity and hospitality once displayed by the old culture hero Maushop. Sakonnet Rock once testified that wives should not anger their husbands. Spruce trees invoke a history of injustice as well as reassurance that Indians will endure. Assuredly the symbolic content of Indian identity is becoming more and more like that of other New Englanders, Americans, and Indians in general, but symbols and motifs persist that their seventeenth-century ancestors would have recognized, even after centuries of change. In the words of the "Old Indian Hymn" that the Narragansett and other tribes "heard in the air" many years before the arrival of whites, and despite the many pronouncements about the disappearance of New England Indian cultures, "There is a stream that issues forth" (Commuck 1845:63). The stream bed is shaped by the racial, economic, and political terrain of the larger society. The stream is the Indian people themselves. Their folklore, which follows them like a mist, is a key into understanding their course through history and is the primary domain where an Indian spirit still survives.

Appendix

This section includes texts, or small clusters of texts, that did not fit neatly into the previous key subject categories and that were too few in number to warrant separate chapters. They are not any less interesting or important than the texts incorporated into the body of this book, and each has something to contribute to our understanding of the folklore, symbolism, and world view of the historic period of the southern New England Algonquian area.

I

The weeks prior to King Philip's War (1675–76) were an ominous time both for English and Indians as both sides anticipated war. The English near Boston heard a gun go off in the air, bullets whistle overhead, and the drums of ghostly armies marching through the woods, while on the same day at Plymouth they heard invisible troops of horses riding back and forth (Mather [1702] 1820, 2:486). Wampanoag shamans prophesied that Indians would win the inevitable struggle if the English fired the first shot and were disheartened to learn that an Indian had fired it (Callender 1838:127–28). According to English legend, Philip's shamans assured him that no Englishman would kill him, which proved to be the case, for a Sakonnet Indian named Alderman fired the fatal shot, shortly after Philip had recounted a dream in which he foresaw his own capture (Mather [1702] 1820, 2:498–99). Some visions are a kind of collective dream. The Wampanoag warriors who besieged Bridgewater in 1676 suddenly withdrew because of an unfavorable vision they saw in the sky overhead (see chapter 3, p. 51). In 1700 a joint military expedition of English and Indians marched from New London to Woodstock, Connecticut, where they reported a curious Indian vision of an Englishman and an Indian fighting in the sky.

1700

The Indians have a notion of a sight seen in the ayr about a twelve-month agoe Last Octobr, of an English man armed, and an Indian wth Bow & Arrows, that they mett wth their heads together

271

*wth some violence, and then parted: Layed down their arms and
Combated wth each other, untill they both fell; the Englishman
Upermost; but striving on the ground, the Indian got above; they
parted againe, and fought wth their Arms, until the Indian van-
quished the Englishman: wch they look upon, to portend the
downfall of the English.*   (Mason 1867:477)

II

The previous vision is reminiscent of a Narragansett memorate re-
garding soldiers seen in the sky as an omen of impending war. Laura
Mars described one such sighting that took place shortly before
World War I.

1983

*They said that during the First World War, I heard mother and
dad both, we used to sit around the table and listen to them talk,
and they said that the sky was just illuminated with northern light,
and they marched like soldiers. And that was before the First
World War. And they said the northern lights was what they went
by in regards to war, if there was going to be a war.*   (L. Mars 1983)

III

Samson Occom noted that the Montauk believed in an afterworld
where good people enjoyed themselves by singing and dancing and
the bad slaved away at hard labor and impossible tasks, such as carv-
ing a dugout canoe with a round stone or fetching water in a loosely
woven basket (Occom 1809:110). The task of carrying water in a basket appears in one subsequent Mohegan legend and in a Yankee legend about the western Niantic. In the Mohegan text, collected by
Gladys Tantaquidgeon, an old Indian man figured out a clever solution to the problem. In the Yankee legend, the ability to make a wa-
tertight basket is seen as a reflection of the Indian basket maker's
virtue (Peale 1939:147–48). The motif, carrying water in a basket or
sieve, is probably indigenous to New England Indian and Yankee
folklore and also is documented in British sources (Briggs 1970:267–
68; 1971, 1:66–67).

1925   THE WATERTIGHT BASKET

*An old Indian man wanted some cider. He went to a neighbor's
house and was told that he could have as much as he could carry
in his basket. It was a very cold day. The old man took his basket
and went down to the brook and dipped the basket in the water.*

Then he took it out and let the water freeze on it. This he did many times until there was a thin coating of ice on the basket. Then he went back to show it to the man. This time he filled the basket with cider and the old man went home. (Speck 1928b:278)

IV

Speck collected a western Niantic legend from Mercy Nunsuch Matthews, the last of her people, about how they once tricked enemy warriors into giving up a siege.

CIRCA 1905

A short distance from the [Niantic] river there is a ridge of rock in which is a small cavern known locally as the Devil's Den. In this, a band of Niantic retreated on one occasion when hard pressed by an enemy, some say Mohawks. Fortunately, expecting a siege, the Niantic carried some mortars and pestles with them, but they had no corn. The enemy, unable to dislodge them, settled down outside to starve them out. Soon, however, they heard the sounds of corn pounding and merriment from the cave and thinking the Niantic were provided with grain they gave up the siege and left. Local tradition attributes mysterious noises in the cave to the Devil.

(Speck 1909:210)

V

Fidelia Fielding was the major authority on Mohegan tradition in her generation, and when she died in 1908, much of the tradition died with her. Speck collected three narratives from Fielding about a trickster named Chahnameed, whose name means great eater or glutton. Surprisingly and inexplicably, these tales are attested only in the Mohegan area, and Speck is the only author to have mentioned them. The Chahnameed texts are folktales, not memorates or legends, and are entirely fictitious. The first text is the only known southern New England example of a widespread type known as obstacle flight, in which the pursuer is impeded by a series of magical objects thrown in his or her path. Obstacle flight, or magical flight, is almost worldwide in its distribution and is known among other northeastern Algonquian people. Chahnameed overcomes three obstacles but is felled by the fourth, a magical hair. Four obstacles rather than three is characteristic of American Indian as opposed to European tales of this sort, and the magical hair resembles seventeenth-century shamanistic sorcery techniques practiced in this area.[1]

1903   THE TALE OF CHAHNAMEED

Long ago there lived a man upon an island some distance from the mainland. His name was Chahnameed, the great eater, the glutton. On the island he had a house, and in a cove near by he kept two canoes. One day, as he stood on the beach looking toward the mainland, he saw something moving, but he could not make out what it was. He looked for some time, and then saw that it was a beautiful young girl walking along the beach. He said to himself: "She is looking for shells to put on her dress;" for her garment was of buckskin covered with colored beads, shells, and fringe. She was very beautiful, and Chahnameed thought so. So he put his hands about his mouth, and called to her. When she looked up, he called to her, and asked her to come over and live with him. The girl hesitated, but Chahnameed urged her, and at last she consented. Then he got into one of the canoes, and paddled to the mainland. When he got there, the girl said: "I will come back, but first I must go and get my mortar and pestle." So she went away to her village, and Chahnameed waited for her. When she came back, she had a mortar, a pestle, and some eggs. Then he took her in the canoe, and paddled to the island, and after that they lived together for a long time.

Now Chahnameed was accustomed to stay away from home for long periods, during which his wife did not know what he did, or where he went. She did not like this, but said nothing to him about it. After a while, however, she made up her mind that she would leave him, for she did not like to be left alone so long. Quietly she set about making some dolls. She made a great many, decorating them with paint and shells, but one doll was made larger than the rest. These she put away, so that her husband should not find them. Waiting until he had departed as usual one day, she took her mortar and pestle and some eggs down to the canoe. This canoe Chahnameed had left at home. Then she went back to the house, and got the dolls, which she put against the walls in different places, all facing the centre. The large one she put in the bed, and covered it up with robes. Before she left, she put a little dried dung about each doll, and then crawled into the bed, and voided her excrement where the large doll lay. She then left her handiwork, went down to the canoe, and paddled away towards the mainland. In the canoe were the mortar, pestle, and eggs.

By and by Chahnameed came home. When he got to the house he looked for his wife, but did not find her. Then he went in and looked around. He saw the dolls, and went over towards one. Immediately the one against the wall behind him began to scream. When he turned around to look at it, the first one began to scream. Every time he turned to look at one doll, the one that was behind him would begin to scream. He did not know what they were. Soon he saw that something was in the bed, and, taking a big stick, he went over to it. He struck the large doll that was under the robes, thinking that it might be his wife. The large doll then screamed louder than the others. He pulled down the robes, and saw that it was only a doll. Then he threw down his stick, and ran down to his canoe. He knew that his wife had departed, for he saw that the mortar and pestle were gone.

When he got to the shore, he put his hands to his eyes, and looked for a long time toward the mainland. Soon he saw her paddling very hard for the land. He leaped into his canoe, and went after her. He soon began to gain, and before long he was almost up to her, and would have caught her, had she not suddenly crept to the stern of her canoe, and, lifting up the mortar, thrown it out into the water. Immediately the water where the mortar fell became mortars. When Chahnameed got there, he could go no farther. But he jumped out of his canoe and dragged it over the mortars, then pushed it into the water and jumped into it again. He paddled very hard to catch her up. His wife paddled very hard, too. But again he began to gain, and soon almost caught her. As before, however, she crept back to the stern, and raising the pestle, threw it over. Where it fell, the water became pestles. Then she paddled on again, very hard. Chahnameed could not pass these pestles either, so he jumped out and dragged the canoe over them; then jumped in and paddled as hard as he could to catch up. Again he began to gain, and almost caught her. But his wife crept to the stern of her canoe, and threw out all the eggs. Where the eggs fell, the water turned to eggs. Chahnameed could not get through these either. So he jumped out and dragged the canoe over them as before. This time he had to work very hard to get through the eggs, but at last succeeded. He paddled harder than ever, and soon began to catch up again. Now he would have caught her, for she had nothing more to throw out. But she stopped paddling, and stood up. Quickly she raised her hand to her head, and from the top pulled out a long hair. Then she drew it through her fingers, and immediately it became stiff like a spear. Chahnameed thought he was going to catch her now; he did not see what she was doing. When he got quite near, she balanced the hair-spear in her hand, and hurled it at him. She

*threw it straight; it hit him in the forehead, and he fell out of the
canoe, and sank. He was dead. This all happened a very long time
ago, back in the beginning of the world. The woman went back to
her people. She was a Mohegan.* (Speck 1903c:104–6)

VI

In the second tale, Chahnameed wins an eating contest by deceiv-
ing his rival and then tricks him into fatally wounding himself by
imitation. Even though these motifs (J 2401. *Fatal imitation;* K 81.1.
Deceptive eating contest: hole in bag) are known in British folklore,
they occur in the folklore of other northeastern Indian groups and
may be indigenous (Briggs 1970:147–48, 190; Dixon 1909:5; Thompson [1929] 1966:330, 353).

1904   CHAHNAMEED THE GLUTTON
WINS THE EATING MATCH

*Chahnameed and another man had a dispute. Each said that he
could eat more than the other, so it was soon decided to hold a
contest. But before the time came, Chahnameed went home and got
a large bag. He fastened it under his coat with the opening near
his throat so that he could pour food into it. He wanted to deceive
them, so he did it well.*

*Now they held the contest. A barrel of soup was brought, and the
two began to eat. It was only that other man who ate, because
Chahnameed was really stuffing the soup into the bag. But the
people did not know that. He was fooling them. Now the other man
could eat no more. He had to give up. But Chahnameed laughed
and said:—*

"Come on! Don't stop! I am not full yet."

*All the people laughed, but they did not know why. Soon even
Chahnameed stopped. The bag was nearly full.*

"Now I will show you. Give me that knife," said Chahnameed.

"Will you do what I do?" he asked the other man.

*Then he made ready to stick the knife they gave him into his
stomach. But he would only stick it into the bag. The people did
not know that. The other man was beaten, but now he said that he
would do what Chahnameed did. Then Chahnameed stabbed the
bag where his stomach was. And the soup ran out. Everybody
thought that he really stabbed himself, but Chahnameed laughed
at them all. Then the other man stabbed his stomach. But he died.*

(Speck 1904b:183–84)

VII

In the third Chahnameed tale the trickster again wins a contest by deception, in this case by appearing to squeeze water from a stone. The motif, K 62. *Contest in squeezing water from a stone*, is well known in European and American folklore but is not widespread, to my knowledge, among northeastern Indians, which suggests that the Mohegan borrowed it from white sources.

1904   CHAHNAMEED SQUEEZES THE STONE

Once there was a man who thought he knew more tricks than Chahnameed. He told him so. Now Chahnameed said:—
"Can you squeeze water out of a stone?"
And taking a piece of curd with him he began to climb a tree. Every one thought that he had a stone in his hand, but he didn't. The curds looked just like a white stone. When he got to the top of the tree he stretched out his hand and squeezed. Water dripped from the curds and fell down on the ground. All the time the people thought that he was squeezing water out of a stone. Then he came down. The other man was there.
"Well! Do that now," said Chahnameed.
And the other man picked up a stone that was lying near by and started up the tree. When he got to the top he held out his hand and squeezed the stone. But no water came. Then he squeezed harder, and soon he squeezed so hard that the sharp edges of the stone cut his hand until it bled. He had to come down. That made the people more afraid of Chahnameed then ever.   (Speck 1904b:184)

VIII

The early nineteenth-century Nantucket legend of Mudturtle is a curious mélange of Indian folklore and white improvisations. Although Mudturtle's fantastic appearance is unprecedented in Indian and English legends from this area, he could be a distorted memory of Maushop or a Chahnameed-like trickster. Like Maushop, he is a powerful creature who scoops out a den in a cliff overlooking the ocean and smokes pokeweed. Like Chahnameed, he dies trying to abduct a woman who rejected his companionship. Nantucket was divided in the earliest historic period into rival eastern and western sachemdoms, but the author's names for these, Khauds and Taumkhods, are fictitious. Indian sources may have contributed to this legend, but they are mixed with other currents that originated from white narrators.

1827

Belonging to the Taumkhod tribe, there was a kind of soothsayer, called by an Indian name that signified Mudturtle. He dealt in rat-skins, smoked snakes, poke-weed, and future events. A more un-couth animal nature never undertook to manufacture: for his frame seemed to have been compounded of limbs and organs picked up at the four corners of the earth, and huddled together without order or object. No one part tallied with another—his feet, legs, hands, arms, ears and eyes, though coupled, were not mates—not did they appear to act in concert; each individual agent being, as it were, independent of its neighbour, and having to perform separate and peculiar functions. His feet diverged at unmeasurable angles; one knee curved inward, and the other had its joint in the rear; the palm of his right hand faced outwardly, and the thumb of his left stood in the centre;—his arms differed a foot in length, the shortest measuring an English ell—they seemed hung upon axles, for he could twirl them about, laterally, and in opposite directions, like the shafts of two windmills in a hurricane; his ears were either inverted or misplaced; and his eyes, one yellow and the other brown, stood awfully apart, so that when the yellow optic looked East, the other stretched off in a four-point course. His dark copper visage, speckled with green spots, seemed in a state of oxydation; and his black bristly hair, twisted into thongs resembling rat's tails, gave his head the appearance of a caulker's mop. Moreover, there was an enormous hump upon his back—and finally, an inhuman elongation of the spine—something like the appendages worn by demonds—to which adjunct, the credulous natives were wont to ascribe his extraordinary powers.

He dwelt alone, under a high cliff overhanging the sea, some twenty furlongs northwest from Brant Point—where he scooped a large cave, the foundations of which, consisting of several huge rocks, may now be seen, partly sunk in the tide upon the beach below; all other traces having long since been obliterated by the perpetual dashings of the restless surge. Although no apparent connection could be discerned among the divers members of this shapeless figure: yet, there was an intimate correspondence be-tween soul and body—the mind being equally warped and con-vulted. His malicious temperament, united to his prodigious per-sonal strength, rendered him an object of dread and hatred to both man and beast; and whenever he moved—which was neither straight-forward, sidewise, nor diagonally, but in a direction par-taking of each, like that of a knight on a chess board—all classes

*of beings hurried fearfully out of his way. If nature had any design
in the construction of this paragon of ugliness, it was, it may be
safely surmised, that he might dig clams, overtake bull-frogs, and
frighten owls.*

*The king of the Khauds resided at Skwom, a hamlet lying far up
the harbour of Khoartoo. He was a warrior of great prowess, though
peaceably disposed: and his picture is preserved to this day upon
the Commonwealth's escutcheon, with the motto, "ense petit placi-
dam, sub libertate quietem." The hand of his only daughter had
been successfully solicited by a young chief of that tribe. He was
tall and agile—she, gentle and squaw-like. A certain evening was
appointed for the nuptials. Mudturtle knew it, and bent on schemes
the most diabolical, launched his canoe after sunset, and paddled
towards Skwom. It was a voyage of some miles, and the tide set
against him, so that he did not land until midnight. Before him lay
the unguarded wigwams, silently basking in the white effulgence
of a full round moon. Prowling through the village, he at length
entered the open cabin of the young couple. All was still. Taking
from his neck a huge bag made of the skins of rats and squirrels, he
hastily drew it over the head of the slumbering bride; and before
she was fairly awake, he had seated her in his canoe, and pushed
from the shore.*

*Having torn off this suffocating head dress, she succeeded in
alarming by violent shrieks, her sleeping friends. They soon mus-
tered upon the strand, whence they could distinguish the unearthly
yell of Mudturtle mingling exultingly with the cry of terror. A vigorous chase immediately commenced, and the monster, finding himself nearly overtaken, when off the peninsula of Khoartoo, plunged
his affrighted captive into the deep, and scrambled with redoubled
diligence to escape his enraged pursuers. This he effected while
they were engaged in seeking the half drowned female; but he dare
not approach his own domicil—for, in the hurry of his flight, he
had unhinged an elbow and dislocated an ancle. So villainous an
enterprise as that which he had undertaken, lived not among the
most ancient traditions of his tribe. Stung with this reflection, he
looked upon his wounds as evil omens, portentous of horrible
consequences—and in a fit of despair, he whirled himself overboard.*

*Meantime, morning dawned—the tawny damsel, being a swim-
mer, had reached land, whence, after some hours, she arrived
among her astonished kindred. The Khauds, exasperated at this
unexampled outrage, resolved on obtaining full satisfaction. A*

*large body, armed with deadly weapons, hastened forthwith to the
Taumkhod encampment, and demanded the head of Mudturtle.
What could be done? No one dare approach his den—in fact it was
inaccessible to all but its zig-zag proprietor. The aggrieved
insisted—the assailed remonstrated—and agreed to transmit their
ultimatum in two days. Numbers of the Taumkhods then assembled
round the accustomed abode of Mudturtle, shouting, and occasionally darting arrows into the cave, in order to bring him forth; but
he appeared not—and the tribes prepared for battle. They met, at a
place called the valley of Mattekajahm—and the Taumkhods fell
on that day, like the Ephraimites at the passes of Jordan, in the
days of Jophtha judge of Israel.*

*Having inflicted ample vengeance, the Khauds granted a truce.
Some days had elapsed, when, after a violent storm, the body of
Mudturtle was thrown upon Brant Point, where it was buried without delay at low-water mark. It was again cast up, and again in-
terred, three several times—whereupon a council was called,
which decreed that the corpse should be buried with the face
downward, and a conch-shell in each hand. This was accordingly
done, and Mudturtle has by this time dug his way through the
exterior stratum of our onion-shaped planet. It should not be forgotten by the faithful historian, that at the final inhumation of this
naughty necromancer, the reputed engine by which he wrought
all manner of magic and mischief, the os coccygis, was abscinded,
and sent as a peace-offering to the King of the Khauds,—who,
ever after, wore it as a trophy, and a charm against the nightmare.*

(Jenks *1827*)

IX

Nineteenth- and early-twentieth-century antiquarians reported a
number of purportedly Indian legends about lovers' leaps and other
tragic and sentimental love stories. One of these, attributed to the
late-eighteenth- or early-nineteenth-century Nantucket Wampanoag,
could be Indian in origin, for the text resembles a Penobscot story in
which the Mohawk came to kill the Penobscot, and a Mohawk warrior warned a Penobscot woman about the attack in advance (Speck
1919:284–85; see also Day 1972:99–107).

1807

*Tradition has preserved a pleasing instance of the force of love.
The western tribe having determined to surprise and attack the
eastern tribe, a young man of the former, whose mistress belonged*

to the latter, being anxious for her safety, as soon as he was concealed by the shades of night, ran to the beach, flew along the shore below the limit of high water, saw his mistress a moment, gave her the alarm, and returned by the same route before day-break: the rising tide washed away the traces of his feet. The next morning he accompanied the other warriors of the tribe to the attack: the enemy was found prepared; and no impression could be made on them. He remained undetected, till several years after peace being restored between the two tribes, and the young man having married the girl, the truth came to light.   (Freeman 1815b:35)

X

The Reverend Stephen Badger of Natick reported one of the few proverbs attributable to a southern New England Indian. A reputable Indian deacon, when asked why his countrymen reverted to Indian habits even after they had been raised in English society, compared their Indian nature to biological instinct. Of course the deacon was an exception to his own generalization, but it reveals an Indian folk impression regarding the unchangingness of culture. The English author shared the deacon's view, but compared Indians to plants rather than ducks.

1797

The general disposition and manners of Indians are so distinguishingly characteristic, that a very worthy Indian, of good understanding, who was a deacon of the church in this place, and an ornament to the christian society for many years, and who, from the first of his making a christian profession to the end of his life, was an example of seriousness and temperance, of a regular conversation, and a constant, grave, and devout attendant on the public institutions of religion, upon being asked how it was to be accounted for, that those Indians, when youths, and were put into English families, chiefly in other towns, for education; who had free access to such liquors as are the produce of the country, and intoxicating when taken to excess, but who refrained therefrom, and were regular and steady in their attention to business, yet soon after they had the command of themselves and of their time, and had associated with those who were of the same complexion, became Indians in the reproachful sense of the word, were idle, indolent, and intemperate, and became habituated to all the excesses of those who had not been favoured with such advantages, made this laconic reply, Ducks will be ducks, notwithstanding they are

hatched by the hen *(In his own broken English dialect, Tucks will
be tucks for all ole hen he hatch um.) And I myself have thought,
that by the peculiarity of their natural constitution, in whatever it
consists, and by whatever it is discriminated from that of others,
they are addicted to, and actually contract, such habits of indolence and excess, as that they cannot, without the greatest efforts,
which they seem not much disposed to make, give up, if ever they
entirely get rid of them. They seem to be like some plants, that
thrive best in the shade; if the overgrowth is cut off, they wither
and decay, and by degrees are finally rooted out.* (Badger 1798:41–42)

XI

An early-nineteenth-century white author wrote of a large benevolent trout that plowed a channel from the sea almost to Santuit
Pond in Mashpee and then died. This Wampanoag legend explains
the origin of Santuit River and a mound of earth near its source
where the trout was said to be buried. Other folklorists, beginning
with James A. Jones and including Red Shell, enlarged upon this
legend by adding Little People and a woman who was transformed
into a fish in order to marry the trout (Digges 1937:343–44; Jones
1829, 3:305–12; Reynard 1934:31–33; chapter 10, VIII). Giant and
helpful fish are known throughout the northern Algonquian area,
and this Mashpee trout is a southern New England survivor of that
broader tradition.[2]

1802

*Before the existence of Coatuit Brook, a benevolent trout, intending
to furnish the Indians with a stream of fresh water, forced his way
from the sea into the land; but finding the effort too great for his
strength, he expired, when another fish took up the work where he
left it, and completed the brook to Sanctuit Pond. The reader may
believe as much of this story as he pleases. He probably would
regard the whole as a fiction, if he was not assured, that thousands
of persons have seen the mound of earth, which covers the grave
of the benevolent trout. It is on the grounds of Mr. Hawley, and not
far from his house; and is twenty-seven feet over, and fifty-four feet
in length.* ("A Description of Mashpee" 1815:7–8)

XII

Tantaquidgeon collected the only Wampanoag folktale known to
have been recorded. Rachel Ryan attributed the tale "Why the
Cricket Is Black" to Daniel Nevers of Gay Head, who died around

1890 in his nineties. Perhaps folktales died out with the native language. Unfortunately, too little data on folktales exists in this region to speculate with confidence on how widespread they may have been or why they disappeared.

1928   WHY THE CRICKET IS BLACK

A cricket and a mosquito were going to have a feast. Cricket sent mosquito to catch some eels while he built a fire. Mosquito came back and cricket asked how many eels he had caught. Mosquito said that he had caught one the size of his leg which caused cricket to laugh so heartily that he fell into the fire and got burned. That is why the cricket is black.   (*Tantaquidgeon 1928*)

XIII

Rachel Ryan attributed the legend of the cormorant or haglet to Thomas Manning of Gay Head, who died around 1880 in his eighties. The humor in this legend is premised upon a cultural assumption that women received smaller portions of food than did the men. The legend is a fragment of an earlier Wampanoag folklore which we can only glimpse from the few texts that happened to be recorded.

1928

One time in the winter men were down on one of the ponds getting eels beneath the ice and they had caught a great many which they had thrown out on the ice and they were all strewn around. An old "haglet" came flying by and he was very hungry as the ponds had all been frozen up and he couldn't catch any fish. When he saw the eels on the ice he thought to himself, "There's my chance, there's plenty down there, and they can't hurt me because they haven't any guns." So he drove down. So down he flew, grabbed up one of the small eels and gulped it down whole, as those birds do. Now the "haglet" has very quick digestion and whatever he eats passes through him very quickly and as he swallowed this eel and flew up with it, it digested so quickly that it passed through him and fell down over the men before the old haglet had gotten away. "Ha, Ha," they called out! "There's something, that one will be for the women folks." An old woman came along and said there's a little eel for my supper so she gathered up what the haglet had dropped and put it in to soup. They meant by that, that when fishing the smaller fish were left out for the women to cook for the table and the same is true of the ears of corn

*in the harvest season. "Haglet" is a local name for the "shag" or
American Cormorant.*   (Tantaquidgeon 1928)

XIV–XV

Pearl Ryan of Gay Head told Tantaquidgeon how an old Indian woman drove away blacksnakes with pipe smoke, and Rachel Ryan spoke of one snake that may have been a king. Clearly the biological environment continued to occupy an important place in late historic Wampanoag imagination and thought.

XIV

1928   TO DRIVE AWAY BLACKSNAKES

When going berrying the women would sniff the air near a berry patch and they could detect a blacksnake by its peculiar odor which is like that of a cucumber. Mrs. Pearl Ryan said that her Grandmother Abiah T. Diamond when she smelled a blacksnake would sit down, light up her pipe and smoke for a while. Soon the snakes would leave the patch. It is believed that snakes do not like tobacco smoke.   (Tantaquidgeon 1928)

XV

1928   KING OF THE SNAKES

On Snake Hill somewhere there is a boulder full of holes that rings when struck with stones. Mrs. Ryan's aunt was up there berrying and she saw a great lot of snakes all over the rock. There were all kinds. One of them larger than the rest had a crescent on the upright top of its head. It shone like a piece of polished metal. It might have been their king.   (Tantaquidgeon 1928)

XVI

Nosapocket of Mashpee, who saw Maushop in the form of a bird, reported an incident that happened in 1840 when the Mashpee proprietors finally took control of their meeting house from the English minister, Reverend Phineas Fish. This was an important occasion for the Mashpee people, who had struggled for years to reclaim their church and parsonage lands. One could say that it was a transforming experience, at least for one of them, who performed an old shamanistic feat, in church, before everyone's eyes. The timing of this Mashpee incident affirms Honko's suggestion that spirits appear with "great changes of life" such as home building and moving (Honko 1965:172)

1981

We have a meeting house in Mashpee. The old Indian church as some call it, built in around 1680 I believe, and it was in around, I'd have to say around 1880 that this story took place because when we regained control of the meeting house there was a gathering held on Sunday afternoon and the native people were assembled in the building which has a balcony and there's a male entrance and a female entrance like an old style longhouse would have. And in through the male door swung open with quite a bash comes running a weasel. It ran right up into the front of the congregation, spun around, and stopped. And after it had gathered everyone's attention started up into the balcony and stood on the bannister and transformed itself into a male, a man, just brief enough not for anyone to know and recognize him as what family he came from or anything. Just that it was an Indian man, he just, poof, and then he collapsed back into the weasel form and darted out the door never to be seen again.   (Nosapocket 1981)

Notes

PREFACE

1. I am very grateful to many individuals and institutions for permission to quote published passages. These include Dorothy Scoville for texts from *Indian Legends of Martha's Vineyard* (1970); Gale Huntington for passages from *An Introduction to Martha's Vineyard, and a Guided Tour of the Island* (1969); Gladys Tantaquidgeon and the Museum of the American Indian for selections from "Notes on the Gay Head Indians of Massachusetts" (1930b) and Tantaquidgeon for a passage from *Folk Medicine of the Delaware and Related Algonkian Indians* (1972); the Dukes County Historical Society for legends from Edward S. Burgess's "The Old South Road of Gay Head" ([1926] 1970); Gladys M. Burgess and the Bourne Historical Society for selections from Betsy D. Keene's *History of Bourne from 1622 to 1937* ([1937] 1975); Frank Hutchings and the Chatham Historical Society for Elizabeth Reynard's Mashpee legends from *The Narrow Land: Folk Chronicles of Old Cape Cod* (1934); and Ethel Boissevain for the two texts from "A Week in the Life of a Narragansett Indian in March, 1864" (1973). Samson Occom's diary passages were reprinted from Harold Blodgett's *Samson Occom* by permission of University Press of New England, copyright 1935 by Dartmouth College. Cambridge University Press permitted me to use a passage from *The Journal of George Fox*, edited by John L. Nickalls (1952). The quotations from William Wood were reprinted from *New England's Prospect*, edited by Alden T. Vaughan (Amherst: University of Massachusetts Press, 1977), copyright © 1977 by the University of Massachusetts Press. The Gay Head legends published by Mabel Knight were reproduced by permission of the American Folklore Society from *Journal of American Folklore* 38(147):134–37 and are not for further reproduction. The Mohegan legends from Frank Speck's *Native Tribes and Dialects of Connecticut: A Mohegan-Pequot Diary* are reproduced with the consent of the United States Government Printing Office and the Smithsonian Institution.

CHAPTER 1. INTRODUCTION

1. Indian place names survived comparatively well in this part of the country. New Englanders and their neighbors have often written about these place names, and their publications occasionally contain folklore material. Two recent works on this subject are Grumet 1981 and Huden 1962.
2. For a recent account of Squanto's interesting life, see Salisbury 1981.
3. In *Jonathan Draws the Long Bow*, a synthesis of New England folklore, Richard Dorson commented on Reynard's method: "What could have

been a genuine contribution, *The Narrow Land: Folk Chronicles of Old Cape Cod* by Elizabeth Reynard (1934), suffers from an absurdly over-written style and an unjustifiable fusion of oral and literary sources" (Dorson 1946:262).

4. Tantaquidgeon's father was the last Mohegan basket maker, and her great-aunt, Fidelia Fielding, was the last native speaker. Her publications include Tantaquidgeon 1930a, 1930b, 1935, and 1972. See also her chapter entitled "Mohegan Medicinal Practices" in Speck 1928b:264–76, and Speck 1915b: 317–20, and 1928a. For a sensitive synopsis of Tantaquidgeon's career, written by a member of her family, see Fawcett 1984.

5. Helen Attaquin of Gay Head and Amelia Bingham of Mashpee published histories of their respective communities, which included some folklore material (Attaquin 1970, Bingham 1970).

6. Although it seems likely that early New England Indians distinguished between different types of narratives, in the way, for example, that the Eastern Cree distinguish between stories about people who lived before living memory and stories about people who lived more recently, we have no direct evidence that they did so (Preston 1975:288–92). Historic New England Indians referred to their narratives interchangeably as fables, legends, traditions, superstitions, and so on, terms that they acquired from English usage. For some recent discussions of folklore genres and of memorates, see Ben-Amos 1976, Dégh and Vázsonyi 1974, Honko 1968, and Pentikäinen 1973.

7. Like the Grimm brothers and Malinowski, Åke Hultkrantz suggested that "The function of legend is to strengthen the solidarity in the group and the group values by maintaining the continuity between the current religious belief and conduct and the religious world of the ancestors of the group" (Hultkrantz 1957:13). For additional sources on legend, see Dégh 1971, 1978; Dégh and Vázsonyi 1976; Dundes 1971; and Hand 1965.

8. I have tried to use the earliest recorded example of each text. Many authors of historical, travel, folklore, and popular literature on New England retold Indian legends often without identifying the written sources of their materials. In the course of this research I have compared these many texts to determine their earliest known dates and the primary sources from which later authors obtained their texts. I did not include this information in the book except in a few cases, such as when Indian narrators borrowed from earlier published sources.

9. Ernest Baughman defined the motif as "a concept, or phenomenon, a characteristic, a power, a happening, a creature, or an object" (Baughman 1966:xi). For convenience I cite motif index numbers and headings in the text as bibliographical references. For Thompson motifs I cite index numbers only, but add *Baughman* before his categories and *Simmons* before the few cases where I coin a motif. Where the Thompson and Baughman motifs do not fit the New England materials, I do not attempt to enlarge or perfect their schemes but use straightforward ethnographic comparison, for the motifs are a tool and not an end in themselves.

Scholars have criticized motif analysis for reasons that echo earlier critiques of traits in diffusionist anthropology. Dundes, for example, has argued that Thompson's motifs are not mutually exclusive, that they are not all the same kinds of entities, and that it is incorrect to assume that motifs are isolable units free to recombine in limitless ways, for their order in the narrative may be fixed (Dundes 1962:97). Similarly, Ben-Amos has asserted that motifs are not free to diffuse in and out of the narratives, "for there is an intrinsic literary regulatory system that governs the migration of motifs . . . their diffusion is not erratic, nor necessarily influenced by social and cultural contacts, but has a folkloric-literary basis" (Ben-Amos 1980:29). He further adds that motifs are not the constituent units of folklore but scholarly constructions that represent real narrative elements. Dundes's and Ben-Amos's warnings that motifs are not free floating and that they combine and recombine in fixed ways according to constraints in the narrative itself would be difficult to confirm or challenge with the New England materials. Since most of these texts are second- and third-hand deliveries that are often distorted through cross-cultural transmission, their value for structural analysis is questionable. Also, we have only the disembodied texts to consider, removed in most cases from the interactional settings in which they were spoken. I will be less concerned with the internal, literary, or structural qualities of the texts than with their explicit content, and with the relationships between this content and the social and historical forces that acted upon the Indian communities.

10. The Iroquois area of northern New York is another region where the ethnohistoric record may be rich and deep enough for a historical analysis of this sort. Edward Spicer's important ethnohistorical work on the Yaqui of northern and western Mexico and Arizona takes account of the interaction between Indian and Christian symbolism, ritual, and mythology in historic perspective, but he is not primarily concerned with folklore (Spicer 1980).

CHAPTER 2. FROM THE PAST TO THE PRESENT

1. A large and excellent literature is accumulating on the archaeology of southern New England. Dean Snow's The Archaeology of New England (1980) is the most comprehensive and up-to-date synthesis since Charles C. Willoughby's earlier classic, Antiquities of the New England Indians (1935). Other syntheses include Fitting 1978, Funk 1978, Russell 1980, Snow 1978, and Tuck 1978. Among the more specialized studies, Dincauze 1968, 1976; Gibson 1980; Ritchie 1969; Robbins 1960; Simmons 1970; Turnbaugh 1984; and Williams 1972 are particularly important.

2. The most up-to-date discussions of the social and political organization of the early historic southern New England tribes are in Bragdon 1981; Grumet 1980; Salisbury 1982:30–49; and Salwen 1978.

3. Modern accounts of the Massachusett include Bragdon 1981; Conkey, Boissevain, and Goddard 1978; Salisbury 1974; Speck 1928c; and Vaughan 1979. Note a distinction between the Massachusett language, which included the Pawtucket, Massachusett, and Wampanoag, and the group of sachemdoms around Massachusetts Bay, also known as Massachusett. Primary sources on the Massachusett and Wampanoag sachemdoms include Gookin 1836, [1792] 1970; Johnson [1654] 1910; Josselyn [1675] 1833; Lechford [1642] 1867; Morton [1632] 1947; Winslow [1624] 1910; and Wood [1634] 1977). Ethnographic summaries of these and many other primary sources are available in Marten 1970 and Quinn 1981.

4. The events and significance of King Philip's War are portrayed in Ellis

and Morris 1906; Jennings 1975; Leach 1963, 1966; and Washburn 1978:92–94. Many earlier accounts, such as those by Church [1716] 1827; Hubbard [1865] 1969; I. Mather [1676] 1862, [1677] 1864; and C. Mather [1702] 1820, 2, continue to be interesting reading.

5. See Ayer 1908 and Dykes [1920] for details of Bourne's life. This discussion of Mashpee history owes much to the recent work of Hutchins 1979 and Mazer 1980.

6. Bragdon 1981 and Levitas 1980 provide original syntheses of Gay Head history. For more information on the conversion of the Martha's Vineyard Indians see Ronda 1981 and Simmons 1979a. For additional documentary sources on Gay Head see Bird, Griswold, and Weekes 1849; Earle 1862; and Pease 1871.

7. The key secondary sources on Narragansett culture and history are Boissevain 1975; Campbell and LaFantasie 1978; Chapin 1931; Simmons 1978, 1983; and Simmons and Simmons 1982. Roger Williams's *A Key into the Language of America*, first published in 1643, mainly describes the Narragansett and is the most important seventeenth-century primary source on the language and culture of southern New England.

8. This synthesis of Mohegan history derives mainly from De Forest 1853; Love 1899; Prince and Speck 1903; Speck 1928b; Smith 1950:422–42; and Conkey, Boissevain, and Goddard 1978. I am grateful to Neal Salisbury for bringing Joseph H. Smith's account of the Mohegan and Mason land controversy to my attention and to David W. Conroy for allowing me to read his manuscript account of Mohegan legal history in the seventeenth and eighteenth centuries. For modern sources on the Pequot War, see Jennings 1975; Salisbury 1982; and Washburn 1978:89–92.

CHAPTER 3. WORLDVIEW

1. A more detailed consideration of Puritan ethnographic bias can be found in Simmons 1981.

CHAPTER 4. THE FIRST EUROPEANS

1. For discussions of the meaning of *manitou*, see Gatschet 1899 and Trumbull 1870.

2. A version of this interpretation of the plague survived as late as 1890 in Mashpee, where Solomon Attaquin observed, "There had been a famine before the English came, and our people were dispirited. Some said that it was because a white man had been killed years before" (Soper 1890:278).

3. As did many others before and since, Kendall wondered about the origin and meaning of the pictographs on the large rock, known as Dighton Rock, on the east bank of the Taunton River. White inhabitants of the area thought that the markings could have been made by the Indians in memory of their victory over the white abductors from the bird. This is one of many unlikely explanations of the curious carvings, which are probably prehistoric Indian in origin. Wampanoag descendants lived in this area when Kendall visited, and some live there even today.

The Penobscot of Maine also perceived the first European ships as birds (swans), whose arrival they believed was the fulfillment of shamanistic prophecy. White swans would have symbolized bad luck to the Penobscot (Speck 1919:266; 1935:24).

Although the Nantucket historian James Freeman did not identify his source, persons of Indian descent lived on Nantucket until the mid-nineteenth century, when the last two, Abram Quary and Dorcas Honorable, died (Simmons 1982a: 83–84).

4. In addition to his collection of Indian hymns, Commuck wrote two articles on the history of the New England Indians who settled at Brotherton, Wisconsin (Commuck 1855, 1859).

Attributing significance to a sound in the air is probably an aboriginal pattern. An Indian woman who died on Martha's Vineyard in 1709 "plainly heard a Voice in the Air over the Top of the House" shortly before she died. The voice assured her in her own language that she would be saved (Mayhew 1727:147).

CHAPTER 5. CHRISTIANITY

1. For an early interpretation of the epidemic of 1617–19 see Arber 1910:933. Additional perspectives on the miraculous rain at Plymouth and the impression it made on neighboring Indians can be found in Bradford 1966:130–32; and Winslow [1624] 1910:334–36.

2. The Nauhaught legend appears in a number of later publications about Cape Cod. The Reverend Timothy Alden, son of the ninth minister of Yarmouth, wrote a similar version of the legend which he attributed to some elderly people, particularly Deacon Isaac Matthews of Yarmouth, who was a friend of Nauhaught. Alden's account added that Nauhaught was "a very athletick man" and that the snakes approached him "with elevated heads and a tremendous hissing" (Alden 1814:239–40). The Mohegan believed that dreaming of a snake was a sign one had enemies; if in the dream one killed the snake one would overcome the enemies (Speck 1928b:275). The Mohegan also believed that if one caught a blacksnake alive and bit it from head to tail, it would cure toothache (Speck 1915b:320). Finally, the Penobscot and many other North American people believed that one must not tell legends in summer or snakes will overhear and bite the offender (Speck 1935:25). Thus, the deacon's story could have had many possible meanings.

3. Meredith Brenizer, in *The Nantucket Indians: Legends and Accounts before 1659*, attributes this legend to "a story by Andrew Oliver, 1764" (1976:17). I have been unable to locate the manuscript or published source of this reference.

4. Speck or Tantaquidgeon obtained this legend from Fielding, James Rogers, Amy Cooper, or Burrill Fielding, all Mohegan (Speck 1928b:276). For more on Ashbow, see Love 1899:74–78. For a complete listing of Mohegan, Pequot, Wampanoag, and Narragansett autobiographical writing, see Brumble 1981.

5. For example, in an essay on Narragansett traditions, Princess Red Wing refers to the creator as *Gitche Manitou*, the Great Spirit, a name borrowed from Ojibwa (Red Wing 1935). For more examples of signs and providences in conversion, see Simmons 1979a.

CHAPTER 6. SHAMANS AND WITCHES

1. The most accessible selection of primary sources on early New England witchcraft is George Lincoln Burr's *Narratives of the Witchcraft Cases*,

1648–1706 (1946). For a comprehensive cultural study of New English witchcraft, see Demos 1982.

2. Samuel Lee obtained much of his information from an English settler and physician named Arnold who lived in the Narragansett country (Kittredge [1690–91] 1913:152).

3. I have included Occom's text because the Montauk and Mohegan were very close culturally and geographically, and because Occom is one of the few New England Indians to have written on this subject.

4. Speck published a slightly different version of this legend five years later (1909:197).

5. For additional information on Indian basket makers in this region see Smith 1904; Speck 1915a, 1918; Speck and Dexter 1948; and Tantaquidgeon 1930a. Fielding repeated this legend somewhat differently in her diary. There she noted that perhaps people think witches are good because they have money and maybe even belong to a church. She concluded, "Poor Indian! He has not money, he has not anything because he can not steal [or] lie!" (Speck 1928b:245–47). Thus, Fielding seems to attribute witchcraft to whites rather than Indians, and she regards the whites' prosperity as immoral and due to witchcraft.

6. For the historic background to this legend, see De Forest 1853:213–15. Speck published this legend a second time (1928b:258–59).

7. The man who frightens witches and steals their money resembles motifs from a number of European, American, and American Indian sources (K 335. *Thief frightens owner from goods;* K 335.0.12. *Owner frightened away by thief disguised as devil;* K 335.1. *Robbers frightened from goods;* K 335.1.6. *Robbers frightened from goods by hidden man;* K 2320. *Deception by frightening*).

8. For other New England examples, see Botkin 1947:410–11; Dorson 1946:58; 1973:44–45; and Johnson 1897:240–41.

9. Versions of this story persist in Gay Head folklore even today. Witch Pond at Gay Head is said to be the site where witchcraft powers seized an old woman who was too curious and snarled her hair (Scoville 1970:20–21). C. G. Hine, the author of the 1908 text, obtained his information from published sources as well as local Indians, including Joseph Mingo and Mary Vanderhoop (Hine 1908:iv).

10. Tantaquidgeon wrote in her field notes that the Mashpee people made cornhusk dolls with painted faces, braided arms, and wide husk skirts. I have not determined if her informant, Dorcas Coombs Gardner, was the same Mrs. Gardner who provided Reynard with this and the previous legend. The name Coombs, however, is derived from Hiacoomes, the first convert of Martha's Vineyard. (See chapter 5, text II, above.)

CHAPTER 7. GHOSTS AND THE DEVIL

1. By the 1730s a few Narragansetts had converted to the Anglican church, but most resisted conversion until the 1740s (Simmons 1979b, 1983).

2. Related motifs include G 303.3.1.2. *The devil as a well-dressed gentleman* and E 421.3.3. *Ghost with a glowing face.* The devil is widely known to frequent dances and other recreational gatherings (Arnold ca. 1927:18; Jones 1982: 69).

3. Mayhew wrote in 1652, "When the Lord first brought me to these poor

Indians on the *Vineyard*, they were mighty zealous and earnest in the Worship of False gods and Devils; their False gods were many, both of things in Heaven, Earth, and Sea: And there they had their Men-gods, Women-gods, and Children-gods, their Companies and Fellowships of gods, or Divine Powers, guiding things amongst men, besides innumerable more feigned gods belonging to many Creatures, to their Corn, and every Colour of it" (Eliot and Mayhew [1653] 1834:201–2).

4. For more on Mitchell family history, see Hutchins 1979:145–47, Peirce 1878 and Speck 1928c:17, 19, 83, 87.

5. Speck recorded Niantic folklore about food offerings for the dead (1909:209). Some motifs for the Peter Sky text include E 334.1. *Ghost haunts scene of former crime or sin;* E 402.1.1.1. *Ghost calls;* and E 556.1. *Ghost drinks liquor.*

6. Dorothy R. Scoville's later version otherwise follows Vanderhoop (Scoville 1970:6–7). Vanderhoop's Indian word for corn *(yepninwaha)* does not resemble anything from Wampanoag, Massachusett, Narragansett, or Pequot-Mohegan, and its origin is puzzling. About this same time, Fidelia Fielding also wrote about Cheepi (spelled Debe and Jeebi) in her diary. See Prince and Speck 1904:25, 29; and Speck 1928b:249.

7. The ineradicable bloodstain after a tragedy is widely known in American and European folklore (Bacon 1904:351; Dorson 1946:156–57, 1973: 22; E 422.1.11.5.1.).

8. Motifs include E 421.3. *Luminous ghosts;* E 530.1.1. *Ghost light follows ghost;* F 401.2. *Luminous spirits;* and K 1888. *Illusory light.*

9. Speck wrote that the Indian words meaning ghost or spirit fox were among the most persistent survivals known to the New England tribes and that such phenomena are signs of death among the Mashpee and other Wampanoag (Speck 1928b:263). Interestingly, the Minnesota Chippewa in the 1960s perceived such fireballs to be bad omens and also shot at them to drive them away (Paredes 1980:381).

10. For English and Afro-American sources on jack-o'-lanterns and other such phenomena, see Hand 1977; Hughes and Bontemps 1958:166–67; and Kittredge [1929] 1972:215.

11. Puckett [1926] 1968:127; E 334.2.2. *Ghost of person killed in accident seen at death or burial spot;* E 422.1.1. *Headless revenant;* E 521.2.2. *Headless ghost of dog.* Headless ghosts are also common in white as well as black people's lore in this area (Bacon 1904:346–50). Charles Skinner published a North Kingston legend about an Indian skeleton that guards graves. This legend could be Indian in origin (Skinner 1896, 2:30–31).

12. Motifs include D 215. *Transformation: man to tree* and E 631.0.5. *Tree from innocent man's blood.* The bloody heart rhododendrons may have some basis in Pequot legend, but Skinner gave no source for his text. For a historical account of the massacre described in the legend, see Hubbard [1865] 1969, 2:33–37.

13. This Narragansett legend of the ghostly stump, associated symbolically with the spirit Cheepi or Hobbamock, brings to mind a legend from Pembroke, Massachusetts, that is said to be Wampanoag in origin. According to this legend, a stump once stood above the waters of Hobomoc Pond in Pembroke, which represented or embodied the spirit for which the pond was named. Published versions of the legend seem embellished by white

authors to the extent that its authenticity is difficult to evaluate (Litchfield 1909:62–65; Skinner 1903:119–22).

14. I am grateful to Courtland E. Fowler of Uncasville for bringing this text to my attention. He copied it from a typed newsletter circulated by the Federated East Indian League which was founded around 1960.

15. The motifs in the Scoville texts (XLIV–LII) are as follows: E 265.3. *Meeting ghost causes death;* E 332.1. *Ghost appears at road and stream;* E 338.1. *Non-malevolent ghost haunts house or castle;* E 402.1.2. *Footsteps of invisible ghost heard;* E 421.1.3. *Ghost visible to dogs alone;* E 421.2.1. *Ghost leaves no footprints;* E 422.1.1. *Headless revenant;* E 423.1.3. *Revenant as horse;* E 521.2. *Ghost of dog;* E 530.1. *Ghost-like lights;* E 574. *Appearance of ghost serves as death omen;* and G 303.10.4.0.1. *Devil haunts dance halls.* These motifs reveal strong western European and Euro-American influence.

16. The names in Boissevain's texts are pseudonymns. The motifs include E 338.2. *Non-malevolent ghost haunts church;* E 530.1. *Ghost-like lights;* and E 546. *The dead sing.* Ghostly lights and music from churches are also Euro-American and Afro-American (Halpert 1971:49; Puckett [1926] 1968:116–17).

17. Crying Rocks motifs include E 225. *Ghost of murdered child;* E 334.2.1. *Ghost of murdered person haunts burial spot;* E 402.1.1.3. *Ghost cries and screams;* and S 325.0.1. *Monstrous (deformed) child exposed.* Theodore Brown (I do not know if he was an Indian) wrote yet another interpretation of the Crying Rocks: the sounds came from the place where Indian women and children hid during the Indian wars (Brown 1935:12). A few miles east of Crying Rocks is Crying Bog, where an Indian mother is said to weep for the children she abandoned after her white husband left her (Bacon 1904:236–37).

18. E 423.1.3.3. *Revenant as headless horse.* The negative legend is not exclusively Indian, for Dorson (1946:68) and Halpert (1971:54) have drawn attention to the form. A Yankee legend from this same area closely resembles the one narrated by Reverend Mars. In the Yankee legend, a Mr. Gardner believed that he had seen a ten-foot-tall ghost, but then he realized that his neighbor had been walking on a stone wall (Arnold ca. 1927:21).

19. E 423.1.1. *Revenant as dog;* E 565. *Ghosts clank chains.* The Shinnecock of Long Island also told legends of dog ghosts (Carr and Westey 1945:116).

20. The Hazard family is one of the oldest and most prominent white families in the South County area.

21. The important motifs in Laura Mars's texts are as follows: C 12. *Devil invoked: appears unexpectedly;* F 491.1. *Will-o'-the-Wisp leads people astray;* and G 303.6.1.5. *Devil appears when cards are played.* The devil's attraction to card games is well known among whites and blacks (Johnson 1897:237; Jones 1982:66).

22. Motifs in the Melanson texts include the following: E 281. *Ghosts haunt house;* E 422.1.1. *Headless revenant;* E 554. *Ghost plays musical instrument;* and E 599.7. *Ghost carries lantern.*

23. The principal motifs in the Silva texts are as follows: E 332.2. *Person meets ghost on road;* E 421.3. *Luminous ghosts;* E 423.1.1. *Revenant as dog;* and F 402.1.1. *Spirit leads person astray.*

24. Burgess, Huntington, Levitas, Scoville, and others share the perception that ghostlore and other supernatural legends are dying out at Gay Head.

CHAPTER 8. TREASURES

1. Motifs include B 576.2. *Animals guard treasure;* C 401.3. *Tabu: speaking while searching for treasure;* E 291.2.2. *Ghost animal guards treasure;* and N 576. *Ghosts prevent men from raising treasure.*
2. This may be the same treasure hunt recorded by Tantaquidgeon (text I above). The taboo on speaking and the animal that frightens the treasure hunters have been known among non-Indians in this region for many years (Denison 1878:170–71; Dorson 1946:182; Hurley 1951:205). Among the motifs are E 291.2.1. *Ghost in human form guards treasure;* E 442. *Ghost laid by piercing grave (corpse) with stake.*
3. The basic motifs are as follows: D 1314.2. *Magic wand (twig) locates hidden treasure;* M 210. *Bargain with devil;* N 511.1.8. *Treasure buried in chest, cask, kettle, or cannon barrel;* and N 591. *Curse on treasure. Finder or owner to have bad luck.*
4. Tantaquidgeon wrote that among the Mohegan, Gay Head, and Mashpee, the phoebe is called the money bird; "If when you hear the bird call 'phoebe,' you say 'tah but' (thank you), you will receive a gift of money" (Tantaquidgeon 1972:87). This belief existed among the Wampanoag as late as 1930 and continues today among the Mohegan.

CHAPTER 9. GIANTS

1. Despite their impressive historical pedigree, the Maushop legends are essentially unknown to Algonquian scholars. Brinton mentioned Wétucks but not Maushop (Brinton 1882:38–49; 1890:130–34); Dixon left southern New England out of his survey of Algonquian folklore (Dixon 1909); Fisher's synthesis overlooked Maushop and the southern New England region (Fisher 1946); and Flannery did not refer to these materials (Flannery 1947). The first scholarly treatment of this subject is Richard Scaglion's chronological survey of a number of Gay Head texts, in which he draws attention to several changes in the legend over time (Scaglion 1974). See also Simmons 1982b.
2. Maushop and Squant legends did not survive everywhere in southern New England, and whether they existed among the Massachusett and Mohegan is conjectural. Even among the Narragansett, Williams's 1643 statement regarding Wétucks is the only unambiguous source. For the Mohegan, Gladys Tantaquidgeon attributes Devil's Footprint, a large hooflike impression in a stone near the Mohegan chapel at Uncasville, to Maushop. Fidelia Fielding explained to Speck around the turn of the century that the devil left that print when he left Mohegan country for Long Island or England (Speck 1909:203; 1928b:256). Giants of various descriptions roamed the periphery of southern New England. Edward Johnson reported in the seventeenth century that "a very terrible beast for shape and bigness . . . came into a wigwam . . . and took away six men at a time" (Johnson [1654] 1910:263). The Housatonic or Mahican of western Massachusetts reported a man who came "down from Heaven with snowshoes on" who "was esteem'd a Hero and a Prophet. He clear'd their country of monsters that infested their roads" (Hopkins [1753] 1911:26). The

Pocumtuck of northwestern Massachusetts had a tradition of a giant beaver that was killed with the trunk of an enormous oak by an even larger creature (said to be Hobbamock). The dead beaver then turned to stone, which still can be seen (Josselyn [1675] 1833:301; Sheldon 1895:29). The Montauk and other Long Island tribes may have had a rich giant folklore (Ayres 1849:106; Barnes 1975:31–33; Hedges 1897:104; and Overton 1941:213–14; [1938] 1963:102–4). Ezra Stiles reported an early eighteenth-century anecdote of a fisherman who netted in the Hudson River a large tooth that belonged to an Indian monster who "obliged the little Indians to bring him two Deer a day for his daily food, or else he would kill & eat an Indian" (Stiles 1901, 3:122).

3. That Wétucks would be known alternatively as Maushop or big man is supported by the fact that Canonicus, the paramount sachem of the Narragansett, also was known as Mausup (Williams 1874:371).

4. Ethnohistoric sources on the Elizabeth Islands include Gookin 1836, [1792] 1970; Amelia F. Emerson 1935; and Alice F. Emerson 1964.

5. Gluskap also built islands and was fond of a magic stone pipe (Beck 1966:63–78; Day 1976:77; Leland and Prince 1902:182–84).

6. Like Maushop, Gluskap was a great transformer who transformed his wife into stone and other people into fish and other aquatic creatures (Beck 1966:73; Day 1976:81; Leland 1898:122–26; Speck [1940] 1976:82; Thompson [1929] 1966:5–8). The Cooper/Basset text is one of the most often reproduced Maushop legends. Ellen Emerson, who summarized this text, incorrectly located Maushop's home in Narragansett Bay (Emerson 1884:438–39). Hereafter, I only cite sources where a text first appears in print.

7. For sources on the giant cannibal bird in nearby Algonquian-speaking areas, see Adams 1905:55–57; Beck 1966:53, 60, 73–74; and Leland 1898:111–13.

8. Mentor L. Williams, in his edition of Schoolcraft's Indian legends, commented that Jones had a reputation as a fraud (Williams 1956:xviii). Schoolcraft himself, however, rewrote a version of Jones's "The Legend of Moshup" under his own name (Schoolcraft 1846).

9. See Dorson (1946:52) for a New England reference to the devil fleeing at cockcrow. This motif is abundantly attested to in Welsh and English folklore (Davies 1937:42–43; Kittredge [1929] 1972:206; Redmond 1899; Wherry 1904:86). The mock sunrise, including the candle trick, is also British (Briggs 1971, 1:89–90; Leather 1912:164). Although the mock sunrise motif also occurs in Cape Verdean folklore, the Gay Head case more closely resembles the British (Parsons 1923:6). Bargaining with the devil is a widespread Euro-American and English motif, particularly in New England. The Unck of Cheepi Unck may derive from Chepian (i.e., Cheepi), Chippeog (ghosts), or tci pai wanksas (spirit fox or devil) (Prince and Speck 1904:29; Speck 1928b:263; Wilson [1647] 1834:19). Although Cape Verdeans and Portuguese have lived in southeastern Massachusetts since the nineteenth century, little of their folklore is evident in the Indian texts (Parsons 1923; Taft 1923:72–78, 339–42).

10. Although the seventeenth-century Indian men and women in this area wore leather aprons, this specific motif probably diffused from Yankee or British giant or devil folklore, where it had existed for centuries (Ashton

1934:368; Burne [1883] 1973:5, 11; Harland and Wilkinson 1873:77; Leather 1912:164; Motz 1982:72, 83; Sikes 1881:370).

11. See, for example, Gatschet 1973; Prince and Speck 1904:41; Trumbull 1903:307; Williams [1643] 1936:45; Wood [1634] 1977:120. Perhaps Vanderhoop added some innovations of her own.

12. Tantaquidgeon portrays Maushop and Squant as more fearsome than do other authors around this time. The folklore she collected is quite traditional, and perhaps not all was intended for white ears. Yet Tantaquidgeon also mentioned that the devil figured prominently as a culture hero and that devil legends are survivals of earlier Maushop lore. She wrote, "Two versions of the hero transformer cycle were recorded; the original form dealing with the gigantic power of Maushop . . . while in the modern version, the miraculous deeds performed are attributed to the power of . . . the Devil" (Tantaquidgeon 1930b: 21). I found little devil folklore in her field notes, so perhaps these texts represent a combination of the two versions. Unless otherwise indicated, her source was Rachel Ryan.

13. Mrs. Ellis of Gay Head furnished text XXXI; Mrs. Jeffries of Gay Head provided texts XXXII, XXXVI, and XXXVIII; and Mrs. Foster and C. W. Ryan told XXXIX.

14. Weston also misrepresented an Ojibwa legend regarding the origin of corn as Wampanoag (Weston 1906:3–4). Red Shell and Red Wing may have obtained some material from Henry Wadsworth Longfellow, who also wrote of Puk-Wudjies in The Song of Hiawatha ([1855] 1955).

15. David Vanderhoop was quoted in the Vineyard Gazette about this time as saying that "nobody tells these stories any more" because television has taken their place in the family ("Relates the Tales of His Indian Ancestors" 1955).

16. These motifs are as follows: A 523: Giant as culture hero; A 531: Culture hero (demigod) overcomes monsters; A 545: Culture hero establishes customs; A 547: Culture hero dispenses food and hospitality; A 560: Culture hero's (demigod's) departure; A 901: Topographical features caused by experiences of primitive hero; Baughman A 955(b): Indian giant god empties pipe in ocean; Nantucket Island is formed; A 955.3: Origin of island's shape and position; A 955.10: Islands from transformed object or person; A 974: Rocks from transformation of people to stone; A 974.2: Certain stones are transformed giants; A 977.1: Giant responsible for certain stones; Baughman A 977.1(a): Giant throws stone into position where it is now seen; Baughman A 977.1(b): Giant carries stone to its present position; A 977.3: Devil drops stones; A 1134: Origin of mist (fog); A 1710: Creation of animals through transformation; A 2135: Origin of whale; Simmons A 2412.1.7: Markings on whale; B 31.1: Roc. A giant bird that carries off men in its claws; B 472: Helpful whale; B 876.2.1: Giant crab; D 127.3: Transformation: man to whale; D 231: Transformation: man to stone; D 661: Transformation as punishment; D 2125.2: Magic transportation on a sheet of ice; D 2153.1.1: Island created by magic; F 531.0.4: Giant woman; F 531.3.1: Giant wades the ocean; F 531.3.2: Giant throws a great rock; F 531.3.4.3: Giant eats whales as small fry; F 531.3.12.2: Giant fishes whales; Simmons F 531.3.16: Giant smokes pipe: causes fog; F 531.5.1: Giant friendly to man; F 531.5.8.1: Giants hostile to Christianity; F 531.6.6: Giants as builders

of great structures; F 531.6.8.6: Giants have children; F 531.6.12: Disappearance or death of giants; F 621.2: Trees pulled up by giant; F 632: Mighty eater; G 303.9.1.1: Devil as builder of bridges; G 353.1: Cannibal bird as ogre; Simmons G 691.5: Bodies of victims at cannibal bird's nest; J 2136.4: Trickster pinched by shellfish (crab); J 2277.1: Clouds supposed to come from smoke; N 812: Giant or ogre as helper; P 253.0.3: One sister and three (four) brothers; P 532: Payment of tax (tribute); Q 551.3.4: Transformation to stone as punishment; R 13.3: Person carried off by bird; R 164: Rescue by giant.

CHAPTER 10. LITTLE PEOPLE

1. James A. Jones, who published the first Indian Little People legend in 1829, attributed it to "an Indian of the Marshpe tribe, dwelling in the vicinity of the Brook Coatuit" (Jones 1830, 1:xxvii). Although Jones can be counted on to have added numerous personal touches and unacknowledged published details to the narrative, at least part of his "Legend of Coatuit Brook" resembles known Mashpee tradition (see "A Description of Mashpee" 1815:7–8). Jones's text (1829, 3:305–12) is not reproduced here because in my judgment it is more Jones than Indian. To Jones's credit, however, he stocked his story with motifs that are known in Eastern and Western Abenaki and other North American Indian oral traditions.

2. Melissa Fawcett wrote that Fidelia Fielding taught Gladys Tantaquidgeon "the ways of the woodland little people or 'makiawisug'" and that "Gladys vividly remembers having been greatly impressed by one family dinner at which Great Aunt Fidelia abruptly excused herself to talk to these magical mischievous beings" (Fawcett 1984:137). Speck, following Ezra Stiles, noted that Muhkeahweesug probably meant "little boy" and also "whippoorwill" in Pequot, suggesting an analogy "between the bird and the fairies" which he noted in other Algonquian mythologies (Speck 1928b:261–62). The taboo against looking at fairies is also common in Welsh and English folklore (C 311.1.2.).

3. Ryan introduces many new motifs, further confirming that this was a period of rapid change in Gay Head folklore. The principal ones (F 302.3.2. Fairy offers gifts to man to be her paramour; F 328. Fairies entice people into their domain; F 361.1. Fairy takes revenge for being slighted; and F 362.4. Fairy causes mutilation [injury]) occur mainly in English, Scottish, and Irish sources. One motif common to the Ryan and Fielding texts has been noted among American Indians in the Southeast (F 334. Fairy grateful to mortal for healing).

On a separate issue, Ryan's Gay Head text resembles Scandinavian legend in three respects. First, the capture or enticement is carried out by supernatural beings; second, these beings are looking for spouses in the human world; and third, the period of highest vulnerability to capture by supernatural beings is premarriage (Lindow 1978:45). Lindow attributes this Scandinavian pattern to a more general tendency for the principal character in a legend of supernatural experience to be assigned to an important life crisis or rite of passage. The Wampanoag case is consistent with this pattern, for the unfortunate woman appears to have been ready for marriage.

4. Details of Eben Queppish's interesting life can be found in Cobb 1926; Hutchins 1979:137–38, 187; Mazer 1980:88–93; and Speck 1928a:75. He was a major figure in the revival of Mashpee Indian identity in the 1920s and 1930s.
5. Jones had done his homework. He probably obtained the name from Captain Benjamin Church's memoirs or from another history of King Philip's War. See Jones 1829, 3:305–12.

CHAPTER 11. WINDOWS TO THE PAST

1. The Housatonic Indians of southwestern Massachusetts also built such stone memorials because it was the custom of their ancestors to thus express gratitude to the supreme being (Hopkins [1753] 1911:24–25). Gideon Hawley, the missionary to Mashpee, noted comparable practices throughout the Northeast (Hawley 1795:59–60). In 1643 the Narragansett sachem Miantonomi led an expedition against the Mohegan, arrayed in a heavy suit of medieval armor given him by Samuel Gorton of Warwick, Rhode Island. When Uncas's men counterattacked, the Narragansett retreated and the Mohegan sachem Tantaquidgeon captured Miantonomi, who was unable to escape because of the added weight. Shortly thereafter the commissioners of the United Puritan Colonies condemned Miantonomi to death and delegated the responsibility for his execution to Uncas. For many years afterward, parties of Narragansett each September visited the site of Miantonomi's capture and burial to renew their mourning and heap up stones in his memory (Chapin 1931:51; Orr 1897:120). According to a Falmouth tradition, Indians erected piles of brushwood to mark boundaries they had established in land transactions with whites (Corbett 1955:130).

The early eighteenth-century Massachusett inhabitants of Natick had a related custom of planting living trees ("the tree of friendship") at the doorways of living persons whom they wished to honor (Biglow 1830:11–12).

CHAPTER 12. CONCLUSION

1. The Narragansett language also died out before Massachusett, Wampanoag, and Pequot-Mohegan, perhaps because the group was less bounded as a community.
2. In her observations on Italian folklore survivals in Roseto, Pennsylvania, Carla Bianco suggested conditions for the continuation and transmission of traditional lore that overlap those proposed here. "These conditions were: a sense of security stemming from a familiar environment, a non-interrupted cultural identity, a sense of mutual belonging due to strong and extended family ties, a continued relationship with Italy, and a fairly successful and autonomous economy of the group as a whole" (Bianco 1974:74).
3. Samuel Rodman, another Narragansett, also spoke against sale of the reservation and against U.S. citizenship. His words reveal the Indians' deep attachment to their home soil and an egalitarian view of the hereafter: "We do not wish to be citizens. For we know we cannot be so in the full acceptation of that term. . . . And, notwithstanding the deprivations under which we labor, we are attached to our homes. It is the birth-place

of our mothers. It is the last gift of our fathers; and there rest the bones of our ancestors. . . . We do not wish to leave it; but we desire to be 'let alone,' so that when our days of degradation upon earth shall come to an end, our dust may mingle with that of our kindred who have passed . . . to that better land above, where tribes and classes are alike unknown" (Campbell and LaFantasie 1978:78).

4. Others who were politically active did not speak of such experiences but nevertheless took a scholarly interest in the published and oral traditions of Indian people.

5. See Thoresen 1973 on A. L. Kroeber and Sapir 1924:404–9. Spicer also writes of the spirit of the Yaqui people, which he describes as their "feeling about the way they have performed and the values they have stood for in the course of their life history as a people" (Spicer 1980:360).

6. Similarly, Elizabeth Colson wrote of Makah folktales and legends in the Northwest, "The accounts have a wide circulation throughout the group, and thus help to keep alive a feeling of belonging to a tradition other than the American. . . . A knowledge of the incidents also reinforces their sense of belonging to a particular group of people, the Makah" (Colson [1953] 1974:184).

7. Keith Basso, in an important chapter on Apache place names, observed similarly, "The Apache landscape is full of named locations where time and space have fused and where, through the agency of historical tales, their intersection is 'made visible for human contemplation.' It is also apparent that such locations, charged as they are with personal and social significance, work in important ways to shape the images that Apaches have—or should have—of themselves. . . . One forms the impression that Apaches view the landscape as a repository of distilled wisdom, a stern but benevolent keeper of tradition, an ever-vigilant ally in the efforts of individuals and whole communities to put into practice a set of standards for social living that are uniquely and distinctively their own. . . . Features of the landscape have become symbols of and for this way of living" (Basso 1983:45). Basso's words also fit the New England situation, and his Apache ethnographic data give an idea of how pervasive the New England moral landscape may once have been.

APPENDIX

1. The important motifs are D672. *Obstacle flight;* D 1002. *Magic excrements;* and K 525. *Escape by use of substituted object.*

2. See Hultkrantz 1983.

Bibliography

Abbey, Marilyn S. 1982. "I'm Practically the Oldest One in Gay Head Now." *Discovery: The Allstate Motor Club Magazine*, Autumn:15.

Adams, Richard C. 1905. *Legends of the Delaware Indians and Picture Writing*. Washington, D.C.

Alden, Timothy. 1798. Memorabilia of Yarmouth, 1797. *Collections of the Massachusetts Historical Society* 5:54–60.

———. 1814. *A Collection of American Epitaphs and Inscriptions*. Pentade 1, vol. 3. New York.

Allen, Joseph C. 1938. *Tales and Trails of Martha's Vineyard*. Boston: Little, Brown and Company.

American Friends Service Committee. 1978. *Report from Mashpee: A Study of the Impact of the Wampanoag Land Claim on the Economy of Mashpee, Massachusetts*. Philadelphia: American Friends Service Committee.

Arnold, James N. Ca. 1927. Anecdotes of South County, R.I. Knight Memorial Library, Providence. Typescript.

Ashton, J. W. 1934. Jack A. Kent: The Evolution of a Folk Figure. *Journal of American Folklore* 47(186):362–68.

Attaquin, Helen A. 1970. *A Brief History of Gay Head, or "Aquinuih."* Published by the author.

Ayer, Mary F. 1908. *Richard Bourne, Missionary to the Mashpee Indians*. Boston: David Clapp & Son. Reprinted from the *New England Historical and Genealogical Register* for April 1908.

Ayres, J. A. 1849. *The Legends of Montauk*. Hartford, Conn.: Edwin Hunt.

Bacon, Edgar M. 1904. *Narragansett Bay: Its Historic and Romantic Associations and Picturesque Setting*. New York: G. P. Putnam's Sons.

Badger, Stephen. 1798. Historical and Characteristic Traits of the American Indians in General and Those of Natick in Particular. *Collections of the Massachusetts Historical Society* 5:32–45.

Barnes, Gean F. 1975. *Tales of the High Hills: Legends of the Montauk Indians*. Sag Harbor: East Hampton Town Bicentennial Committee.

Bascom, William. 1965. The Forms of Folklore: Prose Narratives. *Journal of American Folklore* 78(307):3–20.

Bassett, Benjamin. 1806. Fabulous Traditions and Customs of the Indians of Martha's Vineyard. *Collections of the Massachusetts Historical Society for the Year 1792* 1:139–40.

Basso, Keith. 1983. "Stalking with Stories": Names, Places, and Moral Narratives among the Western Apache. In *Text, Play, and Story: The Construction and Reconstruction of Self and Society*, Stuart Plattner, ed., pp. 19–55. Washington, D.C.: Proceedings of the American Ethnological Society.

Baughman, Ernest W. 1966. *Type and Motif-Index of the Folktales of En-*

gland and North America. Indiana University Folklore Series, no. 20. The Hague: Mouton & Co.

Baylies, William. 1793. Description of Gay Head, 1786. Memoirs of the American Academy of Arts and Sciences 2(1):150–55.

Beck, Horace P. 1966. Gluskap the Liar and Other Indian Tales. Freeport, Maine: Bond Wheelright Company.

Bell, Michael. 1981. Transcript of interview with Ferris B. Dove, November 3, Rockville, R.I.

Ben-Amos, Dan. 1976. Introduction. In Folklore Genres, Dan Ben-Amos, ed., pp. ix–xlv. Austin: University of Texas Press.

———. 1980. The Concept of Motif in Folklore. In Folklore Studies in the Twentieth Century, Venetia Newall, ed., pp. 17–36. London: Rowman and Littlefield.

Beth. 1794. Joseph Nauhaught. Massachusetts Magazine 6(3):150–51.

Bianco, Carla. 1974. The Two Rosetos. Bloomington: Indiana University Press.

Biglow, William. 1830. History of the Town of Natick, Mass., from the Days of the Apostolic Eliot, MDCL, to the Present Time, MDCCCXXX. Boston: Marsh, Capen, and Lyon.

Bingham, Amelia G. 1970. Mashpee: Land of the Wampanoags. Mashpee: Mashpee Historical Commission.

Bird, F. W., Whiting Griswold, and Cyrus Weekes. 1849. Report of the Commissioners Relating to the Condition of the Indians in Massachusetts. Massachusetts House Document No. 46.

Blodgett, Harold. 1935. Samson Occom. Hanover, N.H.: Dartmouth College Publications.

Boas, Franz. 1898. Introduction. In Traditions of the Thompson River Indians of British Columbia, Collected and Annotated, by James Teit, pp. 1–18. Memoirs of the American Folk-Lore Society, 4. Boston and New York: Houghton, Mifflin and Company.

Boissevain, Ethel. 1973. A Week in the Life of a Narragansett Indian in March, 1864. Paper prepared for the Annual Meeting of the American Society for Ethnohistory, Edmond, Oklahoma.

———. 1975. The Narragansett People. Phoenix: Indian Tribal Series.

Botkin, B. A., ed. 1947. A Treasury of New England Folklore. New York: Crown Publishers.

Boyer, Paul, and Stephen Nissenbaum. 1974. Salem Possessed: The Social Origins of Witchcraft. Cambridge, Mass.: Harvard University Press.

Bradford, William. 1966. Of Plymouth Plantation, 1620–1647. Samuel Eliot Morison, ed. New York: Alfred A. Knopf.

Bragdon, Kathleen J. 1981. "Another Tongue Brought In": An Ethnohistorical Study of Native Writings in Massachusett. Ph.D. diss., Department of Anthropology, Brown University.

Brenizer, Meredith M. 1976. The Nantucket Indians: Legends and Accounts before 1659. Nantucket: Poets Corner Press.

Briggs, Katharine M. 1970. A Dictionary of British Folk-Tales in the English Language. Part A, Folk Narratives, vol. 1. Bloomington: Indiana University Press.

———. 1971. A Dictionary of British Folk-Tales in the English Language. Part B, Folk Legends, vols. 1 and 2. Bloomington: Indiana University Press.

Brinton, Daniel G. 1882. *American Hero-Myths*. Philadelphia: H. C. Watts & Co.

————. 1890. *Essays of an Americanist*. Philadelphia: Porter & Coates.

Brown, Theodore D. 1935. Narragansett Territory. *Narragansett Dawn* 1(3): 11–12.

Brumble, H. David. 1981. *An Annotated Bibliography of American Indian and Eskimo Autobiographies*. Lincoln: University of Nebraska Press.

Burgess, Edward S. [1926] 1970. The Old South Road of Gay Head. Reprint. *Dukes County Intelligencer* 12(1):1–35.

Burne, Charlotte, S., ed. [1883] 1973. *Shropshire Folk-Lore: A Sheaf of Gleanings, I*. Reprint. Wakefield, England: E. P. Publishing Limited.

Burr, George Lincoln, ed. 1946. *Narratives of the Witchcraft Cases, 1648–1706*. New York: Barnes and Noble.

Butler, Eva L. 1947. Some Early Indian Basket Makers of Southern New England. Addendum to *Eastern Algonkian Block-Stamp Decoration: A New World Original or an Acculturated Art*, by Frank G. Speck, pp. 35–57. Trenton: Archaeological Society of New Jersey.

Butterworth, Hezekiah. 1893. The Silver Pipe. In *Exercises under the Auspices of the Thalia Club, Warren, R.I.*, p. 16. Providence: Massasoit Monument Association.

Calef, Robert. [1700] 1946. From "More Wonders of the Invisible World." In *Narratives of the Witchcraft Cases, 1648–1706*, George Lincoln Burr, ed., pp. 289–394. Reprint. New York: Barnes and Noble.

Callender, John. 1838. *An Historical Discourse on the Civil and Religious Affairs of the Colony of Rhode Island*. Collections of the Rhode Island Historical Society, 4. Providence: Knowles, Vose, and Company.

Campbell, Paul R., and Glenn W. LaFantasie. 1978. Scattered to the Winds of Heaven: Narragansett Indians, 1676–1880. *Rhode Island History* 37(3):67–83.

Carr, Lloyd G., and Carlos Westey. 1945. Surviving Folktales and Herbal Lore among the Shinnecock Indians of Long Island. *Journal of American Folklore* 58(228):113–23.

Chaffin, William L. 1886. *History of the Town of Easton, Massachusetts*. Cambridge, Mass.: John Wilson and Son.

Chapin, Howard M. 1931. *Sachems of the Narragansetts*. Providence: Rhode Island Historical Society.

Church, Thomas. [1716] 1827. *History of Philip's War, Commonly Called the Great Indian War, of 1675 and 1676*. Reprint. Boston: J. H. A. Frost.

Clough, Ben C. 1918. Legends of Chappaquiddick. *Journal of American Folklore* 31(122): 553–54.

Cobb, D. J. 1926. Two Indian Chiefs of Mashpee. *Cape Cod Magazine*, August 16: 10, 26, 30.

Colby, Lewis. 1983. Conversation, February, Cranston, R.I.

Colson, Elizabeth. [1953] 1974. *The Makah Indians: A Study of an Indian Tribe in Modern American Society*. Reprint. Westport, Conn.: Greenwood Press.

Commuck, Thomas. 1845. *Indian Melodies*. New York: G. Lane & C. B. Tippett.

————. 1855. Sketch of Calumet County. *Collections of the State Historical Society of Wisconsin* 1:103–6.

———. 1859. Sketch of the Brothertown Indians. *Collections of the State Historical Society of Wisconsin* 4:291–98.

Conkey, Laura E., Ethel Boissevain, and Ives Goddard. 1978. Indians of Southern New England and Long Island: Late Period. In *Handbook of North American Indians: Northeast*, vol. 15, William C. Sturtevant, series ed., Bruce Trigger, vol. ed., pp. 177–89. Washington, D.C.: Smithsonian Institution.

Cook, S. F. 1976. *The Indian Population of New England in the Seventeenth Century*. Berkeley: University of California Press.

Corbett, Scott. 1955. *Cape Cod's Way*. New York: Thomas Y. Crowell Company.

Cushman, Robert. [1622] 1910. The Sin and Danger of Self Love. In *Chronicles of the Pilgrim Fathers*, John Masefield, ed., pp. 229–40. Reprint. New York: E. P. Dutton & Co.

Davies, T. A. 1937. Folklore of Gwent: Monmouthshire Legends and Traditions. *Folk-Lore* 48:41–59.

Day, Gordon. 1972. Oral Tradition as Complement. *Ethnohistory* 19(2):99–108.

———. 1976. The Western Abenaki Transformer. *Journal of the Folklore Institute* 13(1):75–89.

De Forest, John W. 1853. *History of the Indians of Connecticut from the Earliest Known Period to 1850*. Hartford, Conn.: Wm. Jas. Hamersley.

Dégh, Linda. 1971. The "Belief Legend" in Modern Society: Form, Function, and Relationship to Other Genres. In *American Folk Legend: A Symposium*, Wayland D. Hand, ed., pp. 55–68. Berkeley: University of California Press.

———. 1978. The Legend and the Sparrow. In *Studies in Turkish Folklore*, Ilhan Basgoz and Mark Glazer, eds., pp. 78–88. Indiana University Turkish Studies, no. 1. Bloomington: Indiana University Press.

Dégh, Linda, and Andrew Vázsonyi. 1974. The Memorate and the Proto-Memorate. *Journal of American Folklore* 87(345):225–39.

———. 1976. Legend and Belief. In *Folklore Genres*, Dan Ben-Amos, ed., pp. 93–123. Austin: University of Texas Press.

Demos, John Putnam. 1982. *Entertaining Satan: Witchcraft and the Culture of Early New England*. New York: Oxford University Press.

Denison, Frederic. 1878. *Westerly (Rhode Island) and its Witnesses*. Providence, R.I.: J. A. and R. A. Reid.

Denton, Daniel. 1670. *A Brief Description of New York, Formerly Called New-Netherlands*. London: Tho. Hancock.

A Description of Mashpee, in the County of Barnstable. 1815. *Collections of the Massachusetts Historical Society* 3, 2d series:1–12. Written in 1802.

The Devil's Bridge. Ca. 1900. Manuscript in the Dukes County Historical Society Library, Edgartown, Mass.

Digges, Jeremiah. 1937. *Cape Cod Pilot*. Provincetown and New York: Modern Pilgrim Press and Viking Press.

Dincauze, Dena F. 1968. Cremation Cemeteries in Eastern Massachusetts. Cambridge, Mass.: Papers of the Peabody Museum of Archaeology and Ethnology, Harvard University, vol. 59, no. 1.

———. 1976. *The Neville Site: 8,000 Years at Amoskeag, Manchester, New Hampshire*. Cambridge, Mass.: Peabody Museum of Archaeology and Ethnology, Harvard University.

Dixon, Roland B. 1909. The Mythology of the Central and Eastern Algonkins. *Journal of American Folklore* 22(83):1–9.

Dorson, Richard M. 1946. *Jonathan Draws the Long Bow.* Cambridge, Mass.: Harvard University Press.

———. 1973. *America in Legend: Folklore from the Colonial Period to the Present.* New York: Pantheon Books.

Douglas, Mary. 1970. Introduction: Thiry Years after *Witchcraft, Oracles, and Magic.* In *Witchcraft Confessions and Accusations,* Mary Douglas, ed., pp. xiii–xxxviii. London: Tavistock Publications.

Dundes, Alan. 1962. From Etic to Emic Units in the Structural Study of Folktales. *Journal of American Folklore* 75(296):95–105.

———. 1964. *The Morphology of North American Indian Folktales.* Helsinki: Academia Scientiarum Fennica.

———. 1971. On the Psychology of Legend. In *American Folk Legend: A Symposium,* Wayland D. Hand, ed., pp. 21–36. Berkeley: University of California Press.

———. 1983. Defining Identity through Folklore. In *Identity: Personal and Socio-Cultural,* Anita Jacobson-Widding, ed., pp. 235–61. Atlantic Highlands, N.J.: Humanities Press, Inc.

Dykes, Hannah S. B. [1920.] History of Richard Bourne and Some of His Descendants. Cleveland: Benjamin F. Bourne.

Earle, John M. 1862. *Report to the Governor and Council Concerning the Indians of the Commonwealth.* Massachusetts House Document No. 215.

Eliot, John, and Thomas Mayhew. [1653] 1834. Tears of Repentance: Or a Further Narrative of the Progress of the Gospel Amongst the Indians in New-England. Reprint. *Collections of the Massachusetts Historical Society* 4, 3d series, pp. 197–260.

Ellis, George W., and John E. Morris. 1906. *King Philip's War.* New York: Grafton Press.

Emerson, Alice Forbes. 1964. *Three Islands: Pasque, Nashawena, and Penikese.* Private printing.

Emerson, Amelia Forbes. 1935. *Early History of Naushon Island.* Boston: Private printing.

Emerson, Ellen Russell. 1884. *Indian Myths.* Boston: James R. Osgood and Company.

Fawcett, Melissa. 1984. The role of Gladys Tantaquidgeon. In *Papers of the Fifteenth Algonquian Conference,* William Cowan, ed., pp. 135–45. Ottawa: Carleton University.

Federal Writers Project. 1937. *Massachusetts: A Guide to its Places and People.* Boston: Houghton, Mifflin and Company.

Fireside Stories. 1936. *Narragansett Dawn* 1(9):205–8.

Fisher, Margaret W. 1946. The Mythology of the Northern and Northeastern Algonkians in Reference to Algonkian Mythology as a Whole. In *Man in Northeastern North America,* Frederick Johnson, ed., pp. 226–62. Andover, Mass.: Papers of the Robert S. Peabody Foundation for Archaeology 3.

Fitting, James E. 1978. Regional Cultural Development, 300 B.C. to A.D. 1000. In *Handbook of North American Indians: Northeast,* vol. 15, William C. Sturtevant, series ed., Bruce Trigger, vol. ed., pp. 44–57. Washington, D.C.: Smithsonian Institution.

Flanagan, John T. 1939. A Pioneer in Indian Folklore: James Athearn Jones. *New England Quarterly* 12(3):443–53.

Flannery, Regina. 1947. Algonquian Indian Folklore. *Journal of American Folklore* 60(238):397–401.

Folger, Eva C. G. 1911. *Nantucket: The Glacier's Gift*. New Haven: Tuttle, Morehouse, and Taylor Company.

Foster, George. 1967. *Tzintzuntzan: Mexican Peasants in a Changing World*. Boston: Little, Brown and Company.

Fox, George. 1952. *The Journal of George Fox*. John L. Nickalls, ed. Cambridge: Cambridge University Press. Written in 1672.

Freeman, Frederick. 1869. *The History of Cape Cod: Annals of the Thirteen Towns of Barnstable County*. Vol. 1. Boston: W. H. Piper and Co.

[Freeman, James.] 1815a. A Description of Duke's County, 1807. *Collections of the Massachusetts Historical Society* 3, 2d series: 38–94.

―――. 1815b. Notes on Nantucket, 1807. *Collections of the Massachusetts Historical Society* 3, 2d series: 19–38.

Funk, Robert E. 1978. Post-Pleistocene Adaptations. In *Handbook of North American Indians: Northeast*, vol. 15, William C. Sturtevant, series ed., Bruce Trigger, vol. ed., pp. 16–27. Washington, D.C.: Smithsonian Institution.

Gardiner, J. Warren. 1883. The Pioneers of Narragansett. *Narragansett Historical Register* 2(2):112–15.

Gatschet, Albert S. 1899. The Deities of the Early New England Indians. *Journal of American Folklore* 12(46):211–12.

―――. 1973. Narragansett Vocabulary Collected in 1879. *International Journal of American Linguistics* 39(1):14.

Gibson, Susan G., ed. 1980. *Burr's Hill: A 17th Century Wampanoag Burial Ground in Warren, Rhode Island*. Studies in Anthropology and Material Culture, vol. 2. Providence, R.I.: Haffenreffer Museum of Anthropology, Brown University.

Goddard, Ives. 1978. Eastern Algonquian Languages. In *Handbook of North American Indians: Northeast*, vol. 15, William C. Sturtevant, series ed., Bruce Trigger, vol. ed., pp. 70–77. Washington, D.C.: Smithsonian Institution.

Gookin, Daniel. 1836. An Historical Account of the Doings and Sufferings of the Christian Indians in New England, in the Years 1675, 1676, 1677. *Transactions and Collections of the American Antiquarian Society* 2:423–534.

―――. [1792] 1970. *Historical Collections of the Indians in New England*. Jeffrey H. Fiske, ed. Reprint. [No place]: Towtaid.

Grumet, Robert S. 1980. Sunksquaws, Shamans, and Tradeswomen: Middle Atlantic Coastal Algonkian Women during the 17th and 18th Centuries. In *Women and Colonization: Anthropological Perspectives*, Mona Etienne and Eleanor Leacock, eds., pp. 43–62. New York: Praeger Scientific.

―――. 1981. *Native American Place Names in New York City*. New York: Museum of the City of New York.

Hallowell, Irving A. 1967. *Culture and Experience*. New York: Schocken Books.

Halpert, Herbert. 1957. Three Maine Legends. *Journal of American Folklore* 70(276):182–83.

———. 1971. Definition and Variation in Folk Legend. In *American Folk Legend: A Symposium*, Wayland D. Hand, ed., pp. 47–54. Berkeley: University of California Press.

Hand, Wayland D. 1965. Status of European and American Legend Study. *Current Anthropology* 6(4):439–46.

———. 1977. Will-o'-the-Wisps, Jack-o'-Lanterns and Their Congeners: A Consideration of the Fiery and Luminous Creatures of the Lower Mythology. *Fabula* 18(3/4):226–33.

———. 1981. European Fairy Lore in the New World. *Folklore* 92(2):141–48.

Hand, Wayland, Anna Casetta, and Sondra B. Thiederman, eds. 1981. *Popular Beliefs and Superstitions: A Compendium of American Folklore*. Vol. 3. Boston: G. K. Hall and Company.

Harland, John, and T. T. Wilkinson. 1873. *Lancashire Legends, Traditions, Pageants, Sports, Etc.* London: George Routledge and Sons.

Harrington, M. R. 1921. *Religion and Ceremonies of the Lenape*. Indian Notes and Monographs. New York: Museum of the American Indian, Heye Foundation.

Hatch, Moses. [1816] 1948. *Family Memoirs Written for the Use of His Children*. New Haven: Private printing.

Hawley, Gideon. 1795. Letter. In *Collections of the Massachusetts Historical Society for the Year 1795* 4:50–67. Written in 1794.

Hebard, Learned, Thomas Kingsbury, and Henry Haven. 1861. *Report of the Commissioners on Distribution of Lands of the Mohegan Indians*. Hartford, Conn.: Printed by Order of the Legislature.

Hedges, Henry P. 1897. *A History of the Town of East-Hampton, N.Y.* Sag Harbor, N.Y.: J. H. Hunt.

Hine, C. G. 1908. *The Story of Martha's Vineyard*. New York: Hine Brothers.

Hobsbawm, Eric. 1983. Introduction: Inventing Traditions. In *The Invention of Tradition*, Eric Hobsbawm and Terence Ranger, eds., pp. 1–14. Cambridge: Cambridge University Press.

Homtas. 1829. Legend of Nantucket. *Nantucket Inquirer* 9 (February 28):2.

Honko, Lauri. 1964. Memorates and the Study of Folk Beliefs. *Journal of the Folklore Institute* 1(1–2):5–19.

———. 1965. On the Functional Analysis of Folk-Beliefs and Narratives about Empirical Supernatural Beings. *Laographia* 22:168–73.

———. 1968. Genre Analysis in Folkloristics and Comparative Religion. *Temenos* 3:48–66.

Hopkins, Samuel. [1753] 1911. Historical Memoirs Relating to the Housatonic Indians. Reprint. *Magazine of History Extra*, no. 17, New York.

Hosmore, Stephen. 1895. Letter to Rev. Thomas Prince, 1729. *Collections of the Connecticut Historical Society* 3:280–81.

How the Fogs Came to the Cape. 1915. *Cape Cod Magazine* 1(1):15–16.

Hubbard, William. [1865] 1969. *The History of the Indian Wars in New England*. Vols. 1 and 2. Samuel G. Drake, ed. Roxbury: W. Elliot Woodward. Reprinted by Kraus Reprint Co., New York. First edition published in 1677.

Huden, John C. 1962. *Indian Place Names of New England*. New York: Museum of the American Indian, Heye Foundation.

Hughes, Langston, and Arna Bontemps, eds. 1958. *The Book of Negro Folklore*. New York: Dodd, Mead, and Company.

Hultkrantz, Åke. 1957. *The North American Indian Orpheus Tradition: A Contribution to Comparative Religion.* Stockholm: Ethnographical Museum of Sweden.

————. 1983. Water Sprites: The Elders of the Fish in Aboriginal North America. *American Indian Quarterly* 7(3):1–22.

Huntington, Gale. 1969. *An Introduction to Martha's Vineyard, and a Guided Tour of the Island.* Edgartown, Mass.: Dukes County Historical Society.

————. 1980. Letter to W. Simmons, April 5.

Huntoon, Daniel T. 1893. *History of the Town of Canton, Norfolk County, Massachusetts.* Cambridge, Mass.: J. Wilson and Son.

Hurley, Gerard. 1951. Buried Treasure Tales in America. *Western Folklore* 10(3):197–216.

Hutchins, Francis G. 1979. *Mashpee: The Story of Cape Cod's Indian Town.* West Franklin, N.H.: Amarta Press.

The Indian Powow, or Deception Rewarded. 1848. *New England Historical and Genealogical Register* 2(1):44.

Ishonowa. 1935. Christian Indian Homes. *Narragansett Dawn* 1(8):178–79.

Jagendorf, M. 1948. *New England Bean-Pot: American Folk Stories to Read and to Tell.* New York: Vanguard Press.

Jenks, Samuel. 1827. The Tradition of the Taumkhods. *New England Galaxy* 10(486): February 2.

Jennings, Francis. 1975. *The Invasion of America: Indians, Colonialism, and the Cant of Conquest.* Chapel Hill: University of North Carolina Press.

Johnson, Clifton. 1897. *What They Say in New England: A Book of Signs, Sayings, and Superstitions.* Boston: Lee and Shepard Publishers.

Johnson, Edward. [1654] 1910. *Johnson's Wonder Working Providence, 1628–1651.* J. Franklin Jameson, ed. Reprint. New York: Charles Scribner's Sons.

Jones, James Athearn. 1826. Indian Traditions: The Creation of Nantucket. *United States Literary Gazette* 4(9 and 10):357–61.

————. 1829. *Tales of an Indian Camp.* 3 vols. London: Henry Colburn and Richard Bentley.

————. 1830. *Traditions of the North American Indians, Being a Second and Revised Edition of "Tales of an Indian Camp."* 3 vols. London: Henry Colburn and Richard Bentley.

Jones, Louis C. 1944. The Ghosts of New York: An Analytical Study. *Journal of American Folklore* 57(226):237–54.

————. 1982. *Three Eyes on the Past: Exploring New York Folk Life.* Syracuse: Syracuse University Press.

Josselyn, John. [1675] 1833. An Account of Two Voyages to New-England. Reprint. *Collections of the Massachusetts Historical Society* 3, 3d series: 211–396.

Keene, Betsey D. [1937] 1975. *History of Bourne from 1622 to 1937.* Reprint. Bourne Historical Society.

Kendall, Edward Augustus. 1809. *Travels through the Northern Parts of the United States in the Years 1807 and 1808, II.* New York: L. Riley.

Kittredge, George L., ed. [1690–91] 1913. Letters of Samuel Lee and Samuel Sewall Relating to New England and the Indians. Reprint. *Publications of the Colonial Society of Massachusetts* 14 (Transactions 1911–13):142–86.

————. [1929] 1972. *Witchcraft in Old and New England*. Reprint. New York: Atheneum.

Knight, Mabel F. 1925. Wampanoag Indian Tales. *Journal of American Folklore* 38(147):134–37.

Leach, Douglas E. 1963. *A Rhode Islander Reports on King Philip's War: The Second William Harris Letter of August, 1676*. Providence: Rhode Island Historical Society.

————. 1966. *Flintlock and Tomahawk: New England in King Philip's War*. New York: W. W. Norton & Company.

Leather, Ella M. 1912. *The Folk-Lore of Herefordshire: Collected from Oral and Printed Sources*. London: Sidgwick and Jackson.

Lechford, Thomas. [1642] 1867. Plain Dealing: Or, News From New-England. J. Hammond Trumbull, ed. Reprint. Boston: J. K. Wiggin & Wm. Parsons Lunt.

The Legend of Scargo Lake. 1922. *Cape Cod and All the Pilgrim Land*, January:10–11.

Leland, Charles G. 1898. The Algonquin Legends of New England. Boston and New York: Houghton, Mifflin and Company.

Leland, Charles G., and John D. Prince. 1902. Kuloskap the Master: And Other Algonkin Poems. New York: Funk and Wagnalls Company.

Lévi-Strauss, Claude. 1962. La pensée sauvage. Paris: Librairie Plon.

Levitas, Gloria. 1980. No Boundary Is a Boundary: Conflict and Change in a New England Indian Community. Ph.D. diss., Rutgers University. Ann Arbor, University Microfilms International.

Lindow, John. 1978. Rites of Passage in Scandinavian Legends. *Fabula* 19(1 and 2):40–61.

————. 1982. Swedish Legends of Buried Treasure. *Journal of American Folklore* 95(377):257–79.

Litchfield, Henry W. 1909. *Ancient Landmarks of Pembroke*. Pembroke, Mass.: George Edward Lewis.

Little, Elizabeth. 1982a. Drift Whales at Nantucket: The Kindness of Moshup. *Man in the Northeast* 23:17–38.

————. 1982b. Indian Politics on Nantucket. In *Papers of the Thirteenth Algonquian Conference*, William Cowan, ed., pp. 285–97. Ottawa: Carleton University.

Lone Wolf. 1936a. Good Luck. *Narragansett Dawn* 1(11):266.

————. 1936b. On the Tracks. *Narragansett Dawn* 1(11):264–65.

Longfellow, Henry W. [1855] 1955. *The Song of Hiawatha*. Reprint. Grand Rapids, Mich.: Wm. B. Eerdmans Publishing Co.

Love, W. DeLoss. 1899. *Samson Occom and the Christian Indians of New England*. Boston and Chicago: Pilgrim Press.

Lowie, Robert H. 1908. The Test Theme in North American Mythology. *Journal of American Folklore* 21(81–82):97–148.

Madison, Nanetta Vanderhoop. 1955. Manuscript of Gay Head pageant, in possession of Leonard Vanderhoop of Gay Head. Typescript.

Malinowski, Bronislaw. [1922] 1961. *Argonauts of the Western Pacific: An Account of Native Enterprise and Adventure in the Archipelagoes of Melanesian New Guinea*. Reprint. New York: E. P. Dutton & Co.

Manning, Ada. 1983. Interview, April 6, Gay Head, Mass.

Mars, Harold. 1983. Interview, April 20, June 30, Charlestown, R.I.

Mars, Laura. 1983. Interview, April 20, June 30, Charlestown, R.I.

Marten, Catherine. 1970. The Wampanoags in the Seventeenth Century: An Ethnohistorical Survey. Occasional Papers in Old Colony Studies, no. 2. Plimoth Plantation.

Mason, John. 1736. A Brief History of the Pequot War: Especially of the Memorable Taking of Their Fort at Mistick in Connecticut in 1637. Boston: S. Kneeland and T. Green.

Mason, Samuel. 1867. Expedition from New London to Woodstock, Conn., February 1699/1700. Massachusetts Historical Society Proceedings, 1866–1867:473–78.

Mather, Cotton. [1702] 1820. Magnalia Christi Americana: Or, the Ecclesiastical History of New-England, From its First Planting in the Year 1620, Unto the Year of Our Lord, 1698. Vols. 1 and 2. Reprint. Hartford, Conn.: Silas Andrus.

Mather, Increase. [1676] 1862. The History of King Philip's War. Samuel G. Drake, ed. Reprint. Boston: Printed for the Editor.

———. [1677] 1864. Early History of New England; Being a Relation of Hostile Passages Between the Indians and European Voyagers and First Settlers. Samuel G. Drake, ed. Reprint. Albany: J. Munsell.

———. [1684] 1890. Remarkable Providences Illustrative of the Earlier Days of American Colonisation. Reprint. London: Reeves and Turner.

Mayhew, Eleanor R., ed. 1956. Martha's Vineyard: A Short History. Edgartown, Mass.: Dukes County Historical Society.

Mayhew, Experience. 1727. Indian Converts: Or, Some Account of the Lives and Dying Speeches of a Considerable Number of the Christianized Indians of Martha's Vineyard, in New-England. London: Samuel Gerrish.

Mayhew, Matthew. 1694. A Brief Narrative of the Success Which the Gospel Hath Had Among the Indians. Boston: B. Green.

Mazer, Rona Sur. 1980. Town and Tribe in Conflict: A Study of Local-Level Politics in Mashpee, Massachusetts. Ph.D. diss., Columbia University. Ann Arbor, University Microfilms International.

Melanson, Donald. 1983. Interview, April 6, Gay Head, Mass.

Melville, Herman. [1851] 1956. Moby-Dick or, The Whale. Reprint. Boston: Houghton Mifflin Company.

Morton, Nathaniel. [1669] 1826. New England's Memorial. Reprint. Boston: Crocker and Brewster.

Morton, Thomas. [1632] 1947. New English Canaan; or, New Canaan, Containing an Abstract of New England. Reprint. New York: Peter Smith.

Motz, Lotte. 1982. Giants in Folklore and Mythology: A New Approach. Folklore 93(1):70–84.

Narragansett Tribe of Indians. 1880. Report of the Committee of Investigation. Providence, R.I.: E. L. Freeman and Co.

Neesqutton. 1935. The Children of Gitche Manitou. Narragansett Dawn 1(8):187–89.

New England's First Fruits. 1643. London: R. O. and G. D. for Henry Overton.

Nosapocket. 1981. Interview, July 9, Mashpee, Mass.

Occom, Samson. 1809. An Account of the Montauk Indians, on Long-Island. Collections of the Massachusetts Historical Society 10:105–11. Written in 1761.

The Old Mohegan Indian Stone Cutter. Ca. 1960. Newsletter of the Federated East Indian League.
Origin of the Island of Nantucket: An Indian Tradition. 1787. *Columbian Magazine*, July:525.
Orr, Charles, ed. 1897. *History of the Pequot War.* Cleveland: Helman-Taylor Company.
Overton, Jacqueline. 1941. Indian Legends Collected and Retold. *Long Island Forum* 4(9):213–14, 220.
———. [1938] 1963. *Indian Life on Long Island: Family, Work, Play, Legends, Heroes.* Reprint. Port Washington: I. J. Friedman.
Paredes, J. Anthony, ed. 1980. *Anishinabe: 6 Studies of Modern Chippewa.* Tallahassee: University Presses of Florida.
Parsons, Elsie C. 1923. Folk-Lore from the Cape Verde Islands, I. In *Memoirs of the American Folklore Society XV, I.* Cambridge, Mass.: American Folk-Lore Society.
Peale, Arthur L. 1939. *Uncas and the Mohegan-Pequot.* Boston: Meador Publishing Company.
Pease, Richard L. 1871. *Report of the Commissioner Appointed to Complete the Examination and Determination of All Questions of Title to Land . . . at Gay Head.* Boston: Wright & Potter.
———. 1881. James Athearn Jones. In *Memorial Biographies of the New England Historic Genealogical Society*, vol. 2, pp. 204–22. Boston: Published by the society.
Peirce, Ebenezer W. 1878. *Indian History, Biography and Genealogy: Pertaining to the Good Sachem Massasoit of the Wampanoag Tribe, and His Descendants.* North Abington, Mass.: Z. G. Mitchell.
Pentikäinen, Juha. 1973. Belief, Memorate, and Legend. *Folklore Forum* 6(4):217–41.
Preston, Richard J. 1975. *Cree Narrative: Expressing the Personal Meanings of Events.* Ottawa: National Museum of Man Mercury Series.
Prince, J. Dyneley. 1899. Some Passamaquoddy Witchcraft Tales. *Proceedings of the American Philosophical Society* 38:181–89.
———. 1907. Last Living Echoes of the Natick. *American Anthropologist* 9(3):493–98.
Prince, J. Dyneley, and Frank G. Speck. 1903. The Modern Pequots and Their Language. *American Anthropologist*, new series, 5(2):193–212.
———. 1904. Glossary of the Mohegan-Pequot Language. *American Anthropologist*, new series, 6(1):18–45.
Propp, V. [1928] 1979. *Morphology of the Folktale.* Reprint. Austin: University of Texas Press.
Puckett, Newbell N. [1926] 1968. *Folk Beliefs of the Southern Negro.* Reprint. Montclair, N.J.: Patterson Smith.
Quinn, David B. 1981. *Sources for the Ethnography of Northeastern North America to 1611.* Ottawa: National Museum of Man Mercury Series.
Rand, Silas T. 1894. *Legends of the Micmacs.* New York and London: Longmans, Green, and Co.
Rasieres, Isaack de. [Ca. 1628] 1963. Isaack de Rasieres to Samuel Blommaert. Reprint. In *Three Visitors to Early Plymouth*, Sydney V. James, ed., pp. 63–80. Plimoth Plantation.
Redmond, Philip. 1899. Some Wexford Folklore. *Folk-Lore* 10(3):362–64.

Red Wing. 1935. Tradition: Youth Learns the Mysteries of Life from Gitche Manitou, the Great Spirit. *Narragansett Dawn* 1(1):25–27.
———. 1936. Editorial. *Narragansett Dawn* 2(2):20.
Relates the Tales of His Indian Ancestors: David Vanderhoop Tells Them with Veneration and Humour, From the Time of Moshup. 1955. *Vineyard Gazette*, March 25.
Reynard, Elizabeth. 1934. *The Narrow Land: Folk Chronicles of Old Cape Cod*. Boston and New York: Houghton Mifflin Company.
Rickels, Patricia K. 1979. Some Accounts of Witch Riding. In *Readings in American Folklore*, Jan H. Brunvand, ed., pp. 53–63. New York: W. W. Norton and Company.
Ritchie, William A. 1969. *The Archaeology of Martha's Vineyard*. Garden City: Natural History Press.
Robbins, Maurice. 1960. *Wapanucket No. 6: An Archaic Village in Middleboro, Massachusetts*. Attleboro: Cohannet Chapter, Massachusetts Archaeological Society.
Ronda, James P. 1981. Generations of Faith: The Christian Indians of Martha's Vineyard. *William and Mary Quarterly*, 3d series, 38(3):369–94.
Rothery, Agnes. 1918. *Cape Cod New and Old*. Boston and New York: Houghton Mifflin Company.
Rowlandson, Mary. [1682] 1913. Narrative of the Captivity of Mrs. Mary Rowlandson. In *Narratives of the Indian Wars, 1675–1699*, Charles H. Lincoln, ed., pp. 107–67. New York: Charles Scribner's Sons.
Russell, Howard S. 1980. *Indian New England before the Mayflower*. Hanover, N.H.: University Press of New England.
Salisbury, Neal. 1974. Red Puritans: The "Praying Indians" of Massachusetts Bay and John Eliot. *William and Mary Quarterly*, 3d series, 31(1):27–54.
———. 1981. Squanto: Last of the Patuxets. In *Struggle and Survival in Colonial America*, David G. Sweet and Gary B. Nash, eds., pp. 228–46. Berkeley: University of California Press.
———. 1982. *Manitou and Providence: Indians, Europeans, and the Making of New England, 1500–1643*. Oxford: Oxford University Press.
[Saltonstall, Nathaniel]. [1675] 1867. *The Present State of New-England with Respect to the Indian War*. Reprint. In *The Old Indian Chronicle*, Samuel G. Drake, ed., pp. 119–69. Boston: Samuel A. Drake.
Salwen, Bert. 1978. Indians of Southern New England and Long Island: Early Period. In *Handbook of North American Indians: Northeast*, vol. 15, William C. Sturtevant, ed., Bruce Trigger, vol. ed., pp. 160–76. Washington, D.C.: Smithsonian Institution.
Sapir, Edward. 1924. Culture, Genuine and Spurious. *American Journal of Sociology* 29:401–29.
Scaglion, Richard. 1974. The Moshop Tale: A Chronological Analysis of a Wampanoag Myth. *Dukes County Intelligencer* 16(1):19–26.
Schoolcraft, Henry R. 1846. Moshop; Or, The Giant of Nopee. In *The Opal: A Pure Gift for the Holy Days*, John Keese, ed., pp. 197–201. New York: J. C. Riker.
———. 1857. *History of the Indian Tribes of the United States: Their Present Condition and Prospects, and a Sketch of their Ancient Status, VI*. Philadelphia: J. B. Lippincott and Co.
Scoville, Dorothy R. 1970. *Indian Legends of Martha's Vineyard*. Edgartown, Mass.: Dukes County Historical Society.

Seketau, Ella Thomas. 1974. Personal communication.

———. 1984. Interview, June 10, Charlestown, R.I.

Sheldon, George. 1895. *A History of Deerfield, Massachusetts.* Vol. 1. Deerfield: Pocumtuck Valley Memorial Association.

Shepard, Thomas. [1648] 1834. The Clear Sun-Shine of the Gospel Breaking Forth upon the Indians in New England. Reprint. *Collections of the Massachusetts Historical Society* 4, 3d series, pp. 25–67.

Sikes, Wirt. 1881. *British Goblins: Welsh Folk-Lore, Fairy Mythology, Legends and Traditions.* Boston: James R. Osgood and Company.

Silva, Wenonah. 1981. Interview, March 24, Gay Head, Mass.

———. 1983. Interview, April 6, Gay Head, Mass.

Simmons, William S. 1970. *Cautantowwit's House: An Indian Burial Ground on the Island of Conanicut in Narragansett Bay.* Providence, R.I.: Brown University Press.

———. 1971. *Eyes of the Night: Witchcraft among a Senegalese People.* Boston: Little, Brown and Company.

———. 1978. Narrangansett. In *Handbook of North American Indians: Northeast,* vol. 15, William C. Sturtevant, series ed., Bruce Trigger, vol. ed., pp. 190–97. Washington, D.C.: Smithsonian Institution.

———. 1979a. Conversion from Indian to Puritan. *New England Quarterly* 52(2):197–218.

———. 1979b. The Great Awakening and Indian Conversion in Southern New England. In *Papers of the Tenth Algonquian Conference,* William Cowan, ed., pp. 25–36. Ottawa: Carleton University.

———. 1980. Powerlessness, Exploitation, and the Soul-Eating Witch: An Analysis of Badyaranke Witchcraft. *American Ethnologist* 7(3):447–65.

———. 1981. Cultural Bias in the New England Puritans' Perception of Indians. *William and Mary Quarterly,* 3d series 38(1):56–72.

———. 1982a. The Earliest Prints and Paintings of New England Indians. *Rhode Island History* 41(3):73–85.

———. 1982b. Return of the Timid Giant: Algonquian Legends of Southern New England. In *Papers of the Thirteenth Algonquian Conference,* William Cowan, ed., pp. 237–42. Ottawa: Carleton University.

———. 1983. Red Yankees: Narragansett Conversion in the Great Awakening. *American Ethnologist* 10(2):253–71.

Simmons, William S., and Cheryl L. Simmons, eds. 1982. *Old Light on Separate Ways: The Narragansett Diary of Joseph Fish, 1765–1776.* Hanover, N.H.: University Press of New England.

Skinner, Charles M. 1896. *Myths and Legends of Our Own Land, II.* Philadelphia: J. B. Lippincott Company.

———. 1903. *American Myths and Legends, I.* Philadelphia: J. B. Lippincott Company.

Smith, Charles H. 1904. The Last of the Niantics. *Connecticut Magazine* 8(3):455–56.

Smith, John. 1910. *Travels and Works of Captain John Smith, President of Virginia, and Admiral of New England, 1580–1631.* Part 2. Edward Arber, ed. Edinburgh: J. Grant.

Smith, Joseph H. 1950. *Appeals to the Privy Council from the American Plantations.* New York: Columbia University Press.

Snow, Dean R. 1978. Late Prehistory of the East Coast. In *Handbook of North American Indians: Northeast,* vol. 15, William C. Sturtevant, series ed.,

Bruce Trigger, vol. ed., pp. 58–69. Washington, D.C.: Smithsonian Institution.

———. 1980. *The Archaeology of New England*. New York: Academic Press.

Soper, Grace W. 1890. Among the Friendly Indians at Mashpee. *New England Magazine*, new series, 2(3):277–79.

Speck, Frank G. 1903a. "The Last of the Mohegans." *Papoose* 1(4):2–5.

———. 1903b. Mohegan Traditions of "Muhkeahweesug," The Little Men. *Papoose* 1(7):11–14.

———. 1903c. A Pequot-Mohegan Witchcraft Tale. *Journal of American Folklore* 16:(61): 104–6.

———. 1903d. The Remnants of Our Eastern Indian Tribes. *American Inventor* 10:266–68.

———. 1904a. A Modern Mohegan-Pequot Text. *American Anthropologist*, new series, 6(4):469–76.

———. 1904b. Some Mohegan-Pequot Legends. *Journal of American Folklore* 17(66):183–84.

———. 1909. Notes on the Mohegan and Niantic Indians. In *The Indians of Greater New York and the Lower Hudson*, Clark Wissler, ed., pp. 181–210. Anthropological Papers, vol. 3. New York: American Museum of Natural History.

———. 1915a. Decorative Art of Indian Tribes of Connecticut. Geological Survey, Memoir 75, no. 10, Anthropological Series. Ottawa: Canadian Department of Mines.

———. 1915b. Medicine Practices of the Northeastern Algonquians. In *Proceedings of the Nineteenth International Congress of Americanists*, F. W. Hodge, ed., pp. 303–21. Washington, D.C.

———. 1918. Remnants of the Nehantics. *Southern Workman*, February: 65–71.

———. 1919. Penobscot Shamanism. *Memoirs of the American Anthropological Association* 6(4):237–88. Lancaster, Pa.

———. 1928a. Mythology of the Wampanoags. *El Palacio* 25(3,4,5):83–86.

———. 1928b. Native Tribes and Dialects of Connecticut: A Mohegan-Pequot Diary. In *Forty-third Annual Report of the Bureau of American Ethnology, 1925–1926*, pp. 199–287. Washington, D.C.: Government Printing Office.

———. 1928c. *Territorial Subdivisions and Boundaries of the Wampanoag, Massachusett, and Nauset Indians*. Indian Notes and Monographs 44. New York: Museum of the American Indian, Heye Foundation.

———. 1935. Penobscot Tales and Religious Beliefs. *Journal of American Folklore* 48(187):1–107.

———. [1940] 1976. *Penobscot Man: The Life History of a Forest Tribe in Maine*. Reprint. New York: Octagon Books.

Speck, Frank G., and Ralph W. Dexter. 1948. Utilization of Marine Life by the Wampanoag Indians of Massachusetts. *Journal of the Washington Academy of Sciences* 38(8):257–65.

Spicer, Edward H. 1971. Persistent Cultural Systems: A Comparative Study of Identity Systems That Can Adapt to Contrasting Environments. *Science* 174(4011):795–800.

———. 1980. *The Yaquis: A Cultural History*. Tucson: University of Arizona Press.

Stamp, Harley. 1915. The Water Fairies. *Journal of American Folklore* 28(109):310–16.

Stiles, Ezra. 1901. *The Literary Diary of Ezra Stiles, DD., LL.D.* Vols. 1 and 3. Franklin B. Dexter, ed. New York: Charles Scribner's Sons.

———. 1916. *Extracts from the Itineraries and Other Miscellanies of Ezra Stiles, D.D., LL.D., 1755–1794.* Franklin B. Dexter, ed. New Haven: Yale University Press.

Swift, Charles F. 1884. *History of Old Yarmouth.* Yarmouth Port: Published by the author.

Taft, Donald R. 1923. *Two Portuguese Communities in New England.* Studies in History, no. 107. New York: Columbia University Press.

Talcott, John. [1677] 1934. *A Letter Written by Maj. John Talcott from Mr. Stanton's at Quonocontaug.* William D. Miller, ed. Reprint. Providence, R.I.: Society of Colonial Wars.

Tantaquidgeon, Gladys. 1928. Manuscript field notes, Gay Head, Mass.

———. 1928–29. Manuscript field notes, Mashpee, Mass.

———. 1930a. Newly Discovered Straw Basketry of the Wampanoag Indians of Massachusetts. *Indian Notes* 7(4):475–83.

———. 1930b. Notes on the Gay Head Indians of Massachusetts. *Indian Notes* 7(1):1–26.

———. 1935. Location, History, Government, Language, Etc. of the Mashpee Indians. Office of Indian Affairs. Typescript.

———. 1972. *Folk Medicine of the Delaware and Related Algonkian Indians.* Harrisburg: Pennsylvania Historical and Museum Commission.

———. 1981. Tantaquidgeon Indian Museum. Privately published brochure.

Taylor, Theodore W. 1972. The States and Their Indian Citizens. U.S. Department of the Interior. Washington, D.C.: Government Printing Office.

Thompson, Stith. 1919. *European Tales among the North American Indians.* Colorado Springs: Colorado College Publications, Language Series.

———. 1955–58. *Motif Index of Folk-Literature.* 6 vols. Copenhagen: Rosenkilde and Bagger.

———. [1929] 1966. *Tales of the North American Indians.* Reprint. Bloomington: Indiana University Press.

Thoresen, Timothy H. 1973. Folkloristics in A. L. Kroeber's Early Theory of Culture. *Journal of the Folklore Institute* 10:41–55.

Todd, Charles Burr. 1907. *In Olde Massachusetts.* New York: Grafton Press.

A Tradition of Indian Run. 1884. *Narragansett Historical Register* 2(3):225.

Tripp, John. 1893. Native Church at Gay Head. *Magazine of New England History* 3(4):250–53.

Trumbull, James Hammond. 1870. On the Algonkin Name "Manit" (or "Manitou"), Sometimes Translated "Great Spirit," and "God." *Old and New* 1:337–42.

———. 1903. *Natick Dictionary.* Bureau of American Ethnology, bulletin 25. Washington, D.C.: Smithsonian Institution.

Tuck, James A. 1978. Regional Cultural Development, 3000 to 300 B.C. In *Handbook of North American Indians: Northeast,* vol. 15, William C. Sturtevant, series ed., Bruce Trigger, vol. ed., pp. 28–43. Washington, D.C.: Smithsonian Institution.

Turnbaugh, William A. 1984. *The Material Culture of R1-1000, A Mid-17th-Century Narragansett Indian Burial Site in North Kingstown, Rhode Is-*

land. Kingston, R.I.: Department of Sociology and Anthropology, University of Rhode Island.

Tylor, Edward. 1874. *Primitive Culture: Researches into the Development of Mythology, Philosophy, Religion, Language, Art and Custom, I.* Boston: Estes and Lauriat.

Underhill, John. [1638] 1902. Newes from America. Reprint. New York: Underhill Society of America.

Under the Leonard Door-Step. 1936. *Narragansett Dawn* 1(9):204–5.

Updike, Wilkins, II. 1907. *A History of the Episcopal Church in Narragansett, Rhode Island.* Daniel Goodwin, ed. Boston: Merrymount Press.

Vanderhoop, Leonard. 1983. Interview, April 7, Gay Head, Mass.

Vanderhoop, Mary A. Cleggett. 1904. The Gay Head Indians: Their History and Traditions. *New Bedford Evening Standard,* June 25: 10; July 2: 10; July 9: 10, 13; July 16: 10, 14; July 23: 12; July 30: 12; August 6: 12; August 13: 12.

Vaughan, Alden T. 1979. *New England Frontier: Puritans and Indians, 1620–1675.* Rev. ed. New York: W. W. Norton & Company.

Verazzano, John De. 1841. The Voyage of John De Verazzano, Along the Coast of North America From Carolina to Newfoundland, A.D. 1524. *Collections of the New York Historical Society,* 2d series, vol. 1, pp. 37–67.

Visit to the Elizabeth Islands. 1817. *North American Review and Miscellaneous Journal* 5:313–24.

Wampanoag woman. 1983. Interview.

Ward, Donald. 1977. The Little Man Who Wasn't There: Encounters With the Supranormal. *Fabula* 18(3/4):212–25.

———. 1981. *The German Legends of the Brothers Grimm, I.* Donald Ward ed. and trans. Philadelphia: Institute for the Study of Human Issues.

Ward, Edward. 1905. A Trip to New England. In *Boston in 1682 and 1699.* George Parker Winship, ed. Providence, R.I.: Club for Colonial Reprints.

Washburn, Wilcomb E. 1975. *The Indian in America.* New York: Harper & Row.

———. 1978. Seventeenth-Century Indian Wars. In *Handbook of North American Indians: Northeast,* vol. 15, William C. Sturtevant, series ed., Bruce Trigger, vol. ed., pp. 89–100. Washington, D.C.: Smithsonian Institution.

Weston, Thomas. 1906. *History of the Town of Middleboro, Massachusetts.* Boston and New York: Houghton, Mifflin and Company.

Wherry, Beatrix A. 1904. Wizardry on the Welsh Border. *Folk-Lore* 15(1):75–86.

Whitfield, Henry. [1651] 1834a. The Light Appearing More and More Towards the Perfect Day: Or, A Farther Discovery of the Present State of the Indians in New England. Reprint. *Collections of the Massachusetts Historical Society* 4, 3d series, pp. 100–147.

———. [1652] 1834b. Strength Out of Weaknesse: Or a Glorious Manifestation of the Further Progresse of the Gospel among the Indians in New-England. Reprint. *Collections of the Massachusetts Historical Society* 4, 3d series, pp. 149–96.

Widdiss, Gladys. 1981. Interview, March 25, Gay Head, Mass.

Williams, Lorraine E. 1972. Ft. Shantok and Ft. Corchaug: A Comparative Study of Seventeenth-Century Culture Contact in the Long Island Sound

Area. Ph.D. diss., New York University. Ann Arbor, University Microfilms International.

Williams, Mentor L., ed. 1956. Schoolcraft's Indian Legends. East Lansing: Michigan State University Press.

Williams, Roger. 1874. *Letters of Roger Williams, 1632–1682*. John Russell Bartlett, ed. Providence, R.I.: Narragansett Club.

———. [1643] 1936. A Key into the Language of America. Reprint. Providence: Rhode Island and Providence Plantations Tercentenary Committee.

Willoughby, Charles C. 1935. Antiquities of the New England Indians. Cambridge, Mass.: Peabody Museum of American Archaeology and Ethnology.

[Wilson, John]. [1647] 1834. The Day-Breaking, if Not the Sun-Rising of the Gospell with the Indians in New England. Reprint. *Collections of the Massachusetts Historical Society* 4, 3d series, pp. 1–23.

Wing, Daniel. 1915. *West Yarmouth Houses*. Library of Cape Cod History and Genealogy, no. 39. Yarmouthport, Mass.: C. W. Swift.

Winslow, Edward. [1649] 1834. The Glorious Progress of the Gospel, Amongst the Indians in New England. Reprint. *Collections of the Massachusetts Historical Society* 4, 3d series, pp. 69–99.

———. [1624] 1910. Good News From New England. Reprint. In *Chronicles of the Pilgrim Fathers*, John Masefield, ed., pp. 267–357. New York: E. P. Dutton & Co.

Wintemberg, W. J. 1907. Alsatian Witch Stories. *Journal of American Folklore* 20(78):213–15.

Winthrop, John. 1825. *The History of New England From 1630 to 1649*, I. James Savage, ed. Boston: Phelps and Farnham.

———. 1826. *The History of New England From 1630 to 1649*, II. James Savage, ed. Boston: Thomas B. Wait and Son.

Wood, William. [1634] 1977. *New England's Prospect*. Alden T. Vaughan, ed. Reprint. Amherst: University of Massachusetts Press.

Index of Folklore Motifs

The folklore motifs discussed in this book are listed below. Most are found in Stith Thompson's *Motif Index of Folk-Literature* (1955–58). If preceded by Baughman the motif can be located in Ernest Baughman's *Type and Motif-Index of the Folktales of England and North America* (1966). If preceded by Simmons, I created the motif number and name for this book.

General Index

Abel's Spring, Martha's Vineyard, 137
African folk motifs, 91, 97, 98, 99, 100, 104, 116–17, 118, 122, 125, 130, 140, 160, 167, 235, 264, 265
Ahsoo, 243–44
Alden, Rev. Timothy, 177, 204
Alderman (Sakonnet Indian), 141, 271
Algonquians, 11–36, 65–66, 70, 124, 129, 132, 172, 173, 176, 177, 216, 225–26, 235, 246, 265, 273, 282
American folk motifs. *See* Anglo-American folk motifs
Ammons, Fannie, 115
Amos, "Blind Joe," 21–22
Amos, Mathias, Jr., 101
Anglo-American folk motifs, 108–9, 125, 130–31, 141, 143, 155, 156, 163, 165, 171, 191, 193, 197, 207, 215, 261–64, 270, 272–73, 277
Aquinnah, 148, 194–95, 199, 200, 222, 232. *See also* Gay Head; Wampanoag history; Wampanoag texts
Ashbow, Samuel, 84
Assawampsett Pond, Mass., 123, 216
Attaquin, Helen, 149, 221, 224–25
Awashonks, 12, 60, 244

Badger, Rev. Stephen, 281–82
Barnstable, Mass., 204, 245
Bascom, William, 7
Bass River, Mass., 79
Basset, Benjamin, 176–77, 178, 186, 201, 218
Bastard Rocks, Charlestown, R.I., 127
Baxter (pirate), 110
Baylies, Dr. William, 174, 178
Bell, Michael, 151
Bellamy, Black, 110, 111
Bigfoot/Sasquatch, 229–30
Bingham, Amelia G., 23
Black Brook, Martha's Vineyard, 132, 135–37, 148, 158–59
Boissevain, Ethel, 150–51
Boston, Mass., 50, 271
Bourne, Joseph, 19
Bourne, Richard, 17, 18, 85–88, 90

Bourne, Mass., 207, 219
Bournedale, Mass., 207
Boyer, Paul, 116
Bradford, William, 49
Bradford (Niantic), R.I., 115, 139–40
Bragdon, Kathleen, 26
Bran, Joshua, 101
Brant Point, Nantucket, 278, 280
Briant, Solomon, 19, 20
Bridgewater, Mass., 43, 51, 62, 123
Bristol, R.I., 91
British folk motifs, 91, 95, 97–100, 104, 105, 110, 116, 118–19, 122–25, 128–31, 140–43, 146, 153–54, 163, 170, 173, 192, 197, 209, 235, 236, 238, 262–64, 271–73, 276
Brotherton, Wis., 30, 70
Brothertown, N.Y., 30, 34
Bureau of American Ethnology, 123
Burgess, Edward S., 100, 132
Butterworth, Hezekiah, 123–24

Calef, Robert, 119
Canonchet, 29, 58
Canonicus, 55
Cape Cod, Mass., 177, 202, 204–6, 208, 215–19, 232
Cape Verde Islands, 193
Captain Kidd, 110, 163–64
Cautantowwit (Kiehtan, creator deity), 38–39, 41, 44, 49, 66–67
Chahnameed, 260, 273–77
Champlain, Samuel de, 15
Chappaquiddick Island, 80–81, 184, 207, 238
Charlestown, R.I., 6, 29–31, 115, 144, 150
Cheepi, 101, 102, 118–19, 121, 125–27, 128, 133, 138, 139, 149, 156, 160, 193–95, 220, 226, 227, 235, 254, 258–61. *See also* Hobbamock (Cheepi, deity)
Chickadee, 85–87, 167, 207
Chilmark, Martha's Vineyard, 120, 176
Chuatawback, mother of, 248
Church, Capt. Benjamin, 59–60, 62, 141

325

E 78 .N5 S54 1986 c.1
Simmons, William Scranton,
 1938-
Spirit of the New England
 tribes

DATE DUE	
OCT 0 8 1995	
APR 15 1997	
OCT 0 3 1997	
SEP 2 0 2001	
DEC 0 9 2013	

GAYLORD   PRINTED IN U.S.A.